D0646839

Stop and Smell the Rosemary

Recipes and Traditions
to Remember

The Junior League of Houston, Inc., is an organization of women committed to promoting voluntarism, developing the potential of women, and improving the community through the effective action and leadership of trained volunteers. Its purpose is exclusively educational and charitable.

Also by The Junior League of Houston, Inc.:
Houston Junior League Cookbook (1968)
The Star of Texas Cookbook (1983)

First Printing September 1996, 75,000 copies

Library of Congress Cataloging in Publication Data main entry under title
Stop and Smell the Rosemary
96-75927

ISBN #0-9632421-2-1

Printed in the United States of America by Wetmore Printing Company, Inc.

Any inquiries about this book or orders for additional copies, should be directed to:
JLH Publications
1811 Briar Oaks Lane
Houston, Texas 77027
713.627.COOK

Stop and Smell the Rosemary

Recipes and Traditions
to Remember

CONTENTS

FOREWORD 6

♦♦♦

BE OUR GUEST-
ENTERTAINING AND MENUS

RECIPES AND TRADITIONS

♦ ♦ ♦

APPENDIX

PROFESSIONAL CREDITS

CONCEPT, DESIGN, AND
ART DIRECTION
Hill/A Marketing Design Group
Chris Hill
Laura Menegaz

PHOTOGRAPHY
Ralph Smith Photography
Ralph Smith

COPYWRITING
Jolynn Rogers

COPY EDITOR
Polly Koch

PHOTO CONCEPT/STYLING
Linda Hofheinz

FOOD STYLING
Irene G. Bertolucci

FLORAL DESIGN
Open Season on Flowers
Miriam Westmoreland

PRINTING
Wetmore Printing, Inc.

♦ ♦ ♦

The Junior League
of Houston, Inc.
recognizes and thanks
Randalls Food Markets, Inc.
for its generous help in
marketing this book.

FOREWORD

Stop and Smell the Rosemary is based on a very simple premise: that in the art of eating can be found the art of living. A meal is a many-layered experience, a lively sequence of events. It's a feast of the senses - the aroma of garlic, the deep ruby glow of a perfect plum, the taste of sweet corn. It's a celebration of nature's bounty in the foods of the changing seasons. And it's a gathering of the entire family for conversation, reflection, and communion as they share the events of their day.

Certainly nothing we can think of touches the human heart or contributes to creating a fulfilling family life more than the eating rituals we create and the shared joy of a lovingly prepared meal. Even in the midst of the busiest day, it's important to savor the life-enhancing magic of eating. The title of this book reminds all of us to do just that.

Rosemary, with its unforgettable fragrance, is the herb of remembrance. For most of us, food is memory. It has a way of bringing back the past that's different for everyone. For some, it's fried chicken and fluffy mashed potatoes. Others get nostalgic over macaroni and cheese. But that's the wonderful thing about food traditions. It's not how complicated or expensive a dish is - sometimes the plainest food gives us the greatest pleasure - but something more basic and enduring. In the ritual of eating is the comfort of things that are familiar to us, our link

to the past and, through our children and our children's children, our
claim on the future. Year after year, sitting around the family table with
those we love, sharing the same simple food, we experience the joy of
remembrance and the promise of renewal.

Throughout this book is a theme: the belief that wonderful food
and memorable meals can be made an everyday pleasure. So, while
the culinary possibilities presented here can encompass many special
occasions, we've concentrated on those recipes that have led to food
traditions we believe celebrate family ties with the greatest humor,
love, and joy.

For *Stop and Smell the Rosemary*, we received almost 4,000 recipes
from members of the Junior League of Houston, friends, families, and
patrons of the Junior League Tea Room. Of the recipes submitted, we
selected more than 500 of our favorites to be included in this book.
Each recipe was tested at least four times to ensure not only that it
stirred our sense of color, taste, and texture, but that it was easy to
follow. We thank each and every person who shared with us their
cherished family recipes and traditions. Their spirit and generosity
infuse every page of this book. To them and to all of you, we wish
good food, good fun, and many happy memories.

COOKBOOK COMMITTEE

EXECUTIVE STEERING COMMITTEE

CHAIRMAN
Veronica "Roni" Obermayer Atnipp

CO-CHAIRMEN
CHAIRMAN
DEVELOPMENT/MARKETING
Nancy O'Connor Abendshein

CHAIRMAN
PHOTOGRAPHY/PRODUCTION
Cara Okoren Moczulski

♦ ♦ ♦

STEERING COMMITTEE

MANAGING EDITOR
Carol Jones Hoppe

RECIPE TESTING CHAIRMAN
Terry Hastings Dean

PR/MARKETING CHAIRMAN
Beverle Gardner Grieco

PRODUCTION COORDINATOR
Carla Oden Tenison

TREASURER
Clare Wiggins Jackson

SALES MANAGER
Catherine Choate Christopherson

SUSTAINING ADVISOR
Susan Ray Mayfield

SUSTAINING MEMBER - AT - LARGE
Boone Boies Bullington

♦ ♦ ♦

THE JUNIOR LEAGUE
OF HOUSTON, INC.
PRESIDENTS

1994-95
Elizabeth "Betty" Sellingsloh Clarke

1995-96
Pamela Jordan Brasseux

1996-97
Deborah Brown Robinson

BE OUR GUEST

Spring is a celebration of renewal after the dreariness of winter. Once, entire communities would gather to plant the village fields and then take part in a shared revelry at spring's return. Many of these festivities centered around May Day, when young and old attended fairs on village commons and wove ribbons around maypoles in a dance. This spring, as trees begin to bud and tender new vegetation shows its bright green face, plan a lighthearted spring brunch and create your own celebration of renewal. Just gather some good friends around you, fling

Menu

FRESH SQUEEZED ORANGE JUICE
FROZEN BELLINIS

♦ ♦ ♦

CORN, RED PEPPER,
AND LEEK SOUP
OR
COOL SUNSET SOUP

♦

BASIL TOMATO SALAD
WITH HEARTS OF PALM
OR
CHILLED ASPARAGUS
WITH GINGER DRESSING
OR
TOASTED WALNUT SALAD

♦

EGGS SARDOU
OR
TOMATO TART
OR
SAVORY BREAKFAST
STRATA

♦

COOLRISE ORANGE ROLLS
COOLRISE CINNAMON ROLLS

♦ ♦ ♦

FRESH PEACH AND
BLUEBERRY CRÊPES
OR
FRESH STRAWBERRIES AND
CREAMY VANILLA SAUCE
OR
AMARETTO ANGEL
FOOD CAKE

An arrangement of white asparagus tied with French ribbon covers a flower container creating the look of a "vase" right out of nature.

open the windows to the garden, and drink in the joys of a new season with lighter menus, bold flavors, and dazzling colors.

A MAYING WE SHALL GO

We associate the glories of spring with flowers: jolly daffodils and tulips, banks of azaleas that look like clusters of fuchsia and white stars, and pansies with velvety petals. If one of your delights is gardening, your own backyard can provide a beautiful, natural setting for this spring brunch. Our table setting, a profusion of pastel colors, provides the theme for our garden party.

The umbrella-shaded table features a pole bedecked with braided pastel-colored plaid and striped ribbons. It will take more than two

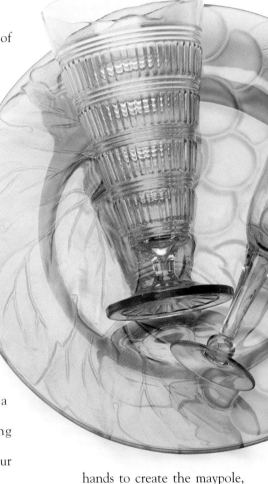

hands to create the maypole, so make it an event. Invite neighborhood children and reward them with cookies

Elegantly folded napkins provide a lively complement to a spring meal and send the message that you took the time to extend a gracious welcome.

and lemonade, or call some friends to help and open a bottle of wine. Complete the maypole by arranging white asparagus decoratively around the container at the center of the table, creating a "vase" right out of nature.

What else? Try adding your grandmother's pastel Fostoria crystal to your own contemporary place setting. It's all in the mix: a layering of textures, a play of patterns, a charming fusion of old and new. Or in the spirit of the season, have a personalized pair of garden gloves waiting at each guest's place setting. And with flowers so abundant, add some to your salads. Try peppery nasturtiums, soft

pansies, marigolds, violets, and rose petals, and urge your guests to please eat the flowers. Use borage blossoms frozen in ice cubes for tea and lemonade. This spring brunch celebrates all growing, living things - including the ties of love and friendship.

◄ *Combine vintage pastel glassware with your contemporary china to enhance the relaxed, festive mood.*

▶ *Try this idea for a truly memorable place card: rosemary tied with a silk ribbon inscribed with the name of each guest and placed in an antique English clay pot.*

SUNNY SIDE UP

ORANGE BLOSSOM PUNCH
3 MUSKETEER MIMOSAS

• • •

BLUEBERRY BISQUE OR
STRAWBERRY SOUP

•

ORANGE PECAN WAFFLES
WITH ORANGE MAPLE SYRUP
OR STONE GROUND
CORNMEAL PANCAKES OR
GERMAN APPLE PANCAKES

•

ORANGE MARMALADE AND
BOURBON GLAZED HAM

•

SEASONAL FRESH FRUIT

• • •

ICED LEMON SOUFFLÉ WITH
RASPBERRY SAUCE OR
LEMON FROZEN YOGURT
WITH BERRIES AND MINT

LINGERING PLEASURES

GIN BREEZE
OLD-FASHIONED LEMONADE
WITH BORAGE BLOSSOM
ICE CUBES

• • •

NUTTY CUCUMBER
SOUP AL FRESCA OR
MANGOSPACHO

•

ORANGE CHICKEN
CASHEW SALAD OR
CHICKEN, RED GRAPE, AND
WATERCRESS SALAD

•

CHILLED HARICOTS
VERTS WITH FETA OR
GRILLED EGGPLANT AND
TOMATO PASTA SALAD OR
ASPARAGUS MUSHROOM
SALAD WITH BASIL
VINAIGRETTE

• • •

BLUEBERRY GLAZE PIE OR
BRANDY GLAZED PEAR CAKE

FAMILY TIES - A CELEBRATION

Summer has a special place in our childhood memories. We remember lazy days with nothing much to do but explore the world around us. Family walks, bicycle rides, fireflies caught in jars, ice cold watermelon, and a fan blowing the hot still air all capture the essence of summertime.

Summers are a family time - a time for gatherings and reunions, visits to grandparents, or long car trips across the country. And for weeks on end in neighborhoods everywhere, the night air is scented with the fragrant aroma of meat cooking over hot coals.

Menu

TROPICAL PUNCH
ICED TEA

◆ ◆ ◆

NUTS ON A
HOT TIN ROOF

WARM BLUE CHEESE,
BACON, AND GARLIC DIP

PARMESAN PITA CRISPS

◆

$10 HAMBURGERS
OR
ORIENTAL FLANK STEAK
OR
CHICKEN AT ATTENTION

◆

GRILLED VEGETABLE SALAD
WITH CITRUS VINAIGRETTE
OR
GRAPEFRUIT, MANGO, AND
SWEET ONION SALAD
OR
FRIED GREEN TOMATOES

◆

CORN AND PEPPER RELISH

UPSIDE DOWN PICKLES

◆ ◆ ◆

APPLE WALNUT PIE

COCONUT
BUTTERMILK PIE

SANTA FE CHOCOLATE
CHIP COOKIES

Fashion a crazy quilt of family memories by using a collection of ties from family members and other brightly colored memorabilia. We mounted ours on plaid shirt fabric and pillow ticking.

To create a watermelon star lantern, use a star-shaped cookie cutter as a pattern. Hollow out the watermelon just as you would a jack-o'-lantern, then use a sharp knife to cut out stars.

Almost at the midpoint of summer comes the Fourth of July. Families and friends across the country reunite to celebrate the holiday with picnics on the lawn, kids playing games, and everyone else relaxing as the long summer day unfolds. A fitting finale is the fireworks display lighting up the night sky.

We've assembled some ideas to help make your next gathering the most memorable one ever. All you need are some treasured family possessions and a few simple materials to create a celebration and a tradition all your own.

Copy family photos on heavy paper and attach them to paint sticks with the date and place of the party as a memento of the day. On a hot July day in Texas, nothing could be more practical.

SETTING A STAR-STUDDED FAMILY PICNIC

It's been said that memory begins in the eye and ends in the heart. For our family picnic feast, we've included things to delight the eye as they touch the heart. Tabletops are a riot of colors and textures in traditional red, white, and blue. Cherished family photographs take on a new twist when used for decorations and keepsakes. Festive holders for silverware and napkins are as close as your kitchen cabinet. We've made our holders by taking empty tin cans, sandpapering them to create an antique look, and then decorating them with designs punched out with an ice pick or cut out with a bottle opener. If

you're feeling particularly ambitious, use a leather design tool and mallet for making star shapes. To celebrate family ties, add a bowtie made from a man's old necktie. At nightfall, fill the cans with votive candles, relax, and enjoy the play of candlelight through the openwork designs.

In this celebration of family, we're making memories with memories in our unusual tablecloth. Take family photos printed on muslin by your local copy shop, stitch them onto fabric, and edge the cloth with points of old ties to create a decorative border. Leave room for your guests to sign their names with washable pens and then embroider or stitch the

names in place. Repeat the tradition every reunion for a colorful running record of gatherings through the years.

Family picnics and ripe red watermelons go hand-in-hand. But at our Fourth of July gathering, watermelons are for more than eating - they're a delicious focal point. Stand a large, hollowed-out watermelon on end and fill it with fresh-cut summer flowers to create a distinctive centerpiece. When it comes to creating your special Family Ties Celebration, let your imagination take you as far as it can go.

ALFRESCO AFFAIR

SUMMERTIME COOLER

♦ ♦ ♦

PEPPERCORN
MARINATED SHRIMP

♦

PIZZA SANDWICH OR
ROASTED VEGETABLE
SANDWICH OR SMOKED
TURKEY AND APPLE
SANDWICH WITH LONE STAR
MAYONNAISE

♦

TUSCAN TOMATO SALAD OR
BLACK BEAN, CABBAGE,
AND DATE SALAD OR
ARTICHOKE POTATO SALAD

♦ ♦ ♦

MINT CHOCOLATE
CUPCAKES OR
CHOCOLATE TOFFEE
BROWNIES

LEMON PECAN WAFERS

LONE STAR BARBECUE

ICE COLD BEER

♦ ♦ ♦

SOUTHWESTERN
CHEESE SPREAD

BLACK BEAN CORN SALSA

♦

LONE STAR BRISKET IN CHILI
SAUCE AND BEER OR
SMOKEY BARBECUED BRISKET

♦

GARDEN POTATO SALAD

CONFETTI SLAW

BARLEY CORN SALAD

♦

HERBED BEER BREAD

♦ ♦ ♦

TOFFEE CHOCOLATE
PECAN PIE

A+ COOKIES

KAHLÚA GINGERBREAD
WITH KEY LIME CURD

For most Americans, the idea of a formal tea may seem as remote as China. Asian and British cultures have long understood the eternal comfort of tea and the enduring pleasures of a ceremony that has continued unchanged for centuries. A tea can be anything: a quiet time for reflection at the end of the day, just you with a friendly cat curled up at your feet; an intimate get-together among friends; or a full-dress tea party with a glittering silver pot, slivers of sandwiches, and little frosted cakes.

Imagine that it's four o'clock, and you're nearing the end of another chilly,

Menu

ENGLISH SCONE CAKE

ORANGE PECAN MUFFINS

LEMON POPPY SEED
TEA BREAD

♦

FRESH FRUIT WITH
POPPY SEED DRESSING

♦

A SELECTION OF
OPEN-FACED
TEA SANDWICHES :

EGG SALAD ON WHITE
ROUNDS WITH
CHOPPED PARSLEY

SUN-DRIED TOMATO,
GOAT CHEESE, AND
WATERCRESS ON TOASTED
WHEAT ROUNDS

DICED SAVORY SHRIMP
SALAD ON TOASTED
WHITE ROUNDS TOPPED
WITH CHOPPED AVOCADO

♦ ♦ ♦

PLUM DANDY

LEMON ORANGE POUND CAKE

♦ ♦ ♦

TEA WITH SLICED LEMONS AND
CLOVES

**TO SET A PROPER
TEA SERVICE**

*Stack a set of dessert plates and
napkins with the butter knives
on top. Next to them place the
sugar bowl, the milk pitcher, the
hot water urn, and the tea pot.
Place the slices of lemon and tea
strainer near the sugar and
cream. On the rest of the tray,
stack the cups and saucers in
pairs with their spoons.*

▶ *The celebration of tea for two
with its quiet companionship
seems to invite informal, intimate conversations as you
catch up on the latest news.*

*An assortment of elegant tea
sandwiches, crusts trimmed,
delicately garnished, and dis-
played on a linen lace doily.*

brisk day. Inside all is warm
and inviting. The kitchen is
filled with the smell of
baking, there's water on to
boil, and a tray holding
teacups, a bowl of sugar, and
a pitcher of milk awaits.
You fill the teapot and let
the tea leaves steep a minute or two. As you
pour your
first cup,
breathing
in the warm
aroma, and take a
sip, all your cares seem
to slip away.

Now you are captivated.
The next step is to plan an

easy-to-host tea party. Start by covering the table, the center of attention, with a traditional white linen or white lace tea cloth. For large parties you may want to use two tea services, one at each end. The tea is always poured by the hostess or a special friend. Place the tea tray, napkins, and plates in an arrangement similar to the one shown on pages 18 and 19. Tea sandwiches, scones, and other refreshments can be artfully positioned nearby, inviting guests to help themselves. Once the party begins, little else needs to be done other than sharing the moment with friends.

Traditional teas to try include old favorites, like English Breakfast, Earl Grey, and Jasmine, or herbal teas made from wild peppermint, spiced citrus, or chamomile blossoms. Or you can make your own distinctive teas. Just add cinnamon sticks, vanilla beans, or other spices to the tea leaves and seal them in airtight containers to create a variety of special blends.

A formal tea plate: a tea or dessert plate, a tea-sized napkin, a delicate china teacup and saucer, a five o'clock silver teaspoon, and a butter knife.

▲ *Giving teacups for special occasions is a lovely tradition you can start now with your daughters, granddaughters, and nieces. You'll be starting a wonderful collection of memories that can be shared with friends and family for generations to come.*

TEA FOR TWO

LEMON YOGURT MUFFINS
ENGLISH MUFFIN BREAD

◆

MINI WHIPPING CREAM
BISCUITS FILLED WITH DICED
CHICKEN PECAN SALAD
WITH CRANBERRIES

◆

FRESH BERRIES AND
CRÈME FRAÎCHE

APRICOT DELIGHT OR
KEY LIME TARTLETS WITH
FRESH RASPBERRIES

◆ ◆ ◆

TEA WITH
SLICED LEMONS

MID-MORNING
MOTHER'S TEA

WALNUT MUFFINS OR
BOUNTIFUL BREAKFAST
MUFFINS

◆

DEWBERRY JEWELS
WITH VANILLA SUGAR

TENDER SCONES WITH
ZILLAH MAE'S JAM

◆

APPLE RAISIN QUICHE

◆

SLICES OF MELON WITH
CHOPPED FRESH MINT

◆ ◆ ◆

TEA

A SPIRITED GATHERING

Cocktail parties bring to mind large gatherings, small talk, and the clinking of glasses. We all remember our parents' parties and how we would slip unnoticed to the top of the stairs to catch a glimpse of neighbors and friends, made newly fascinating by an unfamiliar sophistication. The room below always seemed to be full of laughter and elegance.

Soon after Prohibition, the cocktail party took center stage and has gained in popularity since - and why not? It's a simple way to entertain business clients, repay a large number of social obligations, or celebrate a holiday or special event in a big way. Guests

Menu

GOURMET PECANS

♦

ARTICHOKE CHEESECAKE

♦

BACON TOMATO DIP
WITH ENDIVE

♦

CHERRY TOMATOES
FILLED WITH
BACON TOMATO DIP

♦

CRAWFISH PHYLLO
TRIANGLES

♦

DILLED SCALLOP PUFFS
OR
GINGER SHRIMP TOAST

♦

SALMON PINWHEELS

♦

GARLIC CHICKEN
BITES WITH TOMATO
RAISIN SAUCE

♦

PEPPERCORN-CRUSTED
BEEF TENDERLOIN IN
MILE HIGH BISCUITS

Presentation of food is almost as important as the food itself. An elegant Artichoke Cheesecake with an unusual garnish piques appetites and elicits smiles.

Use your collections as part of the decoration. A group of vintage silver cocktail shakers creates a glittering centerpiece.

usually enjoy attending cocktail parties because it gives them a chance both to meet new people and to renew acquaintances.

For your next cocktail party, be creative: pull out all the stops and turn your home into a truly glamorous setting.

SETTING THE STAGE

Behind every successful party is an organized hostess who has everything planned well in advance and down to the tiniest detail. The first step is to select a date early and decide on the number of guests you want to include. The average room in a house holds 20 people. Keep in mind, though, that having the space slightly crowded creates a convivial, intimate

atmosphere. And while most people have cocktail parties in their homes, don't let that restrict your creativity. How about setting your party in a beach house, at an historic home, on a boat, or at a museum?

The second step is to decide the time of the party. You may choose between a cocktails-only party and a cocktail buffet. The cocktails-only party, usually a prelude to dinner, runs from five to seven o'clock or six to eight o'clock and includes drinks and light appetizers. The cocktail buffet usually begins at seven o'clock and offers food substantial enough to replace dinner. In either case, for a two-hour

Champagne Flute

White Wine

Red Wine

Sherry

Cordial

Sparkling Wine

Brandy

Beer Mug

Double Old Fashioned

Margarita

Pilsner

High Ball

Martini

In keeping with the cocktail party theme, use vases made of cocktail accessories. Shown here are a silver shot glass, a mint julep glass, and a crystal martini glass.

to set up the bar and serve the drinks is a good idea.

Of course, nothing sets the mood of the party more than decorations. We've gone all-out for glamour: a glass table lit from underneath illuminates a collection of unusual glass paperweights and clear glass marbles. Added to this is an assemblage of very tall, elegantly shaped champagne glasses. Look for glasses with interesting shapes and have fun mixing and matching.

Finally, provide music - live music for a truly grand event or "old favorites" played on your home sound system. All that's left is to mix in a group of lively and stimulating guests. The best cocktail parties are those you never want to end.

party, you'll need to count on serving six to eight different appetizers, enough for guests to have three of each kind.

And unless the party is small, it's nice to have help so you can spend more time with your guests. A waitperson can ensure that food trays are replenished and the party area is kept tidy. If more than 20 people are present, having a bartender

SOUTH OF THE BORDER COCKTAIL PARTY

MELBA TOAST WITH TOMATO BASIL SALSA
•
SPICY SALMON TARTARE WITH PLANTAIN CHIPS
•
ROASTED RED PEPPER DIP
•
PACKAGES OF THE SOUTHWEST
•
MEXICAN CHEESECAKE WITH SALSA ROJO AND GUACAMOLE
•
RAJA POBLANO QUESADILLAS
•
TOMATILLO PAPAYA SALSA WITH JICAMA SLICES AND TORTILLA CHIPS

• • •

KAHLÚA BROWNIES
TRADITIONAL MEXICAN CHRISTMAS COOKIES
PECAN PRALINES

TOAST OF THE TOWN COCKTAIL BUFFET

CRAB CAKES WITH ROMA SALSA AND LEMON BUTTER
•
CHÈVRE-FILLED MUSHROOMS
•
SALMON PILLOWS WITH BASIL CREAM SAUCE
•
PORK TENDERLOIN IN CREAMY MUSTARD SAUCE WITH COOLRISE SWEET DINNER ROLLS
•
PESTO, GOAT CHEESE, AND SUN-DRIED TOMATO TORTA
•
OLIVE CAPER CROSTINI
•
HONEY PEPPER PECAN SALAD

• • •

COMPANY CHEESECAKE
CHOCOLATE-COVERED ALMOND MACAROONS
PECAN TORTE

A HARVEST FEAST FOR THE SENSES

As the days grow shorter and the nights snap with the crisp chill of autumn, it's time to pull the curtains, light the fire, and draw together around the table in a celebration of nature's bounty. In earlier times, one great tradition was the harvest banquet, when neighbors took a respite from their work to give thanks for their health and good fortune. They would crowd around a sideboard laden with an array of meats and game dishes, colorful vegetables, and seasonal fruits to discuss the crops and savor the last golden days of autumn. Even without a harvest, fall is a

Menu

CHICKEN LIVER PÂTÉ
OR
MUSHROOM PÂTÉ

◆ ◆ ◆

CHAMPAGNE CAMEMBERT SOUP

◆

SPINACH AND APPLE SALAD

◆

BASIL LEMON GRILLED
VEAL CHOPS
OR
GRILLED MARINATED
VENISON TENDERLOIN

◆

TIED ASPARAGUS BUNDLES
IN CHAMPAGNE SAUCE

COMPOTE OF
GRILLED VEGETABLES IN
ACORN SQUASH

◆

ROASTED NEW POTATOES
WITH BAY LEAVES
OR
ROASTED GARLIC AND GREEN
CHILE MASHED POTATOES
OR
WILD RICE MEDLEY

◆

COOLRISE SWEET DINNER ROLLS
AND SELECTION OF BREADS

◆ ◆ ◆

WHITE CHOCOLATE BROWNIES
WITH VANILLA ICE CREAM
AND CHOCOLATE SAUCE
OR
DIVINE ESPRESSO ICE CREAM
WITH RASPBERRY SAUCE

by its very nature signifies abundance - platters of veal chops, serving dishes filled with grilled vegetables and wild rice, tiny roasted red potatoes placed on a bed of dandelion greens, baskets of breads, and a selection of tempting sweets.

The first objective in setting the table for a buffet meal is to put all of the food in a convenient place, usually on the dining room table or a large sideboard, so that guests can easily help themselves. The basic presentation shown on the preceding page is easy to adapt to your setting, whether you create a buffet around all sides of the table, use two buffet lines, or choose a one-sided arrangement like ours.

great time to recreate this pleasant tradition and to honor a season of gathering inside a loving circle of family and friends.

Cups made from hollowed-out citrus fruits make a delightful display for a special relish. To cut scalloped edges, use a coin as a pattern.

CREATING A CORNUCOPIA OF RICHES

On days when brisk winds herald the coming of winter, there is a longing in each of us for comfortable, informal gatherings that recall older "country" ways. A buffet

The second objective is to arrange the platters of food, plates, napkins, and silver to allow an easy flow for serving. For instance, placing heavier items first on the buffet and lighter items toward the end helps to ensure a balanced plate. Appetizers, beverages, and desserts can be in separate locations. Put napkins and silverware last on the buffet table so that guests have their hands free to serve themselves.

The delightful thing about our harvest buffet is that it is informal, but elegant. Our table setting, from flatware to decorations, preserves a traditional look. To carry out our harvest theme, we've brought together a mix of vintage pewter and period china in rich colors of bittersweet and blue.

We fashioned a topiary for the buffet by anchoring oranges, apples, kumquats, and other fruits of the season to a Styrofoam cone with bamboo skewers. We added pheasant feathers to create a warm fall still life reminiscent of the Dutch masters. For a splash of muted fall colors, we draped an antique paisley shawl over the sideboard. Mellow light cast by massed candles of various heights, combined with the soft glow of a flickering fire, provided the final autumnal touch.

Create a festive frill for veal chops using joss paper, which can be purchased from an oriental market. Make a series of cuts, ¼ inch apart in the gold foil squares, leaving an inch intact at the bottom. Then curl each strip with the blade of a pair of scissors.

AN AUTUMN IDYLL

PENNE À LA VODKA OR
CHILLED SWEET RED PEPPER
SOUP OR OVEN-BAKED
ONION SOUP

•

POACHED PEAR ARUGULA
SALAD WITH CAMBAZOLA
CROSTINI AND SWEET AND
SPICY PECANS

•

MARINATED SALMON SEARED
IN A PEPPER CRUST OR
GRILLED SWORDFISH WITH
AVOCADO BUTTER

•

TWO-BEAN SUCCOTASH
CHÈVRE ZUCCHINI GRATIN
POTATOES AU GRATIN OR
POTATO PUFF

•

FRESH HERB FOCACCIA

• • •

COFFEE ICE CREAM PIE,
DUTCH CHOCOLATE
MOUSSE, OR RHUBARB
CRUMBLE WITH
BOURBON CREAM

SOUTH TEXAS
RANCH BUFFET

MANGO MARGARITAS

•

DETERING RANCH PECANS

• • •

CHILLED GREEN CHILE SOUP
OR MEXICAN GARLIC SOUP

•

ROMAINE AND RED
BELLS WITH CILANTRO
JALAPEÑO DRESSING

•

RANCHO RAMILLETE
FLAUTAS WITH MEXICAN
GREEN HOT SAUCE AND
RAMILLETE RED PICANTE
SAUCE OR BAKED POBLANO
CHILES STUFFED WITH
ARTICHOKES AND TOASTED
WALNUTS

•

BAKED SPICY RICE

BLACK BEAN SALAD

• • •

CINNAMON ICE CREAM
WITH BISCOCHITOS OR
LOW-FAT FLAN

29

JUST DESSERTS

If there's such a thing as heaven on earth, it must surely be an entire meal of nothing but the most sinfully elegant desserts: white chocolate mousse cake with raspberries, towering chocolate tortes on which curls of bittersweet dark chocolate repose, moist chocolate brownies drizzled with a heady sauce. In their secret hearts, your friends would probably savor a few hours of such harmless decadence. As the hostess, don't be afraid to join in with equal abandon. Most desserts can be made ahead of time and served with both a minimum of fuss and a great deal of style.

Menu

OLD-FASHIONED CHOCOLATE
LAYER CAKE

♦

CHOCOLATE LOVERS
DREAM CAKE

♦

FROZEN WHITE CHOCOLATE
MOUSSE CAKE WITH
RASPBERRY SAUCE

♦

CHOCOLATE MOUSSE PIE
WITH CARAMEL PECAN
TOPPING

♦

CAMEO CAKE WITH WHITE
CHOCOLATE FROSTING

♦

COOKIES AND CREAM
CHEESECAKE

♦

CHOCOLATE-GLAZED THREE
LAYER CHEESECAKE

♦

WHITE CHOCOLATE
BREAD PUDDING

♦

PECAN CHOCOLATE
CHUNK BROWNIES

♦ ♦ ♦

FRENCH VANILLA COFFEE

To create white chocolate cups, wrap a tin can in cellophane, then dip it in melted chocolate. When the chocolate hardens, carefully peel the cellophane away, leaving the cups intact.

SWEET INDULGENCES

Gathering a group of friends together on a beautiful day for a feast of treats is reason enough for a party. But any occasion can be an excuse - an anniversary, a birthday, a welcome home for a friend who's been away, or a reunion of old school chums. Whatever the occasion, a party of such grand immoderation deserves appropriate fanfare, beginning with the invitation. After all, a dessert party is all about indulging your deepest cravings for

sugary fare. For instance, if it's an all-chocolate dessert party, why not get your guests in the right frame of mind by sending an invitation tucked inside a box of chocolates or hanging from a chocolate-dipped spoon?

Set your table with the same sense of fun and a lavish hand. A major appeal of any dessert is how enticing and extravagant it looks. We've put together a grouping of uniquely shaped glass vases, containers, and goblets filled with colorful sugar-coated fruits, which gives you a fanciful way of showcasing a rich assortment of sweets, even as it creates a delectable still life of its own.

Luscious fruits and a fluffy mousse show to their best advantage in our edible serving dishes - whimsical baskets made of molded white chocolate. Or dress up desserts

A selection of ripe fruits in festive white chocolate cups enlivens any table.

An ordinary cake can look spectacular with a little ingenuity and a simple vegetable peeler. Choose high fat content chocolate, slightly warm it in the hands, and make curls by gently shaving the chocolate with the peeler.

with curls of chocolate or a splash of gold - edible gold leaves, that is. Books of pure 23-karat gold leaf sheets, available in many fine art shops, invite you to create any number of elegant garnishes.

A dessert party is a special treat, a once-in-a-while exercise in instant gratification. For best results, plan to have eight to ten dessert selections so your guests will have plenty of temptations to give in to - including less familiar confections. As Mae West put it, "When choosing between two evils, I like to try the one I've never tried before."

Use lemons, pears, and oranges to make a festive array of sugared fruits. Try colorful cranberries for the holidays or any fruit that's surprising and different. Coat fruit with egg white (or spray with a strong bonding adhesive), then roll in granulated sugar. If using adhesive method, fruit is not edible.

Rub pieces of gold leaf on top of chocolate-covered espresso beans to achieve a dramatic effect.

Around the first of December, linen cabinets all over America open, and snowy tablecloths and napkins made of the finest damask come down from the uppermost shelf. Mingled smells of silver polish and lemon oil permeate every corner. Children, full of excitement, giggle in anticipation, and soft music plays in the background as scents of cinnamon and nutmeg fill the air. Each year half the fun of the holiday season is in the preparation as the whole house puts on its party finery.

The holidays are a special time of the year, a celebration of the generations. Grandmother's silver, the

Menu

SAVORY RED PEPPER SOUP

◆

SAUTÉED APPLE SALAD WITH
ROQUEFORT AND WALNUTS

◆

RACK OF LAMB WITH PORT AND
ROSEMARY SAUCE
OR
ROSEMARY-SMOKED
LAMB CHOPS
OR
GARLIC ROSEMARY
CORNISH GAME HENS

◆

WILD MUSHROOM AND
ONION RISOTTO

◆

WHIPPED CARROTS
AND PARSNIPS
OR
GLAZED PEARL
ONIONS WITH
RAISINS AND ALMONDS

◆

JALAPEÑO MINT JELLY
OR
ENGLISH MINT SAUCE

◆

SWEET BUTTER HORN
DINNER ROLLS

◆ ◆ ◆

SPICED BREAD PUDDING
WITH BOURBON SAUCE

MINCEMEAT CAKE
OR
APPLE CRANBERRY
CRISP WITH ALMOND
STREUSEL TOPPING

*This sterling service was made in
1899 by Tiffany & Company.
The pattern is Atlantas, also
called Ailanthus, Ailantus, and
B. Tiffany.*

family's heirloom plates,
antique linens, delicate hand-
blown ornaments - all these
precious treasures connect us
with our past.

A CELEBRATION OF HEART AND HOME

Entertaining takes on a
whole new significance
during the holiday
season. Grandparents,
aunts and uncles,
nieces and nephews,
and close family friends
begin to arrive, bearing mysterious packages and bringing
with them the excitement
of other places - and memories
of holidays past.

Such a wonderful time
deserves our best: an elegant
formal table glittering with

polished silver, crystal glasses,
fine china, sparkling ribbons,
and garlands of silver and gold.

Here, we've covered the
table in an antique cloth and
added decorations of gold-
dipped lady apples, fruit
accented with pine boughs,
and golden magnolia leaves.
The menu cards are festooned
with small gold-dipped leaves
and placed between every
two place settings, while a
single large gilded leaf is used
as the place card.

Many of the most dramatic
effects can be achieved without extravagant expense.
Consider what is possible by
simply using gold spray
paint, glass ornaments, ribbons, and greenery. Remember
that it's the small details -

| Master Salt | Individual Salt with Salt Spoon | Nut Cracker | Nut Pick | Escargot Fork | Olive Fork | Fish Fork | Salad or Pastry Fork | Luncheon or Breakfast Fork | Dinner Fork | Butter Spreader | Fish Knife | Cheese or Melon Knife | Game Knife | Fruit Knife | Butter Server | New Style Dinner Knife | Dinner Knife | Luncheon or Breakfast Knife | Dessert Knife | Dessert or Soup Spoon | Teaspoon | Berry Spoon | Ramequin Fork | Melon Spoon | Grapefruit Spoon |

Close-up of an elegant formal place setting with a snowy crisp damask napkin, sparkling wine and water glasses, highly polished silver, fine china, and a gold charger or place plate.

the way you set the table, fold a napkin, or garnish a platter - that best convey warmth and caring.

During holiday parties everyone has a part to play, however large or small. Put the little ones in charge of tree trimming and cookie tasting. Older children can answer the door at party time and take care of the guests' coats. The person with the most elegant handwriting can be enlisted to write the menu cards in black ink. When everyone works together in the spirit of the holidays, it becomes a true family affair.

A menu card in beautiful calligraphy adorned with gold leaves rests between every two place settings.

37

A Taste of Tradition

RITZY OLIVES

•

FIELD GREENS,
CRUMBLED BLUE CHEESE,
AND SPICY PECANS

•

THANKSGIVING TURKEY

•

BAKED SPINACH OR HERB
GARDEN GREEN BEANS

•

YAM AND BUTTERNUT
SQUASH PUDDING OR
LEEKS IN ORANGE
GINGER SAUCE

•

CITRUS CRANBERRY RELISH

•

EASY CORN BISCUITS WITH
WHIPPED BUTTER

• • •

PUMPKIN WALNUT
CHEESECAKE OR
WOODFORD PUDDING CAKE
WITH VANILLA SAUCE

FIRESIDE FARE

WILD RICE SOUP

•

SPINACH AND GOAT CHEESE
SALAD WITH WARM
BALSAMIC VINAIGRETTE

•

MUSTARD PORK ROAST WITH
HONEY APPLES OR APRICOT
AND PECAN-STUFFED
PORK LOIN

•

CREAMY POLENTA WITH
SAGE AND ROASTED
WILD MUSHROOMS

•

CREAMY BRUSSEL SPROUTS
OR WARM RED
CABBAGE WITH GOAT
CHEESE AND PINE NUTS

•

GRANDMA'S CRANBERRY
RELISH

•

CLOVERLEAF DINNER ROLLS

• • •

SWEET POTATO PECAN PIE
WITH CHANTILLY CREAM OR
PRALINE PUMPKIN PIE

FINE BEGINNINGS

*Crab Cakes with Roma Salsa
and Lemon Butter*

Warm Blue Cheese, Bacon, and Garlic Dip

7 slices bacon, chopped
2 cloves garlic, minced
8 ounces cream cheese, softened
¼ cup half and half

4 ounces blue cheese, crumbled (1 cup)
2 tablespoons chopped fresh chives
3 tablespoons chopped smoked
    almonds (1 ounce)

Cook bacon in a large skillet over medium-high heat until almost crisp, about 7 minutes. Drain excess fat from skillet. Add garlic and cook until bacon is crisp, about 3 minutes.

Preheat oven to 350 degrees. Beat cream cheese until smooth. Add half and half and mix until combined. Stir in bacon mixture, blue cheese, and chives. Transfer to a 2-cup ovenproof serving dish and cover with foil. Bake until thoroughly heated, about 30 minutes. Sprinkle with chopped almonds. Serve with sliced apples, toasted pita crisps, or French bread.

Warm Blue Cheese, Bacon, and Garlic Dip may be prepared 1 day in advance. Refrigerate or freeze. Bring to room temperature before baking.

ROASTING SWEET BELL PEPPERS AND CHILE PEPPERS

The most common methods of roasting bell peppers and chile peppers are over the gas stove and under the broiler.

Depending on the method you choose, the steps below should be followed for the best results.

Make a small slice with a sharp knife in all chiles prior to roasting, excluding the bell pepper.

Watch closely while the skins blacken, taking care that the flesh does not bruise or burn.

When the pepper is blackened on all sides, remove from heat and immediately place in a sealed plastic bag. Allow to steam in the bag until cool. Peel, seed, and slice or chop the peppers when cool.

Method 1: Gas Stove
Arrange the peppers on a wire rack or grid above a medium flame. Turn peppers frequently to blacken evenly on all sides. Advantage: Flame-charred peppers have a better flavor and are less likely to have burned flesh. Disadvantage: Can be messy. Bell peppers produce a lot of juice while roasting.

Method 2: Broiler
Place peppers on the rack of a broiler pan 4 to 6 inches under the broiling element. Keep the oven door ajar. Turn to blacken evenly on all sides. Advantage: Can roast several peppers at one time. Disadvantage: Anaheims lose their bright color and broiler can overcook the flesh.

Roasted Red Pepper Dip

2 large red bell peppers, roasted,*
    peeled, and seeded (See accompanying instructions.)
4 ounces sun-dried tomatoes packed
    in oil, drained and patted dry
2 cloves garlic
2 teaspoons ground cumin

1 to 2 pickled jalapeños, coarsely
    chopped
¼ cup chopped fresh cilantro
1 bunch green onions, white part only,
    coarsely chopped
6 ounces cream cheese, softened
½ teaspoon salt

Cool peppers, then press between paper towels to remove excess liquid. Otherwise, the dip will be too runny.

Process peppers, tomatoes, garlic, cumin, 1 jalapeño, cilantro, green onions, cream cheese, and salt in a food processor until smooth. Correct seasonings, adding more jalapeño if desired. Serve with blue corn tortilla chips.

*May substitute a 4-ounce jar of roasted red peppers.

Roasted Red Pepper Dip may be prepared 1 day in advance.

Bacon Tomato Dip

YIELDS 1½ CUPS

10 slices bacon, cooked crisp,
   drained, and cooled
3 large tomatoes, peeled, seeded,
   and chopped
1 cup mayonnaise

1 tablespoon Dijon mustard
¼ cup minced green onions
¼ cup minced fresh parsley
6 drops Tabasco Sauce

Combine bacon, tomatoes, mayonnaise, mustard, onions, parsley, and Tabasco in a food processor. Process until chopped, but not puréed, preserving some of the texture. Adjust seasonings. Serve with crisp, fresh vegetables or melba toast.

Bacon Tomato Dip may be prepared up to 2 days in advance. Refrigerate.

Black Bean Corn Salsa

YIELDS 4 CUPS

2 cans (15 ounces each) black
   beans, drained and rinsed
kernels of 3 ears cooked corn
   (1½ cups)
3 firm tomatoes, peeled,
   seeded, and diced

1 cup fresh cilantro, minced
2 to 4 fresh jalapeños, seeded and diced
¼ cup fresh lime juice
salt
freshly ground pepper
3 avocados, pitted, peeled, and diced

Combine the beans, corn, tomatoes, cilantro, jalapeños, and lime juice in a serving bowl. Season with salt and pepper. Cover and chill. Before serving, toss in avocados. Serve with blue corn tortilla chips.

HANDLING CHILE PEPPERS

As a general rule, the smaller the chile, the hotter it is. The seeds and membranes can contain 80 percent of a chile's capsaicin, the potent compound that gives chiles their fiery nature.

Small chiles, like the serrano and jalapeño, do not need to be peeled. Larger chiles must be peeled, and for that they must be roasted.

Always wear rubber gloves or rub hands generously with oil as capsaicin can burn your skin and irritate your eyes. You can neutralize capsaicin on your hands by washing them in a mixture of 1 quart water and 1 tablespoon bleach.

Do not use wooden cutting surfaces as the oils from the chiles will seep into the wood.

After roasting peppers, snip veins with scissors to release the seeds and place in a colander to rinse. Do not cut chiles under running water as the water vapor carries the oils upward where they can irritate your eyes.

When blending or processing fresh chiles, keep at a safe distance as the blades can disperse the oils and take your breath away.

Neutralize the heat from a chile pepper by placing sugar on the tongue or take a drink of any dairy product. Cold beer or water just keeps the heat going.

Soak chiles in ice water 1 hour before using to lessen the heat. Also do not use the seeds or membrane for a dish with less heat.

Poblano

Scotch Bonnet

Green Habanero

Ancho Chile

Manzana

Rocotillo

Serrano

Jalapeño

Yellow Habanero

Cayenne

Anaheim

Chicken Liver Pâté

1 cup chicken stock
½ pound boneless, skinless
   chicken breasts
½ pound chicken livers, drained
½ cup chopped onion
1½ teaspoons salt
½ teaspoon ground nutmeg
2 teaspoons Dijon mustard
¼ teaspoon ground cloves
pinch cayenne pepper

1 clove garlic, minced
2 tablespoons cognac
2 tablespoons fresh lemon juice
4 large eggs, hard-boiled and chopped
¾ cup (1½ sticks) unsalted
   butter, at room temperature
——
1 cup pistachios, finely chopped
¼ cup minced fresh parsley

Place chicken stock and chicken breasts in a saucepan. Cover and cook over medium-high heat about 15 minutes, or until chicken is tender. Add chicken livers. Reduce heat and simmer 10 minutes. Remove chicken breasts and livers from liquid. Cool. (Reserve stock for another use.)

Chop chicken and livers in a food processor. Add onion, salt, nutmeg, mustard, cloves, cayenne, garlic, cognac, lemon juice, eggs, and butter. Process until smooth. Transfer to a bowl or terrine. Cover and chill.

When ready to serve, sprinkle with pistachios and parsley. Serve chilled with French bread or crackers.

Mushroom Pâté

SELECTING AND CLEANING CULTIVATED MUSHROOMS

Cultivated mushrooms include button, cup, flat, and cremini mushrooms. It is important that mushrooms be fresh, so purchase no more than a few days before intended use. Select firm mushrooms that are evenly colored with tightly closed caps. Clean mushrooms just before using by wiping with a damp paper towel. Never immerse in water as mushrooms are very absorbent and will become mushy.

2 tablespoons plus 2 tablespoons
   unsalted butter, at room temperature
8 ounces fresh mushrooms, minced
1½ teaspoons minced garlic
¼ cup minced green onions,
   white part only
⅓ cup chicken stock
4 ounces cream cheese, softened
2 tablespoons minced green onions,
   green part only

2 teaspoons Worcestershire sauce
2 teaspoons fresh lemon juice
1½ teaspoons minced fresh thyme
1 teaspoon salt
freshly ground pepper
——
chopped fresh parsley, red bell pepper,
   or green onions

Melt 2 tablespoons butter in a medium skillet. Add mushrooms and sauté 2 to 3 minutes. Add garlic and ¼ cup green onions. Sauté 1 minute. Add chicken stock and cook over high heat until all liquid is absorbed. Cool to room temperature.

Blend cream cheese and remaining 2 tablespoons butter in a medium bowl. Add mushroom mixture, 2 tablespoons green onions, Worcestershire, lemon juice, thyme, salt, and pepper. Adjust seasonings. Pour into a 1-cup mold lined with plastic wrap and chill.

When ready to serve, unmold onto a serving plate and sprinkle with parsley, red bell pepper, or green onions. Serve with toast points or crackers.

Mushroom Pâté may be prepared 3 days in advance.

Chèvre-Filled Mushrooms

YIELDS 24 MUSHROOM CAPS

24 large fresh mushrooms, caps
  reserved, stems minced
⅓ cup unsalted butter
2 teaspoons minced onion
¾ cup bread crumbs
2 tablespoons minced fresh parsley

2 tablespoons fresh lemon juice
1 teaspoon salt
3 ounces chèvre, crumbled (¾ cup)
2 ounces blue cheese,
  crumbled (½ cup)
unsalted butter, melted

Place mushroom caps, hollow side up, in a 9 by 13-inch baking dish.
Set aside.

Melt butter in a medium skillet. Add minced stems and onion. Sauté
over medium heat until soft. Remove from heat and add bread crumbs,
parsley, lemon juice, and salt. Mix well, then cool to room temperature.
Stir in cheeses until combined.

Preheat oven to 450 degrees. Spoon cheese mixture into mushroom
caps. Brush with melted butter. Bake 5 to 7 minutes until lightly browned.

Pesto, Goat Cheese, and Sun-Dried Tomato Torta

SERVES 10 TO 12

1 cup coarsely chopped fresh basil,
  loosely packed
1 cup coarsely chopped fresh spinach,
  loosely packed
1½ teaspoons minced garlic
¼ cup virgin olive oil
4 ounces Parmesan cheese, freshly
  grated (1 cup)
freshly ground pepper

8 ounces cream cheese, softened
4 ounces goat cheese, softened
⅓ cup sun-dried tomatoes packed
  in oil, drained, patted dry, and
  minced
¼ cup finely chopped pine nuts
———
thinly sliced sun-dried tomatoes

Chop basil, spinach, and garlic in a food processor. While machine is running,
gradually add olive oil through feed tube. Add Parmesan and process until
almost smooth. Season with pepper. Set aside. Blend cream cheese and goat
cheese in a medium bowl until smooth.

Line a 3-cup bowl with plastic wrap, leaving a 4-inch overhang. Mold
one-third of cream cheese mixture into a disk and distribute evenly in bottom
of prepared bowl. Spread half of basil mixture over cheese. Sprinkle with
half of sun-dried tomatoes and half of nuts. Mold another one-third cheese
mixture into a larger disk and place on top of nuts. Repeat layers with remaining basil mixture, sun-dried tomatoes, pine nuts, and last one-third of cheese.
Tap bowl lightly to allow ingredients to settle. Fold plastic overhang over
top and refrigerate.

Thirty minutes before serving, unfold plastic wrap and invert onto serving
plate. Decorate top with sun-dried tomato slices. Serve at room temperature
with assorted gourmet crackers.

Torta may be prepared 3 days in advance.

Curried Snowball

YIELDS 2 CUPS

8 ounces cream cheese, softened
4 ounces Cheddar cheese,
    shredded (1 cup)
3 tablespoons dry sherry
1 tablespoon Worcestershire sauce
¾ teaspoon curry powder
½ teaspoon garlic powder

½ teaspoon white pepper
pinch cayenne pepper
——
4 to 6 ounces mango chutney
½ cup minced green onions
½ cup finely chopped peanuts
½ cup grated coconut

Combine cheeses, sherry, Worcestershire, curry powder, garlic powder, white pepper, and cayenne in a small bowl. Blend well. Line a 2-cup bowl with plastic wrap, leaving a 4-inch overhang. Press cheese mixture into bowl. Fold plastic overhang over top and cover with another piece of wrap. Refrigerate at least 4 hours. (At this point, it may be frozen.)

When ready to serve, unfold plastic wrap and invert onto a serving plate. Spoon chutney over the top. Sprinkle with green onions, peanuts, and coconut. Serve chilled with crackers.

Curried Snowball is best made a day or two in advance. If frozen, defrost before putting on the topping.

Pesto Parmesan Spread

YIELDS 1½ CUPS

2 tablespoons chopped fresh parsley
½ cup chopped fresh basil
2 tablespoons chopped red or
    green onion
1 clove garlic, chopped
1 ounce Parmesan cheese, freshly
    grated (¼ cup)
8 ounces cream cheese, softened

4 tablespoons unsalted butter,
    at room temperature
——
1 loaf French bread, cut into
    ¼-inch slices
shredded Parmesan cheese
paprika or cayenne pepper

Blend parsley, basil, onion, garlic, and grated Parmesan in a food processor. Add cream cheese and butter, blending thoroughly. Transfer mixture to a bowl. Cover and refrigerate.

Just before serving, spread cheese mixture on French bread slices. Sprinkle with shredded Parmesan. Broil 1 to 3 minutes, or until edges begin to brown. Sprinkle with paprika or cayenne. Serve immediately.

Southwestern Cheese Spread

8 ounces Cheddar cheese,
  shredded (2 cups)
4 ounces Swiss cheese,
  shredded (1 cup)
4 ounces Monterey Jack cheese,
  shredded (1 cup)
2 tablespoons diced green bell pepper
2 tablespoons diced yellow bell pepper
2 tablespoons diced red bell pepper
2 tablespoons chopped green onions

1 ½ teaspoons minced capers
¾ teaspoon minced garlic
¾ teaspoon Worcestershire sauce
1 ½ teaspoons chopped fresh dill
3 tablespoons chopped fresh cilantro
dash Tabasco Sauce
¾ teaspoon Cajun spices
2 to 3 tablespoons Dijon mustard
¼ to ½ cup mayonnaise

Combine cheeses, bell peppers, green onions, capers, garlic, Worcestershire, dill, cilantro, Tabasco, Cajun spices, mustard, and mayonnaise in a large bowl. Stir to blend. Line a 1-quart bowl with plastic wrap, leaving a 4-inch overhang. Press cheese mixture into bowl and fold plastic overhang over top. Cover with another piece of wrap and refrigerate.

    When ready to serve, unfold plastic wrap and invert onto a serving plate. Serve chilled with tortilla chips or assorted crackers. Garnish with Pico de Gallo (page 157).

Baked Chèvre with Sun-Dried Tomatoes and Basil

8 ounces chèvre
4 ounces sun-dried tomatoes packed
  in oil, drained and minced

½ teaspoon minced garlic
½ cup minced fresh basil

Preheat oven to 400 degrees. Lightly coat a small ovenproof serving dish with olive oil. Place chèvre in dish and bake until melted, 15 to 20 minutes. Combine the sun-dried tomatoes, garlic, and basil in a small bowl. Spoon tomato mixture over cheese. Serve with crackers or fresh vegetables.

CHEESE

As children, our taste in cheese was simple: rubbery yellow or white slices, unwrapped from plastic and served with dollops of mayonnaise on spongy white bread. Today, there are infinite varieties of cheeses to discover. They range from delicate fresh cheeses rushed from rural farmhouses and tasting of butter, to rare goat cheeses wrapped in chestnut leaves and tied with straw, to slow-ripening cheeses encased in snowy edible rinds, to magnificently aged straw-colored Parmigiano-Reggiano shaved into tissue-thin slices and eaten with ripe pears. There are hundreds of others too numerous to catalogue here or to count. When serving a cheese course, offer guests at least three cheeses of contrasting color, taste, and texture, around 2 ounces of each cheese per person. Serve unsliced, never cold. Letting cheese come to room temperature releases its flavor.

Salmon Pinwheels

YIELDS 30 PINWHEELS

CAVIAR

Caviar should be kept refrigerated, never frozen. Do not use with silver; it gives caviar a metallic taste. Stainless steel is alright to use. Caviar should not be fishy or salty tasting. It should be shiny, translucent, and large. Do not bruise the eggs. Caviar can be served alone in a glass or crystal bowl surrounded by ice. It can be accompanied by lemon wedges, parsley, sour cream, and hard-boiled eggs.

Dill Cream Cheese:
8 ounces cream cheese, softened
½ cup chopped fresh dill, loosely packed
2 teaspoons fresh lemon juice
¼ teaspoon kosher salt
——

10 slices smoked salmon, each about 3 by 4 inches (⅔ pound)
½ cup Dill Cream Cheese
4 hearts of palm, each cut into 8 equal rounds
——
½ ounce caviar
30 small dill sprigs

Dill Cream Cheese: Blend cream cheese in a food processor until creamy. Add dill, lemon juice, and salt. Process until combined. Store in a tightly covered container in refrigerator up to 1 week.

Cut each salmon slice into 3 equal strips measuring about 1 by 4 inches. Spread ¼ to ½ teaspoon Dill Cream Cheese on each strip. Place 1 heart of palm round at end of strip, spread again with cream cheese, and roll. Continue until all hearts of palm and salmon strips are used. Place pinwheels on a serving tray. Using a pastry bag fitted with a small star tip, pipe a small Dill Cream Cheese star on the top of each pinwheel. Garnish with a small dollop of caviar and a sprig of dill.

Salmon Pillows with Basil Cream Sauce

YIELDS 24 PILLOWS

WON TON WRAPPERS

Made from eggs and flour, won ton wrappers may be purchased fresh or frozen. These thin, pastry-like wrappings should be stored in a tightly sealed plastic bag and frozen or refrigerated. They will stay fresh for 5 days if refrigerated.

Basil Cream Sauce:
1 cup fresh basil, loosely packed
¼ cup olive oil
1 tablespoon pine nuts
2 cloves garlic
¼ teaspoon white pepper
1 cup half and half
½ cup heavy whipping cream
4 ounces Romano cheese, freshly grated (1 cup)

Salmon Pillows:
6 ounces smoked salmon, sliced
4 ounces cream cheese, softened
2 teaspoons fresh lemon juice
⅛ teaspoon white pepper
cornstarch
24 won ton wrappers
1 large egg white, beaten
——
chopped red onion
chopped tomatoes
capers

Basil Cream Sauce: Process basil, olive oil, pine nuts, garlic, and white pepper in a food processor until basil is finely chopped. Combine half and half and whipping cream in a saucepan. Bring to a simmer, but do not boil. Whisk in basil mixture and Romano. Heat until cheese melts. Keep warm.

Salmon Pillows: Process salmon, cream cheese, lemon juice, and white pepper in a food processor. Line a baking sheet with waxed paper and lightly sprinkle with cornstarch. Place 1 rounded teaspoon of salmon mixture in the center of a won ton wrapper. Place on prepared baking sheet and fold in half diagonally, pressing edges to release any air. Brush and seal edges with egg white. Repeat with remaining won tons. Cook in batches in a large pot of boiling water, about 3 minutes. Transfer to serving plate. Top with sauce and garnish with red onion, tomatoes, and capers.

Spicy Salmon Tartare with Plantain Chips

SERVES 12

Plantain Chips:
4 green plantains, peeled
4 cups peanut oil
salt

Spicy Salmon Tartare:
1½ pounds fresh salmon fillets

¼ cup Dijon mustard
¼ cup puréed chipotle chile peppers,
   canned in adobo sauce
½ cup capers, rinsed and drained
½ cup minced green onions
¼ cup extra virgin olive oil

PLANTAINS

The plantain is related to the banana. It can be cooked when ripe or unripe, but is never eaten raw.

Plantain Chips: Cut plantains in half against the grain and slice lengthwise into paper thin slices. Heat oil to 375 degrees in a large skillet over high heat. Fry plantains a few at a time so as not to decrease the oil temperature. Take care not to let them touch while frying. Fry slices 3 minutes, or until crisp. Drain on paper towels and season with salt while still hot.

Spicy Salmon Tartare: Remove all gray matter, skin, and fat from salmon fillets. Cut fillets into very thin strips, then finely dice. Cover and refrigerate. Combine mustard, chipotles, capers, green onions, and olive oil in a nonmetallic bowl. Mix well. Stir in diced salmon. Serve immediately with Plantain Chips.

Ginger Shrimp Toast

YIELDS 60 TOASTS

1 loaf white bread, very thinly sliced
6 tablespoons unsalted butter,
   at room temperature
¼ teaspoon salt
¾ pound fresh medium shrimp,
   boiled (page 48), peeled, deveined,
   and minced

1 clove garlic, minced
2 tablespoons minced fresh parsley
1 teaspoon grated ginger, minced

Preheat broiler. Using a 1½ to 2-inch round cookie cutter, cut bread slices into rounds. Toast on one side. Cream butter and salt until light and fluffy in a medium bowl. Stir in shrimp, garlic, parsley, and ginger. Blend well. Spread shrimp mixture on untoasted side of bread rounds. Place on baking sheet and broil until lightly browned. Serve immediately.

Peppercorn Marinated Shrimp

1 gallon water (no salt added)

1 bag (3 ounces) Zatarain's
  Crab Boil

1 lemon, cut in half, not squeezed

6 to 10 bay leaves

3 tablespoons white distilled vinegar

1 tablespoon unsalted butter

4 to 5 tablespoons Old Bay
  Seasoning (optional)

———

1½ pounds fresh medium shrimp,
  heads off, not peeled, never frozen

Place water, crab boil, lemon,
bay leaves, vinegar, and butter
in a large Dutch oven or soup pot.
Stir the crab boil bag around to
release flavoring. Cover loosely.
When water has boiled 1 to
2 minutes, add ½ to ¾ pound
shrimp. Continue to heat, even
allowing a rolling boil to develop.
When shrimp float to the top and
have turned pink, they are ready
to come out. Remove shrimp with
a slotted spoon to a serving platter.
Add additional batches of shrimp
into same broth, repeating until all
the shrimp are cooked. Sprinkle
generously with Old Bay Seasoning,
adding more or less as desired.
Peel and eat.

No-No's:

◆ Don't overcook the shrimp
  (remove promptly)

◆ Don't add salt to water
  (harder to peel)

◆ Don't use liquid seasonings

◆ Don't add vegetables
  (onions, carrots, corn)

¾ cup balsamic vinegar

3 tablespoons Dijon mustard

¼ cup Worcestershire sauce

3 cloves garlic, minced

juice of 1 lemon or lime

2½ cups virgin olive oil

———

5 pounds fresh medium shrimp,
  boiled, peeled, and deveined

6 bay leaves

6 tablespoons capers

1 large red onion, minced

6 tablespoons black and green
  peppercorns

———

lemon slices

chopped fresh basil

Combine vinegar, mustard, Worcestershire, garlic, and lemon juice in a small bowl. Whisk in olive oil. Set aside.

Layer one-third shrimp, 2 bay leaves, 2 tablespoons capers, one-third red onion, and 2 tablespoons peppercorns in a nonmetallic bowl. Repeat layers until all shrimp are used. Pour marinade over shrimp. Cover and refrigerate 8 to 10 hours. Remove bay leaves. Serve chilled. Garnish with lemon slices and sprinkle with basil.

Golden Baked Shrimp

1 teaspoon salt

½ teaspoon freshly ground pepper

¼ cup fresh lemon juice

2 tablespoons balsamic vinegar

3 cloves garlic, minced

¼ cup mayonnaise

2 pounds fresh large shrimp, peeled
  and deveined

1½ cups fine bread crumbs

1 tablespoon chopped fresh basil

2 tablespoons chopped fresh parsley

1½ teaspoons chopped fresh dill

½ cup (1 stick) unsalted butter,
  melted

¼ cup extra virgin olive oil

Combine salt, pepper, lemon juice, vinegar, garlic, and mayonnaise in a large bowl. Add shrimp to marinade and stir to coat. Cover and refrigerate 1 to 2 hours.

Preheat oven to 450 degrees. Combine bread crumbs, basil, parsley, and dill in a small bowl. Roll each shrimp in crumb mixture and place in a single layer in a 9 by 13-inch shallow baking dish. Add butter and olive oil to reserved marinade and pour over shrimp. Bake 12 to 15 minutes, or until golden.

Crab Cakes with Roma Salsa and Lemon Butter

YIELDS 12 SMALL CRAB CAKES

Roma Salsa:
2 cups diced Roma tomatoes
½ cup diced yellow onion
¼ cup chopped fresh cilantro
1 tablespoon minced garlic
¼ cup fresh lemon juice
2 tablespoons fresh lime juice
1 tablespoon salt
½ teaspoon freshly ground pepper

Lemon Butter:
1 lemon, peeled and quartered
1 shallot, minced
¼ cup white wine
1 bay leaf
1 ½ teaspoons whole black
   peppercorns
2 cups (4 sticks) unsalted butter,
   cut into pieces
1 ½ teaspoons salt
¼ teaspoon white pepper

Crab Cakes:
2 tablespoons plus 3 tablespoons extra
   virgin olive oil
½ cup diced red bell pepper
½ cup diced green bell pepper
½ cup diced yellow onion
2 tablespoons minced garlic
2 tablespoons Creole mustard
2 tablespoons Worcestershire sauce
pinch cayenne pepper
1 tablespoon salt
½ teaspoon freshly ground pepper
½ cup bread crumbs
2 large eggs, lightly beaten
1 ½ pounds fresh lump crabmeat,
   shells removed
½ cup minced green onions
3 tablespoons unsalted butter

REMOVE BAY LEAF
When cooking with bay leaves, always remove from dish before serving. They do not soften during cooking and cannot be eaten.

Roma Salsa: Combine tomatoes, onion, cilantro, garlic, lemon juice, lime juice, salt, and pepper in a small serving bowl. Cover and chill.

Lemon Butter: Combine lemon, shallot, white wine, bay leaf, and peppercorns in a heavy saucepan. Reduce liquid over low heat until mixture is almost dry. Strain liquid, removing bay leaf, peppercorns, and any large lemon particles. Whisk butter, one piece at a time, into strained lemon mixture. Let butter melt before adding additional pieces. Do not allow mixture to boil as butter will break down. Add salt and pepper. Set aside and keep warm.

Crab Cakes: Heat 2 tablespoons olive oil in a large skillet. Add bell peppers, onion, and garlic. Sauté until tender. Add mustard, Worcestershire, cayenne, salt, and pepper. Stir to combine. Add bread crumbs and sauté 1 to 2 minutes. Remove from heat. Place mixture in a large bowl. Fold in eggs, stirring to blend. Stir in crabmeat and green onions. Mix well. Chill 30 to 40 minutes. Shape mixture into 12 small crab cakes. Heat 1 tablespoon olive oil and 1 tablespoon butter in a large skillet. Sauté 4 crab cakes on both sides until golden brown. Repeat with remaining crab cakes, adding an additional 1 tablespoon olive oil and 1 tablespoon butter, as needed, with each batch.

To serve, spoon Lemon Butter onto a serving plate, place crab cakes on Lemon Butter, and top with a dollop of Roma Salsa.

Crawfish Phyllo Triangles

2 packages (8 ounces each) cream cheese, softened
1 pound fresh crawfish, cooked, peeled, and coarsely chopped
3 green onions, chopped
1 tablespoon chopped fresh cilantro
1 tablespoon chopped fresh tarragon
1 teaspoon minced garlic
½ teaspoon curry powder
½ teaspoon crushed red pepper flakes
¼ teaspoon salt
2 tablespoons fresh lime juice
1 pound frozen phyllo dough, thawed (page 55)
1 cup (2 sticks) unsalted butter, melted
1 cup fine bread crumbs

Combine cream cheese, crawfish, green onions, cilantro, tarragon, garlic, curry, red pepper flakes, salt, and lime juice in a large bowl. Set aside.

Preheat oven to 400 degrees. Place 1 sheet of phyllo on a lightly floured surface. Brush with melted butter and sprinkle with bread crumbs. Repeat with 2 more sheets of phyllo. With a sharp knife, cut across horizontally to make 3 rectangles. (Cover remaining phyllo with a damp towel while working on the first.) Place 1 rounded tablespoon of crawfish mixture on a corner of each rectangle and fold up "flag style" to form triangular packages. Repeat with remaining crawfish and phyllo. Place triangles on a greased baking sheet and brush lightly with butter. Bake 12 minutes, or until golden brown. Serve immediately.

Crawfish Phyllo Triangles may be frozen unbaked, then cooked frozen.

Dilled Scallop Puffs

3 tablespoons unsalted butter
1 pound fresh bay scallops, minced
2 teaspoons minced lemon zest
3 cloves garlic, minced
3 tablespoons chopped fresh dill
6 to 8 ounces Baby Swiss cheese, shredded (1½ to 2 cups)
1 cup mayonnaise
½ teaspoon freshly ground white or black pepper
2 loaves white bread, very thinly sliced
paprika

Melt butter in a medium saucepan. Add scallops, lemon zest, and garlic. Sauté 2 to 3 minutes. Add dill and sauté 30 seconds. Cool. Add cheese, mayonnaise, and pepper to cooled mixture. Stir to combine.

Preheat broiler. Using a 1½ to 2-inch round cookie cutter, cut bread slices into rounds. Transfer rounds to a baking sheet and toast on one side in the oven. Mound scallop mixture on untoasted side of each bread round. Sprinkle with paprika. Broil 2 to 3 minutes, until light brown and bubbly. Serve immediately.

Raja Poblano Quesadillas

YIELDS 30 QUESADILLA WEDGES

3 to 5 poblano chile peppers, roasted
  (page 40), peeled, and seeded
3 tablespoons unsalted butter
3 mild white onions, thinly sliced
2 cloves garlic, minced
1 cup sour cream
4 ounces Queso Chihuahua or
  Monterey Jack cheese, shredded
  (1 cup)

¼ cup minced fresh epazote (optional)
salt
freshly ground pepper

——

10 flour tortillas
3 tablespoons unsalted butter
3 tablespoons vegetable oil

EPAZOTE

Epazote, native to tropical America, is a bitter herb with pointed, serrated leaves. It is also known as Mexican tea or wormseed. Epazote is used in many Mexican dishes and soups and with cheese in quesadilla fillings. It is frequently used in bean soups as it is believed to take the wind out of beans. Store fresh epazote in a sealed plastic bag in the refrigerator.

Slice roasted poblanos into ½-inch strips or "rajas." Melt 3 tablespoons butter in a large skillet. Add poblanos, onions, and garlic. Sauté until onions become translucent. Stir in sour cream. Add cheese and epazote. Stir until thoroughly melted. Season with salt and pepper.

Spread 1 tablespoon cheese mixture on half of each tortilla. Fold tortilla in half. Heat 1 tablespoon butter and 1 tablespoon oil in a large skillet over medium-high heat until hot. Cook each quesadilla until it turns golden brown. Flip and brown other side. Slide quesadilla onto a warm serving plate and pat with paper towel to remove excess oil. Cut into 3 wedges. Repeat with remaining cheese mixture and tortillas. Top with Salsa Rojo (page 54).

Blue Cheese Puffs

YIELDS 60 PUFFS

2 packages (8 ounces each) cream
  cheese, softened
1 cup mayonnaise
1 tablespoon minced onion
¼ cup minced fresh chives
3 or 4 ounces blue cheese, crumbled
  (¾ to 1 cup)

½ teaspoon cayenne pepper
1 loaf whole wheat bread, very
  thinly sliced
paprika

Mix cream cheese and mayonnaise in a medium bowl. Stir in onion, chives, blue cheese, and cayenne pepper. Set aside.

Using a 1½ to 2-inch round cookie cutter, cut bread slices into rounds. Spread 1 tablespoon of cheese mixture on each round. Place puffs on a baking sheet and freeze.

When ready to serve, preheat oven to 350 degrees. Remove baking sheet from freezer. Bake 15 minutes. Sprinkle with paprika. Serve immediately.

Blue Cheese Puffs may be stored in sealed plastic bags in the freezer.

Packages of the Southwest

Salsa Fresca:
3 medium tomatoes, peeled, seeded,
    and diced
2 fresh jalapeños, seeded and diced
1 teaspoon minced garlic
½ cup minced onion
1 tablespoon chopped fresh cilantro
½ cup tomato juice
salt

Packages:
2 tablespoons olive oil
1 cup chopped onions

1 tablespoon minced garlic
2 cans (4 ounces each) mild green
    chilies, drained and chopped
½ teaspoon salt
⅛ teaspoon cayenne pepper
¾ teaspoon ground cumin
2 large eggs, lightly beaten
8 ounces Monterey Jack cheese,
    shredded (2 cups)
2 tablespoons all-purpose flour
1 pound frozen phyllo sheets, thawed
1 cup (2 sticks) unsalted butter, melted
2 tablespoons chili powder

Salsa Fresca: Combine tomatoes, jalapeños, garlic, onion, cilantro, and tomato juice in a serving bowl. Season with salt. Cover and chill. Bring to room temperature before serving.

Packages: Heat olive oil in a large skillet. Add onions and sauté until translucent. Add garlic and sauté 2 minutes. Add chilies, salt, cayenne, and cumin. Cook until liquid has evaporated. Cool to room temperature. Add eggs to cooled onion mixture. Toss cheese and flour together in a small bowl. Add to onion mixture. Combine well.

Unwrap phyllo sheets and cover with a damp towel. Arrange 1 sheet of phyllo so that the long end (18 inches) is in front of you. Cut phyllo in half to make two 14 by 9-inch sheets. Brush each sheet with melted butter and sprinkle with chili powder. Fold each sheet in half to make two 14 by 4½-inch pieces. Place 2 tablespoons of filling at one end of piece. Fold in one-half inch of each long side, slightly covering filling, then fold into packages. Continue making packages until filling is used. Place each package seam down on a jelly-roll pan and brush with melted butter. (At this point, the packages may be covered with a damp paper towel, sealed with plastic wrap, and refrigerated up to 1 day in advance.)

When ready to bake, bring the packages to room temperature. Preheat oven to 375 degrees. Bake 15 to 20 minutes until lightly browned. Serve with Salsa Fresca.

The packages may also be folded "flag style" to form triangular packages.

Mango Margaritas and
Packages of the Southwest

Mexican Cheesecake with Salsa Rojo and Guacamole

AVOCADOS

The most common varieties are the dark, bumpy-skinned Haas avocado and the larger, smooth, thin-skinned Fuerte variety. Do not chill avocados as it causes them to blacken. Avocados must be used as quickly as possible, because once peeled, they discolor quickly. Putting the avocado pit in the prepared dish until serving time will help to retard discoloration. Covering the dish with lemon slices, lime slices, or plastic wrap pressed right on the top of the dish can also help. To keep diced avocados green before tossing, float them in water with lemon juice and drain before serving.

Salsa Rojo:
3 large tomatoes, peeled, seeded, and diced
1 red onion, minced
1 clove garlic, minced
2 serrano chile peppers, seeded and minced
1 bunch fresh cilantro, minced
¼ cup fresh lime juice
salt
freshly ground pepper

Cheesecake:
1½ cups crushed tortilla chips
4 tablespoons unsalted butter, melted
2 packages (8 ounces each) cream cheese, softened

8 ounces Monterey Jack cheese or Jalapeño Jack cheese, shredded (2 cups)
3 large eggs
½ cup plus ½ cup sour cream
1 can (4½ ounces) diced green chilies
1 cup picante sauce

Guacamole:
2 avocados, pitted and peeled
2 tablespoons minced onion
1 teaspoon chopped fresh cilantro
juice of ½ lime
dash Tabasco Sauce
1 teaspoon minced fresh jalapeño
salt

Salsa Rojo: Combine tomatoes, onion, garlic, serranos, cilantro, and lime juice in a serving bowl. Season with salt and pepper. Cover and chill.

Cheesecake: Preheat oven to 350 degrees. Combine chips and butter. Press mixture into bottom of a greased 9-inch springform pan. Bake 10 minutes. Combine cream cheese and Monterey Jack in a food processor. Add eggs and ½ cup sour cream and pulse to combine. Add green chilies and picante sauce. Pulse again to thoroughly combine. Pour cheese mixture over crust and spread evenly. Place pan on a baking sheet and bake 40 minutes. Spread remaining ½ cup sour cream on hot cheesecake. Cool to room temperature and chill.

Guacamole: Mash avocados with a fork in a medium bowl. Add onion, cilantro, lime juice, Tabasco, and jalapeño, mixing well. Season with salt.

To serve, unmold cheesecake onto a serving platter. Top with dollops of Salsa Rojo and Guacamole. Serve with tortilla chips.

Artichoke Cheesecake

SERVES 14

4 tablespoons unsalted butter, melted
8 sheets frozen phyllo dough, thawed
3 ounces marinated artichoke hearts
3 packages (8 ounces each) cream
   cheese, softened
5 ounces feta cheese, crumbled
   (1 ¼ cups)
1 ½ teaspoons chopped fresh oregano

¼ teaspoon garlic powder
3 large eggs
¼ cup chopped green onions
——
Roma tomatoes, sliced
Greek olives, pitted
fresh basil leaves

Preheat oven to 400 degrees. Brush bottom and sides of a 9-inch springform pan with butter. Place 1 sheet of phyllo in pan so that phyllo extends up and over the sides of the pan. Brush with butter. Repeat with remaining phyllo and butter. Make 2 slits in the center of phyllo for steam to escape. Bake 9 to 10 minutes, or until lightly browned. Cool on a wire rack. Decrease oven temperature to 325 degrees.

Drain and chop artichokes, reserving 2 tablespoons of the marinade. Set aside. Beat cream cheese, feta, oregano, and garlic powder in a large bowl. Add eggs, beating just until blended. Do not overbeat. Add artichoke hearts, reserved marinade, and green onions. Combine well. Pour mixture into crust and cover loosely with foil. Bake 35 to 40 minutes, until center is soft and sides stay firm when gently shaken. Cool. Cover and chill 2 hours or up to 24 hours.

When ready to serve, remove from pan and garnish with tomatoes, olives, and basil leaves. Serve slightly chilled or at room temperature.

HANDLING PHYLLO

Phyllo is a tissue-thin pastry dough. Originally used in Greece and various Middle Eastern countries, it has become quite popular in the United States. The dough is bought frozen and should be thawed in the refrigerator overnight. Phyllo can be refrigerated up to 1 month or frozen up to 1 year. Once opened, use within 2 to 3 days. Do not unwrap the dough until ready to use as it becomes brittle very quickly. While working with the phyllo sheets, cover those set aside with a damp cloth to keep them from drying out. It is best to brush edges with butter first, then move to the middle, as this prevents the edges from tearing.

Puffed Artichoke Pie

SERVES 6

1 package (11 ¼ ounces) frozen
   puff pastry dough, thawed
2 large eggs, lightly beaten
15 ounces ricotta cheese
4 ounces Parmesan cheese,
   freshly grated (1 cup)

1 ½ cups artichoke hearts,* drained and
   quartered
¼ teaspoon ground nutmeg
salt
freshly ground pepper

Cut two 7-inch diameter circles from each piece of pastry, reserving leftover pastry. Line bottom of a 7-inch springform pan with one of the circles and line sides with 2-inch strips cut from leftover pastry. Refrigerate pan and remaining pastry circle until ready to use. Reserve 2 tablespoons of the beaten eggs. Pour remaining eggs in a medium bowl. Add ricotta, Parmesan, artichoke hearts, and nutmeg. Mix thoroughly. Season with salt and pepper. Spoon evenly into prepared springform pan. Top with remaining pastry circle, pinching edges together to seal. Brush top of pie with reserved 2 tablespoons beaten egg. Refrigerate 20 minutes to firm.

Preheat oven to 400 degrees. Bake 55 minutes to 1 hour, or until golden brown and puffy. Cut into wedges and serve warm.

*Either frozen or canned artichoke hearts may be used. If using frozen, thaw before use. If using canned, they should not be marinated.

Roasted Bell Pepper and Artichoke Pizza

1 teaspoon olive oil
1 clove plus 1 clove garlic, minced
1 red bell pepper, roasted (page 40), peeled, seeded, and cut into strips
1 orange bell pepper, roasted, peeled, seeded, and cut into strips
¼ cup reduced fat mayonnaise
⅛ teaspoon crushed red pepper

¼ teaspoon freshly ground pepper
1 package (9 ounces) frozen artichoke hearts, thawed and drained
1 ready-made pizza crust (1 pound), plain or cheese flavored
2 ounces feta cheese, crumbled (½ cup)
1 teaspoon chopped fresh thyme

Preheat oven to 450 degrees. Heat oil in a nonstick skillet over medium-high heat. Add 1 minced clove garlic and sauté 1 minute. Stir in bell peppers. Set aside.

Place remaining garlic, mayonnaise, red pepper, black pepper, and artichoke hearts in a food processor. Process until finely chopped. Place pizza crust on a greased baking sheet or pizza stone. Spread artichoke mixture over crust, leaving a ½-inch border. Top with bell pepper mixture. Sprinkle with feta and thyme. Bake 14 minutes or until crust is crisp. (Cheese will not melt.) Slice and serve.

Garlic Chicken Bites with Tomato Raisin Sauce

WOODEN SKEWERS

Wooden skewers must be soaked 30 minutes in water before baking or they will burn.

3 tablespoons minced fresh cilantro
2 teaspoons freshly ground pepper
6 cloves plus 2 cloves garlic, minced
1 pound boneless, skinless chicken breasts, cut into 1½-inch pieces

⅓ cup tomato sauce
1 tablespoon brown sugar, firmly packed
1 tablespoon apple cider vinegar
½ cup raisins

Preheat oven to 350 degrees. Combine cilantro, pepper, and 6 minced cloves garlic in a small bowl. Rub mixture over chicken. Thread 1 or 2 pieces of chicken onto each skewer. Place skewers on a lightly greased baking sheet. Bake until chicken is lightly browned and cooked through, 18 to 20 minutes.

Process remaining 2 minced cloves garlic, tomato sauce, brown sugar, vinegar, and raisins in a food processor until raisins are chopped.

Serve Garlic Chicken Bites warm with sauce on the side for dipping.

Venison Meatballs in Sherried Chutney Sauce

1½ pounds ground venison*
1 pound ground spicy sausage
flour
1 cup light sour cream

1 jar (8 ounces) mango chutney,
  chopped
½ cup dry sherry

Combine venison and sausage. Roll venison mixture into 1½-inch meatballs. Roll in flour to lightly coat. Sauté meatballs in a nonstick skillet over medium-high heat until cooked. Drain.

Combine sour cream, chutney, and sherry in a saucepan over medium heat. Stir until blended. Add meatballs and heat thoroughly. Sauce may be thinned with extra sherry. Serve warm in a chafing dish.

*May substitute ground round for the venison.

Oriental Shrimp Dumplings

YIELDS 75 DUMPLINGS

1 large egg, separated
2 green onions, chopped
1 tablespoon sesame oil
1 teaspoon salt
½ teaspoon freshly ground pepper
1¼ pounds fresh medium shrimp,
  uncooked, peeled, deveined,
  and minced
¾ pound lean ground beef

5 dried Chinese mushrooms,
  soaked in water to cover
  20 minutes, squeezed dry,
  and chopped
½ cup chopped fresh cilantro,
  loosely packed
75 won ton wrappers
2 large egg whites, lightly beaten
————
Hot and Spicy Sauce

Lightly beat egg yolk in a large bowl. Add green onions, sesame oil, salt, and pepper. Mix well. Stir in shrimp, beef, mushrooms, and cilantro.

Lay won ton wrappers on a flat surface and brush edges lightly with egg whites. Place 1 tablespoon of filling in middle of each won ton. Bring up opposite corners to meet in middle over filling and pinch firmly to seal. Brush with more egg white, if needed. Repeat until all won tons and filling have been used. Bring a large pot of salted water to boil. Reduce heat until water is simmering. Add won tons and simmer until cooked, 5 to 7 minutes. Drain on paper towels.

Serve warm with Hot and Spicy Sauce on the side for dipping (see accompanying recipe).

HOT AND SPICY SAUCE

6 tablespoons soy sauce
6 tablespoons distilled white vinegar
2 tablespoons sugar
4 tablespoons dry sherry
1 teaspoon cornstarch
6 tablespoons chicken broth
6 tablespoons sesame oil
2 cloves garlic, minced
1 teaspoon chopped fresh ginger
2 green onions, trimmed and
  chopped
½ teaspoon ground Szechuan
  peppercorns
2 tablespoons chili paste
2 tablespoons chopped fresh cilantro

Combine soy sauce, vinegar, sugar, sherry, cornstarch, and chicken broth, whisk well to combine the cornstarch, and set aside. Warm sesame oil in a wok over medium heat. Add garlic, ginger, green onions, peppercorns, and chili paste. Stir fry 15 seconds. Remove from heat. Add soy mixture, then add cilantro. Serve in a small bowl. Yields 3 cups.

Gnarled, windblasted, clinging to rocky soil, olive trees seem as old as time. And well they may be. Some scholars trace their origins back to the Great Flood when a dove carried an olive leaf in its beak to dry land. Olives vary according to the soil and climate of the region where they're grown and the methods used for curing. With their salty taste, earthy colors, and high nutritional content, olives are a delicious beginning to many meals. Some favorites are the small, wrinkled black or mahogany-colored Italian Gaeta olives packed in brine or in oil and herbs; purple-black, almond-shaped Kalamata olives from Greece; tiny, tender black Nicoise olives from the Provence region of France; Royal Victoria olives of red, light-brown or dark-brown hues, similar in taste and richness to Kalamatas; and small, oval, cracked green Sicilian olives spiced with red pepper and oregano or fennel.

Melba Toast with Tomato Basil Salsa

SERVES 4

Melba Toast:
1 loaf white bread, very thinly sliced
½ cup (1 stick) unsalted butter, melted

Tomato Basil Salsa:
½ large red onion, quartered
⅓ cup fresh basil, loosely packed
1 pound Roma tomatoes, peeled, seeded, and halved

3 tablespoons freshly grated Parmesan cheese
¼ cup fresh lime juice
3 tablespoons extra virgin olive oil
2 tablespoons red wine vinegar
¼ teaspoon salt
¼ teaspoon freshly ground pepper

Melba Toast: Preheat oven to 325 degrees. Remove crusts from bread. Cut bread in halves or quarters and place on greased baking sheet. Brush tops with melted butter. Bake until lightly browned, about 10 to 15 minutes.

Tomato Basil Salsa: Coarsely chop onion, basil, and tomatoes in a food processor. Transfer to a bowl. Add Parmesan, lime juice, oil, vinegar, salt, and pepper. Stir to combine.

Serve Tomato Basil Salsa with Melba Toast as an appetizer or over pasta as a refreshing light meal.

Melba Toast may be stored in an airtight container for up to 1 week or up to 1 month in the freezer.

Ritzy Olives

YIELDS 2 CUPS

½ onion, quartered
2 cloves garlic, halved
1 tablespoon chopped fresh fennel
1 teaspoon chopped fresh basil
2 anchovies*
½ teaspoon grated orange zest

pinch freshly ground pepper
½ cup olive oil
½ cup vegetable oil
¼ cup balsamic vinegar
¼ cup white wine vinegar
2 cups green olives, drained

Purée onion, garlic, fennel, basil, and anchovies in a food processor. Add orange zest, pepper, oils, and vinegars. Blend until combined. Transfer mixture to a medium container and carefully stir in olives. Cover and refrigerate 24 hours. Serve olives in the marinade.

*½ teaspoon Worcestershire sauce may be substituted for anchovies.

Olive Caper Crostini

Olive Caper Spread:
½ cup Greek olives, pitted
3 tablespoons extra virgin olive oil
1 tablespoon chopped fresh basil
1 tablespoon capers, drained
2 cloves garlic, minced

Crostini:
1 baguette, sliced ½ inch thick
½ cup (1 stick) unsalted butter, melted

Olive Caper Spread: Process olives, oil, basil, capers, and garlic in a food processor until puréed. Set aside.

Crostini: Preheat oven to 400 degrees. Arrange baguette slices on a baking sheet. Brush both sides with butter. Bake until crisp and golden brown, about 10 minutes. Cool slightly and serve with Olive Caper Spread.

Olive Caper Spread may be prepared up to 4 days in advance and refrigerated. Bring to room temperature before serving. The crostini may be prepared 1 day in advance. Cool crostini completely and store in a sealed plastic bag at room temperature.

PARMESAN PITA CRISPS

3 pita bread rounds
6 tablespoons unsalted butter, melted
3 ounces Parmesan cheese, freshly grated (¾ cup)
½ cup chopped fresh parsley

Preheat oven to broil. Cut around edge of each pita round, making 2 round halves. (There should be 6 rounds.) Place bread smooth side down on a baking sheet. Brush each section liberally with melted butter. Cut each round into eight wedges. Sprinkle Parmesan on top of each wedge. Sprinkle parsley to cover. Broil in oven until hot, golden brown, and bubbly. Serve with dips or as a side with pasta.

Baked Garlic

1 large head elephant garlic*
¼ cup white wine
¼ cup chicken stock
1 tablespoon unsalted butter, melted

salt
cayenne pepper

——

Italian bread

Preheat oven to 300 degrees. Snip off top of garlic. Place the intact head in a small ovenproof serving dish. Add white wine and chicken stock to almost cover garlic. Pour melted butter over garlic. Sprinkle with salt and cayenne pepper. Bake 3 hours.

To serve, pull individual cloves off head and squeeze insides onto Italian bread. Spread the baked garlic as you would spread soft butter. Remaining juice may be used for dipping.

* May also use regular garlic.

ELEPHANT GARLIC

Elephant garlic is not actually garlic, but a relative of the leek. It is the size of an orange and has very large, mild-flavored cloves.

Detering Ranch Pecans

YIELDS 2 CUPS

DON'T GO NUTS

To ease the effort of cracking pecans, place nuts in an appropriate size pot, cover with water, and bring to a boil. Remove from heat, cover, and let stand until cool. Blot the nuts dry and crack, positioning the cracker at opposite ends of the nut.

1 cup water
1 cup sugar
3 to 4 dried red chile peppers*

2 cups pecan halves
¼ cup molasses

Preheat oven to 250 degrees. Combine water, sugar, and chiles in a small saucepan. Bring to a boil. Add pecans and return to a boil. Reduce heat and simmer 10 minutes. Drain pecans. Transfer to a baking sheet. Bake 45 minutes, stirring occasionally. Pour pecans into a small bowl. Add molasses and toss to coat. Return pecans to the baking sheet. Bake an additional 45 minutes, or until pecans are very crisp, stirring occasionally.

* Any variety.

Gourmet Pecans

YIELDS 4 CUPS

PECANS

The pecan derives its name from paccan, an Algonquian word meaning "nut with a hard shell to crack." Pecans grew wild along the riverbanks in Texas and Mexico long before recorded history. Pecans provide protein and fiber, and like most nuts, they are also high in fat.

Two pounds of pecans in the shell equals 1 pound shelled pecans equals 4 cups whole pecans. Nuts will keep for several months if stored in a dry, cool place, but will last up to 1 year in the freezer.

1 cup sugar
½ teaspoon salt
1 large egg white

3 tablespoons Grand Marnier, Kahlúa, or any liqueur with a strong flavor
4 or more cups small pecan halves

Preheat oven to 325 degrees. Line a jelly-roll pan with foil. Combine sugar and salt in a small bowl. Set aside. Whisk egg white and liqueur in a large bowl. Add pecans and stir to coat. Add sugar mixture. Stir thoroughly to blend. Spread pecans in a single layer on prepared pan. Bake 20 to 25 minutes until pecans are toasted and crisp, stirring every 10 minutes. It will look as though all the coating is coming off. Stir from the outside of the pan towards the center as the nuts at the edges brown faster. Watch closely because sugar burns quickly. Remove pan from oven and immediately loosen nuts from foil. Cool on wax paper. Save the seasoned sugar for use as an ice cream topping.

Gourmet Pecans will keep 2 weeks in an airtight container. They make great gifts and are wonderful on ice cream.

Nuts on a Hot Tin Roof

YIELDS 2 CUPS

1½ tablespoons unsalted butter
2 cups salted cashews
¼ teaspoon cayenne pepper

½ teaspoon ground cumin
½ teaspoon ground coriander

Melt butter in a small saucepan. Add cashews and sauté about 3 minutes. Drain on paper towels. Combine cashews, cayenne, cumin, and coriander. Stir well. Store in an airtight container.

Mango Margaritas

SERVES 6

1 jar (26 ounces) mangoes plus juice,
    reserving 3 tablespoons juice
8 ounces gold tequila (1 cup)
1 can (6 ounces) frozen limeade
    concentrate

4 ounces Triple Sec or Cointreau
    (½ cup)
2 ounces Grand Marnier (¼ cup)
crushed ice
coarse sugar

Combine mangoes and juice, tequila, limeade, Triple Sec or Cointreau, and Grand Marnier in a blender. Mix well. Pour half of the liquid in a pitcher and set aside. Dip margarita glass edge in reserved mango juice and then in sugar. Add crushed ice to liquid in blender. Blend until margaritas are slushy. Pour margarita mixture into glasses and serve. Repeat with remaining half.

For a fun touch use tri-colored sugar crystals instead of plain coarse sugar.

Frozen Bellini

SERVES 4

4 ounces vodka (½ cup)
4 ounces peach nectar (½ cup)
4 ounces peach schnapps (½ cup)

4 ounces champagne (½ cup)
5 ounces canned peaches, drained
crushed ice

Combine vodka, peach nectar, peach schnapps, champagne, and peaches in a blender. Mix well. Fill blender with ice to the top. Blend on high speed. Serve immediately. Store unused portion in the freezer.

Gin Breeze

SERVES 6

1 can (12 ounces) frozen limeade
    concentrate
6 ounces gin (¾ cup)

4 ounces Triple Sec (½ cup)
4 cups crushed ice
1 cup fresh mint, loosely packed

Combine limeade, gin, and Triple Sec in a blender. Mix well. Fill blender with ice to the top, add mint, and blend until smooth. Serve immediately.

THE BIRTH OF THE MARGARITA

The year was 1947. An American couple, Mr. and Mrs. Sames, was spending the Christmas holiday at their vacation home in Acapulco where they entertained frequently. Mrs. Sames was particularly fond of a drink favored by the locals: tequila with lime juice. She also enjoyed Cointreau, a liqueur imported from France. During one particularly festive evening, she began experimenting with her two favorite drinks and soon poured a concoction mixed from equal parts tequila, Cointreau, and fresh-squeezed lime juice over ice. The Drink, as it came to be known, was the hit of the season. The following year the Sameses returned. On Christmas Eve, Mr. Sames presented his wife with long-stemmed crystal glasses having shallow, flat bowls, perfect for serving The Drink. Etched into each glass was the name of his beloved wife: Margarita. The rest is history.

The Classic Martini

4 ounces gin
½ ounce dry vermouth
lemon twist, olive, or cocktail onion

Pour gin and vermouth into an ice-filled shaker. Shake, then strain into a glass. Garnish with a lemon twist or olive. Garnishing with an onion makes the drink a Gibson. Vodka may be substituted for gin to make a Vodkatini. Serves 1.

MARTINIS

Every martini is handmade, therefore personal. The martini drinker can look forward to a unique taste through artistic bartending. Experiment with flavored gin or vodka, but for nostalgia's sake, return to The Classic.

2 ounces gin   *dash orange bitters*
1 ounce dry vermouth *lemon peel or olive*

Place gin, vermouth, and bitters into an ice-filled shaker. Shake, then pour into a chilled stemmed glass. Garnish with lemon peel or olive.

This is the martini before Prohibition.

3 Musketeer Mimosa

SERVES 4

4 teaspoons Armagnac, chilled   *1 teaspoon sugar*
4 teaspoons Grand Marnier, chilled *2 cups champagne, chilled*
¼ cup fresh orange juice, chilled   *orange peel, cut into long thin strips*

Combine Armagnac, Grand Marnier, orange juice, and sugar in a pitcher. Add champagne. Place one long orange peel strip into each champagne flute. Fill flutes with champagne mixture. Serve chilled.

Tropical Punch

SERVES 20

½ watermelon, seeded and cut   *4 oranges, each cut into 8 pieces*
* into chunks (8 pounds)*   *2 lemons, sliced*
1 fresh pineapple, cut into chunks *3 star fruit, sliced*
1 liter silver tequila   *6 limes, each cut into 8 pieces*
4 cups fresh orange juice   *3 small ruby grapefruit, each cut into*
½ cup fresh lime juice   * 8 pieces*
1 can (46 ounces) unsweetened   *3 cans (12 ounces each)*
* pineapple juice*   * grapefruit-citrus soft drink*

Place watermelon and pineapple chunks in a 2-gallon jar with a lid. Add tequila, juices, oranges, and lemons. Chill 6 to 8 hours, stirring occasionally. Two hours before serving, add star fruit, limes, and grapefruit.

   Serve punch over crushed ice in a large widemouthed glass, with a generous splash of soft drink and a straw.

Freeze the watermelon rind to use later as a fruit salad bowl.

Summertime Cooler

1 bottle (64 ounces) raspberry-
  cranberry drink, chilled
2 cups water
2 large lemons
2 large limes
1 medium nectarine
½ pound seedless green grapes
½ cup raspberries

lemon leaves
5 tea bags
2 to 4 tablespoons sugar
1 bottle (34 ounces) lemon-lime
  diet soft drink, chilled
1 can (6 ounces) frozen lemonade
  concentrate, thawed

Mix 3 cups raspberry-cranberry drink and 2 cups water. Pour 3½ cups of this mixture into a 6-cup ring mold and freeze. Refrigerate remaining 1½ cups. Cut a continuous 1-inch wide strip of peel from each lemon and each lime. Set aside. Squeeze juice from lemons and limes to equal ¼ cup each. Refrigerate to use in punch later. Trim white membrane from lemon and lime peel strips. Form each strip into a rose by rolling it tightly, skin side out, around finger. Secure with a toothpick. Cover and refrigerate. When juice ring is frozen, cut nectarine into wedges and separate grapes into small clusters. Discard toothpicks from lemon and lime roses. Arrange roses with nectarine wedges, grape clusters, raspberries, and lemon leaves on frozen ring for garnish. Pour in half of remaining drink mixture; freeze about 1 hour to set garnishes in place. Add remaining drink mixture; freeze. In a 4-cup glass measuring cup, pour boiling water over tea bags to equal 4 cups. Let steep 10 minutes. Discard tea bags. Cover and refrigerate tea until ready to complete punch.

Just before serving, mix 2 tablespoons sugar, soft drink, undiluted lemonade, tea, remaining cranberry drink, lemon and lime juices, and 1½ cups cold water in a 6-quart punch bowl (large enough to hold ice ring). Taste, adding more sugar if desired. Unmold the ice ring into your hands, not on a plate because it might break. To loosen the ice ring from mold, place mold in a hot water bath about 30 seconds (do not immerse). Add the ice ring to punch.

Lemon leaves may be purchased at a florist shop.

BEVERAGE GARNISHES

Try adding an extra flourish to drinks served to guests. A small effort can create a very pretty result and turn a simple drink into something special.

- *Freeze berries and drop into each glass*

- *Tie thin slices of lemon or lime zest into bows and place in each glass*

- *Place wedges of lemons, limes, kiwi, or pineapple on the rim of each glass*

- *Float fruit kabobs of melon balls and berries in the drink*

- *Float slices of lemons, limes, oranges (try sticking a clove in the orange slice), blood oranges, or star fruit*

- *Frost glasses in the freezer if cold beverages are to be served*

OLD-FASHIONED LEMONADE

4 cups cold water
¾ cup sugar
1 cup fresh lemon juice
1 lemon, sliced into thin rounds

Bring water to a boil. Add sugar, stirring to dissolve. Cool. Pour water mixture and lemon juice into a large pitcher. Blend well. Serve over ice and garnish with lemon rounds. Serves 6.

Orange Blossom Punch

6 cups fresh orange juice
1 cup fresh lemon juice
4 cups ginger ale
½ cup grenadine

½ cup sugar
4 cups vodka
2 pints lemon or orange sherbet

Combine orange juice, lemon juice, ginger ale, grenadine, sugar, and vodka in a punch bowl. Mix well. Add sherbet, stirring to evenly distribute. Serve immediately.

A TOUCH OF GREEN

Poached Pear Arugula Salad with
Cambazola Crostini and Sweet and Spicy Pecans

Radicchio, Watercress, and Arugula Salad

Dressing:
2 tablespoons white wine vinegar
½ teaspoon Dijon mustard
2 teaspoons minced fresh parsley
⅓ cup extra virgin olive oil
salt
freshly ground pepper

Salad:
2 small heads radicchio, torn
2 bunches watercress, trimmed and
* separated into sprigs*
2 bunches arugula, torn and
* stems discarded*
3 green onions, chopped

———

6 ounces Parmesan cheese, at room
* temperature, shaved into curls*

Combine vinegar, mustard, and parsley in a small bowl. Add oil in a thin stream, whisking continuously until blended. Season with salt and pepper. Set aside. Toss radicchio, watercress, arugula, and green onions in a salad bowl. Add dressing, toss, and top with Parmesan curls. Serve immediately.

Toasted Walnut Salad

Walnut Dressing:
⅔ cup walnut oil
⅓ cup fresh lemon juice
½ teaspoon Dijon mustard
¾ teaspoon sugar
dash salt
dash freshly ground pepper

Salad:
4 heads Boston lettuce, torn
1 cup toasted walnuts, coarsely chopped
2 ounces blue cheese, crumbled
* (½ cup)*
1 pear, peeled, cored, and
* thinly sliced*

Walnut Dressing: Combine walnut oil, lemon juice, mustard, sugar, salt, and pepper in a covered jar. Shake well and refrigerate.

Toss lettuce, walnuts, blue cheese, and pear in a salad bowl. Add dressing, toss, and serve immediately.

Walnut Dressing may be made up to 4 days in advance and kept covered in the refrigerator. Walnut oil should be stored in the refrigerator as it turns rancid quickly.

Strawberry Fields

Strawberry Dressing:
1 cup strawberries, hulled and halved
2 tablespoons raspberry vinegar
2 tablespoons brown sugar,
 firmly packed
¼ cup olive oil
¼ teaspoon sesame oil
½ teaspoon fresh lemon juice
coarse salt
freshly ground pepper

Salad:
4 cups mixed field greens
1 cup strawberries, hulled and halved
1 medium jicama, peeled and
 julienned
———
¼ cup toasted pistachios, chopped

Strawberry Dressing: Process 1 cup strawberries, vinegar, brown sugar, olive oil, sesame oil, and lemon juice in a food processor or blender until smooth. Season with salt and pepper. Set aside.

Combine greens, strawberries, and jicama in a salad bowl. Just before serving, toss dressing with salad and sprinkle with pistachios.

Field Greens, Crumbled Blue Cheese, and Spicy Pecans

Vinaigrette:
⅔ cup sugar
1 teaspoon dry mustard
1 teaspoon salt
⅔ cup distilled white vinegar
3 tablespoons apple cider vinegar
4½ teaspoons onion juice
2 tablespoons Worcestershire sauce
1 cup vegetable oil

Salad:
4 cups mixed field greens
2 green onions, chopped
4 ounces blue cheese, crumbled
 (1 cup)
1 Granny Smith apple, cored,
 seeded, and chopped
¼ cup coarsely chopped Spicy Pecans

Combine sugar, dry mustard, salt, and vinegars. Stir until sugar is dissolved. Whisk in onion juice and Worcestershire. Add oil slowly, whisking continuously until blended.

Toss greens, green onions, blue cheese, apple, and pecans in a salad bowl. Add vinaigrette, tossing to coat.

Spicy Pecans:
2 large egg whites
1½ teaspoons salt
¾ cup sugar
2 teaspoons Worcestershire sauce
2 tablespoons Hungarian paprika
1½ teaspoons cayenne pepper
4½ cups pecan halves
6 tablespoons unsalted butter, melted
 and cooled

Preheat oven to 325 degrees. Beat egg whites with salt until foamy. Add sugar, Worcestershire, paprika, and cayenne. Fold in pecans and melted butter. Spread pecans evenly on a baking sheet. Bake 30 to 40 minutes, stirring every 10 minutes. Remove from oven and cool. Store pecans in an airtight container. Yields 4½ cups.

There was a time when a garden salad meant iceberg lettuce and a wedge of tomato. The wide variety of greens now available in the local supermarket has brought a welcome change to salad making. More flavorful and nutritious than ordinary iceberg, arugula, Belgian endive, chicory, escarole, radicchio, or watercress add color and texture to the salad bowl. Greens once considered weeds, like sorrel or dandelion, introduce a refreshingly tart taste and extra nutrition - like other greens, they're high in vitamins A and C. Combined and tossed with a superb vinaigrette, these field greens turn a salad into the highlight of any meal. Indeed, with a little imagination a simple garden salad can be such a treat, you may never again have to admonish your family to eat their greens.

EDIBLE FLOWERS

Imagine a meal of violets, rose petals, and forget-me-nots. It sounds like something from a charming children's tale. The truth is flower cookery has been around for centuries, reaching a peak of artistry in medieval and Elizabethan times. Herbal teas have been popular for centuries as a natural remedy for a variety of ailments. Today that lost art is being revived as carnations, chrysanthemums, nasturtiums, and marigolds add piquancy to salads, while tea roses float lazily in a glass of champagne. If the idea of dining on flowers has its appeal, among the most flavorful are chives, calendulas, daylilies, marigolds, mint, nasturtiums, pansies, roses, sage, squash blossoms, or sweet borage blossoms, which add a cool cucumber flavor to drinks. Not all flowers are edible, so be sure to shop for yours in a gourmet supermarket.

Poached Pear Arugula Salad
with Cambazola Crostini and Sweet and Spicy Pecans

SERVES 4

Poached Pear:
2 cups dry red wine
½ cup port
2 whole cloves
½ cup sugar
2 Anjou or Bartlett pears,
  peeled, cored, and halved

Roasted Garlic Dressing:
2 tablespoons raspberry vinegar
1 small shallot
1 small clove roasted garlic
6 tablespoons walnut oil
2 tablespoons vegetable oil
salt

Cambazola Crostini:
2 ounces Cambazola cheese
4 baguette slices, toasted

Salad:
4 to 6 cups arugula, torn and
  stems discarded
¼ cup Sweet and Spicy Pecans,
  coarsely chopped

———
1 star fruit, thinly sliced
edible flowers

Poached Pear: Combine wine, port, cloves, and sugar in a medium saucepan. Bring to a boil. Reduce heat and add pears, cut side down. Simmer 10 to 15 minutes, or until tender. Remove pears, reserving liquid, and set aside.

Pour off all but 1 cup of the poaching liquid and reduce it to 2 tablespoons over medium heat. Transfer reduced liquid to a blender or food processor.

Roasted Garlic Dressing: Add vinegar, shallot, and garlic to reduced liquid. Blend until smooth. With machine running, add oils in a thin steady stream. Season with salt.

Cambazola Crostini: Preheat oven to 400 degrees. Spread Cambazola evenly on baguette slices and bake until cheese is slightly melted.

Place arugula in a large bowl. Add dressing and toss to coat. Divide the arugula among 4 plates and sprinkle with Sweet and Spicy Pecans. Place a pear half at the top of the plate (cut into a fan if desired) and the Cambazola Crostini on the side. Garnish with slices of star fruit and edible flowers.

Sweet and Spicy Pecans:
2 tablespoons unsalted butter
3 cups pecan halves
½ cup light brown sugar,
  firmly packed
1 teaspoon paprika

2 teaspoons chili powder
1 tablespoon ground cumin
¼ cup apple cider vinegar
salt

Preheat oven to 350 degrees. Melt butter in a large skillet over medium heat. Add pecans and sauté until lightly browned, about 3 minutes. Add brown sugar and cook until lightly caramelized. Stir in paprika, chili powder, and cumin. Combine well. Add vinegar and cook until all liquid has evaporated. Season with salt. Spread pecans evenly on a baking sheet and bake until crisp, about 3 to 5 minutes. Cool. Yields 3 cups.

Sautéed Apple Salad with Roquefort and Walnuts

Dressing:
¼ cup sherry or red wine vinegar
1 tablespoon chopped fresh thyme
½ cup extra virgin olive oil
salt
freshly ground pepper
————
1 tablespoon extra virgin olive oil
1½ pounds Golden Delicious
  apples, peeled, cored, and cut
  into ½-inch slices
1 tablespoon sugar

Salad:
6 cups mixed salad greens
3 cups watercress,
  coarse stems discarded
1 Belgian endive, sliced
4 ounces Roquefort cheese,
  crumbled (1 cup)
½ cup toasted walnuts,
  chopped

Whisk vinegar and thyme in a small bowl. Gradually whisk in ½ cup oil. Season with salt and pepper. Set aside.

Heat 1 tablespoon olive oil in large nonstick skillet over medium-high heat. Add apples and sugar. Sauté until apples are almost tender, about 8 minutes. Increase heat and sauté until golden brown, about 5 minutes.

Combine salad greens, watercress, and endive in a large salad bowl. Toss in apples. Sprinkle with Roquefort and walnuts. Toss with enough dressing to coat.

ENDIVE

Belgian endive is a salad green originally grown near Brussels that is a member of the chicory family. The compact, spear-shaped shoots with yellow-tinged leaf tips owe their pallor to growing conditions. They are grown in sandy soil in the dark, similarly to mushroom cultivation. Look for tissue-wrapped Belgian endive, as the leaves can discolor and turn bitter with long exposure to light.

Greek Salad with Hearts of Palm and Avocado

Dressing:
juice of 1 large lemon
1 tablespoon fresh fines herbs
1 teaspoon Dijon mustard
1 teaspoon Worcestershire sauce
1 teaspoon salt
½ teaspoon freshly ground pepper
3 cloves garlic, minced
1¼ cups extra virgin olive oil
4 to 6 ounces feta cheese, crumbled
  (1 to 1½ cups)

Salad:
1 large head iceberg lettuce, torn
2 large heads red leaf lettuce, torn
15 green olives with pimentos, sliced
1 can (14 ounces) hearts of palm,
  drained and sliced into rounds
2 avocados, pitted, peeled, halved,
  and sliced

Combine lemon juice, fines herbs, mustard, Worcestershire, salt, pepper, and garlic in a small bowl. Whisk in olive oil. When combined, stir in feta. Set aside.

Toss all lettuce in a salad bowl. Add olives, hearts of palm, and avocados. Pour dressing over salad and toss to coat.

FINES HERBS

Fines herbs is a delicate blend of fresh herbs which may be used to season soups, savory sauces, and cheese and egg dishes. To make fresh fines herbs, mix equal parts minced fresh chervil, chives, parsley, and tarragon.

Honey Pepper Pecan Salad

SERVES 4 TO 6

Honey Pepper Dressing:
1 cup honey
½ cup toasted sesame seeds
½ cup chopped onion
1 large egg
1½ cups Hot Pepper Vinegar

Salad:
2 heads Boston lettuce, torn
kernels of 3 ears cooked corn
  (1½ cups)
1¼ cups chopped toasted pecans
½ red onion, halved and thinly sliced
2 avocados, pitted, peeled, and diced

Honey Pepper Dressing: Process honey, sesame seeds, onion, egg, and Hot Pepper Vinegar in a blender or food processor until smooth. Cover and refrigerate until ready to use.

Toss lettuce, corn, pecans, red onion, and avocado in a salad bowl. Pour dressing over salad and toss to coat.

Hot Pepper Vinegar:
1 cup plus 2 tablespoons water
6 tablespoons distilled white vinegar
4 fresh jalapeños, quartered
¾ teaspoon cayenne pepper
⅛ teaspoon salt

Combine water, vinegar, jalapeños, cayenne, and salt in a saucepan. Bring to a boil over high heat. Boil 2 minutes. Cool. Strain before using. Yields 1½ cups.

Toasted Seed Salad

SERVES 8 TO 10

Dressing:
2 tablespoons fresh lemon juice
dash Tabasco Sauce
⅛ teaspoon dry mustard
¼ teaspoon salt
2 to 3 cloves garlic, minced
¼ cup vegetable oil

Salad:
1 head Boston lettuce, torn
½ head romaine lettuce, torn
½ head red leaf lettuce, torn

½ cup grated carrot
2 tablespoons toasted sesame seeds
2 tablespoons toasted pumpkin seeds
2 tablespoons toasted shelled
  sunflower seeds
2 tablespoons sliced or slivered toasted
  almonds
1 ounce Parmesan or Romano cheese,
  freshly grated (¼ cup)
2 Roma tomatoes, diced
1 avocado, pitted, peeled, and diced

Combine lemon juice, Tabasco, dry mustard, salt, and garlic in a small bowl. Whisk in oil. Cover and chill.

Toss all lettuce in a salad bowl. Sprinkle in carrots, seeds, almonds, and Parmesan. Add tomatoes and avocado. Pour dressing over salad and toss to coat. Serve immediately.

Spinach and Goat Cheese Salad with Warm Balsamic Vinaigrette

SERVES 6 TO 8

Warm Balsamic Vinaigrette:
⅓ cup balsamic vinegar
1 tablespoon Dijon mustard
1 tablespoon honey
½ teaspoon poppy seeds
⅔ cup extra virgin olive oil

Salad:
2 pounds fresh spinach, torn and
    coarse stems discarded
2 red bell peppers, roasted (page 40),
    seeded, and cut into strips
4 ounces goat cheese, crumbled (1 cup)
1 red onion, halved and thinly sliced

SPINACH

Depending on the variety, spinach leaves may be curly or smooth. Choose spinach with crisp, dark green leaves. To store, remove leaves with any sign of yellowing or wilting, loosely place in a tightly sealed plastic bag, and refrigerate for up to 3 days.

Warm Balsamic Vinaigrette: Combine vinegar, mustard, honey, and poppy seeds in a small saucepan. Whisk in oil. Bring to a boil over medium-low heat. Remove from heat.

Arrange spinach on individual plates and drizzle with vinaigrette. Top with red pepper strips, goat cheese, and red onion.

Spinach Dill Salad

SERVES 6

Dressing:
½ cup extra virgin olive oil
¼ cup red wine vinegar
¼ cup sugar
2 cloves garlic, minced
¼ teaspoon salt
¼ teaspoon freshly ground pepper
¼ teaspoon dry mustard
¼ teaspoon onion powder

Salad:
2 pounds fresh spinach, torn and
    coarse stems discarded
1 bunch green onions, chopped
½ cup toasted slivered almonds
1 pint strawberries, hulled and sliced
¼ cup chopped fresh dill

Whisk oil, vinegar, sugar, garlic, salt, pepper, dry mustard, and onion powder until blended. Cover and chill.

Toss spinach, green onions, almonds, strawberries, and dill in a salad bowl. Just before serving, pour dressing over salad and toss.

Spinach and Apple Salad

Dressing:
1 cup white wine vinegar
1 ⅓ cups vegetable oil
2 tablespoons minced chutney
2 teaspoons curry powder
2 teaspoons salt
2 teaspoons dry mustard
½ teaspoon Tabasco Sauce

Salad:
4 pounds fresh spinach, torn and
    coarse stems discarded
1 Red Delicious apple, cored and
    thinly sliced
1 Granny Smith apple, cored and
    thinly sliced
1 cup toasted slivered almonds
1 cup raisins
⅔ cup thinly sliced green onions
¼ cup toasted sesame seeds

Whisk vinegar, oil, chutney, curry powder, salt, dry mustard, and Tabasco until blended. Set aside.

Toss spinach, apples, almonds, raisins, green onions, and sesame seeds in a salad bowl. Just before serving, pour dressing over salad and toss.

Basil Tomato Salad with Hearts of Palm

HEARTS OF PALM

Not all hearts of palm are edible. The hearts that are most common are from the palmetto which is indigenous to Brazil and Florida.

Dressing:
2 tablespoons plus 1 cup extra
    virgin olive oil
½ cup red wine vinegar
2 tablespoons Dijon or Creole
    mustard
1 teaspoon salt
1 teaspoon freshly ground pepper
2 cloves garlic, minced

Salad:
5 heads red leaf lettuce, torn
8 large tomatoes, cut into wedges
4 cans (14 ounces each) hearts of
    palm, drained and cut into rounds
18 fresh basil leaves, chopped
8 ounces Roquefort cheese,
    crumbled (2 cups)

Combine 2 tablespoons olive oil, vinegar, mustard, salt, pepper, and garlic in a small bowl. Whisk in remaining 1 cup olive oil in a thin stream. Set aside.

Combine lettuce, tomatoes, hearts of palm, and basil in a salad bowl. Pour dressing over salad and toss. Sprinkle with Roquefort and serve.

Tuscan Tomato Salad

SERVES 8

6 Roma tomatoes, coarsely chopped
12 Greek olives, pitted and halved
¼ cup capers, rinsed and drained
¼ cup chopped fresh parsley
¼ cup minced green onions
2 ribs celery, chopped
¼ cup fresh basil, chopped

½ teaspoon salt
½ teaspoon freshly ground pepper
3 tablespoons red wine vinegar
6 tablespoons extra virgin olive oil
——
lettuce leaves

Combine tomatoes, olives, capers, parsley, green onion, celery, basil, salt, pepper, vinegar, and olive oil in a large bowl. Cover and marinate at least 30 minutes in the refrigerator.

To serve, line serving plate with lettuce leaves and top with tomato salad.

VARIATIONS

Tuscan Tomato Salad may also be served as a cold pasta sauce, a condiment for sandwiches, a topping for grilled vegetables and meats, or a spread on toasted sourdough bread.

Fresh Tomato Slices with Basil Mayonnaise

SERVES 4

Basil Mayonnaise:
2½ tablespoons white wine vinegar
1 large egg
1½ tablespoons whole
   grain mustard
1 tablespoon chopped fresh basil
½ teaspoon salt

½ teaspoon freshly ground pepper
1 cup vegetable oil
——
2 to 3 large tomatoes, sliced
   ½ inch thick
lettuce leaves

Basil Mayonnaise: Blend vinegar, egg, mustard, basil, salt, and pepper in a food processor until smooth. With machine running, add oil slowly in a thin stream until thickened. Refrigerate.

To serve, line individual plates with lettuce and top with 2 tomato slices and a dollop of Basil Mayonnaise.

Chilled Asparagus with Ginger Dressing

SERVES 6 TO 8

Ginger Dressing:
¼ cup white wine vinegar
2 teaspoons Dijon mustard
3 tablespoons minced crystallized
   ginger
¼ teaspoon salt

½ teaspoon freshly ground pepper
½ cup vegetable oil
——
2 pounds fresh asparagus, trimmed,
   blanched, and chilled
lettuce leaves

Ginger Dressing: Blend vinegar, mustard, ginger, salt, and pepper in a food processor. With machine running, add oil slowly in a thin stream.

When ready to serve, arrange asparagus on a bed of lettuce and drizzle with Ginger Dressing.

BLANCHING

Blanch vegetables by placing them in boiling water 1 to 2 minutes. Plunge into ice water, drain, and chill.

VINEGAR

The vinegar that most of us are familiar with from our mothers' and grandmothers' pantries is the colorless, highly acidic variety used in salad dressings, for pickling, or as a household cleaning agent. One of the oldest fermented foods, vinegar was made by the Chinese over 3000 years ago. Vinegars available today offer infinite possibilities for the creative cook. They include wine vinegars made from sherry, champagne, and red and white wines; malt vinegars; vinegars made from fruits like raspberries, blueberries, cranberries, or strawberries; sharp, clean rice vinegars from China and Japan; and the extraordinary balsamic vinegar of Modena, Italy. This last vinegar is a complex, sweet-tart vinegar with a heady fragrance, made from the unfermented juice of the white Trebbiano grape aged in wooden casks for a minimum of 6 years up to 120 years. Unopened vinegars will keep almost indefinitely if kept in a dark, cool place.

Asparagus Mushroom Salad with Basil Vinaigrette

SERVES 6

Basil Vinaigrette:
1 tablespoon Dijon mustard
1 large egg yolk
2 shallots, chopped
1 clove garlic, chopped
1 ½ cups extra virgin olive oil
¼ cup fresh lemon juice
½ cup balsamic vinegar
½ cup minced fresh basil
salt
freshly ground pepper

Salad:
1 pound fresh asparagus, trimmed
   blanched, and chilled
8 ounces fresh cremini mushrooms
   (brown caps), sliced paper thin
½ medium red onion, diced
¼ cup diced tomato
2 tablespoons chopped fresh parsley
salt
freshly ground pepper
——
12 radicchio leaves

Basil Vinaigrette: Blend mustard, egg yolk, shallots, and garlic in a food processor. With machine running, add oil slowly in a thin steady stream. Transfer mixture to a small bowl and whisk in lemon juice, vinegar, and basil. Season with salt and pepper. Cover and refrigerate.

When ready to serve, cut asparagus diagonally into 1-inch pieces. Combine asparagus, mushrooms, onion, tomato, and parsley. Toss with vinaigrette and season with salt and pepper. Mound asparagus mushroom salad into radicchio cups and place on a serving platter.

Carrot Orange Salad with Fresh Dill

SERVES 4

1 ¼ pounds carrots, grated
1 to 2 tablespoons balsamic vinegar
½ cup fresh orange juice
½ teaspoon grated orange zest

1 orange, segmented, or 1 small
   can mandarin orange segments,
   drained
1 tablespoon plus 1 tablespoon
   chopped fresh dill

Combine carrots, vinegar, orange juice, and orange zest in a serving bowl. Stir to combine. Add orange segments and 1 tablespoon dill. Lightly toss. Cover and chill thoroughly.

Just before serving, sprinkle with remaining 1 tablespoon dill.

Grapefruit, Mango, and Sweet Onion Salad

SERVES 6

Dressing:
2 tablespoons fresh lime juice
¼ teaspoon salt
⅛ teaspoon freshly ground pepper
¼ teaspoon chili powder
1 tablespoon minced red bell pepper
3 tablespoons minced fresh cilantro
½ cup extra virgin olive oil

Salad:
1 small head leaf lettuce, torn
2 medium pink seedless grapefruits,
   segmented and cut into 1-inch pieces
1 large or 2 medium mangoes, peeled,
   pitted, and chopped
1 large 1015 onion, or any other sweet
   onion, halved and thinly sliced
¼ cup chopped fresh cilantro

Whisk lime juice, salt, pepper, chili powder, bell pepper, cilantro, and olive oil until combined. Cover. Set aside for at least 1 hour to allow flavors to blend.

Layer lettuce, grapefruit, and mango in a salad bowl and top with onion. Sprinkle with cilantro. Cover and refrigerate until chilled.

Just before serving, pour dressing over salad and toss to coat.

TEXAS SWEETS

The 1015 onion derives its name from the fact that it should be planted on October fifteenth. These onions are prized for their sweet taste. As sweetness shouldn't make you cry, cut the top from the onion and peel the skin downwards. Chop or slice as much as possible before trimming off the base and root because this is where the sulfuric cells cluster. To remove the smell of onions from your hands and cutting board, rub with salt or lemon juice.

Chilled Haricots Verts with Feta

SERVES 6 TO 8

Lemon Vinaigrette:
3 tablespoons fresh lemon juice
3 tablespoons white wine vinegar
1 tablespoon Dijon mustard
½ teaspoon sugar
½ cup vegetable oil
¼ teaspoon salt
freshly ground pepper

Salad:
1½ pounds haricots verts,*
   tips removed
1 small red onion, minced

———

4 ounces feta cheese, crumbled (1 cup)
½ cup coarsely chopped walnuts

Lemon Vinaigrette: Whisk lemon juice, vinegar, mustard, and sugar until combined. Add oil in a thin stream, whisking continuously until blended. Season with salt and pepper. Set aside.

Plunge green beans into boiling salted water. Cook 3 minutes. Drain and rinse with ice water. Pat dry. Cover and chill thoroughly.

Transfer beans to a shallow serving bowl, add onion, and toss with ½ cup vinaigrette, adding more if desired. Sprinkle feta and walnuts on top. Serve chilled.

Green beans may be substituted for the haricots verts. Increase cooking time to 5 minutes.

Grilled Vegetable Salad with Citrus Vinaigrette

SERVES 4 TO 6

BEYOND ICEBERG

Use the following as a guide to experimenting with a variety of lettuces:

Batavia - compact head with soft, tender leaves. Toss with Boston, romaine, endive, watercress, or radicchio.

Bibb - small head of loosely grouped light green leaves. Use like Batavia.

Boston - soft head with loose leaves, which lend themselves to lining salad bowls or platters. Combine with oak leaf lettuce, endive, and spinach.

Frisee - slightly bitter with frilly, light green leaves and firm white ribs. Mix with arugula, oak leaf lettuce, and radicchio.

Oak leaf lettuce - soft, dark green leaves which resemble oak leaves.

Radicchio - deep crimson, cupped leaves with white ribs on a tightly bunched head.

Romaine - long, flat leaves often used in Caesar salad because of their crunchy nature.

1 teaspoon minced garlic
½ teaspoon minced fresh oregano
½ teaspoon minced fresh basil
2 tablespoons distilled white vinegar
2 tablespoons extra virgin olive oil
salt
freshly ground pepper

———

1 large red bell pepper, seeded and
  sliced into 1½-inch strips
1 large yellow bell pepper, seeded
  and sliced into 1½-inch strips
1 zucchini, sliced lengthwise into
  ¼-inch strips
1 yellow squash, sliced lengthwise
  into ¼-inch strips

Citrus Vinaigrette:
¼ cup fresh orange juice
¼ cup plus 1 tablespoon rice vinegar
¼ cup canola oil
½ teaspoon soy sauce
¼ teaspoon salt
zest from 1 lemon, minced
1 clove garlic, flattened to release
  flavor
freshly ground pepper

———

3 slices fresh pineapple
4 cups mixed salad greens
½ cup pine nuts

Combine garlic, oregano, basil, and vinegar. Whisk in olive oil. Season with salt and pepper. Set aside.

Combine bell peppers, zucchini, and squash in a shallow nonmetallic bowl. Pour marinade over vegetables, toss, and cover. Let marinate at least 1 hour.

Citrus Vinaigrette: Whisk orange juice, vinegar, oil, soy sauce, salt, lemon zest, garlic, and pepper in a small bowl. Cover. Set aside 1 hour to allow flavors to blend.

Prepare grill. Remove vegetables from marinade and grill until tender. Grill pineapple unseasoned. Remove vegetables and pineapple from grill. Slice into 1-inch pieces.

Combine salad greens, grilled vegetables, pineapple, and pine nuts in a large serving bowl. Remove garlic from vinaigrette and discard. Pour vinaigrette over salad and toss. Serve immediately.

Also good as a main course salad.

Barley Corn Salad

Salad:
1 cup barley
kernels of 4 to 5 ears cooked corn*
   (2 cups)
½ cup thinly sliced green onions
1 large tomato, peeled, seeded,
   and minced
1 to 2 fresh jalapeños, seeded
   and minced
¼ cup minced fresh cilantro

Dressing:
2 cloves garlic, peeled and boiled
   10 minutes
3 tablespoons white wine vinegar
½ teaspoon ground cumin
⅓ cup extra virgin olive oil
salt
freshly ground pepper

Sprinkle barley into large pot of boiling salted water. Cook, skimming the foam, for 30 minutes, or until just tender. Barley should be firm. Drain in a colander and rinse with cold water. Let cool. Transfer barley to a large serving bowl. Add corn, green onions, tomato, jalapeños, and cilantro. Toss to combine.

Purée garlic, vinegar, and cumin in a food processor. With machine running, slowly add oil in a thin stream until combined. Season with salt and pepper. Pour dressing over salad and toss.

*May substitute a 10-ounce package of frozen corn, cooked and drained.

Barley Corn Salad may be made a day ahead and stored in the refrigerator, but omit cilantro and add it right before serving.

Minted Tabbouleh

1 heaping cup bulgur wheat
1 cup cold water
½ cup fresh lemon juice
¼ cup plus ¼ cup
   extra virgin olive oil
1 cup chopped fresh mint
1½ cups chopped fresh parsley
½ cup minced red onion
2 teaspoons minced garlic

½ teaspoon salt
1 teaspoon freshly ground pepper
4 Roma tomatoes, peeled, seeded
   and diced
1 large cucumber, peeled, seeded,
   and diced
——
1 large cucumber, peeled and sliced
2 to 4 tablespoons chopped fresh mint

Combine bulgur, water, lemon juice, and ¼ cup olive oil in a large bowl. Cover. Let marinate 30 minutes, then fluff with a fork. Add remaining ¼ cup olive oil, mint, parsley, onion, garlic, salt, and pepper. Toss mixture with a fork. Add tomatoes and cucumber. Toss again. Adjust seasonings. Let marinate at least 30 minutes before serving to allow flavors to blend.

To serve, mound tabbouleh on a serving plate, surround with cucumber slices, and sprinkle with mint.

Delicious with lamb.

GRAINS

It is believed that civilization began some 10,000 years ago when wheat and barley were first planted and culti-vated for food. Delicious and deeply satisfying, rich in protein, vitamins, minerals, and fiber, grains are still among our greatest food sources. Thousands of varieties of grain are grown around the world. Some of the more common grains available are wheat, includ-ing whole or cracked wheat, bulgur, bran, and semolina, which is the hard heart of durum wheat used for pasta or couscous; barley, which comes polished or pearled in three sizes - coarse, medi-um, or fine; corn, including cornmeal, hominy, and hominy grits; oats, found in whole oat groats and oatmeal; rice, both white and brown (or unpolished), available in long-grain and short-grain varieties; buck-wheat groats or kasha, a nutty-flavored grain high in protein; and quinoa, known as the "supergrain" for sup-plying many of the nutrients needed to sustain life.

Black Bean, Cabbage, and Date Salad

SERVES 40

TO QUICK SOAK BEANS

Place beans and 3 cups water in a saucepan. Bring to a boil. Boil, uncovered, 2 minutes. Remove from heat, cover, and let stand 1 hour.

Salad:
1 cup dried black beans
   (3 cups cooked)
3 sticks cinnamon
6 cloves garlic
6 tablespoons minced fresh basil
1 teaspoon salt
1 head green cabbage, cored and
   shredded
1 head red cabbage, cored and
   shredded
1 red onion, chopped

1 white onion, chopped
1 lemon, segmented and chopped
1 orange, segmented and chopped
2 cups chopped walnuts
1 pound dates, seeded and chopped

Dressing:
1 cup frozen orange juice concentrate
1 cup balsamic vinegar
½ cup extra virgin olive oil
1 tablespoon freshly ground pepper

Clean and rinse beans thoroughly. Cover with water and soak 8 to 12 hours. Transfer beans and liquid to a large saucepan. Add cinnamon, garlic, basil, and salt. Bring to a boil. Reduce heat. Simmer partially covered 1 to 1½ hours, or until just tender. Drain beans and plunge into ice water to prevent further cooking.

Toss beans, cabbage, onions, lemon, orange, walnuts, and dates in a serving bowl. Set aside.

Process orange juice concentrate, balsamic vinegar, olive oil, and pepper in a food processor. Pour dressing over salad and toss to coat. Cover and chill 6 to 8 hours to allow flavors to blend. Toss before serving.

Any leftover salad can be used as a hot vegetable the next day. Stir fry salad until steamy.

Black Bean Salad

SERVES 6 TO 8

Dressing:
2 tablespoons extra virgin olive oil
1 tablespoon red wine vinegar
3 to 4 tablespoons fresh lime juice
1 teaspoon salt
½ teaspoon freshly ground pepper

Salad:
2 cans (15 ounces each) black
   beans, drained and rinsed

kernels of 3 ears cooked corn*
¼ cup chopped fresh cilantro
1 small red onion, chopped
1 avocado, pitted, peeled, and chopped
2 large tomatoes, peeled, seeded, and
   chopped
2 fresh jalapeños, seeded and minced

Whisk olive oil, vinegar, lime juice, salt, and pepper until combined. Set aside.

Combine black beans, corn, cilantro, onion, avocado, tomatoes, and jalapeños in a large serving bowl. Toss salad gently to mix. Pour dressing over salad and toss gently to coat.

* May substitute a 10-ounce package of frozen corn, cooked and drained.

Mediterranean Lentil Salad

Salad:
1 tablespoon vegetable oil
1 onion, chopped
2 cloves garlic, chopped
1 teaspoon crushed red pepper
1 ½ cups green lentils
1 bay leaf
2 slices lemon, about ½ inch thick
salt
freshly ground pepper

Dressing:
3 tablespoons fresh lemon juice
1 tablespoon grated lemon zest
½ cup extra virgin olive oil
1 tablespoon chopped fresh oregano

——————

6 ounces feta cheese, crumbled
  (1 ½ cups)
½ cup black olives, pitted and sliced
2 teaspoons chopped fresh oregano
½ red bell pepper, seeded and diced
½ green bell pepper, seeded and diced
½ yellow bell pepper, seeded and diced

Heat oil in a large skillet over medium heat. Add onion and garlic and sauté 2 minutes, or until fragrant. Stir in red pepper flakes and lentils until coated with seasonings. Add water to just cover lentils. Add bay leaf and lemon slices, squeezing gently to release juice. Bring to a boil, then reduce heat to medium-low. Cover and simmer 35 to 45 minutes, or until lentils are tender. Drain, removing lemons and bay leaf. Season with salt and pepper. Transfer to a serving bowl and set aside.

Whisk lemon juice, lemon zest, olive oil, and oregano until combined. Pour dressing over warm lentils, tossing to coat. Cool. Top with feta, olives, oregano, and bell peppers. Toss again. Adjust seasonings.

A wonderful accompaniment to grilled lamb or chicken.

LEMONS

Lemons are an amazingly versatile fruit. They can add a refreshing flavor to food and beverages or can be used in kitchen cleanups. Try adding a squirt of lemon juice to fruits and vegetables, seafood, and soups, and in a variety of drinks. While tasting good, the juice also prevents discoloration in many foods. On the other hand, as a kitchen helper, lemons can be used to remove odors from hands and counter tops and can even polish copper pots. When shopping for lemons, buy those which are smooth, bright yellow, plump, and heavy for their size. To get more juice from each lemon, microwave for 15 seconds on high and then roll the lemon on the counter top.

Artichoke Potato Salad

1 can (14 ounces) artichoke hearts,
  drained and diced
1 pound red potatoes, cooked,
  peeled, and diced
1 bunch green onions, chopped
3 ribs celery, chopped
3 cloves garlic, minced
1 cup mayonnaise

2 teaspoons Dijon mustard
1 tablespoon sugar
3 tablespoons chopped fresh chervil
1 tablespoon chopped fresh parsley
2 tablespoons chopped fresh dill
juice of ½ lemon
salt
freshly ground pepper

Combine artichoke hearts and potatoes. Set aside. Combine green onions, celery, garlic, mayonnaise, mustard, sugar, chervil, parsley, dill, and lemon juice in a large bowl. Add potato mixture and stir gently. Season with salt and pepper. Cover and refrigerate several hours before serving.

Garden Potato Salad

SERVES 10 TO 12

INFUSED VINEGARS

Flavored vinegars have long been used in cooking and can take the place of ordinary vinegar in most recipes, providing that the marriage of flavors is compatible. Good quality wine or cider vinegars are the best choice for flavoring and should be poured into a sterilized bottle over the flavoring of choice. To seal the bottles, push sterilized new corks into the bottles. Using a rubber mallet, pound the cork into the neck of the bottle leaving ¼ inch of cork exposed. Tip the top of the bottle into melted paraffin and twist so paraffin covers the cork and the top of the bottle, forming a tight seal. Try experimenting with white wine, cider, or red wine vinegars, and one or more of the following: fresh dill, mint, thyme, chives, lemongrass, rosemary, tarragon, basil, nutmeg, or ginger; cranberries, blueberries, raspberries, cherries, or fruit peels; and garlic, chile peppers, sliced horseradish, shallots, or peppercorns.

¼ cup vegetable oil
2 cloves garlic, halved
30 to 40 new potatoes, skins on,
  cut into ½ to ¾-inch cubes
½ cup tarragon vinegar
2 teaspoons salt
2 teaspoons sugar
3 to 4 tablespoons chopped
  fresh dill

———
⅔ to 1 cup mayonnaise
2 bunches green onions, chopped

———
1 tablespoon chopped fresh dill
1 bunch radishes, sliced

Combine oil and garlic in a small bowl. Set aside.

Boil potatoes in salted water until just tender. Drain. Transfer to a large bowl.

Remove garlic from oil and discard. Whisk vinegar, salt, sugar, and dill into oil. Pour dressing over warm potatoes and toss to coat. Cover and marinate several hours in the refrigerator. (Can be refrigerated for several days.)

When ready to serve, drain excess liquid. Toss marinated potatoes with mayonnaise and green onions. Garnish with dill and sliced radishes.

Confetti Slaw

SERVES 10 TO 12

Slaw:
1 small head cabbage, cored and
  chopped
3 medium carrots, chopped
  (about ¾ cup)
¾ cup chopped celery
1 large green bell pepper,
  seeded and chopped
1 large red bell pepper,
  seeded and chopped
1 small cucumber,
  peeled and chopped

1 large bunch radishes, chopped
  (about ¾ cup)
1 large onion, chopped (about ¾ cup)

Dressing:
1 cup plus 2 tablespoons distilled white
  vinegar
⅓ cup vegetable oil
¾ cup sugar
1 teaspoon salt
¼ teaspoon freshly ground pepper

Toss cabbage, carrots, celery, bell peppers, cucumber, radishes, and onion in a serving bowl. Set aside.

Whisk vinegar, oil, sugar, salt, and pepper until combined. Pour dressing over vegetables and toss evenly. Cover and refrigerate. When ready to serve, drain excess dressing and toss.

Broccoli Slaw in Chipotle Mayonnaise

Chipotle Mayonnaise:
1 cup mayonnaise
½ cup plain yogurt
2 tablespoons fresh lemon juice
2 cloves garlic
½ to 1 teaspoon salt
1 to 2 chipotle chile peppers, canned
   in adobo sauce

Slaw:
4 large broccoli stalks, florets
   removed, peeled and julienned
4 large carrots, peeled and
   julienned or grated
½ head red cabbage, cored and
   shredded

CHIPOTLE PEPPERS IN ADOBO SAUCE

These are dried jalapeños, canned in a very hot orange-red sauce with a strong smoky flavor.

Chipotle Mayonnaise: Combine mayonnaise, yogurt, lemon juice, garlic, salt, and 1 chipotle in a food processor. Process until smooth. Adjust seasonings, adding more chipotle if desired. Cover and chill.

Combine broccoli, carrots, and cabbage in a serving bowl. Pour Chipotle Mayonnaise over slaw. Toss to blend. Cover and chill until ready to serve.

Won Ton Chicken Salad

Sweet and Sour Dressing:
¼ cup plus 2 tablespoons water
3 tablespoons sugar
3 tablespoons ketchup
1 tablespoon soy sauce
½ cup rice vinegar
1 teaspoon cornstarch

———

½ package won ton wrappers
peanut oil

Salad:
4 whole boneless, skinless chicken
   breasts
2 ribs celery
1 onion, halved
1-inch piece fresh ginger
1 teaspoon salt
⅛ teaspoon freshly ground pepper
1 small head iceberg lettuce, torn
1 head red leaf lettuce, torn
4 green onions, thinly sliced
2 tablespoons toasted sesame seeds
3 to 4 tablespoons sliced almonds

Sweet and Sour Dressing: Combine ¼ cup water, sugar, ketchup, soy sauce, and vinegar in a saucepan. Blend cornstarch with 2 tablespoons water and whisk into dressing mixture. Simmer until thickened. Set aside to cool.

Cut won ton wrappers into ⅛-inch strips and fry in oil until golden brown. Drain on paper towels.

Boil chicken with celery, onion, ginger, salt, and pepper until done, about 20 minutes. Drain, discarding celery, onion, and ginger. Cool. Cut chicken into 1-inch pieces. Toss chicken, all lettuce, green onions, sesame seeds, and almonds in a large salad bowl. Pour dressing over salad and toss to coat. Top with won tons. Serve immediately.

Greek Pasta Salad

SERVES 8 TO 10

PEPPERONCINI

Almost neon red in color and shaped like long cones, these peppers are also known as Tuscan peppers. They are mildly hot. Pepperoncini are most often sold pickled when still green and used as part of an antipasto.

Dressing:
⅔ cup extra virgin olive oil
6 tablespoons fresh lemon juice
¼ cup red wine vinegar
4 cloves garlic, minced
3 tablespoons minced fresh oregano
1 teaspoon salt
1 teaspoon freshly ground pepper

Salad:
12 ounces spiral, rotini, or shell
  pasta, cooked al dente

2 regular or 4 Roma tomatoes, chopped
3 ribs celery, chopped
1 cucumber, peeled, seeded, and
  chopped
5 green onions, chopped
2 small green bell peppers, seeded and
  chopped
1½ cups chopped fresh parsley
12 ounces feta cheese, crumbled
  (3 cups)
20 Greek olives, pitted
12 fresh pepperoncini,* minced

Whisk oil, lemon juice, vinegar, garlic, oregano, salt, and pepper until combined. Set aside.

Combine pasta, tomatoes, celery, cucumber, green onions, bell peppers, parsley, feta, olives, and pepperoncini in a large serving bowl. Pour dressing over salad and toss to coat. Cover and refrigerate 2 to 3 hours to allow flavors to blend.

* May substitute pickled pepperoncini.

Grilled Eggplant and Tomato Pasta Salad

SERVES 8

Salad:
1 medium eggplant, peeled, cut into
  ¼-inch slices, brushed with olive
  oil, and grilled until tender
4 medium tomatoes, seeded and
  sliced, grilled and peeled
2 large red bell peppers, roasted
  (page 40), peeled, and seeded
8 ounces penne pasta, cooked
  al dente

Dressing:
½ cup extra virgin olive oil
3 tablespoons red wine vinegar
1 tablespoon minced shallot
½ teaspoon minced garlic
1 teaspoon salt
½ teaspoon freshly ground pepper
————
chopped fresh parsley

Chop eggplant, tomatoes, and bell peppers. Place in a large bowl. Add pasta. Set aside.

Whisk oil, vinegar, shallot, garlic, salt, and pepper until combined in a separate bowl. Pour dressing over vegetables and pasta. Toss thoroughly and garnish with parsley. Serve at room temperature.

Orange Chicken Cashew Salad

Dressing:
½ cup fresh cilantro
¼ cup fresh parsley
¼ cup vegetable oil
¼ cup fresh orange juice or
  orange pineapple juice
1½ teaspoons red wine vinegar
1½ teaspoons Dijon mustard
1 teaspoon salt
2 teaspoons sugar
1 teaspoon Tabasco Sauce
freshly ground pepper

Salad:
1¼ pounds boneless, skinless
  chicken breasts, poached (page 161)
3 ribs celery, sliced
½ head romaine lettuce, torn
1 large red bell pepper, seeded and
  chopped or julienned
4 green onions, sliced
½ to 1 cup salted cashew halves
——
orange slices
fresh cilantro or parsley

Process cilantro, parsley, oil, orange juice, vinegar, mustard, salt, sugar, and Tabasco in a food processor. Season with pepper. Set aside.

Slice chicken into ¼-inch pieces. Place in a large bowl. Add celery, romaine, bell pepper, green onions, and cashews. Toss with dressing. Serve on a platter garnished with orange slices and cilantro or parsley.

Chicken, Red Grape, and Watercress Salad

Dressing:
2 tablespoons fresh lime juice
1 tablespoon chopped mango
  chutney
1 clove garlic, minced
¼ teaspoon salt
2 tablespoons sour cream
3 tablespoons vegetable oil
1 to 2 drops Tabasco Sauce

Salad:
1½ cups shredded cooked
  chicken breast
1 cup halved seedless red grapes
½ cup roasted and salted
  cashew halves
2 cups watercress, coarse stems
  discarded
salt
freshly ground pepper

WATERCRESS
Dark green, glossy leaves and a spicy flavor typify watercress. For maximum flavor, use within 1 day of purchase as watercress is fragile and does not keep well.

Whisk lime juice, chutney, garlic, salt, and sour cream in a small bowl. Add oil in a thin stream, whisking continuously, until smooth and thoroughly blended. Whisk in Tabasco. Set aside.

Combine chicken and grapes in a serving bowl. Add dressing and toss. Let marinate 15 minutes. Gently toss cashews and watercress with chicken. Season with salt and pepper. Serve immediately.

Chicken Pecan Salad with Cranberries

SERVES 4

Dressing:
2 large egg yolks
2 tablespoons apple cider vinegar
2 tablespoons sugar
1 teaspoon Dijon mustard
¼ teaspoon salt
¾ cup vegetable oil

Salad:
2 whole boneless, skinless chicken
　breasts, poached (page 161) and diced
¾ cup fresh or dried cranberries
3 ribs celery, diced
1 cup pecans, coarsely chopped
——
1 head red leaf lettuce, torn

Blend egg yolks, vinegar, sugar, mustard, and salt in a food processor. With machine running, add oil slowly in a thin stream. Refrigerate.

　Place chicken, cranberries, and celery in a serving bowl. Add dressing and toss to coat. Cover and refrigerate 8 to 10 hours.

　Just before serving, add pecans and toss gently. Serve over lettuce.

Southwestern Chicken Salad

SERVES 6

Dressing:
½ cup fresh lime juice
¼ teaspoon ground cumin
1 tablespoon Durkee dressing
½ cup extra virgin olive oil
salt
white pepper

Salad:
3 whole chicken breasts, poached
　(page 161) and shredded
1 small bunch fresh cilantro, minced
　(about ½ cup)

2 cloves garlic, minced
1 small red onion, julienned
5 poblano chile peppers, roasted
　(page 40), peeled, seeded, and
　julienned
4 Roma tomatoes, chopped
——
red leaf lettuce
goat cheese
pickled nopales (cactus)

Whisk lime juice, cumin, Durkee, and oil until combined. Season with salt and pepper. Set aside.

　Combine chicken, cilantro, garlic, onion, and chiles in a large serving bowl. Pour dressing over salad and toss. Just before serving, toss in tomatoes. Serve on a bed of lettuce garnished with medallions of goat cheese and nopales.

Southwestern Chicken Salad

Wild Rice and Chicken Salad

SERVES 6

Dressing:
½ cup extra virgin olive oil
¼ cup white wine vinegar
1 tablespoon chopped fresh tarragon
1 teaspoon salt
1 teaspoon freshly ground pepper

Salad:
¾ cup raw wild rice,
  cooked (page 200) in 2¼ cups
  chicken stock

4 whole boneless, skinless chicken
  breasts, poached (page 161)
  and cubed
½ cup minced celery
½ cup slivered almonds, sautéed
  lightly in butter
½ cup minced green onions
  ——
4 cups watercress, coarse stems
  discarded

Whisk oil, vinegar, tarragon, salt, and pepper until blended. Set aside.

Combine wild rice, chicken, celery, almonds, and green onions. Pour ½ cup dressing over mixture. Cover and refrigerate 8 to 10 hours, or overnight, to allow flavors to blend.

Just before serving, add remaining ¼ cup dressing. Mix well. Divide watercress among 6 small plates and top with salad.

Chicken and Pecan Rice Salad

SERVES 6

BROWN RICE

Long-grain or medium-grain brown rice has the nutritious, high-fiber bran attached as opposed to white rice which is polished. Brown rice has a firm texture and a nutty taste. Do not stir simmering rice as this will mash the grains and make the rice gummy. If rice is cooked but watery, fluff with a fork over low heat to evaporate the excess water.

4 cups chicken stock
1 cup raw wild rice
1 cup raw long-grain brown rice
4 boneless, skinless chicken breast
  halves, poached (page 161)
  and cubed
1 cup toasted and coarsely
  chopped pecans
3 green onions, sliced
½ cup golden raisins
½ cup chopped celery
2 teaspoons minced orange zest

Vinaigrette:
¼ cup rice vinegar
¼ cup fresh orange juice
2 tablespoons Dijon mustard
2 tablespoons mango chutney
½ teaspoon salt
¼ teaspoon white pepper
½ cup canola or vegetable oil
  ——
2 tablespoons minced fresh chives

Bring chicken stock to a boil in a large saucepan. Stir in wild rice. Reduce heat and simmer covered 10 minutes. Add brown rice and simmer covered an additional 30 to 35 minutes, or until liquid is absorbed. Remove from heat. Cool to room temperature. Combine rice, chicken, pecans, green onions, raisins, celery, and orange zest in a large bowl.

Whisk vinegar, orange juice, mustard, chutney, salt, and pepper until combined in a small bowl. Add oil slowly, whisking constantly, until slightly thickened and thoroughly combined. Pour vinaigrette over rice and chicken mixture. Toss gently. Marinate at least 4 hours, or overnight, in the refrigerator.

Before serving, bring to room temperature and sprinkle with chives.

Oriental Chicken Pasta Salad

12 ounces thin spaghetti
1 chicken bouillon cube
dash sesame oil

——

1¼ cups light teriyaki sauce
¼ cup sesame oil
3 tablespoons grated fresh ginger

2 whole boneless, skinless chicken
  breasts
1 package (.88 ounces) dried enoki
  mushrooms, rehydrated
3 tablespoons toasted sesame seeds
3 green onions, sliced diagonally

——

lettuce leaves

Cook spaghetti al dente, adding bouillon cube and sesame oil to cooking water. Drain, rinse, and chill.

Combine teriyaki sauce, sesame oil, and ginger. Pour half of the marinade over chicken, reserving other half. Marinate 1 hour. Grill chicken, slice into strips, and chill.

Just before serving, toss spaghetti with remaining marinade. Add chicken strips, mushrooms, sesame seeds, and green onions. Toss gently to combine. Serve over a bed of lettuce.

Seafood Salad with Papaya Salsa

Papaya Salsa:
2 medium papayas, peeled, seeded,
  and coarsely chopped
2 green onions, thinly sliced
2 tablespoons minced red onion
1 teaspoon grated lime zest
¼ cup fresh lime juice
1 tablespoon chopped fresh basil
1 tablespoon chopped fresh cilantro
1½ teaspoons extra virgin olive oil
1½ teaspoons grated fresh ginger
1 fresh jalapeño, seeded and minced

1 to 2 cloves garlic, minced
salt
freshly ground pepper

Salad:
1½ pounds fresh halibut or swordfish
  steaks, 1 inch thick
1 pound fresh shrimp, boiled (page 48),
  peeled, and deveined

——

lettuce leaves

PAPAYAS

Although not a staple in American kitchens, papayas are a tropical fruit enjoyed in many countries throughout the world. The variety commonly sold in the United States is yellow and pink. Ripen the fruit in a paper bag until just soft to the touch. Peel with a sharp knife. The edible black seeds in the center can be used as a garnish or added to salad dressings. A papaya can make a traditional meal more exotic when served with meats or used in salads and salsas. It is delicious simply eaten alone.

Papaya Salsa: Combine papayas, green onions, red onion, lime zest, lime juice, basil, cilantro, olive oil, ginger, jalapeño, and garlic in a medium bowl. Season with salt and pepper. Cover and refrigerate at least 2 hours or up to 3 days.

Preheat oven to 450 degrees. Bake fish steaks, uncovered, in a greased dish 10 to 12 minutes. Flake fish with a fork into 1-inch pieces, removing bones and skin.

Arrange fish and shrimp on a bed of lettuce and spoon Papaya Salsa in the center. Serve immediately.

Savory Shrimp Salad

SERVES 8

2 cups mayonnaise

1 cup sour cream

1 tube (1.5 ounces) anchovy paste

1 cup chopped fresh parsley

2 tablespoons chopped fresh chives

3 or 4 teaspoons fresh lemon juice

salt

freshly ground pepper

———

5 pounds fresh small shrimp, boiled (page 48), peeled, deveined, and chilled

4 avocados, pitted, peeled, and chopped into ½-inch squares

———

lettuce leaves

Combine mayonnaise, sour cream, anchovy paste, parsley, chives, and lemon juice in a large bowl. Season with salt and pepper. Cover and chill at least 2 hours.

When ready to serve, add shrimp and avocados. Toss gently and serve on a bed of crisp lettuce leaves.

Palm Crab Salad

SERVES 6

Dressing:

½ teaspoon Dijon mustard

¾ cup distilled white vinegar

¼ teaspoon salt

¼ teaspoon freshly ground pepper

⅛ teaspoon sugar

2 cups vegetable oil

1 medium onion, diced

1 clove garlic, minced

½ cup chopped fresh chives

2 tablespoons diced red bell pepper

1 tablespoon fresh lemon juice

1 teaspoon minced fresh tarragon

2 tablespoons minced fresh parsley

Salad:

lettuce leaves

6 tomatoes, sliced ½ inch thick

6 hearts of palm, sliced lengthwise

1 pound fresh lump crabmeat, shells removed

———

fresh parsley sprigs

lemon wedges

Combine mustard, vinegar, salt, pepper, and sugar in a small bowl. Gradually add oil to the mixture, whisking until smooth. Add onion, garlic, chives, bell pepper, lemon juice, tarragon, and parsley. Stir to combine. Refrigerate at least 2 hours to blend flavors.

Assemble salad by lining individual plates with lettuce. Layer tomatoes, hearts of palm, and crabmeat on each bed of lettuce. Drizzle with chilled dressing. Garnish with parsley and lemon wedges.

Basic Vinaigrette with Variations

⅓ cup vinegar, or fresh lemon or lime juice, or a combination of vinegar and citrus juice
1 teaspoon sugar (optional)

½ teaspoon salt
½ teaspoon freshly ground pepper
⅔ cup extra virgin olive oil

Basic Vinaigrette: Blend vinegar or juice, sugar (if desired), salt, and pepper in a food processor. With machine running, add oil in a thin steady stream. Use vinaigrette immediately or let sit at room temperature for up to 10 hours.

Using this Basic Vinaigrette recipe, try the following substitutions or additions for variation.

Orange Vinaigrette: Use equal parts sherry and balsamic vinegars. Add 1 tablespoon orange-flavored liqueur, 2 tablespoons fresh orange juice, and 1 tablespoon minced fresh thyme. Use light olive oil.

Berry Vinaigrette: Use blueberry, raspberry, or strawberry-flavored vinegar. Add a little ground cinnamon and ¼ cup crushed fresh or frozen berries (same as the flavor of the vinegar). Use equal parts olive oil and vegetable oil. Blend in food processor or blender.

Cheese Vinaigrette: Stir in 3 tablespoons crumbled blue cheese, goat cheese, or freshly grated Parmesan.

Mustard Vinaigrette: Use balsamic vinegar, wine vinegar, or fresh lemon juice. Add 1 tablespoon Dijon mustard and 2 cloves garlic. Include sugar. Use extra virgin olive oil.

Curried Vinaigrette: Use fresh lemon juice. Add 1 teaspoon freshly grated ginger, 1 teaspoon minced garlic, 1 teaspoon curry powder, and ½ teaspoon dry mustard. Use vegetable oil.

Raspberry Dressing

2 large eggs
⅓ to ½ cup raspberry vinegar
½ teaspoon minced shallot
3 tablespoons strained raspberry juice

½ to ¾ cup peanut oil and ½ to ¾ cup light olive oil
salt
white pepper
heavy whipping cream

Process eggs, vinegar, shallot, and raspberry juice in a food processor until blended. Slowly add oil in a thin stream until combined. Add salt and pepper. Thin with cream if necessary. Store covered in refrigerator.

OLIVE OIL

With its slightly nutty flavor and its delicious aroma when heated, olive oil is fast becoming a staple in many American kitchens. It's been that way in other parts of the world for at least 5000 years. Long before fuel oil was black gold, olive oil was liquid gold to the ancient world and the backbone of Mediterranean trade. One of the most delicious and nutritious food products, olive oil is the only oil of culinary importance pressed from the flesh of a ripe fruit instead of a seed or a nut. Olive oils are graded according to color (ranging from deep green to light yellow), aroma, flavor, and acidity. Extra virgin, superfine virgin, fine virgin, and virgin oils are processed from hand-picked olives that are cold pressed without heat or chemicals in huge stone presses. The best oils are made from perfectly ripe olives that are usually green, sometimes bordering on greenish black.

French Dressing

YIELDS 4 CUPS

¾ cup apple cider vinegar
2 teaspoons tarragon vinegar
¾ cup powdered sugar
1 teaspoon dry mustard
1 teaspoon salt

1 teaspoon paprika
1 teaspoon Worcestershire sauce
juice of 2 to 3 oranges
juice of 1 lemon
2 cups vegetable oil

Whisk vinegars, powdered sugar, dry mustard, salt, paprika, Worcestershire, orange juice, and lemon juice in a medium bowl until combined. Slowly add oil, whisking constantly until blended. Cover and refrigerate.

French Dressing is delicious drizzled over orange segments and a thin slice of Bermuda onion.

Poppy Seed Dressing

YIELDS 3 CUPS

½ cup fresh lime juice
½ cup honey
⅓ cup distilled white vinegar
1 teaspoon salt
1 cup sugar

1 tablespoon ground ginger
1 tablespoon dry mustard
2 cups vegetable oil
1 tablespoon poppy seeds

Process lime juice, honey, vinegar, salt, sugar, ginger, and dry mustard in a food processor. With machine running, slowly add oil in a thin steady stream. The dressing should be thick and translucent and should not separate. Stir in poppy seeds. Cover and refrigerate for up to 2 weeks.

Poppy Seed Dressing may be served with fresh fruit on a bed of lettuce.

Blue Cheese Dressing

YIELDS 3 CUPS

⅓ cup red wine vinegar
⅛ teaspoon freshly ground pepper
1 teaspoon onion salt
¼ teaspoon paprika

¼ teaspoon sugar
¼ cup virgin olive oil
4 ounces blue cheese, mashed

Combine vinegar, pepper, onion salt, paprika, and sugar in a small bowl. Whisk in oil and blend. Stir in blue cheese.

Blue Cheese Dressing is wonderful drizzled over thick slices of tomato and avocado.

Creamy Parmesan Dressing

YIELDS 2 CUPS

3 large eggs, at room temperature
1½ teaspoons minced garlic
¾ teaspoon salt
¾ teaspoon white pepper
1½ teaspoons Worcestershire sauce

¼ cup fresh lemon juice
2 ounces Parmesan cheese, freshly
  grated (½ cup)
1 cup vegetable oil

Process eggs, garlic, salt, pepper, Worcestershire, lemon juice, and Parmesan in a food processor. With machine running, add oil in a thin stream until blended. The dressing will be smooth and pale. Cover and refrigerate.

Creamy Parmesan Dressing is especially good tossed with romaine and red leaf lettuce, then sprinkled with croutons.

Matilda's Garlic Dressing

YIELDS 1 CUP

½ cup sour cream
⅓ cup mayonnaise
¼ cup half and half
3 large cloves garlic, chopped
2 tablespoons white wine vinegar

2 tablespoons vegetable oil
1½ teaspoons sugar
½ teaspoon salt
freshly ground pepper

Process sour cream, mayonnaise, half and half, garlic, vinegar, oil, sugar, salt, and pepper in a food processor. Cover and refrigerate at least 1 hour to chill. Adjust seasonings before serving.

Cilantro Jalapeño Dressing

YIELDS 1 CUP

1 cup mayonnaise
¼ cup buttermilk
½ cup chopped fresh parsley
1 bunch fresh cilantro, chopped
3 tablespoons apple cider vinegar
3 green onions, chopped

1 large clove garlic
½ to 2 fresh jalapeños with seeds
2 tablespoons Worcestershire sauce
1 teaspoon paprika
¾ teaspoon salt
½ teaspoon freshly ground pepper

PAPRIKA

Paprika is a powder made by grinding dried sweet red peppers. Most paprika comes from Spain, South America, and Hungary. The Hungarian variety, which comes in mild and hot forms, packs a punch similar to cayenne. To enhance paprika's flavor, roast the powder in a dry skillet for a few minutes and cool thoroughly before using.

Process mayonnaise, buttermilk, parsley, cilantro, vinegar, green onions, garlic, ½ jalapeño, Worcestershire, paprika, salt, and pepper in a food processor. Adjust seasonings, adding more jalapeño if desired. May thin with more buttermilk. Cover and refrigerate.

Cilantro Jalapeño Dressing over romaine lettuce with julienned red bell peppers makes a delicious combination.

SIMPLE PLEASURES

Roasted Vegetable Sandwich

A mainstay of countless brown bag lunches carried each day to schools and offices, sandwiches have been around in one form or another since Roman times. But it wasn't until an incident associated with John Montagu, fourth Earl of Sandwich and British first Lord of the Admiralty during the American Revolution, that the sandwich took its place in our food lexicon. A notorious eighteenth-century gambler, Montagu often refused to leave the gaming tables even for meals. Once in 1762, he spent 24 straight hours gambling, ordering sliced meats and cheeses served between pieces of bread. This method, which allowed him to eat with one hand and gamble with the other, had long been his playing trademark. But with that one infamous episode, the favorite food of children, hurried parents, and midnight snackers was established forever as "the sandwich."

Roasted Vegetable Sandwich

SERVES 4

1 small eggplant, thinly sliced
1 zucchini, thinly sliced
1 yellow squash, thinly sliced
1 red bell pepper, seeded and thinly sliced
2 teaspoons extra virgin olive oil
2 cloves garlic, minced
salt
freshly ground pepper

¼ cup nonfat sour cream
2 tablespoons reduced-fat mayonnaise
1 tablespoon chopped fresh basil
1 teaspoon fresh lemon juice

1 16-inch long baguette, split lengthwise and cut into 4 sections, or bread of your choice
1 bunch watercress, coarse stems discarded (2 cups)

Preheat oven to 450 degrees. Combine eggplant, zucchini, squash, and bell pepper in a large roasting pan. Add oil and garlic. Toss to coat. Season with salt and pepper. Roast vegetables 30 to 35 minutes, or until tender. Cool.

Combine sour cream, mayonnaise, basil, and lemon juice in a small bowl. Spread mayonnaise mixture on baguette. Assemble sandwiches using watercress and roasted vegetables.

The Best B.L.T. with Hill Country Basil Mayonnaise

SERVES 6

Hill Country Basil Mayonnaise:
1 large egg, at room temperature
1 tablespoon fresh lemon juice
1 teaspoon Dijon mustard
¼ teaspoon salt
½ cup vegetable oil
½ cup extra virgin olive oil
1 cup chopped fresh basil

12 slices bread
1 pound bacon, cooked crisp
1 head Boston lettuce
2 large tomatoes, thinly sliced

Hill Country Basil Mayonnaise: Process egg, lemon juice, mustard, and salt in a food processor or blender. With machine running, add oils in a thin stream until mayonnaise has thickened. Add basil leaves and process until smooth. Cover and refrigerate. Yields 1½ cups.

Spread Hill Country Basil Mayonnaise on bread and assemble sandwiches using crisp bacon, lettuce, and tomatoes.

An old favorite is back!

Sun-Dried Tomato, Goat Cheese, and Watercress Sandwich

SERVES 4

Sun-Dried Tomatoes:*
8 Roma tomatoes
2 cups extra virgin olive oil
3 large cloves garlic, minced
2 sprigs fresh rosemary, chopped
2 sprigs fresh thyme, chopped
2 sprigs fresh parsley, chopped

———

8 ounces goat cheese
2 teaspoons minced fresh rosemary

2 teaspoons minced fresh thyme
2 teaspoons minced fresh parsley
salt
freshly ground pepper

———

8 slices black olive bread
2 bunches watercress,
    coarse stems discarded
1 teaspoon olive oil

TIPS ON HERBS

◆ 1 tablespoon fresh herbs =
  1 teaspoon dried herbs

◆ Dried herbs in clear glass containers should be stored in a cabinet as exposure to light causes rapid deterioration.

◆ Refrigerate fresh herbs up to 5 days. Wrap loosely in a damp paper towel and tightly seal in a plastic bag. Alternatively, place a small bunch of herbs in a small vase of water and set out of direct sunlight.

Sun-Dried Tomatoes: Cut tomatoes in half lengthwise and place in a non-metallic bowl or container. Whisk oil, garlic, rosemary, thyme, and parsley in a separate bowl. Pour over tomatoes and marinate 8 to 12 hours. Preheat oven to 200 degrees. Drain tomatoes and arrange in a single layer, cut side up, on a baking sheet. Place on the center rack and roast 5 to 6 hours, until firm but not leathery or dry. Cool.

Blend goat cheese, rosemary, thyme, and parsley in a food processor. Season with salt and pepper.

Generously spread goat cheese on olive bread. Assemble sandwiches by layering sun-dried tomato halves and watercress. Sauté sandwich on both sides with a touch of olive oil until golden. Serve warm.

* May substitute sun-dried tomatoes packed in oil, patted dry.

Egg Salad Sandwich

SERVES 4

4 large eggs, hard-boiled and peeled
2 to 3 green onions, minced
2 ribs celery plus some leaves,
    chopped
⅓ cup mayonnaise
1 tablespoon Dijon mustard
salt
freshly ground pepper

———

8 slices whole wheat bread
mayonnaise
1 head Boston lettuce
2 large tomatoes, thinly sliced

While eggs are still warm, place in a bowl and chop with a pastry cutter. Add onions, celery, mayonnaise, and mustard. Season with salt and pepper. Combine well and chill.

Assemble sandwiches using whole wheat bread, additional mayonnaise, lettuce, and tomatoes.

Olive "Po" Boy

OLIVADA

¾ cup plus ¾ cup large pitted
  black olives, drained
¾ cup plus ¾ cup pitted
  Greek olives, drained
1 clove garlic, chopped
2 tablespoons pine nuts
1 to 2 tablespoons extra
  virgin olive oil

Process ¾ cup black olives, ¾ cup
Greek olives, garlic, pine nuts,
and 1 tablespoon olive oil in a
food processor until somewhat
smooth. (If mixture is too stiff,
add additional 1 tablespoon olive
oil.) Transfer mixture to a bowl.
Set aside. Coarsely chop remaining
¾ cup black olives and ¾ cup
Greek olives. Stir into processed
olive mixture. Cover and refrigerate
up to 1 week. It is best served at
room temperature.

USES FOR OLIVADA

Olivada is an olive paste with a
variety of uses. Try these or create
your own combinations.

◆ Layer on crostini spread with
  soft cheese

◆ Toss with pasta and tomato sauce

◆ Use as a pizza topping

◆ Add to salad dressings

◆ Stir into freshly cooked vegetables

◆ Add to baked potatoes as
  a topping

◆ Spread on chicken breasts and
  roast

◆ Use as topping for grilled fish

Olive Mixture:
1 head cauliflower, florets only,
  or 1 jar (16 ounces) pickled
  cauliflower
1 jar (5 ounces) green olives
  with pimentos, drained
1 can (8 ounces) pitted black olives,
  drained
1 jar (3½ ounces) small capers
1 teaspoon freshly ground pepper
1 tablespoon chopped fresh oregano

3 cloves garlic, crushed
dash cayenne pepper
olive oil
——
6 French rolls or pita bread rounds
6 slices baked ham
6 slices salami
6 slices Swiss cheese
6 slices American cheese
1 tomato, thinly sliced
red leaf lettuce

Olive Mixture: Chop cauliflower in a food processor until finely textured.
Transfer to a bowl. Place green and black olives in food processor and chop
until finely textured. Combine olives with cauliflower. Add capers and
juice, pepper, oregano, garlic, and cayenne. Blend well. Fill a 32-ounce jar
three-fourths full with mixture. Top with olive oil to the neck of the jar.
Cover and refrigerate. This will keep several weeks in the refrigerator.
Stir before using. Yields 4 ½ cups.

Spread Olive Mixture on bread and assemble sandwiches using ham,
salami, Swiss and American cheeses, tomato, and lettuce.

Crab Sandwich

1 pound fresh lump crabmeat,
  shells removed
1 bunch green onions, minced
1 cup bread crumbs *
8 ounces cream cheese, softened
1 cup mayonnaise
juice of ½ lemon
2 to 4 tablespoons dry sherry

¼ teaspoon cayenne pepper
salt
white pepper
——
6 English muffins, sliced and toasted
1 large tomato, sliced
Cheddar or Swiss cheese, sliced
  or shredded

Gently combine crabmeat, green onions, and bread crumbs in a large
bowl. Set aside. Blend cream cheese, mayonnaise, lemon juice, sherry,
and cayenne pepper in a separate bowl. Add cream cheese mixture to
crabmeat mixture. Season with salt and pepper. Blend well.

Preheat broiler. Top English muffin slices with a tomato slice, a
dollop of crab mixture, then cheese. Place on baking sheet and under
broiler long enough to melt the cheese. (Can also bake at 350 degrees
10 minutes.) Serve immediately.

*The best bread crumbs are made from leftover toasted French bread.

Mediterranean Turkey Meatball Sandwich

SERVES 3 TO 4

Meatballs:
1¼ pounds ground turkey
¼ cup minced onion
1½ teaspoons chopped fresh
    oregano
2 tablespoons chopped fresh mint
2 tablespoons chopped fresh parsley
1 teaspoon lemon pepper
1 large clove garlic, minced
1 teaspoon fresh lemon juice

Cucumber Sauce:
½ cup nonfat sour cream
½ medium cucumber, peeled and
    minced
1½ teaspoons fresh lemon juice
⅛ teaspoon freshly ground pepper
——
3 pita bread rounds, cut in half
6 lettuce leaves, torn
1 medium tomato, diced

Combine turkey, onion, oregano, mint, parsley, lemon pepper, garlic, and lemon juice in a large bowl. Mix well and shape into 1¼-inch balls (about 18). In a nonstick skillet, brown meatballs over medium heat, 8 to 10 minutes. Set aside.

Combine sour cream, cucumber, lemon juice, and pepper in a small bowl.

Assemble sandwiches by placing 3 meatballs in each pita half, topped with cucumber sauce, lettuce, and tomato.

Smoked Turkey and Apple Sandwich with Lone Star Mayonnaise

SERVES 4 TO 6

Lone Star Mayonnaise:
1 cup nonfat mayonnaise
1 tablespoon Dijon mustard
3 drops liquid smoke
juice, pulp, and zest of 1 lime
1 tablespoon chipotle chile peppers,
    canned in adobo sauce,
    plus 1 tablespoon sauce

——
12 slices whole wheat farm bread
2 green apples, cored, seeded,
    and thinly sliced
6 to 8 slices smoked turkey breast
6 to 8 slices Muenster cheese

Lone Star Mayonnaise: Blend mayonnaise, mustard, liquid smoke, lime, and chipotles in a food processor. Cover and refrigerate. Yields 1½ cups.

Spread Lone Star Mayonnaise on bread and assemble sandwiches using apples, turkey, and cheese.

Lone Star Mayonnaise is also great with fresh vegetables or as a dip for cold shrimp.

Every year across America, one of the surest signs of summer is not white shoes or the opening of the neighborhood swimming pool, but the sight of Dad standing over the backyard grill, spatula in hand as the mouth-watering smell of charcoal-grilled meat fills the air. The hamburger, that most American of food traditions, had its origins far from America. It began as a medieval culinary practice of Mongolian and Turkish tribes in which low-quality, tough meat from Asian cattle grazing on the Russian steppes was shredded to make it more palatable. Tartare steak, as it was known, traveled to Germany sometime before the fourteenth century where it was flavored with spices and called "Hamburg steak" after the seaport town of Hamburg. It wasn't until after it came to America with the wave of German immigrants in the 1880s, when the hamburg steak was put in a bun, that it became the hamburger Americans know and love.

$10 Hamburgers

SERVES 4

8 ounces fresh mushrooms, sliced
2 tablespoons vermouth
¼ cup unsalted butter
½ teaspoon garlic salt
——
1 pound ground round beef
1 green bell pepper, seeded and diced
1 small white onion, diced
¼ cup half and half

salt
freshly ground pepper
——
4 slices cheese (provolone, Jarlsberg, Swiss, or Brie)
4 English muffins, split and toasted
Dijon mustard or Hill Country Basil Mayonnaise (page 94)

Combine mushrooms, vermouth, butter, and garlic salt in a saucepan. Sauté until mushrooms are soft. Set aside.

Combine beef, bell pepper, onion, and half and half. Season with salt and pepper. Mix thoroughly. Form four patties from meat mixture. Cook patties on grill or on stove in skillet. During the last few minutes of cooking, place cheese slices on patties, cover, and allow cheese to melt.

Assemble hamburgers by spreading English muffins with Dijon mustard or Hill Country Basil Mayonnaise. Add meat and a spoonful of sautéed mushrooms.

Pizza Sandwich

SERVES 4

½ package dry yeast
2 tablespoons plus ¾ cup warm water
2 cups plus 1 to 2 cups sifted all-purpose flour
1 teaspoon vegetable oil
2 teaspoons cornmeal
4 ounces provolone cheese, sliced
2 ounces Italian ham, thinly sliced

2 ounces boiled ham, thinly sliced
2 to 3 slices American cheese
4 ounces hard Italian salami, thinly sliced
1 can (4 ounces) sliced black olives or Italian olives, drained
1 can (2 ounces) anchovies, drained (optional)

Dissolve yeast in 2 tablespoons warm water. Mix ¾ cup warm water with 2 cups flour in a large bowl until blended. Add yeast mixture and 1 to 2 cups flour to form a stiff dough. Knead well. Place mixture in a bowl greased with vegetable oil, turning dough over to grease top, and leave in a warm place to rise, about an hour. When dough has doubled in size, punch down and let rest another hour to rise again. Separate dough into two equal parts. On a baking sheet sprinkled with cornmeal, press down one ball of dough to form a flattened round, about ¼ inch thick.

Preheat oven to 400 degrees. On dough round, layer provolone cheese, Italian ham, boiled ham, American cheese, salami, black olives, and anchovies. On floured board, roll out remaining dough to form another round and place on top of sandwich. Press edges together to seal. Cut a small hole in the center to allow steam to escape. Bake 20 to 25 minutes until golden brown. Remove sandwich from baking sheet, place directly on the oven rack, and bake 10 minutes. Remove from oven and cut into wedges. Serve immediately.

Tomato Basil Soup

10 to 12 Roma tomatoes, peeled,
   or 1 can (28 ounces) whole
   tomatoes, drained
3 cups tomato juice
2 cups chicken stock
15 or more fresh basil leaves
1½ cups heavy whipping cream

¾ cup (1½ sticks) unsalted butter,
   cut into pieces
½ teaspoon salt
½ teaspoon freshly ground pepper
——
freshly grated Parmesan cheese

Combine tomatoes, tomato juice, and chicken stock in a large saucepan. Simmer 30 minutes. Add basil. Transfer soup in batches to a food processor or blender and process until smooth. Return to saucepan over low heat. Whisk in cream, butter, salt, and pepper. Whisk until butter is melted and soup is thoroughly heated. Garnish with Parmesan.

Cream of Poblano Soup

2 tablespoons unsalted butter
3 poblano chile peppers, roasted
   (page 40), peeled, seeded,
   and diced
½ cup chopped onion
¼ cup chopped carrots
2 tablespoons all-purpose flour
4 cups water
2 cups chicken stock
¾ cup half and half

1 tablespoon plus 2 tablespoons
   minced fresh cilantro
1 teaspoon salt
1½ cups crushed tortilla chips
6 ounces Monterey Jack cheese,
   shredded (1½ cups)
½ pound chorizo (Mexican sausage),
   casings removed, crumbled, browned,
   and drained

Melt butter in a large saucepan. Add poblanos, onion, and carrots. Sauté 5 minutes, or until vegetables are soft. Sprinkle with flour. Sauté an additional 5 minutes. Whisk in water and chicken stock until blended. Simmer uncovered for 30 minutes. Transfer soup in batches to a blender or food processor. Process until smooth. Return to saucepan. Add half and half, 1 tablespoon cilantro, and salt. Heat to a simmer. Ladle soup into individual bowls. Top with tortilla chips, cheese, remaining 2 tablespoons cilantro, and chorizo.

Corn, Red Pepper, and Leek Soup

SERVES 6 TO 8

CHICKEN STOCK

4 pounds chicken, necks, wings,
  backs, and other scraps
1 onion, coarsely chopped
3 ribs celery, chopped
1 carrot, chopped
1 bay leaf
1 teaspoon salt
¼ teaspoon peppercorns

*Place chicken, onion, celery,
carrot, bay leaf, salt, and peppercorns in a large saucepan. Add
cold water to cover, about
1 inch above chicken. Bring to
a boil, reduce heat, and simmer
loosely covered for 2 hours.
Occasionally skim off the foam
that rises to the surface. Using a
colander, strain and reserve the
liquid. Cool and degrease. May
be refrigerated or frozen. Yields
1½ to 2 quarts.*

2 tablespoons unsalted butter
3 tablespoons vegetable oil
2 medium leeks, white part only,
  coarsely chopped
1 large red bell pepper, seeded and
  coarsely chopped
kernels of 5 ears corn (reserving
  ¼ cup)
6 cups chicken stock

½ cup heavy whipping cream
½ teaspoon salt
⅛ teaspoon white pepper
pinch cayenne pepper

——

2 tablespoons minced fresh parsley
red bell pepper, chopped
crème fraîche (page 102)

Heat butter and oil in a large saucepan. Add leeks and sauté 5 minutes, stirring occasionally. Add bell pepper and sauté until slightly soft, about 5 minutes. Add corn and sauté 3 minutes. Add stock and bring to a boil. Reduce heat and simmer uncovered 30 minutes. Transfer soup in batches to a blender or food processor. Process until smooth. Return to saucepan over low heat. Stir in cream, salt, pepper, and cayenne. Adjust seasonings.

Place ¼ cup corn in a strainer and submerge in boiling water 2 minutes. Drain. Ladle soup into individual bowls and top with corn, parsley, bell pepper, and a dollop of crème fraîche.

Savory Red Pepper Soup

SERVES 8 TO 12

½ cup (1 stick) unsalted butter
2 large onions, chopped
2 cloves garlic, minced
4 large carrots, peeled and chopped
1 large russet potato, peeled
  and chopped
6 red bell peppers, roasted (page 40),
  peeled, seeded, and chopped
2 firm pears, peeled, cored,
  and chopped

5 cups chicken stock
1 tablespoon chopped fresh parsley
salt
freshly ground pepper

——

crème fraîche (page 102)
  or sour cream
fresh Italian parsley sprigs

Melt butter in a large saucepan. Add onion and garlic and sauté 10 minutes. Add carrots and sauté an additional 10 minutes. Add potato and bell peppers and sauté 10 minutes. Add pears, chicken stock, and parsley. Bring to a boil. Reduce heat. Simmer uncovered 20 minutes, or until vegetables are tender. Season with salt and pepper. Transfer soup in batches to a food processor or blender. Process until smooth. Reheat.

Ladle soup into individual bowls and garnish with crème fraîche and sprigs of parsley.

Corn, Red Pepper and Leek Soup

Cream of Carrot and Lemon Soup

SERVES 6 TO 8

CRÈME FRAÎCHE

2 cups heavy whipping cream,
  at room temperature
½ cup sour cream, at room
  temperature

Whisk heavy cream and sour
cream in a large bowl. Cover with
plastic wrap and let stand in a
warm, draft-free place 12 hours
or overnight. (A gas stove with
a pilot light on is ideal.) Store,
covered, in the refrigerator up to
2 weeks. Serve chilled. Crème
fraîche is also available in your
local supermarket.

Crème fraîche has a slightly
tangy, nutty flavor and has a
variety of uses:

◆ Topping for fresh berries or
  fruit desserts

◆ Topping for puddings or rich
  chocolate desserts

◆ Thickener for salad dressings

◆ Sauce over warm vegetables

◆ Garnish for soups

---

4 tablespoons plus 2 tablespoons
  unsalted butter
1 large onion, chopped
1 large clove garlic, sliced
1½ pounds carrots, peeled
  and sliced
3 tomatoes, chopped
1 russet potato, peeled and sliced
¼ cup chopped fresh basil or
  Italian parsley
4 cups chicken stock or 3 cups canned
  chicken broth and 1 cup water

1½ teaspoons salt
¼ teaspoon freshly ground pepper
1 cup crème fraîche
  (see accompanying recipe)
¼ teaspoon Tabasco Sauce
¼ cup fresh lemon juice

———

carrot curls
crème fraîche
fresh Italian parsley

Melt 4 tablespoons butter in a large saucepan. Add onion and garlic. Sauté
until softened, but not browned. Add carrots, tomatoes, potato, basil, stock,
salt, pepper, and remaining 2 tablespoons butter. Bring to a boil, then
reduce heat and simmer covered 45 minutes. Strain soup, reserving broth
and vegetables. Purée vegetables in a food processor until smooth. Return
puréed vegetables and broth to saucepan. Add crème fraîche and Tabasco.
Simmer uncovered 15 minutes. (The recipe can be made up to 2 days ahead
and refrigerated at this point.) Remove from heat and add lemon juice.
Serve in individual bowls garnished with a carrot curl, a dollop of crème
fraîche, and a sprig of parsley.

Champagne Camembert Soup

SERVES 4

A UNIQUE SOUP BOWL

A unique way to serve cheese soup
is in a hollowed-out round loaf of
bread. Brush the insides with olive
oil and toast the top and bottom in a
350 degree oven 10 minutes. Ladle
soup into bread bowls and serve
immediately.

---

4 tablespoons plus 6 tablespoons
  unsalted butter
1 tablespoon all-purpose flour
1 cup chicken stock
1 cup heavy whipping cream
⅔ cup whole milk
4½ ounces Camembert cheese,
  rind removed and quartered

⅔ cup champagne
salt
white pepper

———

chopped fresh parsley

Melt 4 tablespoons butter in a large heavy saucepan. Sift in flour and
whisk to blend. Gradually add stock, whisking constantly until just boiling.
Remove from heat. Stir in cream and milk. Return to heat. Just before
boiling, remove from heat. Add remaining 6 tablespoons butter,
Camembert, and champagne. Return to medium heat and stir until cheese
is melted. Season with salt and pepper. Garnish each serving with parsley.

You may thin this with additional chicken stock if soup is too rich.

Smooth Black Bean Soup

SERVES 8 TO 10

1 can (6 ounces) tomato paste
6 cans (15 ounces each) black beans,
   rinsed and drained
4 cans (14½ ounces each)
   beef broth
3 beef bouillon cubes
1 teaspoon paprika
dash cayenne pepper
1 teaspoon onion powder

1 teaspoon garlic salt
¾ teaspoon white pepper
½ bunch fresh cilantro, chopped
2 fresh jalapeños, seeded and sliced
1 bunch green onions, chopped

——

sour cream
chopped fresh cilantro

Combine tomato paste, black beans, broth, bouillon cubes, paprika, cayenne, onion powder, garlic salt, and pepper in a large saucepan. Bring to a boil, reduce heat, and simmer 15 minutes. Add cilantro, jalapeños, and green onions. Simmer 2 minutes more. Transfer to a food processor and process in batches until smooth. Reheat. Garnish each serving with sour cream and cilantro.

IS IT CORIANDER OR CILANTRO?

Fresh coriander, called cilantro in Spanish and also known as Chinese parsley, is a parsley-like plant with bright green, round, lightly fringed, fragile leaves and wispy stems. It has a distinctive flavor and a peppery aroma, which has a cooling effect on highly spiced foods. It is widely used in Asian, Caribbean, and Latin American cooking. The ground coriander seeds sold in the spice section at the supermarket are not interchangeable with the fresh green leaves found in the produce department. Their flavors are quite different.

Tortilla Soup

SERVES 6

6 tablespoons vegetable oil
8 corn tortillas, chopped
6 cloves garlic, minced
½ cup chopped fresh cilantro
1 medium onion, chopped
1 can (28 ounces) diced tomatoes
2 tablespoons ground cumin
1 tablespoon chili powder
3 bay leaves
6 cups chicken stock

1 teaspoon salt
½ teaspoon cayenne pepper
4 to 6 cooked chicken breast halves,
   shredded or cubed

——

Monterey Jack cheese, shredded
avocado, pitted, peeled, and cubed
sour cream
2 corn tortillas, sliced and fried crisp

Heat oil in a large saucepan over medium heat. Add tortillas, garlic, cilantro, and onion. Sauté 2 to 3 minutes. Stir in tomatoes. Bring to a boil and add cumin, chili powder, bay leaves, and chicken stock. Return to a boil. Reduce heat. Add salt and cayenne. Simmer 30 minutes. Remove bay leaves and stir in chicken. Reheat. Garnish with Monterey Jack, avocado, sour cream, and tortilla chips.

Since before recorded history, garlic has been used as a seasoning and as a medicine. Ancient Mediterranean cultures subscribed to its curative powers: Aristophanes claimed it gave courage, Pliny that it cured consumption, and Mohammed that it eased pain. All we know is that this member of the lily family, sometimes called "the stinking rose," adds a wonderful flavor to many dishes as it fills the kitchen with a seductive fragrance. On their own, whole garlic heads roasted in their skins make a perfect accompaniment to grilled or roasted meats. Garlic can be mild like the white variety or strong like the rose-colored variety, with a range of intensity and hue in between. Whichever you prefer, the garlic you use should be firm, crisp, and fresh. The fresher the garlic, the milder the taste.

Mexican Garlic Soup

SERVES 8 TO 10

2 boboli or hard rolls
1 tablespoon plus ⅓ cup olive oil
5⅓ tablespoons unsalted butter
3 heads garlic, cloves peeled
 and minced
4 large tomatoes, puréed
 and strained

14 cups beef broth
8 sprigs fresh cilantro, chopped
2 large eggs, beaten
4 ounces feta cheese, crumbled (1 cup)
3 serrano chile peppers or 1 to 2 fresh
 jalapeños, seeded and minced

Preheat oven to 350 degrees. Slice rolls and brush with 1 tablespoon olive oil. Bake 10 minutes, or until crisp. Set aside. Heat ⅓ cup olive oil and butter in a large soup pot. Add garlic and sauté until lightly browned. Add tomatoes and cook until mixture thickens. Stir in beef broth. Cook 20 minutes. Add cilantro and bring to a boil. Whisk in eggs. Add cheese, chiles, and baked roll slices to soup just before serving.

Oven-Baked Onion Soup

SERVES 6

4 tablespoons unsalted butter
6 cups thinly sliced yellow onions
2 tablespoons all-purpose flour
6 cups beef broth
½ cup dry white wine
½ teaspoon salt

½ teaspoon freshly ground pepper
3 tablespoons brandy
6 slices French bread, toasted
6 slices Gruyère cheese
2 ounces Parmesan cheese, freshly
 grated (½ cup)

Melt butter in a soup pot. Add onions and sauté over medium heat until lightly browned. Add flour and blend. Stir in beef broth, wine, salt, and pepper. Bring to a boil. Reduce heat and simmer 10 minutes. Remove from heat and add brandy.

Preheat oven to 375 degrees. Place slices of bread in the bottom of 6 individual ovenproof soup bowls. Ladle soup over bread, top with Gruyère, and sprinkle with Parmesan. Bake until cheese melts, about 5 minutes. Serve immediately.

Italian Tortellini Soup

4 cans (14½ ounces each) Italian-style stewed tomatoes, coarsely chopped, plus liquid

2 cans (14½ ounces each) low-salt beef broth

2 tablespoons chopped fresh basil

½ teaspoon freshly ground pepper

1 medium zucchini, halved and thinly sliced

¾ pound green beans, snapped and cut into thirds

¾ pound Italian sausage, casings removed, crumbled, browned, and drained

1 package tortellini with cheese (6 to 8 ounces)

——

freshly grated Parmesan cheese

Combine tomatoes plus liquid, broth, basil, and pepper in a Dutch oven. Bring to a boil. Reduce heat. Add zucchini, green beans, sausage, and tortellini. Cook approximately 10 to 15 minutes, or until tortellini is tender. Serve with grated Parmesan.

Vegetable Garden Soup

1½ cups water

5 cans (14½ ounces each) vegetable broth

2 cans (10 ounces each) diced tomatoes with green chilies

2 medium zucchini, coarsely chopped

2 medium yellow squash, coarsely chopped

1 red onion, coarsely chopped

1 bunch green onions, chopped

¼ cup chopped fresh cilantro

1 tablespoon minced garlic

½ cup raw instant brown rice

——

2 avocados, pitted, peeled, and chopped

tortilla chips, crushed

Combine water, broth, tomatoes, zucchini, squash, red onion, green onions, cilantro, garlic, and rice in a large saucepan. Bring to a boil, reduce heat, and simmer 1 to 2 hours. Just before serving, top with avocados and tortilla chips.

Wild Rice Soup

**GARNISHING
YOUR SOUP**

*Soup garnishes add contrasting
flavor and texture to the soup, as
well as enhancing its visual appeal.*

*Some suggested garnishes include
toasted coconut, chopped peppers,
crème fraîche, shredded cheese,
bacon, sesame seeds, chopped
herbs, thinly sliced fruit, capers,
chopped nuts, peppercorns, avocado slices, or crumbled corn chips.*

*A decorative garnish would
be to squeeze sour cream through
a plastic bottle with a small
opening, then drag a wooden pick
through the sour cream drops for
a swirled effect.*

½ cup raw wild rice, rinsed*
2 cups water
3 tablespoons unsalted butter
1 medium onion, chopped
3 carrots, peeled and chopped
½ cup chopped celery
¼ cup chopped green bell pepper
1 slice ham (1 inch thick), cubed

4 large fresh mushrooms, sliced
½ cup all-purpose flour
3 cans (14½ ounces each) chicken
  broth
1 tablespoon minced fresh chives
1 cup half and half
2 to 4 tablespoons dry sherry

Bring rice and water to a boil in a medium saucepan. Boil 45 minutes.
Set aside. Melt butter in a large saucepan. Add onion, carrots, celery, bell
pepper, ham, and mushrooms. Sauté until vegetables are tender. Add flour
and stir until liquid has evaporated. Slowly add chicken broth, whisking
to blend thoroughly. Add wild rice and chives. Slowly add half and half.
Do not allow to boil. Add sherry just before serving.

*Best if soaked for 8 hours before cooking.

Chilled Sweet Red Pepper Soup

½ cup (1 stick) unsalted butter
3 large red bell peppers,
  seeded and sliced
1 cup chopped leeks, white part only
1½ cups chicken broth

3 cups buttermilk
⅛ teaspoon white pepper
———
chopped fresh chives

Melt butter in a large saucepan. Add bell peppers, leeks, and broth.
Bring to a boil. Reduce heat and simmer covered 30 minutes, or until
vegetables are tender, stirring occasionally. Transfer mixture to a blender
or food processor. Process until smooth, stopping once to scrape down the
sides. Strain. (Should be 3 cups liquid.) Combine liquid, buttermilk, and
white pepper in a large bowl. Cover and chill at least 2 hours. Sprinkle
with chives when ready to serve.

Forgo the usual soup bowl and serve instead in bright yellow bell pepper halves.

Cool Sunset Soup

5 tablespoons unsalted butter
1½ cups chopped leeks,
  white parts only
3 cups chopped carrots (about
  1¼ pounds)
5 cups chicken stock
1 tablespoon fresh lemon juice

¼ cup minced fresh cilantro
salt
freshly ground pepper
———
½ cup sour cream
6 sprigs fresh cilantro

Melt butter in a large saucepan. Add leeks and sauté about 4 minutes.
Add carrots and sauté 5 minutes. Add stock. Simmer uncovered
25 minutes. Remove from heat and purée in batches in a food processor.
Cover and refrigerate. Whisk in lemon juice and cilantro when ready
to serve. Season with salt and pepper. Garnish each serving with a dollop
of sour cream and a cilantro sprig.

*For a creamier soup, add ½ cup sour cream and ½ cup half and half when adding lemon juice
and cilantro.*

Chilled Green Chile Soup

1½ cups chicken stock
¼ cup minced onion
3 ounces cream cheese, softened
1 cup sour cream
2 cans (4½ ounces each) diced
  green chilies

¼ teaspoon ground cumin
1 teaspoon minced garlic
1 cup heavy whipping cream
½ teaspoon salt

Bring stock and onion to a boil. Reduce heat and simmer 5 minutes. Cool.
Blend cream cheese and sour cream in a medium bowl. Add chilies, cumin,
and garlic. Stir in stock, whipping cream, and salt. Transfer to a blender in
batches and process until smooth. Cover and chill until ready to serve.

Chilled Green Chile Soup will keep up to 1 week in the refrigerator.

Chilled Yellow Pepper Soup with Scallop Ceviche Verde

¼ teaspoon saffron threads
1 tablespoon warm water
3 medium yellow bell peppers,
  roasted (page 40), peeled,
  and seeded
½ cup chopped onion
¼ cup chopped carrot
1 clove garlic, minced
½ serrano chile pepper or fresh
  jalapeño, seeded

1 ½ cups chicken stock
½ cup heavy whipping cream
½ cup milk
salt

——

Scallop Ceviche Verde
¼ cup sour cream

Soak saffron in warm water 10 minutes. Transfer to a medium saucepan and add bell peppers, onion, carrot, garlic, serrano, and chicken stock. Bring to a boil. Reduce heat and simmer 5 minutes. Transfer mixture to a blender or food processor. Process until smooth. Chill.

When ready to serve, stir in cream and milk. Season with salt. Ladle soup into chilled bowls, and top with Scallop Ceviche Verde and a dollop of sour cream.

CEVICHE

Ceviche is seafood that has been "cooked" in citrus juice.

Scallop Ceviche Verde:
½ pound fresh sea scallops, thinly
  sliced
¼ cup plus 1 tablespoon fresh
  lime juice
3 medium tomatillos, husked,
  rinsed, and minced
1 clove garlic, minced
½ small tomato, seeded and diced
¼ cup diced green onions

1 tablespoon extra virgin olive oil
3 serrano chile peppers, seeded
  and minced
1 small ripe avocado, pitted, peeled,
  and diced
1 tablespoon minced fresh basil
  or 2 teaspoons minced fresh cilantro
salt
freshly ground pepper

Marinate scallops in ¼ cup lime juice at least 1 hour in the refrigerator. Drain. Combine marinated scallops with 1 tablespoon lime juice, tomatillos, garlic, tomato, green onions, olive oil, serranos, avocado, and basil. Season with salt and pepper. Chill 30 minutes before serving.

Spicy Shrimp Gazpacho

SERVES 6 TO 8

1 teaspoon salt
2 cloves garlic, minced
1½ cups cubed white bread,
    crusts removed
¼ cup red wine vinegar
2 tablespoons balsamic vinegar
¼ cup extra virgin olive oil
1 teaspoon ground cumin
1 cup plus 1½ cups tomato juice
2 pounds tomatoes, peeled,
    seeded, and diced
1 green bell pepper, diced
1 red bell pepper, diced

⅓ cup minced green onions
1 cucumber, peeled, seeded,
    and minced
⅓ cup minced red onion
½ to 1 cup ice water
½ pound fresh shrimp, boiled (page 48),
    peeled, deveined, and chopped
¼ cup minced fresh parsley
dash Tabasco Sauce
salt
freshly ground pepper
——
croutons

Make a paste with salt and garlic, rubbing the flat side of a knife back and forth over ingredients. Combine paste, bread, vinegars, olive oil, cumin, and 1 cup tomato juice in a food processor. Blend until smooth. Transfer mixture to a large bowl and add tomatoes, bell peppers, green onions, cucumber, and red onion. Stir in remaining 1½ cups tomato juice and chill 3 hours. Thin soup with ice water to desired consistency. Add shrimp, parsley, and Tabasco. Season with salt and pepper. Serve with croutons.

Nutty Cucumber Soup al Fresca

SERVES 6 TO 8

3 cucumbers, peeled, seeded,
    and chopped
1½ cups plus 1½ cups chicken
    broth
3 cups light sour cream
3 tablespoons distilled white vinegar
2 teaspoons garlic powder,
    or 3 teaspoons minced garlic

2 tomatoes, peeled, seeded,
    and chopped
¼ cup slivered almonds
½ cup minced green onions
½ cup chopped fresh parsley
salt
freshly ground pepper

Blend cucumbers and 1½ cups chicken broth in a blender. Transfer mixture to a medium bowl. Stir in remaining 1½ cups chicken broth, sour cream, vinegar, and garlic powder. Chill several hours. Just before serving, add tomatoes, almonds, green onions, and parsley. Season with salt and pepper.

Remember coming home from school on a cold winter's day to discover the heady aroma of soup simmering on the stove? As you were embraced by its warmth and comforting smells, enticed by its promise of goodness, suddenly all seemed right with your world. For most of us, no matter what age, that still holds true. Hot or cold, soup is the perfect food to spark the appetite, balance a menu, and soothe the soul. Serve a light consommé to complement a rich main course, or a hearty tortellini soup to round out a light meal, while chilled gazpachos and fruit soups like strawberry and blueberry bisques add a refreshing lift to meals on a hot summer day. And on those gray winter afternoons, there's nothing like a sturdy vegetable or baked onion soup as a heartwarming main dish.

Mangospacho

MANGOES

The mango is a tropical fruit originally grown in India and Southeast Asia. Although not one of the more common fruits in the United States, it is actually one of the most popular fruits enjoyed worldwide. Try substituting the mango for tomatoes, pineapple, or peaches in traditional salsas and relishes to add a refreshing tropical twist. To prepare the mango, use a sharp paring knife to cut the flesh vertically from the fibrous pit, then peel.

2 large mangoes plus 2 large
   mangoes, peeled, pitted, and diced
2 tablespoons grated fresh ginger
½ cup rice vinegar
½ cup olive oil
2 cups water
2 tablespoons brown sugar,
   firmly packed
1 teaspoon salt
½ teaspoon white pepper

1 medium red onion, diced
1 cup strawberries, hulled and diced
2 cucumbers, peeled, seeded,
   and diced
½ cup chopped fresh cilantro
½ cup chopped fresh chives

———

chopped fresh cilantro
crème fraîche (page 102)

Blend 2 diced mangoes, ginger, vinegar, olive oil, water, brown sugar, salt, and pepper in a blender until smooth. Transfer mixture to a large bowl and add remaining 2 mangoes, onion, strawberries, cucumber, cilantro, and chives. Adjust seasonings. Chill several hours to let flavors blend. Let rest at room temperature 15 to 20 minutes before serving. Ladle into bowls and garnish with cilantro and crème fraîche.

Mangospacho is especially pretty served in clear bowls.

Blueberry Bisque

2 cups blueberries, fresh or frozen
1 cup fresh pineapple juice
1 cup sour cream

———

lime sherbet
chopped fresh tarragon

Process blueberries in a food processor until smooth. Add pineapple juice and sour cream. Process to blend. Transfer mixture to a saucepan and bring to a boil. Gently boil 15 minutes. Cool slightly. Strain. Chill 8 to 10 hours.

    Mix sherbet with tarragon and freeze to set. When ready to serve, pour bisque into bowls and garnish with a dollop of sherbet.

Strawberry Soup

SERVES 6 TO 8

1 quart strawberries, hulled
1 cup plus 3 cups buttermilk
¾ cup sugar
⅔ cup sour cream

3 tablespoons kirsch
_____
fresh mint sprigs

Process strawberries, 1 cup buttermilk, and sugar in a food processor. Set aside. Combine remaining 3 cups buttermilk, sour cream, and kirsch in a large bowl. Pour the strawberry mixture into the sour cream mixture. Stir to combine. Cover and chill. Serve chilled and garnish with mint sprigs.

KIRSCH

A clear brandy distilled from cherry juice and pits.

Norwegian Fruit Soup

SERVES 10

⅓ to ¾ cup quick cooking
   tapioca
8 cups water
1 can whole pitted prunes, drained,
   or 12 ounces dried prunes, halved
¼ cup raisins
¼ cup golden raisins
1 cup whole dried apricots
2 sticks cinnamon, broken

½ teaspoon salt
juice of 1 lemon
1 can (16 ounces) pitted cherries
   plus juice
1 can (16 ounces) peach halves
   plus juice
1 cup sugar
2 cups grape juice
2 cups red wine

Place tapioca and water in a large saucepan. Add prunes, raisins, apricots, cinnamon sticks, and salt. Bring to a boil. Reduce heat to a simmer. Cover and cook until tapioca is clear, stirring occasionally. Add lemon juice, cherries, peaches, sugar, grape juice, and wine. Bring to a boil. Remove from heat. Serve hot or cold.

Use less tapioca for a thinner soup and more for a thicker soup.

Upside Down Pickles

YIELDS 46 OUNCES

1 jar (46 ounces) whole dill pickles, drained
2½ cups sugar
6 tablespoons apple cider vinegar

1 teaspoon celery seeds
2 tablespoons prepared horseradish
1 small onion, chopped

Slice pickles. Put them back in jar and set aside. Combine sugar, vinegar, celery seeds, horseradish, and onion. Pour mixture over pickles. Turn jar upside down and refrigerate 24 hours. Serve chilled.

Zucchini Pickles

YIELDS 2 PINTS

4 cups sliced zucchini
2 medium onions, sliced
½ cup salt

1 cup apple cider vinegar
1 cup sugar
1 tablespoon pickling spice

Toss zucchini and onions in a medium bowl and sprinkle with salt. Let stand 30 minutes. Rinse with cold water, drain thoroughly, and set aside. Combine vinegar, sugar, and pickling spice in a medium saucepan. Bring to a boil. Add drained zucchini and onion, and return to a boil. Remove from heat, and cool to room temperature. Spoon into sterilized jars. Cover and refrigerate.

Corn and Pepper Relish

YIELDS 2 PINTS

2 cups apple cider vinegar
1⅓ cups sugar
1 tablespoon chopped fresh basil
¼ teaspoon freshly ground pepper

1 cup diced green bell pepper
1 cup diced red bell pepper
kernels of 4 ears cooked corn (2 cups)

Combine vinegar, sugar, basil, and pepper in a medium saucepan. Bring to a boil. Reduce heat and simmer 10 minutes. Add bell peppers and simmer 3 minutes. Stir in corn. Cool to room temperature. Spoon into sterilized jars. Cover and refrigerate.

Grandma's Cranberry Relish

YIELDS 2½ QUARTS

1 pound fresh cranberries, rinsed
3 medium Winesap apples, peeled, cored, and sliced
3 medium oranges, peeled, seeded, and sliced
1 can (40 ounces) crushed pineapple, drained
2 cups sugar
1 cup chopped pecans

Chop cranberries, apples, and oranges in a food processor, preserving the texture. Stir in pineapple, sugar, and pecans. Cover and chill overnight.

Citrus Cranberry Relish

YIELDS 1 QUART

1½ cups sugar
¾ cup water
1 bag (12 ounces) fresh cranberries
½ cup orange marmalade
juice of 1 large lemon
½ cup chopped walnuts

Combine sugar and water in a medium saucepan. Make a simple syrup by bringing to a boil, then simmering 5 minutes. Add cranberries. Stir over medium heat about 20 minutes, or until all berries burst. Remove from heat. Add marmalade, lemon juice, and walnuts. Stir to combine. Cool. Transfer to a serving bowl. Cover and chill thoroughly. Serve chilled.

Spiced Pineapple and Apricots

YIELDS 2 PINTS

1 cup apricot nectar or pineapple juice
⅔ cup distilled white vinegar
1¼ cups sugar
2 teaspoons ground ginger
2 teaspoons ground cinnamon
2 teaspoons ground cloves
2 cups cubed fresh pineapple
2 cups pitted and halved fresh apricots

Heat nectar, vinegar, sugar, ginger, cinnamon, and cloves in a medium saucepan. Bring to a boil, reduce heat, and simmer uncovered 5 minutes. Stir in pineapple and apricots, bring to a boil, reduce heat, and simmer uncovered until fruit is just tender, 8 to 10 minutes more. Remove from heat and cool to room temperature. Spoon into sterilized jars. Cover and refrigerate.

CRANBERRIES

Cranberries are one of only three major fruits native to North America. (The other two are blueberries and Concord grapes.) The Pilgrims called them crane berries, possibly because of the crane's affection for the red berries. Some people call them bounce berries because when ripe, they bounce. The peak season for cranberries is from October through December. Look for bright red berries that are firm and glossy. A time-tested rule when cooking is that they are done when they pop open.

Three-Pepper Chutney

YIELDS 1 QUART

CHUTNEY

Chutney, from the East Indian word chatni, means spicy condiment containing fruit, vinegar, sugar, and spices. Chutney can range in texture from chunky to smooth and can be very spicy or mild. It can be eaten hot or cold and is delicious with roasted meat or poultry. Use it as a spread for sandwiches or as a sauce for omelets, or spread it over cream cheese and serve with crackers.

3 red bell peppers, seeded and chopped
3 green bell peppers, seeded and chopped
3 fresh jalapeños, seeded and minced
1 onion, chopped
1 ½ cups brown sugar, firmly packed
1 ½ cups apple cider vinegar
1 teaspoon salt

Combine bell peppers, jalapeños, onion, brown sugar, vinegar, and salt in a medium saucepan. Bring to a boil. Reduce heat. Simmer uncovered 1 to 2 hours, or until syrupy. Transfer chutney to a serving bowl. Cover and chill thoroughly.

Serve with grilled seafood, chicken, beef, and pork, or as a relish for hamburgers and hot dogs.

Mango Chutney

YIELDS 5 PINTS

6 cups brown sugar, firmly packed
2½ cups distilled white vinegar
salt
8 cups diced mangoes*
1 cup raisins
1 large piece fresh ginger, chopped
3 cloves garlic, minced
3 fresh red chile peppers

Combine sugar, vinegar, and salt in a saucepan. Bring to a boil and boil 20 minutes. Add mangoes, raisins, ginger, garlic, and chiles. Boil until thick, about 50 minutes. Spoon into sterilized jars. Cover and refrigerate.

Peaches may be substituted for all or some of the mangoes.

Dried Fruit Chutney

YIELDS 1 PINT

2 cups dried cherries, blueberries, or cranberries
1¼ cups sugar
¾ cup distilled white vinegar
¼ cup chopped celery
¼ cup minced fresh ginger
6 tablespoons fresh apple juice
3 tablespoons fresh lemon juice
½ teaspoon crushed red pepper flakes

Combine berries, sugar, vinegar, celery, ginger, juices, and red pepper flakes in a large saucepan over medium heat, stirring until sugar dissolves. Continue to cook 8 to 10 minutes, stirring frequently. Allow to cool to room temperature. Cover and refrigerate.

Serve with meat or game.

Tomato Chutney

YIELDS 1½ PINTS

1-inch piece fresh ginger
8 to 10 cloves garlic
1 teaspoon cumin seeds
1¾ cups apple cider vinegar
3 cans (14 ounces each) whole
 tomatoes, drained and cut
 into chunks
6 fresh jalapeños, seeded and
 slivered

1½ cups sugar
2 tablespoons raisins
1 tablespoon slivered almonds
10 peppercorns
2 cinnamon sticks, 3 to 4 inches
 long, cut into smaller sections
½ teaspoon hot Hungarian paprika
8 whole cloves
¼ teaspoon salt

Process ginger, garlic, and cumin seeds in a food processor. Process until blended, adding a little vinegar if necessary. Set aside. Combine vinegar, tomatoes, and jalapeños in a large saucepan. Stir until blended. Add sugar, raisins, almonds, peppercorns, cinnamon sticks, paprika, cloves, salt, and garlic mixture. Stir until completely blended. Cook on low heat, stirring frequently, until mixture thickens, approximately 2 to 2½ hours. Cool.

Sun-Dried Tomato Pesto

YIELDS 3 CUPS

½ cup sun-dried tomatoes packed
 in oil, drained
¾ cup toasted walnuts
1 cup fresh basil, loosely packed
6 ounces Parmesan cheese, freshly
 grated (¾ cup)

¾ cup olive oil
6 cloves garlic
1 teaspoon freshly ground pepper
salt

Combine sun-dried tomatoes, walnuts, basil, Parmesan, olive oil, garlic, and pepper in a food processor. Process until ingredients are thoroughly chopped, but not puréed. Add salt to taste. Cover and refrigerate or freeze.

PESTO

Pesto originated in Genoa, Italy, and is an uncooked sauce made with fresh ingredients such as basil, garlic, mint, cilantro, and olive oil. Be creative when using pesto. It can be used as a topping over cream cheese or a sandwich spread, whisked into eggs as they are scrambled, tossed over potatoes, served over pasta, or brushed over broiled chicken or fish.

Fresh Cilantro Mint Pesto

YIELDS 1 CUP

4 large bunches fresh cilantro,
 stems discarded
½ cup fresh mint or ¼ cup
 bottled mint sauce
1-inch piece fresh ginger, diced
6 cloves garlic

1 teaspoon ground cumin
½ teaspoon salt
juice of 1 large lemon or lime
1 to 4 serrano chile peppers, seeded
 and chopped
3 tablespoons canola oil

Blend cilantro, mint, ginger, garlic, cumin, salt, lemon or lime juice, and serranos in a food processor until smooth. Slowly add the oil in a fine stream until well blended. Cover and refrigerate.

AL DENTE

Light Pasta with Tomato Basil Sauce

To the Italians it was pomodoro or golden apple. To the French and to the British, it was a love apple. By any name, a tomato plucked from the vine and eaten on the spot, still tasting of the warmth of the midday sun, is a vivid childhood memory. Even today in supermarket produce sections with more and more varieties coming in from afar, we can find excellent fresh tomatoes year round. Beefsteak tomatoes are best used sliced or chopped for salads. Bite-size cherry tomatoes offer consistently good quality and a nice alternative in winter when beefsteak tomatoes are tasteless. The bright red Roma tomatoes are usually flavorful, and green tomatoes are excellent when fried or cooked into relishes. For Mexican and Southwestern cooking, the yellow or green tomatillo tomatoes in papery husks are the highlight of many recipes.

Light Pasta with Tomato Basil Sauce

SERVES 2 TO 4

2 teaspoons olive oil
½ cup minced onion
1 large clove garlic, minced
2 small zucchini, thinly sliced
   into ½-inch rounds
½ cup chicken broth
10 Roma tomatoes, peeled, seeded,
   and chopped, or 1 can (14½
   ounces) whole tomatoes, drained,
   seeded, and chopped

¼ cup coarsely chopped fresh basil
½ teaspoon salt
½ teaspoon freshly ground pepper
8 ounces penne pasta, cooked al dente

——

freshly grated Parmesan cheese

Heat olive oil in a large skillet over medium-high heat. Add onion and garlic. Sauté until onion is translucent, about 2 minutes. Stir in zucchini, chicken broth, and tomatoes. Bring to a boil, reduce heat, and simmer 5 minutes. Stir in basil, salt, and pepper. Serve over pasta and sprinkle with Parmesan.

Angel Hair Pasta with Herbed Marinara

SERVES 2 TO 4

10 cloves garlic, crushed
3 tablespoons olive oil
1 onion, minced
½ cup white wine
½ cup chicken stock
1 can (14½ ounces) whole
   tomatoes, seeded and chopped,
   plus liquid
2 tablespoons goat cheese

2 tablespoons chopped fresh basil
1 tablespoon chopped fresh thyme
9 ounces angel hair pasta, cooked
   al dente

——

chopped fresh basil
sliced black olives
freshly grated Parmesan cheese

Stir garlic into olive oil in a medium saucepan. Let marinate 30 minutes. Sauté garlic in oil over low heat until soft. Add onion and sauté until translucent. Add wine and chicken stock. Simmer over low heat about 10 minutes. Stir in tomatoes plus liquid. Simmer 10 minutes, or until liquid is slightly reduced. Remove from heat. Add goat cheese, basil, and thyme. Stir until goat cheese is melted. Toss with hot pasta. Garnish with basil, olives, and Parmesan.

Boiled shrimp may be added for a heartier dish. The sauce may also be used over baked chicken breasts.

Rigatoni with Olives, Arugula, and Herbs

SERVES 2

3 tablespoons extra virgin olive oil

1½ teaspoons minced garlic

⅛ teaspoon crushed red pepper flakes

¼ cup minced pitted green olives

1 tablespoon capers, rinsed, drained, and minced

¼ cup minced fresh parsley

¼ cup minced fresh basil

¼ teaspoon freshly ground pepper

6 ounces rigatoni or other tubular pasta, cooked al dente

1 cup chopped fresh arugula

freshly grated Parmesan cheese

Heat olive oil in a large skillet over medium-low heat. Add garlic and red pepper flakes. Sauté until garlic is soft, but not browned, 1 to 2 minutes. Add olives and capers. Sauté 1 minute, stirring constantly. Stir in parsley and basil. Season with pepper. Toss pasta, sauce, arugula, and Parmesan until combined. Serve immediately.

COOKING PASTA AL DENTE

The best method for cooking pasta is to bring at least 1 gallon of water per pound of pasta to boil. Add the pasta all at once and stir frequently while boiling. The key is not to overcook the pasta. Do not rely on the time given in the directions. Always taste the pasta to determine doneness. The pasta should be tender, but firm.

Penne à la Vodka

SERVES 4 TO 6

7 tablespoons unsalted butter

¾ teaspoon crushed red pepper flakes

¾ cup vodka (Russian or Polish)

2 cups canned puréed or crushed Italian tomatoes

¾ cup heavy whipping cream

1 teaspoon seasoned salt

1 pound penne pasta, cooked al dente

4 ounces Parmesan cheese, freshly grated (1 cup)

8 fresh basil leaves, chopped

Warm a serving bowl for the pasta. Melt butter in a large skillet. Stir in pepper flakes and vodka. Simmer 2 minutes. Stir in tomatoes and cream. Simmer 5 minutes. Add seasoned salt and stir well. Lower heat and gently stir in pasta. Add Parmesan. Pour into prepared serving bowl, toss with basil, and serve immediately.

Creamy Artichoke and Mushroom Penne

SERVES 6 TO 8

ARTICHOKES

Artichokes should be cut and cooked with stainless steel utensils. If artichokes were left on the stem, they would blossom into gorgeous flowers.

3 tablespoons unsalted butter
¼ cup minced onion
1 clove garlic, crushed
8 ounces fresh mushrooms, sliced
1 cup artichoke hearts, chopped
1 cup heavy whipping cream
2 tablespoons capers, rinsed and drained

salt
freshly ground pepper
12 ounces penne pasta, cooked al dente
1 ounce Parmesan cheese, freshly grated (¼ cup)
2 tablespoons chopped fresh parsley

Melt butter in a large skillet over medium-high heat. Add onion and garlic. Sauté until tender, but not brown. Add mushrooms. Sauté 5 minutes. Stir in artichokes, heating thoroughly, about 2 to 3 minutes. Place artichoke mixture in a bowl and set aside. Return skillet to heat and add cream. Boil until cream is reduced to one half. Add artichoke mixture and capers to cream. Stir until combined. Season with salt and pepper. Toss warm sauce with pasta. Gently stir in Parmesan and parsley. Serve immediately.

Pasta Capri

SERVES 4

PEELING TOMATOES

To peel and seed tomatoes, cut a shallow X through the skin at the bottom of each tomato. Drop the tomatoes into boiling water for 10 to 20 seconds. Remove with a slotted spoon and put in a bowl of ice water until cool. Peel off the skin, cut in half, and gently squeeze out the seeds.

14 ounces linguini pasta, cooked al dente
1 tablespoon plus 2 tablespoons extra virgin olive oil
½ cup (1 stick) unsalted butter
12 ounces fresh large shrimp, boiled (page 48), peeled, and deveined
6 Roma tomatoes, peeled, seeded, and diced (2 cups)

¾ cup thinly sliced green onions
1 can (4 ounces) sliced black olives
4 teaspoons minced shallots
¾ cup white wine
½ teaspoon salt
½ teaspoon freshly ground pepper
—————
1 lemon, thinly sliced

Toss pasta lightly with 1 tablespoon olive oil. Set aside. Heat remaining 2 tablespoons olive oil in a large skillet over high heat. Add butter, shrimp, tomatoes, onions, olives, and shallots. Sauté 1 minute. Stir in wine, lower heat, and simmer until creamy and slightly thickened. Add more wine if sauce becomes too dry. Season with salt and pepper. Place pasta in a serving bowl, add sauce, and toss. Garnish with lemon slices.

Chicken Pasta with Sun-Dried Tomatoes

SERVES 2

1 teaspoon extra virgin olive oil
3 shallots, minced
1 (8 ounce) boneless, skinless
chicken breast, cooked and
julienned
4 ounces sun-dried tomatoes
packed in oil, drained

½ cup heavy whipping cream
8 ounces penne pasta, cooked al dente
½ tablespoon unsalted butter, melted
2 tablespoons freshly grated
Parmesan cheese
3 tablespoons chopped fresh basil
½ teaspoon salt

Heat olive oil in a large skillet over medium heat. Add shallots and sauté
2 minutes, or until soft. Add chicken and tomatoes and cook 2 minutes.
Stir in cream. Cook an additional 2 minutes, stirring occasionally. Toss
sauce, pasta, butter, Parmesan, basil, and salt in a large serving bowl.
Serve immediately.

Spicy Chicken and Black Bean Fettucine

SERVES 4

¼ cup extra virgin olive oil
4 boneless, skinless chicken breast
halves, cut into bite-size pieces
1 tablespoon chili powder
2 teaspoons ground cumin
1 tablespoon minced garlic
2 to 3 fresh jalapeños, seeded
and sliced
1 bunch green onions, chopped

1 can (15 ounces) black beans,
drained and rinsed
8 to 10 ounces feta cheese,
crumbled (2 to 2½ cups)
2 small Roma tomatoes, chopped
1 pound black pepper fettucine pasta,
cooked al dente
——
½ cup chopped fresh cilantro

Heat olive oil in a medium skillet over medium heat. Add chicken,
chili powder, cumin, and garlic. Sauté until cooked through, but not
browned. Remove chicken and set aside. Return skillet to heat. Add
jalapeños and green onions. Sauté 3 to 4 minutes. (It is best if jalapeños
are still crunchy.) Stir in black beans. Heat about 3 minutes. Add feta
and chicken, and heat thoroughly. Remove from heat and stir in tomatoes. Toss pasta gently with sauce and sprinkle with cilantro.

Delicious served with a crusty bread and a salad.

PASTA

*Although it's claimed that
pasta originated in China,
you might have a hard
time convincing the Italians,
Japanese, Koreans,
Germans, and French,
each of whom insist their
countries invented the dish.
Not even the Italians know
how many shapes pasta
comes in. Many descriptions
of pasta mention size as
well as use. The following
illustrations show some of
the more popular, or interesting, pasta shapes.*

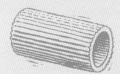

RIGATONI

FARFALLE

ELICHE

RAVIOLI

CAVATAPPI

Fettucine with Smoked Turkey in Black Peppercorn Sauce

SERVES 4 TO 6

2 tablespoons unsalted butter
2 tablespoons minced shallots
½ to 1 tablespoon black
 peppercorns, crushed
1 cup dry white wine
3 cups whipping cream
½ teaspoon ground nutmeg
salt

1 pound fettucine pasta, cooked
 al dente
1 pound smoked turkey breast,
 julienned
————
¼ cup chopped fresh chives
freshly grated Parmesan cheese

Melt butter in a large skillet over medium heat. Add shallots and peppercorns. Sauté 20 seconds. Add wine. Boil until almost no liquid remains, 6 or 7 minutes. Stir in cream and nutmeg. Boil until reduced to sauce consistency, about 5 minutes. Season with salt. Thoroughly toss sauce, pasta, and turkey. Sprinkle with chives. Serve, passing the Parmesan separately.

Fettucine and Salmon in Scotch Cream Sauce

SERVES 2 TO 4

1 cup heavy whipping cream
1 cup milk
6 tablespoons unsalted butter
2 tablespoons plus 1 tablespoon
 minced green onions
2 tablespoons Scotch whiskey
2 ½ tablespoons all-purpose flour

1 tablespoon minced
 fresh parsley
⅛ teaspoon white pepper
½ pound smoked salmon or lox,
 cut into ¼-inch pieces
8 ounces fettucine pasta, cooked
 al dente

Scald cream and milk in a medium saucepan. Set aside. Melt butter in a large skillet over medium heat. Add 2 tablespoons green onion and sauté 2 minutes. Remove pan from heat. Add Scotch and stir to blend. Return skillet to medium heat. Stir in flour and cook until golden brown, about 2 minutes. Gradually whisk in cream mixture. Cook until thickened, whisking constantly, about 5 minutes. Stir in 1 tablespoon green onion, parsley, and pepper. Fold in salmon. Toss pasta with sauce. Serve immediately.

PASTA

Fresh and dry pasta is available in a variety of shapes, categorized in the following list as ribbons, strands, tubes, and special shapes:

Ribbons - linguine, fettucine, tagliatelle, and lasagna. Linguine is the narrowest, and lasagna is the widest.

Strands - capelli, cappellini, vermicelli, and spaghetti. Capelli is the thinnest, and spaghetti is the thickest.

Tubes - cannelloni and manicotti are used for filling, ziti are straight-cut narrow tubes, and penne are diagonally cut with smooth or ridged sides.

Special shapes - farfelle are bowtie shaped, fiochetti are bow shaped, ravioli are stuffed squares, rotini are little corkscrews, and tortellini are small, stuffed twists.

*Fettucine and Salmon in
Scotch Cream Sauce*

Crabmeat Saffron Fettucine

SERVES 6 TO 8

⅛ teaspoon saffron
1 tablespoon dry sherry
½ cup (1 stick) unsalted butter
2 tablespoons chopped shallots
3 cups whipping cream
¼ teaspoon salt

⅛ teaspoon white pepper
1 pound fresh lump crabmeat,
   shells removed
10 ounces fettucine pasta, cooked
   al dente
¼ cup chopped fresh parsley

Mix saffron and sherry. Set aside. Melt butter in a large saucepan over moderate heat. Add shallots and sauté until soft. Stir in cream. Turn heat to low. Simmer until reduced, about 30 minutes. Stir in sherry mixture and simmer 5 minutes. Season with salt and pepper. Gently toss in crabmeat and warm only (do not cook). Add pasta and toss over low heat. Place in serving bowls and sprinkle with parsley.

Creamy Crawfish Tortellini

SERVES 6

½ cup (1 stick) unsalted butter
1 medium onion, minced
2 cloves garlic, minced
1 pound fresh crawfish tails
4 ounces Parmesan cheese, freshly
   grated (¼ cup plus ¼ cup)
2 tablespoons chopped fresh parsley

2 cups whipping cream
¼ cup dry sherry
9 ounces tortellini pasta, cooked
   al dente
salt
cayenne pepper

Melt butter in a large skillet. Add onions and garlic. Sauté until translucent. Add crawfish and cook 5 minutes. Add ¼ cup Parmesan, parsley, whipping cream, and sherry. Simmer until thickened. Fold tortellini into crawfish mixture. Season with salt and cayenne pepper. Serve with remaining ¼ cup Parmesan.

Pasta with Basil and Pine Nuts

SERVES 6

1 tablespoon olive oil
3 tablespoons minced garlic
3 cups chopped tomatoes
¾ cup sun-dried tomatoes packed in
   oil, drained and thinly sliced
½ cup chopped fresh basil

½ cup chopped pine nuts
1 cup chicken stock
½ teaspoon salt
¼ teaspoon freshly ground pepper
1 pound fedelini or vermicelli pasta,
   cooked al dente

Heat oil in a large skillet. Add garlic and sauté until translucent. Add tomatoes, basil, and pine nuts. Cook 2 to 3 minutes. Add chicken stock, salt, and pepper. Heat thoroughly. Place pasta in a serving bowl, add sauce, and toss. Serve immediately.

Cannelloni with Besciamella Sauce

Italian Tomato Sauce:
¼ cup extra virgin olive oil
1 cup minced onion
4 cups canned chopped tomatoes
1 can (15 ounces) tomato sauce
2 tablespoons chopped fresh basil
1 teaspoon salt
freshly ground pepper

——

Filling:
2 tablespoons extra virgin olive oil
¼ cup minced onion
1 teaspoon minced garlic
1 box (10 ounces) frozen
    chopped spinach, thawed
    and squeezed dry
½ pound ground round beef
½ pound Italian sausage, casings
    removed, crumbled
1 ounce Parmesan cheese, freshly
    grated (¼ cup)

2 tablespoons whipping cream
2 large eggs, lightly beaten
2 teaspoons chopped fresh oregano
salt
freshly ground pepper

Besciamella Sauce:
4 tablespoons unsalted butter
¼ cup all-purpose flour
1 cup milk
1 cup whipping cream
1 teaspoon salt
1 teaspoon white pepper

——

1 pound lasagna noodles, cooked
    al dente
1 ounce Parmesan cheese, freshly
    grated (¼ cup)

Italian Tomato Sauce: Heat oil in a large saucepan. Add onion and sauté until translucent. Stir in tomatoes, tomato sauce, and basil. Season with salt and pepper. Reduce heat. Simmer 40 minutes, stirring occasionally. Purée tomato mixture in a blender. Adjust seasonings. (Tomato sauce may be made ahead and chilled.)

Filling: Heat olive oil in a large skillet over moderate heat. Add onion and garlic. Sauté until soft, about 8 minutes. Add spinach and cook 4 minutes, stirring constantly. When all liquid has cooked away, transfer to a large bowl. Set aside. Brown beef and sausage. Drain. Add meat to spinach mixture. Stir in cheese, cream, eggs, and oregano. Season with salt and pepper.

Besciamella Sauce: Melt butter in a large saucepan over moderate heat. Remove from heat and stir in flour. Add milk and cream, whisking constantly. Return to heat and continue stirring. When sauce boils and is smooth, reduce heat. Simmer, still stirring, until sauce is thick enough to coat spoon, about 3 minutes. Remove from heat. Season with salt and white pepper.

Preheat oven to 375 degrees.

Pour a light film of tomato sauce into a shallow 10 by 18-inch baking dish. Cut each lasagna noodle into 3 rectangular sections. Place 1 tablespoon meat filling on bottom one-third of each pasta rectangle and roll it up. Lay side by side, seam-side down, in one layer on tomato sauce. Top with Besciamella Sauce, then tomato sauce. Sprinkle with Parmesan. Bake uncovered 20 minutes, or until cheese is melted and sauce is bubbling.

Cannelloni may be frozen unbaked. If frozen, increase baking time to 40 minutes.

WHAT TYPE OF SAUCE TO USE WITH DIFFERENT PASTA:

Thin ribbons, like linguine - light vegetable or light cream sauce

Thick ribbons, like lasagna - meat, game, hearty vegetable, or heavy cream sauce

Thin strands, like capelli - light vegetable sauce (or in soups)

Thick strands, like spaghetti - seafood, hearty vegetable, or heavy cream sauce

Small tubes, like penne - creamy cheese sauce (or in soups or salads)

Large tubes, like cannelloni - hearty vegetable, chunky meat, or heavy cream sauce

Small shapes, like bowtie - light vegetable or light cream sauce or vinaigrette (or in soups or salads)

THE MAIN EVENT

Rack of Lamb with Port and Rosemary Sauce

MEAT

Basic Beef Tenderloin with
Cranberry Wine Sauce

Basic Beef Tenderloin

SERVES 10 TO 12

1 whole beef tenderloin
seasoned salt
freshly ground pepper

Salt and pepper tenderloin. Let rest 30 minutes at room temperature.
(Can cover and refrigerate.)

Preheat oven to 500 degrees. Bake 5 minutes, then reduce heat to
400 degrees. Bake an additional 40 to 45 minutes, or to desired
doneness. Tenderloin may also be grilled over medium heat, about
20 minutes. Try topping the tenderloin with one or a combination of
the following sauces:

Cranberry Wine Sauce:

3 cups fresh cranberries
1½ cups sugar
1¼ cups port

¼ cup cold water
4½ teaspoons cornstarch

Combine cranberries, sugar, and port in a large saucepan. Bring to a
boil. Cook 5 to 7 minutes, or until cranberry skins pop. Combine water
and cornstarch. Stir into cranberry mixture. Bring to a boil and cook
1 minute, stirring constantly. (This can be made ahead, refrigerated, and
reheated.) Yields 2 cups.

Orange Béarnaise Sauce:

¼ cup white wine vinegar
2 tablespoons minced shallot
½ teaspoon minced orange zest
3 tablespoons fresh orange juice
¼ teaspoon salt

¼ teaspoon white pepper
3 large egg yolks
1 cup (2 sticks) unsalted butter, melted
   and slightly cooled

Combine vinegar, shallot, orange zest, orange juice, salt, and pepper in a
small saucepan. Bring to a boil. Continue cooking over moderately high
heat until liquid reduces to 2 tablespoons. Transfer mixture to a blender,
add egg yolks, and pulse once. With the machine running, add butter in
a stream. Transfer sauce to a bowl and serve immediately. Also delicious
over vegetables. Yields 1 cup.

Roasted Shallot and Butter Sauce:

2 tablespoons unsalted butter
12 small shallots, peeled and halved
   through root end
½ cup dry white wine

6 tablespoons unsalted butter, chilled
   and cut into tablespoon-size pieces
salt
freshly ground pepper

Melt 2 tablespoons butter in large skillet. Add shallots and cook about
10 minutes, stirring occasionally. Remove shallots and set aside. Add wine
to skillet and bring to a boil, scraping up any browned bits. Pour into
small saucepan. Cook over high heat until liquid is reduced to 2 tablespoons. Remove from heat and whisk in 2 tablespoons butter. Return pan
to low heat and whisk in remaining butter, 1 tablespoon at a time. If sauce
breaks down at any point, remove from heat and whisk in 2 tablespoons
cold butter. Season with salt and pepper. Stir in shallots and any juices
that may have accumulated. Serve immediately. Yields ½ cup.

**BEEF ROASTING
GUIDE**

Thermometer reading of the meat's
internal temperature:
Rare - 135 to 140 degrees
Medium - 155 to 160 degrees
Well done - 165 to 170 degrees

Peppercorn-Crusted Beef Tenderloin
in Blackjack Bourbon Sauce

SERVES 4 TO 6

FOUR-PEPPERCORN MIX

Four-peppercorn mix is a combination of green, black, white, and pink peppercorns. The pepper plant is native to the equatorial forests of India and will bear for up to 20 years. Green peppercorns are harvested while still unripe. Sun-dried green peppercorns are commonly known as black peppercorns. Berries left on the plant until fully ripe, then soaked, peeled, and dried are white peppercorns. Pink peppercorns are not a true peppercorn but are the dried, pungent berry from a South American tropical rose. The culinary value of pink peppercorns is primarily visual.

Blackjack Bourbon Sauce:
1½ pounds beef neck bones
4 large shallots, coarsely chopped
6 cloves garlic, coarsely chopped
2 large carrots, coarsely chopped
1 cup bourbon
1 tablespoon tomato paste
4 sprigs fresh thyme
2 teaspoons four-peppercorn mix
2 cups chicken stock
2 cups beef stock
salt

Beef:
¼ cup four-peppercorn mix, lightly crushed
1 tablespoon cornstarch
2 teaspoons chopped fresh thyme
1 teaspoon chopped fresh oregano
1 tablespoon plus 1 tablespoon vegetable oil
1 beef tenderloin (about 2 pounds)
coarse salt

Blackjack Bourbon Sauce: Brown beef bones, shallots, garlic, and carrots in a heavy saucepan over medium heat, stirring occasionally, about 20 minutes. Add bourbon. Increase heat and boil until liquid is reduced to one-half, about 5 minutes. Mix in tomato paste, thyme, and peppercorns. Add chicken stock and beef stock. Boil until liquid is reduced to 1 cup, about 20 minutes. Strain through a fine sieve into a small saucepan. Season with salt.

Preheat oven to 350 degrees. Mix peppercorns, cornstarch, thyme, and oregano on a large plate. Brush 1 tablespoon oil over beef. Roll beef in peppercorn mixture, coating completely. Season with salt.

Heat remaining 1 tablespoon oil in a heavy, large ovenproof skillet over medium-high heat. Add beef and brown on all sides, about 5 minutes. Transfer skillet to oven and roast until meat thermometer inserted into center of beef registers 135 degrees for rare, about 30 minutes, or to desired doneness.

Slice beef and arrange on plates. Bring sauce to simmer. Spoon over beef.

Blackjack Bourbon Sauce can be prepared 1 day in advance. Cover and refrigerate until ready to use.

Grilled Filet Mignon with Roasted Tomato and Oregano Sauce

SERVES 6

Roasted Tomato and Oregano Sauce:
5 Roma tomatoes (about 1 pound)
1 pasilla chile pepper
2 tablespoons plus 2 tablespoons
  unsalted butter
½ onion, minced
1 large clove garlic, minced
½ yellow bell pepper, chopped
¼ cup red wine vinegar

¼ cup dry white wine
1 cup chicken stock
2 tablespoons chopped fresh oregano
1 tablespoon chopped fresh thyme
——
6 filet mignon steaks (7 ounces each),
  1 inch thick
salt
freshly ground pepper

Roasted Tomato and Oregano Sauce: Roast tomatoes until skins begin to blacken. Transfer to a bowl and cool. Do not peel. Coarsely chop. Heat a small skillet over medium-high heat. Add pasilla and cook until skin darkens, about 1 minute per side. Transfer to plate and cool. Seed, stem, and cut pasilla into small pieces. Set aside.

Melt 2 tablespoons butter in large saucepan over medium-high heat. Add onion and sauté until brown. Add garlic and bell pepper. Sauté until soft, about 4 minutes. Stir in vinegar and wine and bring to boil, scraping up any browned bits. Boil until liquid is reduced to one-half, about 5 minutes. Add roasted tomatoes, pasilla, and stock. Simmer until sauce thickens and is reduced to ⅔ cup, about 15 minutes. Purée sauce in blender until almost smooth. Stir in oregano and thyme.

Prepare grill to medium-high heat or preheat broiler. Season steaks with salt and pepper. Grill to desired doneness. Transfer to serving plate and keep warm.

Bring sauce to simmer. Remove from heat. Whisk in remaining 2 tablespoons butter. Season with salt and pepper. Spoon sauce next to steaks and serve immediately.

Roasted Tomato and Oregano Sauce can be made 1 day in advance. Cover and chill until ready to use, adding butter at the last minute.

Grilled Marinated Venison Tenderloin

SERVES 10 TO 12

1½ cups vegetable oil
¾ cup soy sauce
¼ cup Worcestershire sauce
2 tablespoons dry mustard
2 teaspoons salt
1 tablespoon freshly ground pepper

½ cup red wine vinegar
2 tablespoons chopped fresh parsley
2 cloves garlic, crushed
⅓ cup fresh lemon juice
——
3 venison tenderloins

Whisk oil, soy sauce, Worcestershire, dry mustard, salt, pepper, vinegar, parsley, garlic, and lemon juice in a small bowl. Pour over tenderloins and marinate 4 to 5 hours, turning occasionally.

Prepare grill. Grill over medium-hot coals 14 to 15 minutes, turning once. Slice tenderloins and serve with Blueberry Barbecue Sauce (at right).

This marinade is good with pork and beef tenderloins, but grill 20 minutes, or to desired doneness.

PASILLA CHILE PEPPER

The pasilla chile pepper is a long, narrow, wrinkled chile. It gets its name from the Spanish word for "raisin." It is used extensively in moles and sauces because of its rich and piquant flavor. Fresh, it is the chilaca chile.

BLUEBERRY BARBECUE SAUCE

1 tablespoon olive oil
¼ cup minced onions
1 tablespoon chopped fresh jalapeño
1 pint fresh blueberries
3 tablespoons brown sugar, firmly
  packed
¼ cup rice vinegar
¼ cup ketchup
3 tablespoons Dijon mustard
1 teaspoon Tabasco Sauce
4 tablespoons unsalted butter
salt
freshly ground pepper

Heat oil in a large skillet. Add onions and jalapeño. Sauté until soft. Stir in blueberries, sugar, vinegar, ketchup, mustard, and Tabasco. Bring to a low boil and cook 15 minutes, stirring constantly. Transfer sauce to a blender and purée until smooth. Strain through a sieve into a small saucepan. Reheat. Add butter, stirring until melted. Season with salt and pepper. Serve immediately. Yields 1½ cups.

May be made in advance, but add the butter at the last minute. You may choose not to add the butter at all; it tastes great without it. Also good with beef and chicken.

Chicken-Fried Sirloin with Peppered Cream Gravy

SERVES 4

PERFECT GRAVY

To prevent lumps, whisk cream gravies vigorously as milk or other liquid is added.

4 boneless sirloin steaks
  (6 ounces each)
1½ cups buttermilk
1 teaspoon Tabasco Sauce
1 teaspoon plus 1 teaspoon salt
¼ teaspoon plus ¼ teaspoon
  freshly ground pepper
1 cup all-purpose flour
1 cup peanut oil

Peppered Cream Gravy:
2 tablespoons unsalted butter
2 tablespoons all-purpose flour
2 cups milk
2 tablespoons heavy whipping cream
1 teaspoon salt
¾ teaspoon freshly ground pepper

Lightly pound steaks with a meat mallet until they are about ¼ inch thick. Mix buttermilk, Tabasco, 1 teaspoon salt, and ¼ teaspoon pepper in a shallow dish.

Combine flour with remaining 1 teaspoon salt and ¼ teaspoon pepper in another shallow bowl. Mix well. Dredge flattened sirloin in flour to coat evenly. Submerge steaks, one at a time, in buttermilk mixture. Return steaks to flour and dredge again. Press flour firmly into surfaces of steaks so it will adhere.

Pour peanut oil into a deep, broad skillet to a depth of ½ inch. Carefully place one coated steak into hot oil. Fry about 3 minutes, turn carefully, and fry other side 3 minutes, or until crust is golden brown and steak is to desired doneness. Transfer steak to a plate lined with paper towels. Keep warm. Repeat procedure for other steaks.

Peppered Cream Gravy: Melt butter in a saucepan over medium-high heat. Whisk in flour and sauté until lightly browned. Remove pan from heat. Pour in milk in a steady stream, whisking vigorously. Return pan to heat and whisk until sauce thickens. Whisk in cream, salt, and pepper. Place steak on plates and top with gravy.

Teriyaki Sirloin Kabobs

SERVES 6

⅓ cup soy sauce
⅓ cup red wine vinegar
¼ cup vegetable oil
3 tablespoons honey
1 tablespoon minced crystallized
  ginger
1 large clove garlic, minced

2½ pounds sirloin beef, cubed
1 fresh pineapple, peeled and cubed
2 Gala or Golden Delicious
  apples, cubed

3 cups steamed rice

Combine soy sauce, vinegar, oil, honey, ginger, and garlic in a blender. Pour into a sealable plastic bag. Add beef and marinate at room temperature 30 minutes or in refrigerator overnight.

Drain beef, reserving marinade. Skewer beef alternately with pineapple and apple cubes. Brush kabobs with marinade and grill 15 to 20 minutes, depending on desired doneness. Baste often with marinade. Serve with steamed rice.

Kentucky Bourbon Roast

1 eye of round roast (2½ pounds),
  scored on both sides
garlic salt
freshly ground pepper
½ cup (1 stick) unsalted butter,
  melted

¼ cup Worcestershire sauce
¼ cup A-1 Steak Sauce
¾ cup bourbon
juice of ½ lemon

Place meat in Dutch oven. Sprinkle garlic salt over roast until meat is white. Add pepper until meat is black. Pour butter over roast. Combine Worcestershire and A-1 in a separate bowl. Pour over roast. Pour bourbon over roast and then lemon juice. Boil over high heat until alcohol is burned off, about 2 minutes. Remove from heat and marinate in the refrigerator about 4 hours, basting occasionally.

Bring roast to room temperature and prepare grill. Grill, basting with marinade, over medium-hot coals 20 to 30 minutes for rare, or to desired doneness.

If you prefer to roast in the oven, preheat to 550 degrees. Reduce to 350 degrees and roast 18 to 20 minutes per pound (approximately 50 minutes). Baste occasionally with marinade.

TO SCORE MEAT

To score means to make shallow cuts in the surface of meats. Scoring assists flavor absorption, tenderizes less tender cuts of meat, and allows excess fat to drain during cooking. For variety, tuck slices of garlic into shallow cuts.

Ginger Marinated Skirt Steak

6 cloves garlic, coarsely chopped
3 ounces fresh ginger, coarsely
  chopped (⅔ cup)
2 to 4 tablespoons dark soy sauce
¼ cup dry sherry
¼ cup rice vinegar

¼ cup olive oil
2 tablespoons sesame oil
———
6 skirt steaks (8 ounces each)

Combine garlic, ginger, soy sauce, sherry, vinegar, and oils in large non-metallic bowl. Add steaks and turn to coat. Cover and marinate 1 hour at room temperature, or as long as 8 hours in refrigerator. Return steaks to room temperature before cooking.

Prepare grill. Scrape garlic and ginger from steaks. Pat dry with paper towels. Grill steaks about 4 inches from heat, turning once, about 3 minutes on each side for rare or 4 minutes per side for medium-rare. Transfer from grill to carving board. Let rest loosely covered 10 minutes before carving. Cut on the diagonal into thin slices. Delicious with Salsa Tropical (see accompanying recipe).

Also a delicious marinade for chicken.

SALSA TROPICAL

1 mango, pitted, peeled, and diced
1 avocado, pitted, peeled,
  and diced
1 small red onion, diced
½ cup chopped fresh cilantro
1 fresh jalapeño, seeded
  and minced
2 to 3 tablespoons fresh lime juice
1½ teaspoons minced fresh oregano

Combine mango, avocado, onion, cilantro, and jalapeño in a small bowl. Stir in lime juice and oregano. Serve immediately. Yields 3 cups.

Oriental Flank Steak

MARINADES

Marinades are often used in preparing foods to be grilled. They tenderize, moisten, and add flavor to meats and vegetables. Marinades are usually a combination of an acid, such as vinegar, lemon juice, wine, or yogurt, an oil, such as olive oil, and a flavoring, such as molasses, spices, or mustard. The food should be covered in the marinade in a nonmetallic container and refrigerated until ready to grill. The length of time required for marinating depends on the type of food. Tougher meats should be marinated overnight, while fish should only marinate a short period of time. If you want to use the marinade for basting, set some aside before adding the meat. Otherwise, the marinade should always be discarded.

½ cup soy sauce
2½ tablespoons brown sugar,
 firmly packed
2 tablespoons fresh lemon juice
1 teaspoon ground ginger

½ teaspoon garlic salt
——
2 pounds flank steak, trimmed of fat
 and scored on both sides

Combine soy sauce, brown sugar, lemon juice, ginger, and garlic salt in a shallow dish. Place steak in dish, cover, and marinate 6 to 8 hours in the refrigerator. Bring to room temperature before cooking.

Prepare broiler. Broil 3 to 4 inches from heat about 5 minutes per side. Slice on the diagonal and serve.

May also be grilled.

Cowboy Steak with Corn Sauce

SERVES 4

SOUTHWEST SEASONINGS

*2 tablespoons chili powder
2 tablespoons paprika
1 tablespoon ground coriander
1 tablespoon garlic powder
1 tablespoon salt
2 teaspoons ground cumin
1 teaspoon cayenne pepper
1 teaspoon crushed red pepper
1 teaspoon freshly ground pepper
1 teaspoon dried oregano*

Combine all ingredients and store in an airtight container.

1 flank steak (about 2 pounds)
¼ cup extra virgin olive oil
1 tablespoon Southwest Seasonings
 (see accompanying recipe)
¼ cup chopped fresh cilantro

Corn Sauce:
kernels of 2 ears fresh corn (1 cup)
½ teaspoon salt
freshly ground pepper
¼ cup chopped onion

¼ cup chopped green onions
1 tablespoon minced garlic
2 cups beef stock
2 Roma tomatoes, peeled, seeded,
 and chopped
2 tablespoons chopped fresh cilantro
——
12 corn tortillas
1 tablespoon unsalted butter, melted

Rub meat with oil and sprinkle with seasoning. Place cilantro around steak and marinate 30 minutes.

Corn Sauce: Heat a medium skillet over high heat. Add corn, salt, and pepper. Blacken corn slightly, about 2 minutes, shaking skillet constantly (the corn will pop a bit). Add onions, green onions, and garlic. Cook 1 minute. Stir in stock, tomatoes, and cilantro. Bring to a boil. Reduce heat and simmer 15 minutes. Keep sauce warm or prepare up to 1 hour ahead and reheat.

Place steak on a rack in a roasting pan. Broil about 7 inches from heat 5 to 7 minutes. Turn and broil 5 minutes more. Move oven rack closer to heat (about 5 inches from source) and broil another 5 minutes. Remove steak from the oven and slice thinly across the grain.

Ten minutes before the steak is ready, heat a heavy skillet over medium heat. Soften each tortilla in skillet, about 1 minute. Just before serving, brush each tortilla with melted butter. Reheat in hot skillet about 15 seconds.

To serve, spoon corn sauce on 4 dinner plates. Top with tortillas and steak slices.

Smokey Barbecued Brisket

1 brisket (8 to 10 pounds), trimmed
green mesquite chips

Basting Sauce:
½ cup water
½ cup vegetable oil
½ cup garlic vinegar
½ cup sugar
¼ cup unsalted butter
¼ cup fresh lemon juice

1 small onion, sliced
1 tablespoon salt
1 tablespoon freshly ground pepper
1 tablespoon Worcestershire sauce

Oven Cooking Sauce:
1 cup Red Hot Barbecue Sauce or
   bottled barbecue sauce
2 cups red wine
2 tablespoons sugar

Combine water, oil, vinegar, sugar, butter, lemon juice, onion, salt, pepper, and Worcestershire in a small saucepan. Cook until onion is soft and fragrant.

Prepare barbecue pit or smoker by adding green mesquite chips to the hot coals. Place brisket in the pit or smoker. Baste meat on all sides with basting sauce. Let smoke 4 hours, turning and basting every hour with sauce. Do not try to brown or tenderize in pit, but give brisket plenty of smoke. Remove brisket from pit and place in large roasting pan that has a fairly tight lid. Preheat oven to 250 degrees.

Combine barbecue sauce, wine, and sugar. Pour sauce over meat. Cover and cook 4 hours, or until fork tender. Remove meat from pan and skim excess grease from gravy. Slice and serve.

Plan ahead on this great dish. It takes 8 hours from start to finish, but it is well worth the effort!

Red Hot Barbecue Sauce:
½ cup sugar
½ cup light brown sugar,
   firmly packed
1 cup beef stock
4 cups water
¾ cup prepared mustard

½ cup distilled white vinegar
⅔ cup Worcestershire sauce
2 cans (6 ounces each) tomato paste
2 to 5 teaspoons chili powder
2 fresh jalapeños, seeded and sliced

Combine sugars, stock, water, mustard, vinegar, Worcestershire, tomato paste, 2 teaspoons chili powder, and jalapeños in a large saucepan. Stir to combine. Adjust seasonings, adding more chili powder if desired. Simmer 2 hours, stirring frequently, until sauce reaches desired consistency.

BARBECUE

Any time of the year is a good time for succulent grilled meat dripping with goodness and brimming with the flavor that only outdoor grilling over fragrant wood gives. All it requires is a long, lazy afternoon (the best barbecue is never rushed) and a gathering of good friends to make a memorable feast. Although the word "barbecue" may come from the French barbe à queue, "from whiskers to tail," meaning the whole animal has been cooked, barbecue is strongly associated with America - especially South Carolina, Alabama, Kansas, and, of course, Texas. True Texas barbecue, which can be brisket, ribs, sausage, chicken, wild game, ham, or seafood, is cooked slowly - some cooks say 12 to 14 hours - at low temperatures over green oak or mesquite embers, and basted now and then with a mixture of oil, vinegar or lemon juice, and seasonings no self-respecting chef would ever divulge. One thing you won't find on Texas barbecue is the spicy sweet bottled "barbecue sauce." Ready-made sauce gives the chef one less thing to brag about, which, after all, is half the fun.

Lone Star Brisket in Chili Sauce and Beer

1 brisket (5 to 7 pounds), trimmed
2½ teaspoons seasoned salt
¼ teaspoon freshly ground pepper
2 cloves garlic, minced
2 onions, sliced and separated
  into rings

2 ribs celery, chopped
1 bottle (12 ounces) chili sauce
¼ cup water
12 ounces beer, at room temperature

Preheat oven to 300 degrees. Sprinkle brisket with seasoned salt, pepper, and garlic. Place brisket in roasting pan, fat side up. Add onions and celery in a single layer over top of brisket, covering brisket completely. Pour chili sauce over brisket. Pour ¼ cup water into chili sauce bottle, shake, and pour over meat. Roast uncovered 1½ hours, basting every 30 minutes. Pour beer over meat. Cover tightly with foil and roast an additional 3 to 4 hours, depending on size of brisket. Remove brisket from gravy and place on a carving board. Refrigerate gravy or chill quickly by placing in freezer. When cooled, slice meat without disturbing the shape of the brisket. Slide the brisket back into pan. When gravy is cold, skim fat and pour gravy over brisket. Put back into the oven to reheat. Serve immediately. This freezes well, already sliced.

Rancho Ramillete Flautas

SERVES 8 TO 10

1 brisket (5 to 7 pounds), trimmed
1 medium onion
1 head garlic
2 teaspoons salt

——

20 flour tortillas
2 tablespoons vegetable oil,
  or more as needed

——

1 to 2 cups fresh Mexican cream
1 head green leaf lettuce, shredded
2 tomatoes, chopped
1 bunch radishes, minced
8 ounces Panela or Monterey Jack
  cheese, shredded (2 cups)

——

Mexican Green Hot Sauce
Ramillete Red Picante Sauce

⅔ cup sour cream
¼ cup whipping cream

Combine sour cream and whipping
cream. Cover and refrigerate.

Trim all fat from brisket and cut into 3 by 3-inch pieces. Cover brisket with water in a large pot. Add whole onion, head of garlic, and salt. Bring to a boil. Cover and reduce heat. Simmer 4 to 6 hours, or until tender, adding more water as needed. Remove meat to a platter and cool. Once cooled, shred brisket, using fingers or fork, and place in a bowl. Set aside.

Warm tortillas and keep warm while making flautas. Fill each tortilla with brisket, roll tightly, and place seam side down in a rectangular dish. Cover with aluminum foil to keep warm.

Heat oil in a large skillet. Fry flautas in batches, starting seam side down, until golden brown. Turn and brown other side. Repeat with remaining flautas, adding more oil as needed. Drain on paper towels.

When ready to serve, place flautas on a serving platter. Cover with cream, lettuce, tomatoes, radishes, and cheese. Serve immediately with Mexican Green Hot Sauce or Ramillete Red Picante Sauce on the side.

Mexican Green Hot Sauce:

15 tomatillos, husked and rinsed
4 serrano chile peppers
2 cloves garlic
¼ medium onion

½ teaspoon salt
½ medium avocado, pitted, peeled,
  and diced
¼ cup chopped fresh cilantro

Cover tomatillos and serranos with water in a medium saucepan. Bring to a boil. Reduce heat and cook until soft. Place tomatillos and 2 serranos in a blender. (Reserve remaining 2 serranos and water that they cooked in.) Blend tomatillos and serranos. Add garlic, onion, salt, and a little bit of the water that the serranos cooked in. Blend until thoroughly combined. Adjust seasonings, adding more serranos if desired. Pour into a decorative bowl and garnish with avocado and cilantro. Yields 1 ½ cups.

Also called Mexican green tomatoes, tomatillos resemble small
green tomatoes except for their thin,
parchment-like husks. They are
very tart and acidic and have a
slightly lemon flavor. Select firm,
evenly colored tomatillos with dry,
tight-fitting husks and store in a
paper bag in the refrigerator for up
to 1 month. Before using, remove
the husk and wash well as they have
a sticky surface. Tomatillos may
be used raw in salads and salsas.
However, cooking will soften the
skin and enhance the flavor.

Ramillete Red Picante Sauce:

10 tomatillos, husked
3 ancho chile peppers or
  cascabel chiles
1 habanero chile pepper

⅛ medium onion
1 clove garlic
¼ teaspoon salt
fresh cilantro

Cover tomatillos, ancho chiles, and habanero with water in a medium saucepan. Bring to a boil. Reduce heat and cook until soft. Place tomatillos, 2 ancho chiles, and habanero in a blender. (Reserve 1 ancho chile and water that chiles cooked in.) Blend tomatillos, ancho chiles, and habanero. Add onion, garlic, salt, and a little bit of water that the chiles cooked in. Blend until thoroughly combined. Adjust seasonings, adding additional ancho chile if desired. Pour into a decorative bowl and garnish with cilantro. Yields 1 cup.

Mexican Tart

SERVES 4 TO 6

1 unbaked 9-inch pastry shell or
  1 large tortilla (12 inches)
1 large egg white, lightly beaten, or
  1 tablespoon vegetable oil
1½ teaspoons paprika
¼ teaspoon chili powder
2 tablespoons vegetable oil
1 boneless chuck roast (1 pound)
1 large onion, chopped
1 large clove garlic, minced
8 ounces Monterey Jack cheese,
  shredded (2 cups)

1 cup sour cream
¾ cup chopped green onions
1 can (4 ounces) whole green chilies,
  drained and coarsely chopped
3 large eggs, beaten
1 teaspoon salt
¼ teaspoon freshly ground pepper

————

sour cream
avocado, pitted, peeled, and sliced
Salsa Fresca (page 52)

Preheat oven to 400 degrees. If using pastry, fit into 9-inch tart or pie pan. Brush with egg white and bake 5 minutes. Let cool. If using tortilla, grease 9-inch pie pan, add tortilla, and brush lightly with oil. Bake until top is very lightly browned, about 5 minutes.

Combine paprika and chili powder. Sprinkle on meat. Heat oil in large skillet over medium-high heat. Add meat, onion, and garlic, and brown well. Reduce heat, cover partially, and cook (do not add liquid) until tender, about 1 to 1½ hours. If meat begins to stick, cover pan completely. If liquid has accumulated when meat is tender, remove lid and cook until moisture is evaporated. Remove from heat. Let meat cool, then coarsely shred, using fingers or fork. Reserve onion and garlic.

Preheat oven to 325 degrees. Combine meat, onion, garlic, cheese, sour cream, green onion, chilies, eggs, salt, and pepper in large bowl. Mix well. Spoon mixture into prepared pastry, spreading evenly. Bake 55 to 60 minutes, or until filling is set and crust is nicely browned. Cool slightly. Garnish with sour cream and avocado slices. Serve with Salsa Fresca.

Sweet and Sour Beef Stew

SERVES 6

6 tablespoons all-purpose flour
1¼ teaspoons ground allspice
1¼ teaspoons ground cinnamon
2 teaspoons salt
1 teaspoon freshly ground pepper
2 pounds beef stew meat, cut into
   1-inch cubes
¼ cup vegetable oil
2 large onions, thinly sliced
   (about 1½ pounds)

1 cup dried apricots,* quartered
2 tablespoons sugar
2 tablespoons red wine vinegar
2 tablespoons water
1 cup red wine
1 cup beef broth
8 ounces fresh mushrooms, quartered

Preheat oven to 350 degrees. Combine flour, allspice, cinnamon, salt, and pepper in a large plastic bag. Add beef and shake, coating pieces evenly with seasoned flour. Heat 1 tablespoon oil in a heavy skillet over medium-high heat. Add one-third beef and cook until brown. Transfer meat to a Dutch oven. Repeat with remaining meat in two batches, adding 1 tablespoon oil to skillet for each batch.

Add remaining 1 tablespoon oil to the same pan. Add onions and apricots. Cook until onions are soft and light brown, stirring frequently, about 12 minutes. Mix in sugar, vinegar, and water. Increase heat to high. Cook until onions are brown, stirring frequently, about 8 minutes. Add onion mixture to beef in Dutch oven. Add wine, broth, and mushrooms. Cover tightly and bake 2¼ hours, or until beef is tender. You can uncover stew during last 30 minutes if the sauce is too thin.

*May substitute dried cherries or a mixture of the two.

Can be prepared 2 days ahead. Bring to room temperature. Reheat over low heat or microwave on high for 7 minutes, stirring once.

Chocolate Chili

SERVES 6

3 pounds ground chuck
1 pound pork, cubed
2 cans (28 ounces each) peeled and
   diced tomatoes
4 cloves garlic, minced
2 teaspoons ground coriander
2 tablespoons all-purpose flour

4 teaspoons ground cumin
4 teaspoons salt
2 large onions, chopped
1 teaspoon ground oregano
6 tablespoons chili powder
4 bay leaves
2 ounces semi-sweet chocolate

Cook beef in a large skillet until brown. Add pork and brown. Stir in tomatoes, garlic, coriander, flour, cumin, salt, onions, oregano, and chili powder. Simmer 1 hour. Add bay leaves and cook 10 minutes. Remove bay leaves and add chocolate. Stir to combine. Cook 10 minutes longer to blend flavors.

IS IT CHILI?

The origins of chili are vague, but as its popularity spread, the recipe was adapted to local ingredients and tastes. Some use chopped chiles while others use chili powder. The use of chopped beef, cubed steak, or no meat at all depends on the cook. Although chili purists would never concur, some cooks add beans to their recipes.

Spicy Meat Loaf

S E R V E S   6   T O   8

SACK LUNCH

The next day serve a sandwich made with a slice of cold meat loaf and ketchup on white bread.

Seasoning mix:
2 bay leaves
2 teaspoons salt
½ teaspoon cayenne pepper
1 teaspoon freshly ground pepper
½ teaspoon ground cumin
½ teaspoon ground nutmeg
——
4 tablespoons unsalted butter
¾ cup diced onions
½ cup diced celery

½ cup diced green bell peppers
¼ cup diced green onions
2 teaspoons minced garlic
1 teaspoon Tabasco Sauce
1 tablespoon Worcestershire sauce
½ cup evaporated milk
½ cup ketchup
1½ pounds ground chuck
½ pound ground pork
2 large eggs, lightly beaten
1 cup dry bread crumbs

Combine bay leaves, salt, cayenne, pepper, cumin, and nutmeg in a small bowl. Set aside.

Melt butter in a 1-quart saucepan over medium heat. Add onions, celery, bell peppers, green onions, garlic, Tabasco, Worcestershire, and seasoning mix. Sauté until mixture starts sticking excessively, about 6 minutes. Stir occasionally and scrape the bottom of the pan well. Stir in milk and ketchup. Continue cooking 2 minutes, stirring occasionally. Remove from heat and allow mixture to cool to room temperature.

Preheat oven to 350 degrees. Place beef and pork in a large bowl. Add eggs and cooked vegetable mixture. Remove bay leaves. Add bread crumbs. Mix by hand until thoroughly combined. Form mixture into a large loaf shape. Place onto a broiler rack or any large pan with a rack so drippings drop below loaf while cooking. Finish shaping loaf to 12 by 6 inches. Bake uncovered 25 minutes. Raise heat to 400 degrees and continue cooking until done, about 35 minutes.

Basil Lemon Grilled Veal Chops

S E R V E S   4

½ cup olive oil
1 cup chopped fresh basil
juice and grated zest of 1 lemon
2 to 3 cloves garlic, minced
1 tablespoon Dijon mustard

4 veal chops, 1 inch thick
——
fresh basil sprigs
lemon wedges

Process olive oil, basil, juice and zest of lemon, garlic, and mustard in a blender or food processor until basil is minced. Transfer basil mixture to a nonmetallic bowl. Add veal chops. Marinate 30 minutes at room temperature or in refrigerator at least 2 hours.

Prepare grill. Grill over medium-hot coals about 7 minutes per side, turning once and basting with marinade. Garnish with basil sprigs and lemon wedges.

Veal Chops with Salad Greens and Tomatoes

SERVES 4

4 lean loin veal chops
  (8 ounces each)
1 cup all-purpose flour
4 large eggs
½ teaspoon salt
¼ teaspoon freshly ground pepper
3 cups dry bread crumbs
1 cup olive oil
——

4 ounces arugula, torn and stems
  discarded
4 ounces Belgian endive
2 heads radicchio, torn
2 large tomatoes, seeded and coarsely
  chopped (about 1½ pounds)
1 red onion, halved and thinly sliced
½ cup olive oil
½ cup balsamic vinegar

SELECTING VEAL

When purchasing veal, look for ivory-colored meat with a pink tinge and very white fat. If veal is to be cooked within 8 hours of purchase, refrigerate in the store wrapping. Otherwise, remove the packaging, loosely wrap in waxed paper, and refrigerate for no more than 2 days.

Partially scrape meat away from bone, leaving meat attached to the largest part of each bone. Place chops between 2 sheets of wax paper and pound until ¼ inch thick. Dredge chops in flour, pressing with fingers to make sure flour adheres. Shake off excess. Whisk eggs in a small bowl and season with salt and pepper. Dip chops in egg mixture then in bread crumbs. Heat ¾ cup oil in a skillet over medium-high heat. Add 1 chop and cook 1½ minutes. Turn chop and reduce heat to medium, cooking 1 minute longer, until golden brown. Drain chop on paper towels. Repeat cooking process with remaining chops, adding oil and adjusting heat as necessary.

Place arugula, endive, and radicchio in a large salad bowl. Layer with tomatoes and onions. Whisk oil and vinegar in a small bowl. Pour over greens and toss.

To serve, place 1 chop on each of 4 plates and cover with a generous serving of greens.

Veal Scallops with Leeks and Cream

SERVES 2

1 tablespoon plus 1 tablespoon
  unsalted butter
2 large leeks, white and pale green
  parts only, chopped (about 2 cups)
1 teaspoon chopped fresh thyme
6 veal scallops

½ teaspoon salt
¼ teaspoon freshly ground pepper
½ cup heavy whipping cream
——
2 green onions, sliced

VEAL

Veal is generally cooked more like poultry than beef because the meat comes from a young calf and is very lean.

Melt 1 tablespoon butter in a large skillet over medium heat. Add leeks and thyme. Sauté until leeks are tender and just beginning to brown, about 8 minutes. Transfer to a small bowl. Set aside.

Increase heat to high. Melt remaining 1 tablespoon butter in same skillet. Season veal with salt and pepper. Add to skillet and cook until brown and tender, about 2 minutes per side. Transfer veal to serving platter, cover with foil, and keep warm. Add cream and leek mixture to skillet. Boil until reduced to sauce consistency, scraping up any browned bits, about 2 minutes. Adjust seasonings. Pour sauce over veal and garnish with green onions.

Lamb Stew with Rosemary

SERVES 4

2 tablespoons all-purpose flour
¼ teaspoon salt
¼ teaspoon freshly ground pepper
½ pound lean stewing lamb,
  cut into 1-inch cubes
1 tablespoon olive oil
1 can (14 ounces) whole peeled
  tomatoes, chopped, plus liquid
4 ounces fresh mushrooms, quartered

1 clove garlic, crushed
1 bay leaf
¾ teaspoon minced fresh rosemary
1 tablespoon plus 1 tablespoon
  chopped fresh parsley
½ cup frozen peas, thawed
——
2 cups steamed rice

Place flour, salt, and pepper in a large plastic bag. Add lamb, shaking to coat evenly. Heat oil in a large skillet over medium heat. Add lamb, reserving flour. Sauté 5 to 10 minutes, or until lamb is browned evenly. Add reserved flour and stir to blend. Add tomatoes, mushrooms, garlic, bay leaf, rosemary, and 1 tablespoon parsley. Bring to a boil. Reduce heat to medium-low. Cover and simmer 30 minutes. Remove bay leaf. Stir in peas. Cover and let rest 5 minutes. Serve over rice and garnish with remaining 1 tablespoon parsley.

Butterflied Leg of Lamb

SERVES 8

4 cloves garlic

4 sprigs fresh rosemary

⅓ cup Creole mustard

¼ cup soy sauce

¼ cup olive oil

½ teaspoon Tabasco Sauce

2 tablespoons balsamic vinegar

1 leg of lamb (5 to 7 pounds), butterflied

———

Jalapeño Mint Jelly

Chop garlic and rosemary in a food processor. Add mustard, soy sauce, olive oil, Tabasco, and vinegar. Process to combine. Place lamb on a rack in a 9 by 13-inch pan. Rub and coat completely on both sides with the marinade. Refrigerate 2 hours or longer.

Preheat broiler. Broil lamb about 20 minutes on each side for medium-rare, longer for medium or well done. Serve with Jalapeño Mint Jelly.

Jalapeño Mint Jelly:

2 cups water

1 cup distilled white vinegar

¼ cup to ½ cup minced fresh jalapeños

6½ cups sugar

few drops green food coloring

1 cup fresh mint, packed, stems discarded

6 ounces liquid fruit pectin

Combine water, vinegar, jalapeño, sugar, and food coloring in a large saucepan. Bring to a rolling boil, stirring occasionally. Boil 3 minutes. Add mint and pectin. Boil 1 minute. Strain into hot sterilized jars. Yields 9 cups.

Also good over cream cheese served with water biscuits.

LAMB ROASTING GUIDE

Thermometer reading of the meat's internal temperature:
Rare - 130 to 140 degrees
Medium - 150 to 160 degrees
Well done - 160 to 170 degrees

LEG OF LAMB

The most flavorful cut of lamb, the leg can be grilled or roasted whole or boned and butterflied. Select a plump leg of lamb, which will have a high ratio of meat to bone and fat, and have your butcher butterfly it. This process includes deboning and trimming all visible fat and the fell. The fell is the thin parchment-like coating on the leg. If grilling or roasting whole, do not remove the fell as it serves to retain the meat's juices.

Rack of Lamb with Port and Rosemary Sauce

SERVES 4

1 rack of lamb, 8 to 10 ribs

½ teaspoon chopped fresh rosemary

½ teaspoon salt

¼ teaspoon freshly ground pepper

Port and Rosemary Sauce:

1 onion, chopped

2 strips bacon, chopped

1 tablespoon chopped fresh rosemary

½ cup port

¼ cup water

½ cup heavy whipping cream

Preheat oven to 350 degrees. Trim any excess fat from lamb. Sprinkle with rosemary, salt, and pepper. Place lamb in a baking dish. Bake 45 minutes. Set aside. Keep warm.

Port and Rosemary Sauce: Pour any drippings from lamb into a skillet. Add onion and bacon. Cook over medium heat until bacon is crisp. Add rosemary, port, and water. Bring to a boil. Reduce heat. Simmer uncovered until reduced to ½ cup. Add cream and simmer, stirring until slightly thickened. Spoon sauce over lamb. Serve immediately.

MESQUITE CHIPS

Mesquite chips and other grill-compatible woods such as apple, cherry, hickory, peach, pecan, and walnut add a unique smokiness to grilled foods. Wood chips should always be soaked in water for 1 hour before using (wood chunks should soak for 2 hours). Drain thoroughly before sprinkling chips over hot coals. After draining, wood chips can be stored in the freezer indefinitely. Frozen chips should be sprinkled directly on hot coals.

12 ounces beer
juice of 1 large lemon
½ cup virgin olive oil
6 large sprigs fresh rosemary, chopped
2 bay leaves, crumbled
3 cloves garlic, crushed
1 tablespoon sugar
½ cup soy sauce
2 teaspoons dry mustard

———

1 leg of lamb (5 to 6 pounds), butterflied

———

½ cup (1 stick) unsalted butter, melted
2 cloves garlic, crushed
salt
freshly ground pepper

———

English Mint Sauce

Combine beer, lemon juice, olive oil, rosemary, bay leaves, garlic, sugar, soy sauce, and dry mustard in a large nonmetallic bowl. Place lamb in marinade. Cover and refrigerate 6 to 12 hours, turning occasionally.

Prepare grill with mesquite chips and charcoal. Remove lamb from marinade and discard marinade. Grill 15 to 20 minutes. Turn and grill other side 15 to 20 minutes. Set aside and keep warm.

Combine butter, garlic, salt, and pepper in a small bowl. Brush butter over cooked lamb and serve with English Mint Sauce on the side.

English Mint Sauce:
½ cup sugar
½ cup fresh lemon juice
¼ cup water

⅛ teaspoon salt
½ cup minced fresh mint

Heat sugar, lemon juice, water, and salt in a saucepan over low heat, about 5 minutes. Do not boil. Remove from heat. Add mint. Let stand 15 minutes. Yields 1 cup.

Lamb Medallions with Feta and Rosemary

SERVES 4

2 cups fresh bread crumbs
2 ounces feta cheese, crumbled
   (½ cup)
2 tablespoons chopped fresh rosemary
½ cup chopped fresh Italian parsley
salt
freshly ground pepper

4 to 5 pounds loin of lamb, deboned
½ cup all-purpose flour
3 large eggs, beaten
1 cup (2 sticks) unsalted butter,
   clarified*
——

fresh rosemary sprigs

Combine bread crumbs, cheese, rosemary, and parsley. Season with salt and pepper. Set aside. Cut lamb into medallions, each about 1 inch thick. Dredge meat in flour. Dip each piece into beaten eggs and then coat with bread crumb and cheese mixture.

Heat clarified butter in a skillet until it is smoking hot. Add meat and brown on all sides. Repeat until all meat is browned (do not overcrowd the meat in pan). Transfer meat to a roasting rack. Preheat oven to 350 degrees. Just before serving, roast browned meat 7 minutes. Garnish with a small sprig of fresh rosemary. Serve immediately.

*Clarified butter is simply melted butter with the residue removed. It can be heated to higher temperatures. To clarify, melt butter over low heat. Remove from heat and skim the white butterfat from the top. Let it rest several minutes to allow the solids to settle, then pour off the clear yellow liquid.

Rosemary-Smoked Lamb Chops

SERVES 4

6 to 8 sprigs fresh rosemary
——
¼ cup olive oil
2 tablespoons chopped fresh rosemary

½ teaspoon salt
¼ teaspoon freshly ground pepper
8 rib or loin lamb chops, 1 inch thick

Cover rosemary sprigs with water and soak 30 minutes.

Prepare grill. Position rack 4 to 6 inches above coals. Whisk oil, rosemary, salt, and pepper in a small bowl. Rub a small amount of this mixture on each chop. Reserve remainder. Drop a few soaked rosemary sprigs onto the coals. Grill chops, turning occasionally. Brush lightly with remaining rosemary mixture and grill until browned, about 4 minutes. Drop remaining rosemary sprigs on coals. Continue to cook, turning once again and basting with rosemary mixture, another 4 minutes. Serve immediately.

HOT OFF THE GRILL

Grilling food over a fire is probably the oldest form of cooking. Some say it's still the best. Put a cook in front of a grill and you'll see the inner Neanderthal revealed. Grilling is among the most competitive of sports and the occasion of much outsize boasting about skills with the grill. The difference between barbecuing and grilling is a matter of degrees: barbecue is slow-cooked at temperatures ranging from 180 to 250 degrees; grilling sears food quickly at a high temperature to seal in juices. To get the best results, build a fire using charcoal briquettes or, if available, natural lump charcoal processed from hickory, cherry, maple, mesquite, or pecan wood. Coals take 20 to 30 minutes to achieve the gray ash coating ideal for grilling. Scrub the metal bars of the grill with a wire brush and then oil them with a rag to prevent meat from sticking. When turning meat, don't use a fork because juices will run out. Use tongs instead. For extra flavor and tenderness, marinate meat at room temperature for up to an hour.

Roasted Rosemary Pork with Asparagus

SERVES 8

PORK ROASTING GUIDE

Thermometer reading of the meat's internal temperature should read 160 to 165 degrees. Pork should always sit 10 minutes before serving.

3 large cloves garlic, minced
4 teaspoons chopped fresh rosemary
½ teaspoon salt
½ teaspoon freshly ground pepper
3 tablespoons olive oil

2 tablespoons Dijon mustard
2 tablespoons fresh lemon juice
1 center cut pork loin roast (5 pounds)
2 pounds thick fresh asparagus, trimmed and blanched

Preheat oven to 400 degrees. Mix garlic, rosemary, salt, pepper, olive oil, mustard, and lemon juice in a small bowl. Reserve 1 tablespoon of mixture. Spread remainder over fat side of pork. Place pork fat side up on a wire rack in a roasting pan. Place pork in oven. Reduce heat to 325 degrees and cook uncovered 2 hours.

Toss asparagus with 1 tablespoon reserved garlic mixture. Arrange asparagus around roast and cook uncovered 15 to 20 minutes. Serve immediately.

Mustard Pork Roast with Honey Apples

SERVES 10

1 tablespoon dried sage
¼ teaspoon dried marjoram
2 tablespoons soy sauce
1 clove garlic, minced
½ cup Dijon mustard
1 rolled boneless pork loin roast (5 pounds)

Honey Apples:
½ cup honey
¼ teaspoon salt
¼ teaspoon ground cinnamon
2 tablespoons apple cider vinegar
4 Granny Smith apples, peeled, cored, and cut into ½-inch slices

Preheat oven to 325 degrees. Combine sage, marjoram, soy sauce, garlic, and mustard in a small bowl. Mix well. Place roast, fat side up, in a shallow roasting pan. Spread with mustard mixture. Insert meat thermometer, making sure it does not touch fat. Bake uncovered 2 to 2½ hours, or until thermometer registers 160 degrees.

Honey Apples: Combine honey, salt, cinnamon, and vinegar in a large saucepan. Bring to a boil. Add apples. Reduce heat and simmer 10 minutes. To serve, slice roast and top with Honey Apples.

Apricot and Pecan-Stuffed Pork Loin

SERVES 10

1½ cups dried apricots
½ cup pecans
1 clove garlic
½ teaspoon salt
¼ teaspoon freshly ground pepper
2 tablespoons plus 2 tablespoons chopped fresh thyme
1 tablespoon plus 3 tablespoons molasses

2 tablespoons plus 2 tablespoons peanut or vegetable oil
1 boneless pork loin roast (5 pounds), halved
1 cup bourbon
1 cup chicken broth
¼ cup heavy whipping cream
¼ teaspoon salt

Coarsely chop apricots, pecans, garlic, salt, and pepper in a food processor. Add 2 tablespoons thyme, 1 tablespoon molasses, and 2 tablespoons oil. Process until mixture is finely chopped, but not smooth.

Make a lengthwise cut down the center of each roast, cutting to, but not through, the bottom. Starting from center slice, slice horizontally toward one side, stopping ½ inch from edge. Repeat with other loin half. Flatten each half to a ½-inch thickness using a meat mallet or rolling pin.

Spread apricot mixture evenly over pork. Roll each loin half, jelly-roll fashion, starting with long side. Secure with string. Place both rolls, seam side down, in a shallow roasting pan. Brush with remaining 2 tablespoons oil and sprinkle with remaining thyme. Preheat oven to 350 degrees.

Bring bourbon, broth, and remaining 3 tablespoons molasses to a boil in a large saucepan. Remove from heat. Carefully ignite bourbon mixture with a long match. When flames die, pour over roasts.

Bake at 350 degrees 1 to 1½ hours, or until meat thermometer inserted in thickest portion registers 160 degrees. Remove pork from pan, reserve drippings, and keep warm.

Pour reserved drippings in a small saucepan. Add cream and salt. Cook over medium-high heat, stirring constantly, until slightly thickened. Slice pork and serve with sauce.

Honey Sesame Pork Tenderloin

SERVES 4 TO 6

½ cup soy sauce
2 cloves garlic, minced
1 tablespoon grated fresh ginger
1 tablespoon sesame oil
1 to 1½ pounds pork tenderloin

¼ cup honey
2 tablespoons dark brown sugar, firmly packed
¼ cup sesame seeds

Combine soy sauce, garlic, ginger, and sesame oil in large plastic bag. Add tenderloin. Marinate at least 2 hours in refrigerator.

Preheat oven to 375 degrees. Combine honey and brown sugar in a shallow bowl. Remove tenderloin from marinade and pat dry with a paper towel. Roll tenderloin in honey mixture then roll in sesame seeds. Roast in a shallow pan 20 to 30 minutes, or until meat registers 160 degrees on a meat thermometer. Serve immediately.

Grilled Pork Tenderloin

SERVES 4 TO 6

SAGE

Most herbs belong to either the carrot or the mint family. Sage is included in the mint family and has over 3,200 relatives. It is an herb that comes in a number of varieties and grows wild in Texas. It was originally used in ancient times for medicinal purposes, but today is most commonly used to enhance pork, game, and poultry.

2 tablespoons chopped fresh thyme
1 tablespoon chopped fresh sage
pinch salt
1 teaspoon freshly ground pepper
¼ teaspoon ground allspice or cloves
3 cloves garlic, minced
2 tablespoons vegetable oil

1 to 1½ pounds pork tenderloin
½ cup orange marmalade
⅓ cup Dijon mustard
1 tablespoon grated fresh ginger
1 tablespoon Worcestershire sauce
¼ teaspoon salt
¼ teaspoon freshly ground pepper

Mix thyme, sage, salt, pepper, allspice, and garlic in a small bowl. Rub tenderloin in oil then coat evenly in thyme mixture. Cover and marinate at least 1 hour in the refrigerator.

Combine marmalade, mustard, ginger, Worcestershire, salt, and pepper in a small bowl.

Prepare grill. Oil grill rack and position 4 to 6 inches above coals. Place tenderloins on rack so that they are not directly over heat. Close grill and maintain constant temperature. Grill 45 to 60 minutes, basting with marmalade mixture every 10 minutes. Pork is done when a meat thermometer registers 160 degrees. Remove from grill, cover loosely with foil, and let rest 10 minutes. Slice and serve immediately.

Pork Tenderloin in Creamy Mustard Sauce

SERVES 4 TO 6

1 to 1½ pounds pork tenderloin*
½ cup all-purpose flour
¾ teaspoon plus ¼ teaspoon salt
½ teaspoon plus ¼ teaspoon
  freshly ground pepper
3 tablespoons unsalted butter

3 to 6 green onions, white parts
  only, sliced
⅓ cup dry white wine
1 cup heavy whipping cream
¼ cup Dijon mustard

Cut tenderloin crosswise into ½-inch slices. Place pieces between waxed paper and pound to a ¼-inch thickness. Combine flour, ¾ teaspoon salt, and ½ teaspoon pepper in a plastic bag. Add pork in batches and toss to coat. Melt 1 tablespoon butter in a large skillet over medium-high heat and add one-third of pork. Sauté until brown and cooked through, about 3 minutes per side. Transfer pork to a platter and keep warm. Repeat with remaining pork in two more batches, adding 1 tablespoon butter for each batch. Add green onions to skillet. Sauté until tender, about 1 minute. Stir in wine. Bring to a boil. Boil until liquid is reduced to 2 tablespoons, about 3 minutes. Stir in whipping cream and simmer until thick, about 5 minutes. Whisk in mustard. Return pork to the skillet with mustard sauce. Heat thoroughly. Serve immediately.

Can substitute veal scallopini for pork.

Pork with Cassis and Currants

⅓ cup dried currants
1 cup chicken broth
1 cup beef broth
1 to 1½ pounds pork tenderloin
all-purpose flour
2 tablespoons plus 3 tablespoons
   unsalted butter

½ cup Crème de Cassis
3 tablespoons red wine vinegar
salt
freshly ground pepper

CURRANTS

Currants, just like raisins, are made by drying grapes. The difference is in the type of grape used. Currants are usually made from the small Zante grape, which originated in Greece's Zante Gulf.

Soak currants in warm water 30 minutes. Drain and set aside. Combine chicken and beef broths in a medium saucepan. Boil until reduced to 1 cup, about 12 minutes. Set aside.

Preheat oven to 375 degrees. Coat pork with flour, shaking off excess. Melt 2 tablespoons butter in a skillet over medium-high heat. Add pork and brown on all sides. Transfer pork to a roasting pan. Bake 20 to 30 minutes, or until meat registers 160 degrees on a meat thermometer. Tent with foil to keep warm. Set aside.

Drain grease from same skillet. Add currants, Crème de Cassis, and vinegar. Boil until liquid is reduced by one-half, about 5 minutes. Scrape up any browned bits. Add reduced broths. Boil until mixture is slightly syrupy, about 12 minutes. Remove from heat. Whisk in remaining 3 tablespoons butter, cut into pieces. Season with salt and pepper.

To serve, cut pork into slices and top with sauce. Serve immediately.

Pork Tenderloin with Spinach, Pine Nuts, and Garlic

1 tablespoon unsalted butter
3 cloves garlic, minced
¼ cup pine nuts
8 ounces fresh spinach, coarse
   stems discarded
salt

freshly ground pepper
1 tablespoon vegetable oil
1 to 1½ pounds pork tenderloins,
   flattened to ¾ inch
1 cup red wine
2 cups beef broth

PINE NUTS

Also known as piñon nuts or pignolias, pine nuts are tiny seeds that nestle within the cones of the stone pine, which grows on arid mountaintops in the Southwest. They are deep ivory in color with a delicate flavor and can only be harvested by hand. Pine nuts should be refrigerated, but be aware that they turn rancid quickly. They may also be frozen.

Preheat oven to 350 degrees. Melt butter in a large skillet. Add garlic and pine nuts. Sauté 1 minute. Add spinach and cook until spinach is limp. Season with salt and pepper. Transfer to a bowl. Set aside.

Heat 1 tablespoon oil in same skillet over medium heat. Brown tenderloins on one side. Remove and spoon spinach mixture over largest unbrowned side. Wrap with kitchen twine, securing the pieces together. Place in a roasting pan. Add wine. Bake 35 minutes per pound, or until meat thermometer registers 160 to 165 degrees. Remove tenderloin and keep warm.

Return pan to stove top. Add beef broth and cook until sauce is thick, scraping up any brown bits. To serve, slice pork and serve with sauce.

Curried Chutney Pork Tenderloin

1 cup plain low-fat yogurt
1 tablespoon minced fresh parsley
¼ teaspoon crushed red pepper
1½ tablespoons minced chutney

1 teaspoon plus 1 tablespoon
  curry powder
1 to 1½ pounds pork tenderloin
1 large clove garlic, minced

Combine yogurt, parsley, red pepper, chutney, and 1 teaspoon curry powder in a small bowl. Place tenderloin in a shallow dish and pour yogurt mixture over tenderloin, covering completely. Cover and refrigerate at least 2 hours.

Preheat oven to 375 degrees. Remove tenderloin from marinade and sprinkle with remaining curry powder and minced garlic. Place pork in a small roasting pan. Bake 30 minutes, or until meat registers 160 degrees on a meat thermometer. Serve immediately.

Peppered Pork Chops with Balsamic Sage Sauce

SERVES 4

BALSAMIC VINEGAR

The production of balsamic vinegar is said to require an artistry equal to that necessary for the production of fine wines. Good balsamic vinegar is smooth, mellow tasting, and quite expensive.

8 small boneless pork loin rib chops
  (1½ pounds)
salt
2 to 3 teaspoons freshly ground
  pepper
2 to 3 tablespoons olive oil
6 tablespoons balsamic vinegar

¼ cup chicken broth
1 tablespoon chopped fresh sage
2 tablespoons unsalted butter,
  cut in small pieces

——

large fresh sage leaves

Sprinkle chops with salt. Sprinkle half of pepper evenly over one side of chops. Press pepper into surface of each chop so pepper adheres. Sprinkle remaining pepper over other side and press to adhere.

Heat a large skillet over medium-high heat. When hot, add 2 tablespoons olive oil. When oil is hot, add half of chops. Cook until brown, about 6 minutes. Turn and cook on other side, about 5 minutes longer, or until chops are cooked through. Transfer to platter and set aside. Add more oil to pan. Cook remaining chops. Add to platter and keep warm.

Pour off all but 1 tablespoon of drippings from the pan. Add vinegar and broth to pan. Bring to a boil. Stir in chopped sage and any meat juices that have collected on platter. Cook, stirring up any browned bits on bottom of pan, until liquid is reduced by half. Whisk in butter.

To serve, place 2 chops on each of 4 warm dinner plates. Pour sauce over chops and garnish with sage leaves.

Grilled Mustard Pork Chops with Two-Tomato Salsa

SERVES 4

Two-Tomato Salsa:
1½ cups diced Roma tomatoes
8 sun-dried tomato halves packed
 in oil, drained and chopped
¼ cup chopped fresh basil
¼ teaspoon cayenne pepper

——

2 tablespoons Dijon mustard
2 tablespoons honey
1 teaspoon minced garlic
4 boneless pork chops,
 ¾ inch thick

——

fresh basil leaves

Two-Tomato Salsa: Combine tomatoes, sun-dried tomatoes, basil, and cayenne in a medium bowl. Set aside.

Prepare grill. Combine mustard, honey, and garlic in a small bowl. Place chops on uncovered grill directly over medium-hot coals. Grill 4 to 5 minutes and turn. Brush chops with mustard mixture. Grill 4 to 5 minutes, or until chops are faintly pink in center.

If broiling is preferred, place chops in broiling pan on rack 4 to 5 inches from heat. Broil 5 to 6 minutes, or until brown. Turn chops and brush with mustard mixture. Broil 5 to 6 minutes.

Garnish with basil and serve with Two-Tomato Salsa.

USES FOR SUN-DRIED TOMATOES

Sun-dried tomatoes originated in Italy, where the tomatoes were left to dry in the sun and were then packed in olive oil for various uses. Thanks to commercialization, most sun-dried tomatoes now are produced in dehydrators. They should be labeled as dried tomatoes rather than sun-dried tomatoes. Their intensified sweet flavor and chewy texture lend themselves to many uses. Pairing the tomatoes with goat cheese is one of the more popular combinations, but thinking creatively can produce many other taste-tempting alternatives. Try them in omelets or soups, chopped and mixed with butter as a spread, tossed with pasta and pesto, or as a topping on a pizza.

Orange Marmalade and Bourbon Glazed Ham

SERVES 6 TO 8

1 medium ham, butt if possible
whole cloves
1 cup water
1 cup cream sherry
1 tablespoon grated fresh ginger

½ cup orange marmalade
½ cup bourbon
2 tablespoons prepared mustard
¼ cup brown sugar, firmly packed

Preheat oven to 425 degrees. Line roasting pan with foil. Trim rind and fat from ham, if necessary, leaving ¼-inch layer of fat. Score ham in a diamond pattern. Stick cloves into center of each diamond. Place ham in pan. Combine water, sherry, and ginger in a small bowl. Pour sauce over ham. Bake 5 minutes per pound.

Cook marmalade, bourbon, and mustard over medium heat in a small saucepan until warm, stirring occasionally, about 5 minutes (glaze will be thin). Increase oven to 450 degrees. Brush glaze over ham and sprinkle with brown sugar. Bake until deep brown, about 20 minutes. Spoon off fat from the pan juices. Transfer juices to a saucepan and boil until thick, about 10 minutes. Slice ham and serve au jus.

Try a spiral-cut ham for a buffet.

POULTRY

Quail with Onions, Mushrooms,
and Peaches

Herb Roasted Chicken

S E R V E S   4

1 large whole chicken (4 pounds)
1 clove garlic, minced
1 teaspoon chopped fresh rosemary
1 teaspoon chopped fresh thyme
1 teaspoon chopped fresh oregano
   or marjoram

¼ teaspoon freshly ground pepper
½ teaspoon salt
1 tablespoon olive oil

Preheat oven to 375 degrees. Rinse chicken inside and out with cold water. Remove pockets of fat just inside chest cavity. Pat dry.

Blend garlic, rosemary, thyme, oregano, pepper, salt, and olive oil to make an herb paste. Rub herb paste over chicken and under skin. Roast, breast side up, 20 minutes. Turn and roast another 20 minutes. Turn again and roast another 35 minutes. Remove chicken from oven. Cover loosely with aluminum foil and let rest 15 minutes prior to carving. Serve chicken au jus with crusty bread.

Chicken at Attention

S E R V E S   4

1 large whole fryer chicken
2 tablespoons olive oil
seasoned salt

seasoned pepper
garlic powder
1 can (12 ounces) beer, opened

Prepare a low, hot fire in grill, keeping coals as far away from grill as possible.

Wash and clean fryer. Coat fryer with olive oil, inside and out. Wipe excess oil on outside of beer can. Sprinkle entire fryer with seasonings. Insert opened beer can into cavity of fryer (fryer should now be standing upright). Place on grill and smoke at least 3 hours. Depending on bird and fire, cooking time could take up to 5 hours or more. Chicken will darken as it cooks. Monitor chicken carefully! Serve immediately.

Also delicious using duck or Cornish game hens.

TYPES OF CHICKEN

The following is an explanation of the various types of chickens used in cooking:

Capons - 10 weeks old and weighing 8 to 10 pounds. They are quite large and good for stuffing.

Roasters - 10 weeks old and weighing 4 to 8 pounds.

Broiler/Fryers - only 45 days old and weighing 3 to 4 pounds.

Rock Cornish Game Hens - 5 to 6 weeks old and weighing 1 to 2 pounds. They make an elegant entree.

Free-Range Chickens - grain-fed and allowed to roam freely. The result is a much leaner chicken.

Chicken with Tarragon Vinegar

SERVES 4

SHALLOTS

More subtle than onions and less pungent than garlic, shallots are indispensable for many French sauces. They are particularly delicious used in wine cooking.

3 tablespoons extra virgin olive oil
1 tablespoon plus 2 tablespoons
  unsalted butter
1 whole chicken, cut into pieces
salt
freshly ground pepper
½ cup dry white wine

4 shallots, minced
1 can (28 ounces) whole tomatoes,
  drained and chopped
¼ to ½ cup tarragon vinegar
2 to 3 tablespoons minced fresh
  tarragon

Heat oil with 1 tablespoon butter in a deep 12-inch skillet over high heat. Season chicken liberally with salt and pepper. Place in skillet, cooking until golden brown, approximately 10 to 12 minutes on each side. Transfer chicken to serving platter. Cover loosely with foil. Keep warm. Pour fat from skillet. Return skillet to medium-high heat. Add wine, deglazing pan by scraping away any bits clinging to it. Add shallots and tomatoes. Cook 5 to 7 minutes. Increase heat to high, add vinegar, and cook an additional 2 to 3 minutes. Stir in remaining 2 tablespoons butter and cook another minute.

   Return chicken to skillet, coating with sauce. Cover, cook an additional 2 to 3 minutes, or until some of sauce is absorbed. Stir in tarragon. Serve immediately.

Peppercorn Chicken Breasts

SERVES 3 TO 4

4 large boneless, skinless chicken
  breast halves
1 tablespoon crushed whole pink,
  green, or Szechwan peppercorns

2 teaspoons unsalted butter
½ cup dry sherry or orange juice
½ cup heavy whipping cream
½ teaspoon chopped fresh tarragon

Place chicken between sheets of plastic wrap. Flatten to a ¼-inch thickness using a meat mallet or rolling pin. Sprinkle with peppercorns. Melt butter in a large skillet over medium heat. Add chicken. Cook, turning once, until chicken is done, about 10 to 12 minutes. Remove chicken and keep warm.

   Increase heat to high. Add sherry or orange juice to pan. Whisk in cream and tarragon. Boil, stirring constantly, until sauce is glossy and reduced to one-half its original volume. Spoon sauce over chicken. Serve immediately.

Champagne Chicken

SERVES 2

1 cup champagne
12 sprigs fresh thyme, minced
3 tablespoons fresh lime juice
4 cloves garlic, chopped
2 large sprigs fresh rosemary, minced
2 boneless, skinless chicken
  breast halves

½ teaspoon salt
¼ teaspoon freshly ground pepper
——
fresh rosemary sprigs

Combine champagne, thyme, lime juice, garlic, and rosemary in a large bowl. Add chicken breasts. Season with salt and pepper. Cover bowl and refrigerate overnight.

Preheat oven to 350 degrees. Remove chicken from marinade and place in a small roasting pan. Reserve marinade. Roast chicken 20 to 30 minutes, basting occasionally with marinade. Place chicken on a platter and cover to keep warm. Pour pan juices into a saucepan. Add remaining marinade. Cook mixture over medium-high heat until reduced slightly, about 5 minutes. Spoon sauce over chicken and garnish with fresh rosemary sprigs.

Pesto-Stuffed Chicken Rolls

SERVES 4 TO 6

6 boneless, skinless chicken
  breast halves
¼ teaspoon salt
¼ teaspoon freshly ground pepper
3 ounces cream cheese, softened
¼ cup pesto

½ cup minced red bell pepper
¾ cup crushed corn flakes
½ teaspoon paprika
——
fresh basil sprigs

Place each piece of chicken between two sheets of plastic wrap. Flatten to a ¼-inch thickness using a meat mallet or rolling pin. Sprinkle with salt and pepper. Set aside.

Combine cream cheese, pesto, and bell pepper, stirring with a fork until smooth. Spread 2 tablespoons cheese mixture over each chicken breast. Roll up lengthwise, securing with wooden picks. Combine corn flakes and paprika. Dredge chicken rolls in crumb mixture. Place chicken in an 11 by 7-inch baking dish coated with nonstick cooking spray. Cover and refrigerate 8 hours.

Preheat oven to 350 degrees. Bring chicken to room temperature before baking. Bake uncovered 35 minutes. Let stand 10 minutes. Remove wooden picks and slice into 1-inch rounds. Garnish with fresh basil sprigs.

Chicken in Orange Sauce

1 cup fresh orange juice
1 tablespoon minced shallot
4½ teaspoons white wine vinegar
1 tablespoon white wine
1 tablespoon brown sugar,
    firmly packed
2 tablespoons plus 4 tablespoons
    unsalted butter, chilled

4 strips orange zest
½ teaspoon salt
¼ teaspoon freshly ground pepper
¼ teaspoon freshly grated nutmeg
——
4 tablespoons unsalted butter
4 boneless, skinless chicken
    breast halves

Bring orange juice, shallot, vinegar, wine, and sugar to a simmer in a small saucepan over medium heat. Stir until sugar dissolves. Increase heat to high. Boil until sauce is reduced to ⅛ cup, about 15 minutes.

Remove sauce from heat and whisk in 2 tablespoons chilled butter. Set pan over low heat and whisk in remaining 4 tablespoons butter, 1 tablespoon at a time. Remove pan from the heat briefly if sauce breaks down. Mix in orange zest. Season with salt, pepper, and nutmeg. Set aside and keep warm.

Melt 4 tablespoons butter in a large skillet over medium heat. Add chicken and cook about 10 to 12 minutes per side. Transfer chicken to a serving plate and top with orange sauce.

Lime Grilled Chicken with Mango Salsa

PEACH SALSA

2 cups peaches, peeled and
    coarsely chopped
¼ cup chopped red bell pepper
¼ cup chopped green bell pepper
¼ cup chopped yellow bell pepper
¼ cup chopped cucumber
¼ cup sliced green onions,
    white part only
1 to 2 fresh jalapeños, seeded
    and minced
2 tablespoons honey
2 tablespoons fresh lime juice
1 tablespoon minced fresh cilantro

Combine peaches, bell peppers, cucumber, green onions, jalapeños, honey, lime juice, and cilantro. Cover and chill up to 4 hours, stirring once or twice. Yields 2½ cups.

Mango Salsa:
2 mangoes, peeled, pitted,
    and diced
½ red bell pepper, seeded
    and diced
½ cup fresh orange juice
juice of 2 limes
¼ cup minced fresh basil
salt
freshly ground pepper
——

2 tablespoons frozen orange juice
    concentrate, thawed
2 tablespoons frozen limeade
    concentrate, thawed
salt
freshly ground pepper
4 boneless, skinless chicken breast
    halves

Mango Salsa: Combine mangoes, bell pepper, orange juice, lime juice, and basil in a medium bowl. Season with salt and pepper. Cover and refrigerate 2 hours.

Combine orange juice, limeade, salt, and pepper in a plastic bag. Add chicken and marinate 2 hours in the refrigerator.

Prepare grill. Place rack about 3 inches from heat. Grill chicken until brown and firm to the touch, about 7 minutes per side. Top with Mango Salsa and serve. For a variation, serve instead with Peach Salsa (see accompanying recipe).

Chicken with Ancho Chile Sauce and Pico de Gallo

SERVES 3 TO 4

Ancho Chile Sauce:
1 ½ cups water
2 ancho chile peppers
2 cloves garlic, peeled
1 teaspoon salt
1 ½ teaspoons minced fresh
   oregano
1 tablespoon sugar
1 teaspoon olive oil

Pico de Gallo:
1 cup chopped tomatoes
½ cup chopped onion
¼ cup chopped fresh cilantro

½ fresh jalapeño, seeded and minced
1 tablespoon fresh lemon juice
1 tablespoon olive oil
——
4 boneless, skinless chicken breast
   halves
olive oil
salt
freshly ground pepper
6 ounces Monterey Jack cheese,
   shredded (1 ½ cups)
——
1 avocado, pitted, peeled, and sliced

ANCHO CHILE PEPPER

The ancho chile pepper is a broad dried chile, 3 to 4 inches long and a deep reddish brown. It ranges in flavor from mild to pungent. Fresh, it is green and referred to as a poblano chile pepper.

Ancho Chile Sauce: Boil water, chiles, garlic, salt, and oregano in a small saucepan until chiles are tender, about 5 minutes. Remove chiles and garlic from cooking liquid. Reserve cooking liquid. Discard stems and seeds from chiles and coarsely chop. Transfer chiles and garlic to a food processor. Pulse until finely chopped. With machine running, gradually add enough chile cooking liquid (about ⅓ cup) to form a thick sauce. Add sugar and olive oil. Blend until smooth. (Sauce can be prepared 1 day ahead. Cover tightly and refrigerate.)

Pico de Gallo: Combine tomatoes, onion, cilantro, jalapeño, lemon juice, and olive oil in a small bowl. (Can be prepared 4 hours ahead. Cover and refrigerate.)

Preheat broiler. Brush chicken lightly with olive oil. Season with salt and pepper. Broil chicken until just cooked through, brushing occasionally with Ancho Chile Sauce, about 5 minutes per side.

Reduce heat to 400 degrees. Transfer chicken to baking dish. Brush with more sauce. Sprinkle cheese over chicken. Bake just until cheese melts, about 3 minutes.

To serve, arrange chicken on plates, top with Pico de Gallo, and garnish with avocado slices. Serve remaining Ancho Chile Sauce separately.

Piñon-Breaded Chicken with
Ancho Chile Lingonberry Sauce

SERVES 3 TO 4

¾ cup pine nuts, coarsely chopped
⅓ cup bread crumbs
3 cloves garlic, minced
3 tablespoons minced fresh parsley
3 tablespoons minced fresh thyme
½ teaspoon salt
¼ teaspoon white pepper

4 boneless, skinless chicken breast
  halves
½ cup flour
2 large eggs, beaten
⅓ cup olive oil
———
Ancho Chile Lingonberry Sauce

Mix pine nuts, bread crumbs, garlic, parsley, thyme, salt, and white pepper in a small bowl. Dip chicken breasts into flour, beaten eggs, and then bread crumb mixture. Heat olive oil in a large skillet over medium-high heat. Add breaded chicken breasts. Sauté 10 to 12 minutes on each side, or until golden brown. Spoon Ancho Chile Lingonberry Sauce on each of 3 to 4 plates. Place a chicken breast on top.

Ancho Chile Lingonberry Sauce:

2 tablespoons olive oil
2 shallots, minced
2 cloves garlic, minced
½ cup Madeira
2 cups chicken stock
2 ancho chile peppers, softened in
  boiling water 2 minutes, drained

1 jar (4 ounces) lingonberries
  in syrup
¼ cup chopped fresh thyme
½ teaspoon salt
¼ teaspoon freshly ground pepper

Heat olive oil over medium-high heat. Add shallots and garlic. Sauté 2 minutes, or until garlic is brown. Add Madeira, chicken stock, and ancho chile peppers. Cook over high heat 5 minutes, or until the liquid is reduced by one-half and chiles are soft. Remove the chiles from liquid. Remove seeds and stems and discard. Purée chiles in a food processor. Add purée back to liquid. Add lingonberries and thyme. Cook sauce 5 minutes, or until consistency of heavy cream. Add salt and pepper to taste.

LINGONBERRIES

Lingonberries are tart, red berries that grow wild in the mountainous regions of northern Europe, Canada, and Maine in the United States. They can be purchased packed in jars with syrup.

Spicy Yogurt Chicken

2 cups plain yogurt
1 clove garlic, crushed
1 teaspoon ground ginger
1 teaspoon chili powder
1 teaspoon ground cardamom

½ teaspoon ground cloves
½ teaspoon ground cinnamon
2 teaspoons salt
4 bay leaves, crushed
8 to 10 pieces chicken

Mix yogurt, garlic, ginger, chili powder, cardamom, cloves, cinnamon, salt, and bay leaves in a plastic bag. Add chicken and marinate at least 4 hours or overnight.

Prepare grill. Grill chicken about 8 minutes per side. Serve immediately.

Tea Room Chicken and Spinach Crêpes

Basic Crêpes:
1½ cups all-purpose flour
1½ cups milk
6 large eggs
6 tablespoons unsalted butter,
  at room temperature
pinch salt

Filling:
6 tablespoons unsalted butter
1½ cups diced celery

1½ cups diced yellow onion
4 ounces fresh mushrooms, sliced
8 ounces chopped fresh spinach,
  stems discarded
¾ cup all-purpose flour
½ cup milk
1 cup chicken stock
2½ pounds cooked chicken
  breasts, shredded
——
Mushroom Sauce

MUSHROOM SAUCE
½ cup sliced fresh mushrooms
2 tablespoons unsalted butter
2 tablespoons all-purpose flour
¾ cup chicken stock
½ cup heavy whipping cream
salt

Sauté mushrooms in butter until soft. Add flour, stock, and cream, stirring constantly, until thickened. Season with salt. Serve over Tea Room Chicken and Spinach Crêpes.

Basic Crêpes: Beat flour, milk, eggs, butter, and salt in a large bowl until combined. Heat a 7-inch skillet or crêpe pan over moderately high heat. Butter pan with a napkin or paper towel and wipe off any excess. Pan should be hot, but butter should not brown. Pour about ⅛ cup batter into pan. Quickly tilt and turn pan so that it is covered with batter. Cook 45 seconds, or until top is dry. Flip and cook other side about 15 seconds. Remove from pan. Repeat with remaining batter. Yields about 28 crêpes.

Filling: Melt 6 tablespoons butter in a large skillet. Add celery, onion, and mushrooms. Sauté until tender. Add spinach and cook 3 to 5 minutes. Vigorously whisk in flour, milk, and stock. Remove from heat. Add chicken and mix gently. Let cool.

Preheat oven to 350 degrees. Fill each crêpe with ⅓ cup filling. Roll and place seam-side down in a 9 by 13-inch shallow baking dish. Cover and bake 25 to 30 minutes. Serve with Mushroom Sauce (see accompanying recipe).

Middle Eastern Chicken

SERVES 4 TO 6

2 tablespoons unsalted butter
3 whole boneless, skinless
  chicken breasts
1 medium onion, chopped
½ red bell pepper, seeded and
  julienned
2 large garlic cloves, minced

1 ¼ teaspoons curry powder
1 can (14½ ounces) whole
  tomatoes plus liquid
½ cup dried currants
salt
freshly ground pepper
¼ cup toasted slivered almonds

Melt butter in a large skillet over medium-high heat. Place chicken in skillet and brown on both sides, about 4 minutes per side. Transfer chicken to a plate. Add onion and bell pepper to the skillet. Reduce heat to medium. Sauté vegetables until barely tender, about 4 minutes. Add garlic and curry powder. Stir 1 minute. Add tomatoes with their juice, breaking up tomatoes with a spoon. Bring mixture to a simmer. Return chicken to pan, along with any juices that may have accumulated on the plate. Cover skillet and simmer gently about 15 minutes. Uncover and add currants. Cook until chicken is tender, about 5 minutes. Season with salt and pepper. Arrange chicken on a serving platter. Spoon vegetables and sauce over chicken. Sprinkle with almonds and serve.

Chicken Curry

SERVES 6 TO 8

CURRY POWDER

Traditional Indian curry powder is a freshly ground combination of as many as 20 chiles, spices, herbs, and seeds. Commercial curry powder is quite different and comes in two varieties - standard and the hotter Madras. Both the freshly ground and the commercial curry powders vary greatly with region and brand, so experiment and choose your favorite.

4 tablespoons unsalted butter
4 medium onions, chopped
2 tart apples, peeled, cored,
  and chopped
6 ribs celery, chopped
5 tablespoons curry powder
¼ cup all-purpose flour
4 cups chicken stock
4 whole boneless, skinless chicken
  breasts, cooked and diced
½ cup raisins

——
6 cups cooked rice

Condiments:
chutney
grated coconut
peanuts
chopped green onions
pineapple cubes
chopped bacon

Melt butter in a large skillet. Add onions, apples, and celery. Sauté until tender. Combine curry powder and flour. Add to vegetables. Cook 1 minute. Stir in chicken stock until smooth. Add chicken and raisins. Cover and simmer 20 to 30 minutes. Serve with rice and an assortment of condiments.

Curried Chicken Kabobs

½ cup ground cocktail peanuts
1 tablespoon brown sugar,
   firmly packed
1 tablespoon curry powder
½ teaspoon crushed red
   pepper flakes

2 tablespoons fresh lemon juice
¼ cup soy sauce
1 clove garlic, crushed
3 whole boneless, skinless chicken
   breasts, cubed

Combine peanuts, brown sugar, curry, red pepper, lemon juice, soy sauce, and garlic in a large bowl. Add chicken and toss to coat thoroughly. Cover and chill at least 3 hours.

   Prepare grill. Thread chicken on skewers. Grill 8 to 12 minutes, turning frequently.

Chicken Strudel

1½ pounds boneless, skinless
   chicken breasts, poached and
   chopped (See accompanying
   instructions.)
2 tablespoons olive oil
1 medium onion, chopped
1 pound fresh spinach,
   coarse stems discarded
12 ounces Muenster
   cheese, shredded (3 cups)

2 tablespoons dry white wine
½ teaspoon salt
½ teaspoon freshly ground pepper
1 large egg, beaten
1 pound frozen phyllo pastry, thawed
½ cup (1 stick) unsalted butter,
   melted
⅔ cup bread crumbs
paprika

POACHING CHICKEN

Chicken meat used in soups, salads, sandwiches, and curry dishes is usually poached. To poach chicken, simmer the chicken in salted stock or water to which 2 ribs of celery, 1 onion, and 1 bay leaf have been added. Cook the chicken until just tender, approximately 20 to 30 minutes.

Heat oil in a medium skillet. Add onion and sauté until tender. Add spinach and continue to cook 5 minutes, stirring frequently. Remove from heat. Let cool. Stir in cheese, wine, salt, pepper, and egg. Add chicken.

   Preheat oven to 375 degrees. On waxed paper, place 1 sheet of phyllo. Brush with butter and sprinkle with 2 tablespoons bread crumbs. Repeat to make 4 to 5 layers. Spoon half of chicken mixture on one end. Roll and tuck ends under the strudel. Brush with butter and make diagonal cuts on top through dough about 1 inch apart. Sprinkle top with paprika. Repeat process to make the second strudel. Place both strudels on a greased baking sheet. Bake 20 minutes. Cool before slicing.

Texas White Chili

1 pound dried white beans
14 cups chicken broth
1½ medium onions, chopped
2 cloves garlic
1 teaspoon salt
1 tablespoon vegetable oil
1 can (4 ounces) whole green chilies,
    drained and chopped, or 1 poblano
    chile pepper, roasted (page 40)
2 teaspoons ground cumin
2 tablespoons chopped fresh oregano

2 teaspoons ground coriander
pinch ground cloves
pinch cayenne pepper
1 bag (16 ounces) frozen
    white shoepeg corn
4 boneless, skinless chicken breast
    halves, cooked and diced
———
4 ounces Monterey Jack cheese,
    shredded (1 cup)
4 green onions, thinly sliced

Combine beans, stock, half the onions, garlic, and salt in a large soup pot. Bring to a boil. Reduce heat, cover, and simmer 1½ hours, or until beans are very tender. Add more chicken broth as needed.

Heat oil in a large skillet. Add remaining onion, chilies, cumin, oregano, coriander, cloves, and cayenne pepper. Mix thoroughly. Cook 10 minutes. Fold corn into mixture. Continue cooking 12 minutes. Combine corn mixture, bean mixture, and chicken. Spoon chili into 6 individual bowls. Sprinkle with cheese and green onions.

Thanksgiving Turkey

SERVES 12 TO 14

1½ bunches each fresh thyme,
    sage, basil, and oregano,
    coarsely chopped
1½ teaspoons each dried thyme,
    sage, basil, and oregano
2 tablespoons unsalted butter,
    at room temperature
1 tablespoon salt
1 tablespoon freshly ground pepper
1 fresh turkey (12 to 14 pounds)
2 small onions, cut into
    ¼-inch slices
2 carrots, cut into ¼-inch rounds
2 ribs celery, cut into
    ¼-inch pieces
2 leeks, cut into ¼-inch rounds
2 cloves garlic, sliced
olive oil

——

Herb Butter:
1 cup (2 sticks) unsalted butter,
    at room temperature
2 tablespoons minced fresh parsley
2 tablespoons minced fresh sage
2 tablespoons minced fresh thyme
2 tablespoons minced fresh basil
1 tablespoon minced fresh oregano
1 clove garlic, minced
salt
freshly ground pepper

——

Jalapeño and Cranberry Jelly or
Mexican Cranberry Sauce

Preheat oven to 450 degrees. Mix fresh herbs, dried herbs, butter, salt, and pepper. Rub into turkey cavity. Stuff onions, carrots, celery, leeks, and garlic into cavity. Truss with string. Rub outside of bird with olive oil. Place on a rack in a roasting pan. Roast 30 minutes.

Herb Butter: Combine butter, parsley, sage, thyme, basil, oregano, garlic, salt, and pepper in a small bowl. (This can be refrigerated up to 4 days, but bring to room temperature before using.)

Reduce oven to 325 degrees and brush turkey with half of Herb Butter. Roast another 30 minutes and brush with remaining Herb Butter. Continue to roast, basting occasionally with pan juices, until thigh temperature measures 170 degrees on a meat thermometer, about 2¼ hours. Serve with Jalapeño and Cranberry Jelly or Mexican Cranberry Sauce.

Jalapeño and Cranberry Jelly:
6 jalapeños, seeded and quartered
2½ cups cranberry juice cocktail
7 cups sugar

6 ounces liquid fruit pectin
1 cup distilled white vinegar
red food coloring (optional)

Place jalapeños and cranberry juice in blender. Process until jalapeños are finely chopped. Combine jalapeño mixture with sugar in a large Dutch oven. Bring to a full rolling boil. Add pectin. Return to a boil. Cook 2 to 3 minutes. Add vinegar and food coloring if desired. Cool. Spoon into sterilized jars and refrigerate.

Mexican Cranberry Sauce:
1 can (16 ounces) whole berry
    cranberry sauce
1 tablespoon chopped fresh cilantro

1 jar (10½ ounces) hot jalapeño
    pepper jelly, preferably red

Combine cranberry sauce, cilantro, and jelly in a small saucepan. Cook over low heat, stirring often, until jelly melts. Cool. Spoon into sterilized jars. This will keep for several months in the refrigerator.

A THANKSGIVING TRADITION

Since the Pilgrims celebrated their first Thanksgiving, turkey has been an indispensable part of this holiday tradition for almost every American, regardless of their ethnic heritage. Producing a juicy, exquisitely browned bird for appreciative guests takes time, but it's one of the cook's rewards for all her hard work in creating a table laden with good food and good cheer. And that's the real point of Thanksgiving: to share our abundance and celebrate and renew the bonds of friendship and family ties. And most of all, it's about memories - the ones we make and the ones (and they're usually the best ones) that happen without our even trying. This year at Thanksgiving as you polish the glasses and take down your best china and carefully launder your finest linens, relax and enjoy the experience. The memories will take care of themselves.

Garlic Rosemary Cornish Game Hens

SERVES 6

6 fresh Cornish game hens
2 tablespoons minced garlic
2 tablespoons chopped fresh
  rosemary

½ teaspoon freshly ground pepper
¼ teaspoon crushed red pepper
½ teaspoon salt

Preheat oven to 450 degrees. Trim hens of any visible fat. Rinse and pat dry. Combine garlic, rosemary, black pepper, red pepper, and salt. Rub mixture over and under skin of each hen. Rub any excess seasonings into cavities. Close each cavity with a 6-inch bamboo skewer or cooking twine. Place hens in single layer on a rack in a large roasting pan. Roast 15 minutes. Lower temperature to 350 degrees. Roast 35 minutes longer, or until juices run clear when inner thigh is pierced.

Quail with Onions, Mushrooms, and Peaches

SERVES 4

QUAIL AND DOVE

These small game birds are very tender due to their size and flavorful due to the nuts and berries they eat.

8 fresh quail, skinned
2 tablespoons all-purpose flour
1 tablespoon Italian seasoned
  bread crumbs
2 tablespoons olive oil
1 large sweet yellow onion, thinly
  sliced
8 fresh mushrooms, sliced
3 cloves garlic, minced
2 fresh peaches, pitted, peeled, and
  sliced

½ cup dry white wine
½ cup fresh orange juice
1 beef bouillon cube
1 teaspoon ground ginger
½ teaspoon ground cinnamon
salt
freshly ground pepper
2 tablespoons brandy
———
2 cups cooked wild rice

Rinse and pat quail dry. Place quail, flour, and bread crumbs in a brown paper bag. Shake until evenly coated. Heat oil in a large skillet over medium-high heat. Add quail and brown until golden, about 10 minutes on each side. Add onion, mushrooms, and garlic. Sauté another 5 minutes, or until onions are tender. Stir in peaches. Stir in white wine, orange juice, and bouillon cube. Stir until bouillon is dissolved. Add ginger and cinnamon. Season with salt and pepper. Allow liquid to reduce by about one-third, simmering over medium-high heat, about 5 to 7 minutes. Cover and simmer on low heat another 15 minutes. Stir in brandy. Serve with wild rice.

Quail After the Hunt

SERVES 6 TO 8

½ cup (1 stick) unsalted butter
12 fresh quail, breasted
8 ounces Jalapeño Jack cheese,
  shredded (2 cups)
4 ounces Italian sausage, casings
  removed, browned, and crumbled

½ cup chopped fresh herbs
  (a combination of Mexican mint
  marigold, thyme, or cilantro)
24 slices prosciutto

Preheat oven to 350 degrees. Melt butter in a 9 by 13-inch baking dish.
Set aside. Carefully cut a slit into side of each breast. Combine cheese
and sausage with herbs. Stuff each breast with mixture. Wrap stuffed
breast with prosciutto and hold together with wooden picks. Place breasts
in prepared dish and coat with butter. Bake 10 to 15 minutes, turning
breasts once.

MEXICAN MINT MARIGOLD

A beautiful, fragrant plant with an abundance of yellow blossoms, Mexican mint marigold is also known as sweet mace. With its mild anise flavor, it tastes a bit like tarragon.

Dove Madeira

SERVES 4

8 fresh doves
¼ cup fresh lemon juice
1 teaspoon salt
½ teaspoon freshly ground pepper
3 tablespoons plus 2
  tablespoons unsalted butter
3 tablespoons chopped onion

2 tablespoons all-purpose flour
½ cup Madeira
½ cup chicken stock
¼ cup heavy whipping cream
1 tablespoon minced fresh thyme

———

2 cups cooked wild rice

Preheat oven to 350 degrees. Rub doves inside and out with lemon
juice, salt, and pepper. Melt 3 tablespoons butter in a large skillet over
medium heat. Add doves and cook until browned. Add onion and sauté
until transparent. Remove doves and onions to a 7 by 11-inch baking
dish. Set aside.

    Melt remaining 2 tablespoons butter in a separate skillet. Stir in flour
and cook 1 or 2 minutes. Remove from heat. Stir in Madeira, stock, and
cream. Return to heat, stirring until sauce thickens. Pour sauce over birds.
Cover and bake 40 minutes. Serve with wild rice.

SEAFOOD

Shrimp with Tomato Pepper Sauce

Herbed Baked Salmon

SERVES 4

1½ pounds thickly cut fresh
   salmon fillet, skin intact
¾ cup mayonnaise (can use light
   or nonfat)
3 ounces Parmesan cheese,
   freshly grated (¾ cup)
6 tablespoons minced green onions
3 tablespoons chopped fresh herbs
   (basil, dill, parsley, chervil,
   thyme, or a combination)

2 tablespoons minced red bell pepper
juice of ½ lemon
salt
freshly ground pepper
cayenne pepper

SALMON

About 90 percent of North
American salmon come from
Alaskan waters. A firm fish with a
distinctive flavor, common species
include chinook, coho, sockeye,
and chum.

Preheat oven to 350 degrees. Mix mayonnaise, Parmesan, green onions,
herbs, bell pepper, lemon juice, salt, pepper, and cayenne in a small bowl.
Spread over salmon to within ½ inch of edges. Spray shallow baking dish
with nonstick cooking spray and warm in oven 20 minutes. Place salmon
skin side down on dish (it should sizzle). Bake 20 minutes or until just
flaky. Do not overcook. Salmon should be medium-rare to medium. Skin
should be crispy and may be eaten or removed, as desired.

Marinated Salmon Seared in a Pepper Crust

SERVES 2

¾ pound center-cut fresh salmon
   fillet, skin removed and halved
2 tablespoons soy sauce
1 clove garlic, mashed to a paste

2 teaspoons fresh lemon juice
1 teaspoon sugar
4 teaspoons freshly ground pepper
2 tablespoons olive oil

Have butcher prepare salmon fillet. Combine soy sauce, garlic, lemon
juice, and sugar in a plastic bag. Add salmon, shaking to coat evenly.
Marinate in refrigerator 30 minutes. Remove salmon from bag, discard
marinade, and pat dry. Press pepper on each side of fillet. Heat oil in a
large skillet over moderately high heat until it is hot, but not smoking.
Sauté salmon 2 minutes on each side, or until it just flakes. Transfer
salmon to paper towels and drain. Serve immediately.

Grilled Salmon Steaks with Watercress Mustard Butter

SERVES 6

Watercress Mustard Butter:
2 bunches watercress, minced
  (1 cup)
½ cup (1 stick) unsalted butter,
  at room temperature
1 tablespoon minced shallot
1 tablespoon Dijon mustard

¼ teaspoon plus ¼ teaspoon salt
¼ teaspoon freshly ground pepper
——

6 fresh salmon steaks (8 ounces each),
  1 inch thick
——

watercress sprigs

Watercress Mustard Butter: Combine watercress, butter, shallot, mustard, ¼ teaspoon salt, and pepper in a small bowl. Refrigerate at least 1 hour.

Prepare grill. Season fish with remaining salt and dot one side with half of the mustard butter mixture. Arrange fish, butter side up, and grill 4 minutes. Turn and dot with remaining butter mixture. Cook 3 minutes. Garnish with watercress sprigs and serve immediately.

Garlic Ginger Grilled Tuna

SERVES 4

TUNA

Tuna steaks are slices cut cross-wise, ¾ to 1¾ inches thick, and usually boneless and skinless. Varieties of tuna include albacore, yellowfin, bluefin, and bonito, albacore being the mildest flavored and bonito the strongest.

MANGO CHILE SALSA

3 mangoes, peeled, pitted, and chopped
1 small red bell pepper, seeded and minced
½ large red onion, minced
2 tablespoons minced fresh cilantro
1 serrano chile pepper, seeded and minced
¼ cup fresh lime juice
¼ cup fresh pineapple juice

Combine mangoes, bell pepper, onion, cilantro, and serrano pepper. Stir in lime juice and pineapple juice. Blend well. Yields 1 cup.

Serve with Garlic Ginger Grilled Tuna or as a dip.

4 fresh tuna steaks (6 ounces each)
extra virgin olive oil
freshly ground pepper
——
1 teaspoon minced fresh ginger
1 teaspoon minced garlic
salt

½ teaspoon white pepper
¼ cup fresh lemon juice
¼ cup white wine vinegar
¼ cup extra virgin olive oil
——
Southeast Asian Pesto or Mango
  Chile Salsa

Brush tuna steaks with olive oil and season with pepper. Refrigerate until ready to use. Combine ginger, garlic, salt, pepper, lemon juice, and vinegar in a saucepan. Boil 2 to 3 minutes. Remove from heat. Let cool. Whisk in oil.

Prepare grill. Brush tuna with marinade, then grill quickly until it feels springy to the touch, about 5 minutes per side. Serve with Southeast Asian Pesto or Mango Chile Salsa (see accompanying recipe).

Southeast Asian Pesto:
2 or 3 large cloves garlic
½ cup coarsely chopped fresh ginger
¼ cup sliced fresh lemongrass,
  fleshy part only
½ cup chopped green onions
½ cup chopped fresh basil
½ cup chopped fresh parsley

½ cup chopped fresh cilantro
½ to 1 teaspoon chopped fresh jalapeño
½ cup toasted nuts of choice
¼ to ⅓ cup rice vinegar
1 teaspoon salt
⅔ to ¾ cup olive oil
2 teaspoons sesame oil

Process garlic, ginger, lemongrass, green onions, basil, parsley, cilantro, jalapeño, nuts, vinegar, and salt in a food processor until smooth. Add oils gradually, using only enough to allow herbs and vegetables to become a smooth paste. Cover and refrigerate. Bring to room temperature before serving. Yields 3 cups.

Grilled Swordfish

8 fresh swordfish steaks
(6 to 8 ounces each),
1 inch thick
2 tablespoons olive oil
salt

freshly ground pepper
——
8 lime wedges
Avocado Butter or Tomatillo
Papaya Salsa

Pierce steaks on both sides with a fork. Brush with oil and season with salt and pepper. Cover and refrigerate until ready to grill.

Prepare grill or broiler. Discard marinade and arrange steaks on rack. Grill 9 minutes, turning once. Transfer to a warm serving plate. Serve with Avocado Butter or Tomatillo Papaya Salsa. Garnish with lime wedges.

Avocado Butter:

½ cup (1 stick) unsalted butter,
at room temperature
½ cup mashed avocado
5 tablespoons fresh lime juice

2 tablespoons minced fresh parsley
2 cloves garlic, minced
salt

Cream butter in a small bowl. Beat in avocado, lime juice, parsley, and garlic. Season with salt. Cover and refrigerate.

Tomatillo Papaya Salsa:

6 tomatillos, husked, rinsed, and
coarsely chopped
1 papaya, seeded, peeled,
and chopped
½ red onion, minced

1 fresh jalapeño, seeded and minced
2 tablespoons chopped fresh cilantro
2 tablespoons fresh lime juice
1 tablespoon olive oil
½ red bell pepper, seeded and chopped

Combine tomatillos, papaya, red onion, jalapeño, cilantro, lime juice, olive oil, and bell pepper in a medium bowl. Cover and chill 6 to 8 hours.

SALSAS

Salsa is the Spanish word for sauce. Traditionally salsas have consisted of a mixture of chiles, tomatoes, garlic, cilantro, and salt. It is still a diced condiment, but today the ingredients and combinations are creative and endless. Try your favorite combinations of fruits or vegetables, or even a combination of both. Salsas are usually eaten with chips or bread, served as an accompaniment to grilled meats, or spooned over beans or cream cheese.

*If you find the idea of
selecting fresh fish to be
a daunting prospect, your
best course of action may be
to find a good fish market
and make friends with
the owner. If, however,
your nearest fish market
is the seafood section of
your local supermarket,
look for the following signs
of quality and freshness:*

- *Bright, clear, bulging eyes*
- *Rosy, sweet-smelling gills*
- *Shimmery, tightly clinging scales*
- *Firm, springy flesh*
- *Fresh, clean smell (truly fresh fish smell fresh, like the ocean)*

*Plan to use the fish the
day of purchase, or store
fish on ice the way the
markets do. As for quanti-
ties, allow 13 ounces per
serving for whole fish and
6 to 8 ounces per serving
for steaks and fillets.*

Pecan-Crusted Snapper with Chardonnay Butter Sauce

SERVES 4

Chardonnay Butter Sauce:
2 cups plus ¼ cup Chardonnay
½ cup fresh lemon juice
2 tablespoons cornstarch
½ cup (1 stick) unsalted butter,
    cut into 8 pieces
1 teaspoon salt
⅛ teaspoon white pepper

——

2½ cups pecan pieces, finely
    chopped
½ cup cornstarch

2 teaspoons salt
1 teaspoon white pepper
4 fresh snapper fillets (6 ounces
    each), skin removed
3 to 4 tablespoons olive oil

——

bowtie pasta, cooked al dente
leeks, julienned and lightly steamed
carrots, julienned and lightly
    steamed
toasted pecan pieces

Chardonnay Butter Sauce: Combine 2 cups Chardonnay and all but
1 tablespoon of lemon juice in a sauté pan. Boil on high heat until liquid
is reduced to one-half. Blend cornstarch and ¼ cup Chardonnay until
smooth. Add to boiling mixture. Stir and simmer 5 minutes. Turn off
heat. Whisk in butter piece by piece. Whisk in reserved 1 tablespoon
lemon juice. Season with salt and pepper. Remove from heat. Set aside.

Combine pecans, cornstarch, salt, and pepper in a shallow dish. Coat
fillets by turning twice in pecan mixture and pressing lightly into fish.
Heat oil in large sauté pan or skillet over medium-high heat. Place fillets
in pan. Reduce heat to medium. Cook 3 to 4 minutes on each side, or
until done. Remove from heat.

Place ¼ cup sauce in center of each plate. Place snapper on top
of sauce. Garnish with bowtie pasta, leeks, carrots, and pecan pieces.
Serve immediately.

Red Snapper with Tomato Caper Sauce

SERVES 4

Tomato Caper Sauce:
3 tablespoons olive oil
1 onion, chopped
3 cloves garlic, minced
1 can (14 ounces) chopped tomatoes
4 Roma tomatoes, peeled,
    seeded, and diced

¼ cup minced fresh parsley
3 tablespoons capers, rinsed and
    drained
2 teaspoons minced fresh oregano
1½ pounds fresh red snapper fillet,
    skin removed

Tomato Caper Sauce: Heat oil in a medium skillet. Add onion and cook
until transparent. Add garlic, tomatoes, parsley, capers, and oregano.
Bring to a boil. Reduce heat. Simmer covered 5 minutes. Remove lid and
simmer 15 minutes more.

Preheat oven to 450 degrees. Place snapper in a baking dish. Top with
sauce. Bake 12 to 15 minutes. Serve immediately.

Baked Red Snapper with Feta

SERVES 4 TO 6

2 fresh red snapper fillets (1¼
   pounds each), skin removed
2 tablespoons plus 2 tablespoons
   olive oil
¼ cup minced onion
2 cloves garlic, minced
1 can (14½ ounces) whole
   tomatoes
½ cup tomato paste

2 tablespoons capers, rinsed and drained
1 teaspoon dried oregano
¼ teaspoon crushed red pepper
¼ cup plus 2 tablespoons chopped
   fresh parsley
salt
freshly ground pepper
4 ounces feta cheese, crumbled (1 cup)
1 tablespoon ouzo liqueur

Preheat oven to 425 degrees. Pat fish fillets with a damp cloth. Heat
2 tablespoons oil in a medium saucepan over medium heat. Add onion
and garlic. Cook, stirring, until onion is transparent. Add tomatoes,
tomato paste, capers, oregano, red pepper flakes, ¼ cup parsley, salt,
and pepper. Cook 10 minutes.

   Pour remaining 2 tablespoons oil into a baking dish. Add fish in a single
layer. Pour tomato sauce over fillets. Bake 15 minutes. Sprinkle with feta.
Bake 5 minutes. Sprinkle with ouzo and remaining 2 tablespoons chopped
parsley. Serve piping hot.

OUZO

*Ouzo is a clear, sweet, anise-
flavored liqueur from Greece.*

Southwestern Snapper

SERVES 4

6 cups mixed salad greens
½ cup chopped fresh cilantro
1 red bell pepper, seeded and sliced
1 yellow bell pepper, seeded
   and sliced
———
kernels of 2 ears cooked corn (1 cup)
3 Roma tomatoes, peeled, seeded,
   and chopped
¼ cup toasted pine nuts
1 avocado, pitted, peeled, and diced
———

¼ cup fresh lime juice
2 cloves garlic, minced
1½ teaspoons minced fresh oregano
½ teaspoon chili powder
¼ teaspoon salt
¼ teaspoon freshly ground pepper
¼ cup olive oil
———
4 red snapper fillets (6 ounces each),
   skin intact
2 tablespoons olive oil
¼ teaspoon freshly ground pepper

Combine salad greens, cilantro, and bell peppers in a large bowl. Cover
and chill.

   Toss corn, tomatoes, and pine nuts in a small bowl. Set aside.

   Heat lime juice, garlic, oregano, chili powder, salt, and pepper in a
small saucepan over medium heat. Whisk in olive oil. Set aside and
keep warm.

   Preheat broiler. Arrange fillets in a shallow pan, skin side down. Brush
with olive oil and sprinkle with pepper. Broil 6 inches from heat 8 to
10 minutes, or until fish flakes easily.

   When ready to serve, toss avocado into corn mixture. Arrange fillets
on greens. Top with corn mixture, then drizzle with warm dressing.
Serve immediately.

IS IT DONE?

*To test fish for doneness, prod it
with a fork at its thickest point. A
properly cooked fish is opaque, has
milky white juices, and just begins
to flake easily. Undercooked fish is
translucent and has clear and
watery juices.*

Stir Fried Fish with Sweet and Sour Sauce

SERVES 4

HOOKED ON TROUT

Rainbow trout, named for the colorful stripe that runs down its back, or the steelhead trout, which can weigh as much as 40 pounds, definitely conjure up visions of the mountain campsite with a freshly caught trout sizzling in the breakfast frying pan. However, farm-raised trout are the ones we are sure to find at our local fish market, and they usually weigh less than 1 pound. Trout has few bones to tangle with and usually tastes best when cooked simply and quickly.

1½ pounds fresh speckled trout, bass, or other firm fish fillets, cut into ¾-inch slices
2 tablespoons cornstarch
1 cup all-purpose flour
3 tablespoons canola oil
2 teaspoons baking powder
½ teaspoon salt
1 cup water

Sweet and Sour Sauce:
1 cup fresh pineapple juice
1 tablespoon cornstarch

6 tablespoons sugar
¼ cup red wine vinegar
¼ teaspoon Tabasco Sauce
⅛ teaspoon salt
1 tablespoon canola oil
1 teaspoon grated fresh ginger
1 teaspoon grated lemon zest
1 red bell pepper, seeded and julienned

──────
1½ to 3 cups peanut oil (deep frying)
──────

3 cups cooked white rice

Toss fish with 2 tablespoons cornstarch in a medium bowl to coat. Set aside. Mix flour, 3 tablespoons oil, baking powder, and salt in a small bowl. Gradually add water, whisking until batter is smooth. Pour batter over fish and stir gently to coat all pieces. Let stand 15 minutes.

Sweet and Sour Sauce: Whisk pineapple juice, cornstarch, sugar, vinegar, Tabasco, and salt in a small bowl to blend. Set aside.

Heat oil in an electric wok or large skillet on medium-high heat. Add ginger and lemon zest. Stir fry until fragrant, about 30 seconds. Add bell pepper and stir fry just to heat through, about 30 seconds. Add pineapple juice mixture. Cook until sauce is thick and clear, stirring constantly, about 1 minute. Transfer to a bowl. Keep warm.

Wipe wok with paper towel. Heat oil in wok to 375 degrees. Add batter-coated fish pieces in batches. Fry until crisp and golden, about 4 minutes. Transfer fish to paper towel-lined plate. Drain. Reheat oil as necessary between batches.

Arrange fish over rice on platter. Spoon sauce over fish and serve immediately.

Sautéed Trout with Parsley Caper Sauce

SERVES 4

¾ cup all-purpose flour
¼ teaspoon salt
¾ teaspoon freshly ground pepper
¾ cup skim milk
1½ pounds fresh trout fillets
3 tablespoons plus 3 tablespoons
 olive oil

Parsley Caper Sauce:
4 tablespoons unsalted butter

1¼ pounds Roma tomatoes,
 peeled, seeded, and diced
6 tablespoons chopped fresh parsley
2 tablespoons fresh lemon juice
1½ tablespoons capers, rinsed and
 drained

————

1 lemon, sliced
1 tablespoon capers, rinsed and drained

Combine flour, salt, and pepper in a shallow dish. Pour milk into another shallow dish. Dip one fish fillet into milk to moisten, then into flour mixture. Turn to coat completely. Place fillet on large sheet of waxed paper. Repeat procedure with remaining fillets.

Heat 3 tablespoons oil in heavy large skillet over medium heat. Add half of fish to skillet and sauté until light brown and cooked through, about 2 minutes per side. Transfer to a serving platter. Heat 3 more tablespoons oil in same skillet. Sauté remaining fish fillets. Transfer fish to platter. Set aside and keep warm.

Parsley Caper Sauce: Melt butter in same skillet. Add tomatoes and simmer until tomatoes are soft, pressing and stirring occasionally, about 5 minutes. Stir in parsley, lemon juice, and capers. Cook until ingredients are thickened and reduced to sauce consistency, stirring occasionally, about 5 minutes. Spoon Parsley Caper Sauce over fish fillets. Garnish platter with lemon slices and additional capers.

Parmesan-Crusted Catfish

SERVES 4 TO 6

1 cup finely crushed Ritz crackers
1 tablespoon chopped fresh parsley
½ teaspoon salt
¼ teaspoon cayenne pepper
¼ teaspoon freshly ground pepper

6 fresh catfish fillets
½ cup (1 stick) unsalted butter,
 melted
2 ounces Parmesan cheese, freshly
 grated (½ cup)

Combine cracker crumbs, parsley, salt, cayenne, and pepper in a shallow dish. Dip fillets in butter and roll in cracker crumb mixture.

Preheat oven to 400 degrees. Place fillets on baking sheets that have been lined with aluminum foil and sprayed with nonstick cooking spray. Bake 20 minutes or until fish is golden brown. Sprinkle with Parmesan. Serve immediately.

CRABS

From Alaska to northern California, and Canada to the Gulf, the seas yield a great gift to our tables, the popular and versatile crab. The most popular crabs in America are the blue crab, which comes from the Atlantic and Gulf coasts; the incomparable Dungeness crab from the West coast; and the giant Alaskan king crab, which can weigh up to 20 pounds and is prized for its delectable scarlet-skinned white leg meat. Regional favorites include the rock crab taken from New England and California coasts and the stone crab, found mostly off the coast of Florida. Only the heavy, black-tipped claws of these crabs are eaten. There are different ways to go about catching a crab. If you're into it for the experience and you have all the time in the world, the tried and true method of a chicken neck attached to a piece of string will do just fine. More serious crabbers may opt for crab pots or rings baited with fish. Either way, the rewards are a sweet, succulent, delicious dish filled with all the goodness of the sea.

Galveston Crab Cakes

1 pound fresh lump crabmeat, shells removed
¾ cup Italian flavored bread crumbs
1 large egg, beaten
¼ cup mayonnaise
1 teaspoon Worcestershire sauce
1 teaspoon dry mustard
½ teaspoon salt
¼ teaspoon freshly ground pepper
2 tablespoons chopped fresh parsley

¼ teaspoon cayenne pepper
1 teaspoon prepared horseradish
1 tablespoon fresh lemon juice
2 tablespoons unsalted butter
2 tablespoons olive oil
————
lemon wedges
Gulf Coast Tartar Sauce or Roasted Corn and Tomato Tartar Sauce

Place crabmeat in a large bowl. Add bread crumbs and mix gently. Combine egg, mayonnaise, Worcestershire, mustard, salt, pepper, parsley, cayenne, horseradish, and lemon juice in a separate bowl. Gently blend in crabmeat mixture. Form mixture into 6 large crab cakes. Heat butter and oil in a large skillet. Add crab cakes and sauté until golden brown. Garnish with lemon wedges. Serve with Gulf Coast Tartar Sauce or Roasted Corn and Tomato Tartar Sauce.

Gulf Coast Tartar Sauce:
3 tablespoons fresh lemon juice
2 tablespoons Dijon mustard
½ teaspoon cayenne pepper
1 large egg
1 large egg yolk
¼ teaspoon salt
pinch freshly ground pepper
½ cup vegetable oil

½ cup chopped green onions
¼ cup chopped fresh parsley
½ teaspoon soy sauce
1 teaspoon Worcestershire sauce
2 tablespoons minced dill pickle
2 tablespoons chopped fresh dill
1 tablespoon capers, rinsed and drained
1 teaspoon Tabasco Sauce

Blend lemon juice, mustard, cayenne, egg, egg yolk, salt, and pepper in a food processor until smooth. With the machine running, add oil in a thin stream, blending until thickened. Add green onions, parsley, soy sauce, Worcestershire, pickle, dill, capers, and Tabasco. Pulse several times until well combined. (Gulf Coast Tartar Sauce may be made 1 day in advance and refrigerated.) Yields 2 cups.

Roasted Corn and Tomato Tartar Sauce:
1 can (15¼ ounces) corn, drained
¼ cup mayonnaise
2 Roma tomatoes, peeled, seeded, and diced

2 green onions, minced
½ teaspoon Creole seasoning
¼ teaspoon salt
freshly ground pepper

Preheat oven to 350 degrees. Place corn on a baking sheet and roast in oven 15 minutes. Combine corn, mayonnaise, tomatoes, onions, Creole seasoning, and salt. Season with pepper. Cover and refrigerate until ready to use. Yields 2 cups.

Tea Room Crab Cakes

SERVES 4 TO 6

2 tablespoons unsalted butter

1 medium yellow onion, diced

2 large eggs, lightly beaten

¼ teaspoon cayenne pepper

8 ounces mozzarella cheese,
  shredded (2 cups)

½ cup bread crumbs

¼ teaspoon salt

½ teaspoon freshly ground pepper

1 pound fresh lump crabmeat,
  shells removed

———

2 cups all-purpose flour

1 cup milk

1 large egg, lightly beaten

2½ cups bread crumbs

2 tablespoons plus 2 tablespoons
  unsalted butter

2 tablespoons plus 2 tablespoons
  vegetable oil

Rémoulade Sauce

Melt butter in a sauté pan. Add onion and cook until transparent. Combine onion, eggs, cayenne, cheese, bread crumbs, salt, and pepper in a large bowl. Mix well. Gently toss in crabmeat. Form crab mixture into 10 to 12 small crab cakes. Chill covered at least 30 minutes, but no longer than 2 hours.

Place flour in a small bowl. Combine milk and egg in a separate bowl. Place bread crumbs in a shallow dish. Dust crab cakes in flour, dip in milk and egg mixture, then dip in bread crumbs. Heat 2 tablespoons butter and 2 tablespoons oil in a large skillet. Cook half of crab cakes over medium heat, about 4 to 6 minutes per side, or until golden brown. Transfer to paper towels to drain. Add remaining butter and oil to skillet and cook remaining crab cakes. Drain. Serve immediately with Rémoulade Sauce (see accompanying recipe).

RÉMOULADE SAUCE

¼ cup Creole mustard

½ cup prepared mustard

2 tablespoons paprika

⅛ teaspoon cayenne pepper

1 teaspoon salt

½ cup distilled white vinegar

½ cup chopped green onions

dash Tabasco Sauce

½ cup chopped celery

½ cup chopped fresh parsley

½ cup ketchup

2 cloves garlic, minced

3 large eggs, at room temperature

juice of 1 lemon

1⅓ cups vegetable oil

Combine mustards, paprika, cayenne, salt, vinegar, green onions, Tabasco, celery, parsley, ketchup, garlic, eggs, and lemon juice in a blender. Process at high speed until blended. Gradually add oil in a steady stream until sauce thickens to mayonnaise consistency. Cover and chill. Serve with Tea Room Crab Cakes or boiled shrimp. Yields 3 cups.

Shrimp and Crab Picante

SERVES 8

4 tablespoons unsalted butter

3 cloves garlic, minced

1 large onion, chopped

1 large green bell pepper, seeded
  and chopped

1 bunch green onions, chopped

2 cans (10 ounces each) diced
  tomatoes with green chilies

1 can (14 ounces) tomatoes,
  with no salt added

1 teaspoon Worcestershire sauce

1 pound fresh shrimp, boiled (page 48),
  peeled, and deveined

1 pound fresh lump crabmeat,
  shells removed

———

6 cups cooked rice

4 green onions, sliced

Melt butter in a large skillet. Add garlic, onion, bell pepper, and green onions. Sauté until tender. Blend tomatoes in a food processor until smooth. Add to vegetable mixture. Reduce heat and simmer about 30 minutes. Stir in Worcestershire, shrimp, and crabmeat. Continue cooking 20 minutes. Water can be added if mixture is too thick. Serve over rice and garnish with green onions.

Scallops in Creamy Red Chile Sauce

SERVES 4

SCALLOPS

The two best-known species of scallops are the sea scallop and the bay scallop. Bay scallops are smaller, sweeter, and generally more expensive than the sea scallop. Scallops are usually sold shucked as they perish quickly out of water. Look for scallops with a sweet smell and a fresh, moist sheen. If they appear to be melting into one another, they are past their prime. Also avoid those that are stark white, which is a sign that they have been soaked in water to increase their weight.

Creamy Red Chile Sauce:
1 ancho chile pepper
1 ½ cups hot water
1 large red bell pepper, seeded and diced
½ cup diced onions
2 serrano chile peppers, seeded and diced
1 fresh jalapeño, seeded and diced

1 ½ teaspoons toasted coriander seeds
1 clove garlic, minced
½ cup heavy whipping cream
salt
————
2 pounds fresh sea scallops
3 tablespoons vegetable oil
2 tablespoons fresh lime juice
2 tablespoons chopped fresh parsley

Creamy Red Chile Sauce: Place ancho chile in a small bowl and cover with hot water. Soak 30 minutes. Remove ancho chile from water and pour water into a large skillet. Remove seeds and chop ancho chile. Place chopped ancho chile, bell pepper, onions, serranos, jalapeño, coriander, and garlic in water in skillet. Simmer until bell pepper is tender, about 20 minutes. Purée sauce in a blender or food processor until smooth. Return to skillet. Stir in cream. Cook over medium-high heat until sauce is reduced by one-half, about 2 minutes. Season with salt. Keep warm.

Pat scallops dry, cutting any large ones in half. Heat oil in a large skillet over high heat. Add scallops and sauté 2 minutes until opaque. Remove to a serving platter. Sprinkle scallops with lime juice. Boil pan juices 30 seconds, then stir in chile sauce mixture. Heat 2 minutes until warm. Pour sauce over scallops and sprinkle with parsley. Serve immediately.

Seafood Brochette

SERVES 4

½ cup sherry or white wine
¼ cup vegetable oil
¼ cup soy sauce
½ teaspoon ground ginger
1 clove garlic, minced
————
1 pound fresh shrimp, peeled and deveined

½ pound fresh scallops
8 fresh mushrooms
1 onion, cut into chunks
8 cherry tomatoes
1 yellow bell pepper, seeded and cut into 8 chunks
————
3 cups cooked white rice

Combine sherry, oil, soy sauce, ginger, and garlic in small bowl. Pour all but ¼ cup marinade into a plastic bag. Add shrimp and scallops. Marinate 1 hour in refrigerator.

Prepare grill. Drain shrimp and scallops. Thread shrimp and scallops alternately on skewers with mushrooms, onion, tomatoes, and bell pepper. Grill 8 to 10 minutes, turning and basting frequently with reserved ¼ cup marinade. Serve over rice.

Shrimp Olé

¼ cup plus ¼ cup olive oil
2 red bell peppers, roasted (page 40),
    peeled, seeded, and diced
2 poblano chile peppers, roasted,
    peeled, seeded, and diced
½ red onion, diced
1 clove garlic, diced
2 Roma tomatoes, diced

juice of 4 limes
5 pounds fresh large shrimp, peeled
    and deveined
½ cup white wine

——

6 cups cooked brown or wild rice
½ cup chopped fresh cilantro

Heat ¼ cup oil in a large skillet over medium-high heat. Add peppers, poblanos, onion, garlic, and tomatoes. Sauté lightly. Squeeze lime juice over vegetables and remove from heat. Heat remaining ¼ cup oil in a wok or very large skillet over medium-high heat. Add shrimp and stir fry until opaque. Stir in white wine and sautéed vegetables. Serve over rice and garnish with cilantro.

Thai Shrimp

⅓ cup water
2 tablespoons dark brown sugar,
    firmly packed
2 tablespoons minced fresh ginger
½ teaspoon freshly ground pepper
2 cloves garlic, minced
1 pound fresh large shrimp, peeled
    and deveined

3 tablespoons chopped fresh basil
1 teaspoon fresh lime juice

——

3 cups cooked jasmine or
    other long-grain white rice

Combine water, sugar, ginger, pepper, and garlic in a large nonstick skillet over high heat. Cook 5 minutes, or until mixture is slightly thickened. Add shrimp. Cook 3 minutes, or until shrimp turn pink, stirring constantly. Remove from heat. Stir in basil and lime juice. Serve over rice.

Oregano Shrimp

SERVES 4 TO 6

1 ½ pounds fresh large shrimp,
  peeled and deveined
2 tablespoons fresh lemon juice
½ cup bread crumbs
2 cloves garlic, minced
2 tablespoons chopped fresh parsley
2 tablespoons freshly grated
  Parmesan cheese

2 teaspoons minced fresh oregano
½ cup (1 stick) unsalted butter,
  melted
——
1 pound angel hair pasta, cooked
  al dente

Preheat oven to 325 degrees. Place shrimp in a 9 by 13-inch baking dish.
Sprinkle shrimp with lemon juice. Combine bread crumbs, garlic, parsley,
Parmesan, and oregano in a small bowl. Sprinkle bread crumb mixture
over shrimp. Pour butter on top. Bake 10 to 15 minutes, or until hot and
bubbly. Serve over angel hair pasta.

Spicy Baked Shrimp

SERVES 3 TO 4

½ cup olive oil
2 tablespoons Creole seasoning
2 tablespoons fresh lemon juice
2 tablespoons chopped fresh parsley
1 tablespoon honey
1 tablespoon soy sauce

pinch cayenne pepper
1 pound fresh large shrimp, peeled
  and deveined
——
lemon wedges

Combine olive oil, Creole seasoning, lemon juice, parsley, honey, soy
sauce, and cayenne in a 9 by 13-inch glass baking dish. Add shrimp and
toss to coat. Cover and refrigerate at least 1 hour or overnight.

Preheat oven to 450 degrees. Bake shrimp, stirring occasionally, about
6 to 8 minutes. Serve with lemon wedges.

Shrimp with Tomato Pepper Sauce

SERVES 4

Tomato Pepper Sauce:
1 tablespoon unsalted butter
2 large red bell peppers, seeded
   and chopped
1 large tomato, peeled, seeded,
   and chopped
1 tablespoon chopped fresh chives
1 tablespoon chopped fresh dill
juice of ½ lemon

salt
white pepper
——
2 tablespoons unsalted butter
24 to 30 fresh large shrimp, peeled and
   deveined, tails intact
1 shallot, minced
——
fresh dill sprigs

Tomato Pepper Sauce: Melt 1 tablespoon butter in a large skillet over medium-low heat. Add bell peppers and tomato. Cook covered until peppers are soft, about 20 minutes. Transfer bell pepper mixture to a food processor. Purée until smooth. Add chives, dill, and lemon juice. Process again. Season with salt and pepper. Keep warm.

Melt 2 tablespoons butter in a large skillet over medium heat. Add shrimp and shallot. Cook, turning, until shrimp turn pink, about 2 minutes. Coat each individual plate with sauce, place shrimp on sauce, and garnish with dill sprigs. Serve immediately.

Baked Prawns with Tomatoes and Feta

SERVES 3 TO 4

3 tablespoons olive oil
1 large onion, chopped
2 cloves garlic, crushed
1 can (14 ounces) chopped tomatoes
½ cup white wine
3 tablespoons chopped fresh parsley

1 teaspoon chopped fresh oregano
salt
freshly ground pepper
¾ pound fresh medium prawns
4 ounces feta cheese, cut into
   ½-inch cubes

Preheat oven to 450 degrees. Heat oil in a medium saucepan. Add onion and sauté until transparent. Add garlic and cook 2 more minutes. Add tomatoes, wine, parsley, oregano, salt, and pepper. Reduce heat. Cover and simmer until sauce is thick. Divide half of sauce between 4 lightly greased individual ovenproof dishes. Arrange prawns on top of sauce and cover with remaining sauce. Place feta on top. Bake 10 minutes, or until prawns are cooked and cheese begins to brown.

FETA CHEESE

Feta cheese is the most popular of Greek cheeses. It is usually made from sheep's milk, although American feta is made from cow's milk. This white, crumbly cheese is stored in brine to keep it moist. The cheese is an integral part of the Greek salad, but is also delicious served with a little olive oil and sprinkled with fresh herbs.

Sesame Shrimp with Lime Cilantro Butter

SERVES 3 TO 4

Lime Cilantro Butter:
4 tablespoons unsalted butter
2 cloves garlic, crushed
1-inch piece fresh ginger, grated
¼ cup fresh lime juice
¼ cup minced fresh cilantro
2 tablespoons white wine
1 teaspoon Worcestershire sauce

½ teaspoon salt
¼ teaspoon freshly ground pepper
————
1 pound fresh jumbo shrimp, peeled
  and deveined
2 tablespoons sesame oil
2 tablespoons sesame seeds

Lime Cilantro Butter: Melt butter in a medium saucepan. Add garlic and ginger. Sauté until the essence of garlic is released, 2 to 3 minutes. Add lime juice, cilantro, wine, Worcestershire, salt, and pepper. Cook over medium heat, slightly reducing liquid, about 5 minutes.

Place shrimp in a large bowl. Pour half of Lime Cilantro Butter over shrimp and toss gently. Reserve remaining half of Lime Cilantro Butter mixture. Keep warm.

Prepare broiler. Place shrimp in a broiling pan. Brush with sesame oil and sprinkle with sesame seeds. Broil about 5 minutes. Serve immediately with reserved Lime Cilantro Butter.

Shrimp and Mushroom Sauté

SERVES 3 TO 4

½ cup (1 stick) unsalted butter
8 ounces fresh mushrooms, sliced
1 clove garlic, minced
1 pound fresh shrimp, peeled
  and deveined
2 tablespoons fresh lemon juice
2 tablespoons minced fresh parsley
½ teaspoon salt

¼ teaspoon freshly ground pepper
2 tablespoons chopped fresh chives
¼ teaspoon Tabasco Sauce
2 tablespoons bourbon
————
3 cups cooked rice or pasta
1 lemon, quartered

Melt butter in a medium skillet over medium heat. Add mushrooms and garlic. Sauté until tender. Add shrimp and cook until slightly pink. Stir in lemon juice, parsley, salt, pepper, chives, Tabasco, and bourbon. Heat thoroughly, stirring occasionally. Serve over rice or pasta and garnish with lemon wedges.

Bayou Dinner

2 packages frozen corn with
   small "coblets" (about 24)
4 to 5 pounds fresh large shrimp,
   heads removed
1 cup (2 sticks) unsalted butter,
   cut into slices
¼ cup olive oil
¼ cup Worcestershire sauce
¼ cup soy sauce
2 cloves garlic, minced

1 teaspoon Tabasco Sauce
2 teaspoons Creole seasoning
¼ cup minced fresh rosemary
¼ cup minced fresh oregano
1 teaspoon cayenne pepper
2 teaspoons salt
2 teaspoons freshly ground pepper
4 lemons, sliced in rounds
————
6 cups cooked rice

Preheat oven to 500 degrees. Boil corn in water 5 minutes. Place shrimp
and corn in a large deep roasting pan. Top with butter slices. Combine
oil, Worcestershire, soy sauce, garlic, and Tabasco. Pour over shrimp.
Combine Creole seasoning, rosemary, oregano, cayenne, salt, and pepper
in a small bowl. Sprinkle over shrimp. Top shrimp with lemon slices.
Bake 8 to 10 minutes, turning and basting often, until shrimp turn pink.
Serve over rice.

WHAT'S A BAYOU?

*For all you folks not from the
South, marshy creeks or "bayous"
meander casually throughout
Houston. A bayou is what Texans
have called these minor rivers that
are tributaries to another body of
water.*

South Texas Crawfish Boil

1 bottle ice cold beer
————
5 pounds fresh crawfish
1¼ cups salt, plus more as needed
————
8 lemons, quartered
2 ribs celery, chopped
4 onions, quartered

4 heads garlic
6 bay leaves
3 to 4 sprigs fresh thyme
4 bags crab boil
1 to 2 teaspoons cayenne pepper
8 small red potatoes
3 ears corn, cut into thirds

Pop the beer and have a drink to prepare for some fun. Cover crawfish
with cold water and add salt. Purge 10 minutes, drain, and rinse. Add
more water and salt to crawfish, rinse, and drain, until water is no
longer muddy.

   Place 4 to 5 quarts cold water in a large soup pot. Add lemons, celery,
onions, garlic, bay leaves, thyme, crab boil, and cayenne pepper. Bring to
a boil. Add potatoes. Boil 7 minutes. Add corn. Boil 3 minutes. Add
crawfish and enough water to cover. Return to a boil. Cook 4 to 6 minutes, depending on size of crawfish. (Crawfish will turn bright red when
done.) Drain. Discard bay leaves, thyme, and crab boil bags.

   Pour crawfish and vegetables onto a table that has been covered with
plastic and newspaper. Serve immediately. Have several rolls of paper
towels handy and be sure to try the onions and garlic!

This is a lot of fun to cook outside with a group of friends. Use a large pot and a propane-lighted fire.

ON THE SIDE

*Creamy Polenta with Sage and
Roasted Wild Mushrooms*

Asparagus in Champagne Sauce

SERVES 4

PREPARING ASPARAGUS

Gently bend each stalk, which will cause the woody end to break off at just the right spot. Wash in ice water. Tough spots on the stalk may be removed with a vegetable peeler.

Champagne Sauce:
1 cup champagne
5 large egg yolks
dash tarragon vinegar
¼ teaspoon salt

⅛ teaspoon white pepper

———

1 pound fresh asparagus, trimmed
and steamed

Champagne Sauce: Combine champagne, egg yolks, and vinegar in the top of a double boiler. Season with salt and pepper. Cook over simmering water, stirring constantly, until sauce thickens. Remove from heat and stir. Serve sauce immediately over asparagus.

For asparagus bundles, dip long strips of leeks into boiling water. Cool and tie.

Marinated Asparagus

SERVES 4

1 cup extra virgin olive oil
⅓ cup red wine vinegar
1 tablespoon salt
1 teaspoon sugar
¼ cup chopped green bell pepper
1 tablespoon chopped fresh parsley

2 tablespoons chopped pimento
2 tablespoons chopped green onion

———

1 pound thin fresh asparagus, trimmed
and blanched

Combine oil, vinegar, salt, sugar, bell pepper, parsley, pimento, and green onion in a shallow nonmetallic bowl. Add asparagus, tossing to coat. Cover and marinate several hours in the refrigerator. Serve chilled or at room temperature.

Dilled Broccoli and Leek Purée

4½ tablespoons unsalted butter
1¼ pounds leeks, white and
   pale green parts only, halved
   and thinly sliced (5 cups)
1 large russet potato, peeled
   and quartered
1 pound broccoli, florets separated
   from stems, stems peeled
   and chopped

6 tablespoons heavy whipping cream
1 tablespoon minced fresh dill
salt
freshly ground pepper

Melt butter in a large skillet over medium heat. Add leeks and cook until very soft, about 20 minutes. Stir often to prevent burning. Cook potato in boiling salted water until almost tender, about 15 minutes. Stir in broccoli stems and cook 5 minutes. Add broccoli florets and cook 5 additional minutes, or until all vegetables are tender. Drain. Purée leeks, potato, and broccoli in a food processor. Transfer to a large saucepan. Stir in cream and dill. Season with salt and pepper. Warm over low heat, stirring often. Serve immediately.

This dish may be prepared ahead and refrigerated or frozen.

Creamy Brussel Sprouts

5 tablespoons unsalted butter
1 pound fresh mushrooms, sliced
2 cans (14 ounces each) artichoke
   hearts, drained and quartered
1½ to 2 pounds brussel
   sprouts, steamed

½ cup (1 stick) plus 1 tablespoon
   unsalted butter
½ cup plus 1 tablespoon all-purpose
   flour

1½ cups milk
1½ cups heavy whipping cream
½ cup dry sherry
2 tablespoons Worcestershire sauce
½ teaspoon salt
¼ teaspoon freshly ground pepper

----

4 ounces Parmesan cheese, freshly
   grated (1 cup)

Preheat oven to 350 degrees. Melt butter in a large skillet. Add mushrooms and sauté until soft. Layer mushrooms, artichokes, and brussel sprouts in a baking dish.

   Melt butter in a large skillet. Stir in flour, milk, and cream. Cook, stirring constantly, until slightly thickened. Add sherry, Worcestershire, salt, and pepper. Stir to blend. Pour sauce over layered vegetables. Sprinkle with Parmesan. Cover and bake 45 minutes.

Sweet and Sour Braised Red Cabbage

SERVES 4

½ cup raspberry or red wine vinegar
3 tablespoons dark brown sugar,
   firmly packed
1 cup chicken stock
1 teaspoon caraway seeds

1 large head red cabbage, cored
   and shredded
salt
freshly ground pepper

Combine vinegar, sugar, stock, caraway seeds, and cabbage in a large saucepan. Season with salt and pepper. Bring to a boil. Cover and simmer, stirring occasionally, 50 minutes. Uncover and boil until liquid has evaporated.

This dish can be made 1 day in advance. Keep covered and chilled. Reheat before serving.

Warm Red Cabbage with Goat Cheese and Pine Nuts

SERVES 4 TO 6

¼ cup extra virgin olive oil
2 small shallots, thinly sliced
1 head red cabbage, cored and
   thinly shredded
juice of 1 lemon
2 tablespoons balsamic vinegar
1 tablespoon capers, rinsed and
   drained

salt
¼ cup toasted pine nuts or
   walnut pieces
2 ounces goat cheese or feta cheese,
   crumbled (½ cup)
2 tablespoons chopped fresh parsley

Heat olive oil in a skillet over medium-high heat. Add shallots and cabbage. Toss quickly until slightly wilted, but still crisp. Add lemon juice, vinegar, and capers. Toss until mixed. Remove from heat and season with salt. Transfer to a serving bowl. Sprinkle with nuts, cheese, and parsley.

Whipped Carrots and Parsnips

SERVES 8

1½ pounds carrots, peeled and
   sliced into ½-inch pieces
2 pounds parsnips, peeled and
   sliced into ½-inch pieces

½ cup (1 stick) unsalted butter, at
   room temperature and cut into pieces
freshly grated nutmeg
salt
freshly ground pepper

Place carrots in a large pot of boiling salted water. Lower heat, cover partially, and cook 5 minutes. Stir in parsnips. Simmer until vegetables are tender, about 15 minutes. Drain. Return vegetables to pot. Stir over medium heat until excess moisture has evaporated. Purée vegetables and butter in a food processor until smooth. Season with nutmeg, salt, and pepper. Serve warm.

This dish can be prepared up to 4 hours ahead. Warm over low heat, stirring often.

Chèvre Zucchini Gratin

2 pounds zucchini, cut diagonally
   into ¼-inch slices
3 tablespoons unsalted butter
1 large onion, halved and
   thinly sliced
salt
freshly ground pepper

8 ounces chèvre, at room temperature
½ cup heavy whipping cream
1 ounce Parmesan cheese, freshly
   grated (¼ cup)
¼ cup dry bread crumbs

Preheat oven to 350 degrees. Grease a 9 by 13-inch baking dish. Boil zucchini in salted water until tender, but still crisp, about 2 minutes. Drain and pat dry.

Melt butter in a skillet. Add onion and sauté until translucent. Arrange one-third of zucchini in prepared dish. Season with salt and pepper. Spread half of onion over zucchini. Repeat layers, seasoning with salt and pepper, and end with zucchini on top.

Crumble chèvre into top of a double boiler. Stir in cream. Cook until smooth and thick, 3 to 4 minutes. Thin with an additional 2 to 4 tablespoons cream if too thick. Pour over zucchini layers. Combine Parmesan and bread crumbs. Sprinkle over gratin. Bake 35 to 40 minutes.

Chèvre Zucchini Gratin may be prepared in advance and refrigerated or frozen. Bring to room temperature before baking.

Corn and Black Bean Tamale Pie

kernels of 4 ears fresh cooked
   corn (2 cups)
1 cup chicken or vegetable stock
1 cup masa harina*
1 can (16 ounces) creamed corn
1 teaspoon baking powder
2 tablespoons unsalted butter, melted
2 cans (15 ounces each) black
   beans, rinsed and drained

1 teaspoon ground cumin
1 teaspoon chili powder
¼ teaspoon garlic powder
pinch cayenne pepper
½ teaspoon oregano
¼ cup tomato purée
1 can (4½ ounces) diced green chilies
8 ounces Cheddar cheese, shredded
   (2 cups)

CUTTING CORN FROM THE COB

To remove corn kernels from the cob, hold the cob vertically on a flat surface. Using a sharp knife, slice downward, removing several rows of kernels at a time. When finished, use the back side of the knife to scrape in a downward motion to capture the milk of the corn.

Preheat oven to 350 degrees. Spray a 7 by 11-inch baking dish with nonstick cooking spray. Purée corn briefly in a food processor. Combine puréed corn, stock, masa, creamed corn, baking powder, and butter in a bowl. Set aside. Combine black beans, cumin, chili powder, garlic powder, cayenne, oregano, tomato purée, and green chilies in a large bowl. Spread two-thirds of masa corn mixture in bottom of prepared baking dish. Layer bean mixture and cheese. Top with remaining masa corn mixture. Bake 1 hour. Serve with Mexican Green Hot Sauce and Ramillette Red Sauce (page 137).

Masa harina is available in the flour section of your local supermarket.

CORN

One of the joys of summer is a fresh ear of sweet corn dripping with butter and eaten when it's piping hot. Corn is available year round, but it's best in the summer, especially when it comes straight from the fields to the cooking pot. A gift of America to the world, corn was first cultivated by the Indians in the Mexican highlands as many as 5000 years ago. Tradition has it that the crow brought the first corn and bean from the Creator's fields in the Southwest - the corn in one ear and the bean in the other. With increased interest in Southwestern cooking, ancient varieties of Indian corn are again being cultivated: Black Aztec, which dries purplish black and can be ground into purple cornmeal; Rainbow Inca, a multicolored sweet corn; and the blue corn traditionally revered by the Hopis and Zunis.

Toasted Corn Pudding

SERVES 4 TO 6

7 ears fresh corn, husked
3 tablespoons unsalted butter
5 to 6 ounces goat cheese, cream cheese, or a mixture of the two
¼ cup all-purpose flour
2¼ cups low-fat milk
1 can (4½ ounces) diced green chilies
¼ teaspoon cayenne pepper
¼ teaspoon salt
4 large eggs, lightly beaten

Preheat oven to 350 degrees. Grease a 7 by 11-inch baking dish. Toast corn, a few ears at a time, in a large skillet until half the kernels are brown. Cool. With a sharp knife, cut kernels from ears into same skillet. With dull side of knife, scrape the ears lengthwise, adding pulp to skillet. Add butter and cheese. Stir over medium heat to melt. Stir in flour. Remove pan from heat. Stir in milk, chilies, cayenne, and salt. Whisk in eggs. Pour mixture into prepared baking dish. Bake uncovered until center is firm and edges are brown, about 55 to 65 minutes.

Jalapeño Cheese Cornbread Pudding

SERVES 8

1 tablespoon vegetable oil
½ cup diced yellow onions
kernels of 3 to 4 ears fresh corn (1½ cups)
4 large eggs, lightly beaten
2 cups heavy whipping cream
4 cups cornbread, crumbled
8 ounces Jalapeño Jack cheese, shredded (1 cup plus 1 cup)
salt
freshly ground pepper
1 to 2 fresh jalapeños, seeded and thinly sliced

Preheat oven to 300 degrees. Grease an 8-inch square baking pan. Heat oil in a large skillet. Add onions and corn. Sauté until onions are translucent. Remove from heat. Stir in eggs, cream, cornbread, and 1 cup cheese. Season with salt and pepper. Pour pudding into prepared pan. Sprinkle with remaining 1 cup cheese and top with jalapeño slices. Place pan in a water bath. Bake 1 hour, or until firm.

Use as an alternative to stuffing on Thanksgiving. Great side dish for a Mexican buffet or an outdoor barbecue.

Italian Gnocchi

4 cups whole milk

1 cup regular or quick-cooking farina,
   or Cream of Wheat (not instant)

4 ounces Parmesan cheese, freshly
   grated (⅔ cup plus ⅓ cup)

2 teaspoons salt

2 large egg yolks, lightly beaten

2 tablespoons plus 5 tablespoons
   unsalted butter, melted

⅓ cup minced sun-dried
   tomatoes packed in oil, drained

¼ cup minced fresh basil

Heat milk in a heavy saucepan over medium heat until hot, but not
boiling. Lower heat. Add farina in a thin, slow stream, whisking constantly. Continue whisking until it forms a thick mass on whisk, 5 to 10 minutes for regular and less time for quick-cooking. Remove from heat. Add
⅔ cup Parmesan, salt, egg yolks, and 2 tablespoons butter. Mix rapidly
until well blended. Stir in sun-dried tomatoes and basil.

Moisten counter top with water and spread farina mixture on it. Use a
spatula to spread it into an even thickness of ½ inch. Let mixture cool
completely. (Farina mixture can also be spread in a baking dish and placed
in refrigerator 30 minutes.)

Preheat oven to 350 degrees. Grease a baking sheet. Cut shapes out
of farina mixture using a 2-inch diamond-shaped cookie cutter. Place on
baking sheet. Dot with remaining 5 tablespoons butter. (At this point,
farina mixture can be covered with plastic wrap and refrigerated. Remove
farina mixture from refrigerator 30 minutes prior to baking.) Bake 30 to
40 minutes, or until lightly browned. Remove from baking sheet. Sprinkle
with remaining ⅓ cup Parmesan. Serve immediately.

GNOCCHI

*Lightness is the key to these
traditional Italian dumplings
(pronounced nō´key). Serve
instead of potatoes or as a garnish
for soup.*

Two-Bean Succotash

SERVES 2

FAVA BEANS

A fava bean is a flat bean that resembles a large lima bean. They can be purchased dried, canned, and infrequently, fresh. Choose pods that are not bulging with beans. Their tough skin should be removed by blanching before cooking.

1 tablespoon unsalted butter	¼ cup blanched fava beans
1 tablespoon diced red bell pepper	¼ cup fresh corn kernels
2 tablespoons diced red onion	salt
¼ cup blanched haricots verts*	freshly ground pepper

Melt butter in a medium skillet. Add bell pepper and onion. Sauté until tender. Add haricots verts, fava beans, and corn. Sauté 1 minute. Season with salt and pepper. Toss quickly and serve.

* Green beans may be substituted for haricots verts.

Herb Garden Green Beans

SERVES 4 TO 6

CHIFFONADE

Roll basil leaves up tightly and thinly slice crosswise. The resulting strips are called chiffonade. This process is usually used for basil and sage, so that leaves are not bruised.

4 tablespoons unsalted butter	1 teaspoon chopped fresh rosemary
⅓ cup minced onion	2 cloves garlic, minced
¼ cup minced celery	1 teaspoon salt
¼ cup minced fresh parsley	1 teaspoon freshly ground pepper
¼ cup fresh basil chiffonade	1 pound green beans, snapped
(See accompanying instructions.)	and blanched

Melt butter in a large skillet. Add onion and celery. Sauté until soft. Add parsley, basil, rosemary, garlic, salt, and pepper. Cook, stirring constantly, 3 minutes. Gently stir in beans. Cook uncovered until beans are thoroughly heated.

Oriental Green Beans

SERVES 4

1 tablespoon vegetable oil	½ teaspoon sugar
1 tablespoon chopped fresh chives	1 pound green beans, snapped
1 tablespoon minced garlic	and steamed
1 tablespoon soy sauce	2 teaspoons toasted sesame seeds

Heat oil in a wok or large skillet. Add chives and garlic. Sauté until garlic is soft. Stir in soy sauce and sugar. Add beans and cook 1 minute, tossing lightly to coat. Sprinkle with sesame seeds. Serve immediately.

Leeks in Orange Ginger Sauce

12 small to medium leeks
1 tablespoon distilled white vinegar
2½ quarts plus 4 quarts water
6 tablespoons unsalted butter
5 tablespoons minced fresh ginger

1 teaspoon ground ginger
1 cup fresh orange juice
1 tablespoon plus 1 tablespoon
  orange zest, minced

Trim root ends off leeks. Cut an X in bottom of each leek. Remove any tough or discolored leaves. Trim tops, leaving 2 inches of green. Cut an X lengthwise through green part.

Combine vinegar, leeks, and 2½ quarts water in a large soup pot. Soak 30 minutes. Drain and rinse leeks under cold water to thoroughly clean. Bring remaining 4 quarts water to a boil in a large saucepan. Add leeks. Reduce heat and simmer until tender, 5 to 7 minutes. Drain and pat dry.

Melt butter in a large skillet over low heat. Add fresh and ground ginger. Cook 1 minute, stirring constantly. Add leeks and increase heat to medium. Cook leeks until slightly browned on both sides, stirring occasionally, 5 to 7 minutes. Place leeks on a warmed serving dish, decoratively fanning out green ends. Keep warm.

Add orange juice and 1 tablespoon orange zest to skillet. Increase heat to medium-high. Whisk sauce until slightly thickened, about 3 minutes. Spoon sauce over leeks. Sprinkle with remaining 1 tablespoon orange zest. Serve immediately.

LEEKS

Leeks are members of the lily family. They have a mild, almost sweet onion-like flavor. Leeks are very sandy and must be rinsed thoroughly before using. First trim the root end and the dark green leaves, leaving only the white and light green parts. Halve the stalk lengthwise and rinse under cold water, spreading the leaves to remove all trapped sand. Pat dry.

Leek and Gruyère Pie

4 tablespoons unsalted butter
8 leeks, thinly sliced
2 large eggs
2 large egg yolks
1 cup heavy whipping cream
1 cup half and half
½ teaspoon salt

¼ teaspoon freshly ground pepper
freshly grated nutmeg
1 10-inch deep dish pie shell,
  partially baked
2 to 4 ounces Gruyère cheese,
  shredded (½ to 1 cup)

Melt butter in a large skillet. Add leeks and cover. Cook over low heat, stirring frequently to prevent scorching, about 30 minutes, or until leeks are tender. Remove from heat and cool. Set aside.

Preheat oven to 300 degrees. Combine eggs, yolks, cream, and half and half in a bowl. Whisk until blended. Add salt, pepper, and nutmeg. Stir to blend. Spoon leek mixture into pie shell. Pour cream mixture over leeks to ½ inch from the top of crust. Sprinkle cheese evenly over top of pie. Place pie on middle rack in oven. Bake until top is browned and filling is completely set, 35 to 45 minutes. Cool 10 minutes. Serve warm.

The pie shell may be baked in a quiche pan, a 10-inch round deep dish pie pan, or a 9 by 12-inch casserole.

Southern Lima Beans

SERVES 8

1 pound dried lima beans
6 cups water
½ pound bacon, thickly sliced
  and diced
1 onion, chopped
1 green bell pepper, seeded
  and chopped
1 tablespoon all-purpose flour

2 teaspoons seasoned salt
½ teaspoon salt
¼ teaspoon freshly ground pepper
2 teaspoons prepared mustard
1 teaspoon Worcestershire sauce
2 tablespoons brown sugar,
  firmly packed
1 can (14½ ounces) crushed tomatoes

Cover beans with water and boil 2 minutes. Remove from heat. Cover
and let stand 1 hour. Test beans. If not tender, cook until tender. Drain.
Cook bacon in a large skillet until crisp. Drain and set aside. Add onion
and bell pepper to bacon drippings. Sauté 5 minutes. Stir in flour,
seasoned salt, salt, pepper, mustard, Worcestershire, brown sugar, and
tomatoes. Simmer uncovered 10 minutes. Place beans in a 9 by 13-inch
baking dish. Pour sauce over beans. Sprinkle with bacon. Warm in a
300 degree oven or microwave before serving.

Gram's Fried Okra

SERVES 4 TO 6

OKRA

*The viscous sap given off when okra
is sliced will thicken the liquid in
which it is cooked. Select firm,
brightly colored pods under 4 inches
in length. Store unwashed okra in
a plastic bag in the refrigerator for
up to 3 days.*

1 pound fresh okra, sliced
2 cups buttermilk
¼ cup flour
½ cup cornmeal

salt
freshly ground pepper
dash cayenne pepper
oil

Place okra in a medium bowl. Cover with buttermilk. Cover with plastic
wrap and refrigerate 30 minutes. Mix flour and cornmeal in a separate
bowl. Season with salt, pepper, and cayenne. Dip okra in flour mixture,
coating evenly. Heat oil in a large skillet. Add okra and fry until golden
brown. Drain on paper towels. Serve immediately.

Fresh Okra and Tomatoes

SERVES 8

1 tablespoon olive oil
1 small onion, chopped
1 pound fresh okra, sliced
4 large Roma tomatoes, peeled,
  seeded, and chopped

2 teaspoons Creole seasonings
salt
freshly ground pepper
Tabasco Sauce

Heat oil in a large skillet over medium heat. Add onion. Sauté until
soft and transparent. Add okra. Cook 3 minutes. Stir in tomatoes. Cook
3 minutes. Add Creole seasonings, stirring to combine. Cook to let flavors
blend. Season with salt, pepper, and Tabasco. Serve immediately.

Glazed Pearl Onions with Raisins and Almonds

SERVES 8

2 pounds pearl onions
1 cup dry sherry
½ cup raisins
¼ cup honey
¼ cup water
2 tablespoons unsalted butter

1 teaspoon minced fresh thyme
salt
freshly ground pepper
⅔ cup toasted slivered almonds
4 teaspoons red wine vinegar

Bring a pot of salted water to a boil. Add onions. Cook 3 minutes to loosen skins. Drain and cool slightly. Cut root ends from onions. Squeeze onions at stem end. (Onions will slip out of skins.) Combine onions, sherry, raisins, honey, water, butter, and thyme in a large skillet. Bring to a boil over medium-high heat. Reduce heat. Cover and simmer until liquid evaporates and onions begin to caramelize, stirring often, about 45 minutes. Season with salt and pepper. Remove from heat. Stir almonds and vinegar into onions. Add a few teaspoons of water if mixture is too dry. Serve warm.

This dish can be prepared up to the point when the onions have begun to caramelize and set aside for up to 6 hours. Store at room temperature. Rewarm over low heat before continuing.

Can be served with roasted duck, ham, or a traditional Thanksgiving turkey.

Plum Creek Onions

SERVES 4

4 onions, yellow or white
4 beef bouillon cubes

1½ tablespoons unsalted butter
¼ cup Worcestershire sauce

Preheat oven to 350 degrees. Carve a small, marble-size well into the top of each onion. Slice a bit off bottom so it will not roll. Place 1 onion on an 8-inch aluminum foil square. Form foil around onion, but leave access to well. Place 1 bouillon cube and 1 teaspoon butter into well. Pour 1 tablespoon Worcestershire into well. Seal foil over onion. Repeat procedure on other onions. Place onions in an 8 by 8-inch baking dish. Bake 1 hour.

ONIONS

Onions, like garlic, chives, scallions, leeks, and shallots, are members of the extensive lily family. Extremely versatile and rich in vitamin C, nothing enlivens recipes like onions. Early Egyptian peasants used them to relieve a monotonous diet of fish and dates and were paid for their labor on the pyramids in onion, garlic, and parsley. Up to the last century, onions also accompanied sailors on their long voyages because they prevented scurvy. Onions fall into two classifications: green onions and dry onions. Of the dry onions, the mild type can be stored up to 6 months. These include most of the common cooking varieties like yellow, white, Spanish, and red. The other type of dry onion is the sweet onion. These are usually large, high in water and sugar, and low in the sulfur compounds that irritate the eyes and make you cry. Sweet onions are delicious eaten raw, on burgers, or in salads. The most popular include Texas's 1015, Georgia's Vidalia, and Washington's Walla Walla.

Baked Poblano Chiles Stuffed with Artichokes and Toasted Walnuts

SERVES 8

FRESH ARTICHOKE HEARTS

To prepare fresh artichoke hearts, break off the stem so that the fibers are pulled out. Remove the tough outer leaves. Using a sharp knife, trim the bottom neatly and rub with lemon to prevent discoloration. Trim off the top third of the remaining leaves. Simmer until fork tender, 30 to 40 minutes, in a pot of water to which about 1 tablespoon lemon juice has been added. Cool submerged in the liquid and refrigerate covered until ready to use. Remove the remaining leaves and choke just before serving.

8 poblano or Anaheim chile peppers, roasted (page 40) and peeled, leaving tops and stems attached

Basic Tomato Sauce:
1 tablespoon vegetable oil
2 cloves garlic, minced
6 fresh tomatoes, peeled, seeded, and chopped, or 2 cans (14½ ounces each) Italian-style tomatoes plus liquid, chopped
3 tablespoons minced fresh basil or cilantro
½ teaspoon salt
¼ teaspoon freshly ground pepper

Cheese Filling:
½ tablespoon unsalted butter
½ cup toasted walnuts
8 ounces mozzarella cheese, shredded (2 cups)
4 ounces Monterey Jack or Asiago cheese, shredded (1 cup)
4 ounces cream cheese, softened
2 to 3 tablespoons sour cream, as needed
6 freshly cooked artichoke hearts, diced, or 1 can (15¾ ounces) artichoke hearts, drained, rinsed, and diced

Using a sharp knife, make a lengthwise cut down each chile. Remove seeds and avoid tearing. Set aside.

Basic Tomato Sauce: Heat oil in a large skillet over medium heat. Add garlic and tomatoes. Sauté 2 to 4 minutes. Add basil, salt, and pepper. Remove from heat. Set aside and keep warm.

Cheese Filling: Heat butter in a small skillet over medium heat. Add walnuts. Sauté 2 to 4 minutes. Cool and coarsely chop. Set aside. Mix cheeses in a medium bowl. Add just enough sour cream to bind filling. Fold in walnuts and artichokes. Carefully stuff each chile, leaving it partially open.

Preheat oven to 350 degrees. Lightly grease a 9 by 13-inch baking dish. Place stuffed chiles in prepared dish. Bake until cheese is melted and creamy, 10 to 15 minutes. Serve Basic Tomato Sauce over chiles or on the side.

Tamale Stuffing

SERVES 8 TO 10

4 tablespoons unsalted butter
1 large onion, chopped
36 tamales, broken into pieces
8 cups day old cornbread
½ pound seasoned sausage, browned, drained, and crumbled

2 large eggs, beaten
½ jar (5 ounces) mild enchilada sauce
¼ teaspoon cayenne pepper
½ teaspoon ground cumin
salt
freshly ground pepper

Preheat oven to 350 degrees. Lightly grease a 9 by 13-inch baking dish. Melt butter in a medium skillet. Add onions and sauté until translucent. Crumble tamales and cornbread into a large bowl. Add sausage, onions, eggs, enchilada sauce, cayenne, cumin, salt, and pepper. Mix gently. Place stuffing in prepared dish. Bake 25 minutes.

Creamy Polenta with Sage and Roasted Wild Mushrooms

SERVES 4

Polenta:
1 ¾ cups water
1 ¾ cups chicken broth
1 teaspoon minced garlic
¾ cup polenta*

Sage:
½ cup extra virgin olive oil
⅓ cup fresh sage leaves
salt

⅔ cup crème fraîche (page 102)
 or sour cream
1 ounce Monterey Jack cheese,
 shredded (¼ cup)
1 ounce Parmesan cheese,
 freshly grated (¼ cup)
3 tablespoons unsalted butter, melted
¼ teaspoon salt
⅛ teaspoon freshly ground pepper

Roasted Wild Mushrooms

Preheat oven to 350 degrees. Bring water, broth, and garlic to a boil in a large ovenproof saucepan over medium-high heat. Slowly mix in polenta. Reduce heat to medium. Cook 5 minutes, stirring constantly. Cover and place in oven. Bake until thick, but still creamy, stirring occasionally, about 45 minutes. (Add more water if mixture appears dry.)

Heat oil in a small skillet over medium-high heat. Add sage leaves. Fry until crisp, about 10 seconds. Drain on paper towels. Season with salt. Set aside.

Combine polenta, crème fraîche, Monterey Jack, Parmesan, butter, salt, and pepper. Spoon polenta onto serving plates. Top with Roasted Wild Mushrooms. Garnish with sage leaves. Serve immediately.

*Cornmeal may be substituted for the polenta.

Roasted Wild Mushrooms:
8 cloves garlic, thinly sliced
3 tablespoons olive oil
3 tablespoons balsamic or
 red wine vinegar
3 sprigs fresh rosemary, chopped

3 sprigs fresh thyme, chopped
1 pound large fresh wild mushrooms
 (shiitake, oyster, or cremini)
¼ teaspoon salt
⅛ teaspoon freshly ground pepper

Preheat oven to 425 degrees. Line 2 baking sheets with foil. Combine garlic, olive oil, vinegar, rosemary, and thyme in a large bowl. Add mushrooms and toss to coat. Season with salt and pepper. Arrange mushrooms in a single layer on prepared baking sheets. Roast until mushrooms are tender and slightly crisp on edges, about 25 minutes. Serve immediately.

The mushrooms are also delicious served with roasted meats.

Succulent, earth-toned, with a haunting woodsy fragrance, mushrooms are a rich, delicious treat. To the ancient Egyptians, they were "sons of Gods" sent to earth on thunderbolts because of their mysterious habit of appearing after a rainstorm. Mushrooms can be found today in the white domestic variety and in the almost countless species of wild mushrooms native to humid regions in every latitude on earth. Since some species are poisonous, it's best to concentrate on commercially grown wild mushrooms available fresh or dried, including rich, meaty-tasting cèpes from France and their Italian cousins, porcini; frilly, sweet-tasting chanterelles from the Pacific Northwest; firm, brown cremini that are great eaten raw or sautéed in butter; slender, white-capped enoki; morels from Europe, the king of the mushroom family; tawny shiitake with their rich smoky flavor; and dark, delicately flavored truffles from the Perigord region in France - always expensive and best eaten fresh.

Polenta Soufflé

POLENTA

Polenta originated in Italy in the sixteenth century. It quickly became a favorite of the northern Italians. Polenta is simply cornmeal stirred and simmered in salted water until all the liquid is absorbed. The cornmeal can be the traditional white or yellow variety or the coarser polenta cornmeal. This dish can be eaten in the creamy stage, or it can be firmed up on a flat surface and cut into shapes for grilling, broiling, or frying.

4½ tablespoons unsalted butter
¾ cup polenta*
1¾ cups chicken broth
1 cup heavy whipping cream
2 ounces Parmesan cheese,
  freshly grated (½ cup)

½ teaspoon salt
4 large egg yolks, beaten
5 large egg whites, very stiffly beaten

Preheat oven to 375 degrees. Grease a 2½ to 3-quart casserole dish. Melt butter in a large skillet. Add polenta and cook 2 minutes. Stir in broth and cream. Bring to a boil. Simmer uncovered 5 minutes. Remove from heat. Add cheese, salt, and egg yolks. Stir until combined. Fold in egg whites. Spoon into prepared casserole dish and bake 35 minutes.

Cornmeal may be substituted for the polenta.

New Potatoes with Herbs

ROASTED NEW POTATOES WITH BAY LEAVES

*8 medium fresh new potatoes
15 bay leaves
¾ cup chicken stock
½ cup olive oil
salt
freshly ground pepper*

Preheat oven to 350 degrees. Starting at one end of potato and moving to the other end, make a crosswise slit every ½ inch. Cut bay leaves lengthwise into thirds. Place a piece of bay leaf into each slit. Place potatoes in an oiled baking dish. Heat chicken stock to boiling and pour over potatoes. Drizzle with oil. Season with salt and pepper. Bake until potatoes are tender and cooking liquid has evaporated, about 40 minutes. Remove bay leaves before serving. Serves 4.

1½ pounds small red new potatoes
2 tablespoons unsalted butter
salt
freshly ground pepper

2 tablespoons plus 2 tablespoons
  chopped fresh basil
2 large shallots, minced
2 large cloves garlic, minced

Pierce potatoes in several places with a fork. Melt butter in a large skillet over medium heat. Add potatoes. Season with salt and pepper. Cover and cook potatoes until almost tender, shaking skillet occasionally, about 25 minutes. Add 2 tablespoons basil, shallots, and garlic. Reduce heat to medium-low. Cook until potatoes are very tender and brown, about 10 minutes. Transfer to a serving bowl. Sprinkle with remaining 2 tablespoons basil. Serve immediately.

Try substituting other fresh herbs for the basil such as rosemary, oregano, thyme, dill, or fennel.

Potato Puff

SERVES 4 TO 6

½ cup milk
3 large eggs
¼ cup chopped fresh parsley
½ to 1 small onion, halved
1½ teaspoons salt

freshly ground pepper
4 tablespoons unsalted butter, melted
4 ounces Cheddar cheese, diced (1 cup)
3 medium russet potatoes, peeled
  and quartered

Preheat oven to 350 degrees. Grease a 1½-quart casserole. Blend milk, eggs, parsley, onion, salt, pepper, butter, and cheese in a food processor. Add potatoes, 1 cup at a time, until potatoes are blended. Pour into prepared casserole. Bake 1 hour.

Potatoes Au Gratin

SERVES 8

3 pounds russet potatoes, peeled,
  quartered, and sliced wafer thin
½ teaspoon salt
⅛ teaspoon freshly ground pepper
¼ teaspoon ground nutmeg

8 ounces Gruyère cheese, shredded
  (2 cups)
½ to 1 can (14 ounces) chicken broth
2 tablespoons unsalted butter

Preheat oven to 450 degrees. Grease a 9 by 13-inch baking dish. Gently toss potatoes with salt, pepper, and nutmeg. Layer one-third of potatoes in prepared dish. Sprinkle with one-third of cheese. Repeat layers. Cover potatoes with chicken broth. Dot with butter. Bake uncovered 15 minutes. Reduce heat to 375 degrees. Bake 1 to 1½ hours, or until top is golden and crusty. Serve immediately.

Mashed Potatoes with Rosemary Butter

SERVES 4 TO 6

4 tablespoons unsalted butter
1 tablespoon chopped fresh rosemary
1¾ pounds russet potatoes,
  peeled and cut into 1-inch cubes
1 teaspoon salt

½ cup warm milk
2 ounces Parmesan cheese,
  freshly grated (½ cup)
salt
freshly ground pepper

Melt butter in a small saucepan. Add rosemary and set aside. Place potatoes in a medium saucepan. Cover with cold water and add salt. Boil over medium-high heat until tender, about 15 minutes. Drain. Transfer to a large bowl. Add milk and mash with a potato masher. Add Parmesan and rosemary butter. Mix with an electric mixer until smooth. Season with salt and pepper.

HOT POTATOES

The potato is one of the world's great comfort foods. Served baked with all the toppings, fried crisp and golden, or whipped into fluffy, white, buttery-tasting mounds, the first bite makes us instantly relax and go ahhh. Perhaps it's because potatoes are linked to our earliest memories: standing in the kitchen by our mother's side watching her turn plain potatoes into something magical. Where once only russets, white-skinned potatoes, and red potatoes were available in supermarkets, we're now seeing less usual varieties like Maris Peer, Golden Wonder, Kerr's Pink, and Romano. But don't let the unfamiliar names keep you from buying them. Potatoes are either the thin-skinned waxy variety, best for boiling or steaming, or the mealy kind used for baking or mashing. Blue potatoes, with their grayish blue skin and sometimes inky-blue flesh, are a delicious treat, boiled or baked and served with butter.

Roasted Garlic and Green Chile Mashed Potatoes

SERVES 4 TO 6

ROASTING GARLIC

Roasted garlic is delicious spread on bread, whipped into potatoes, or simply mixed into soups and salads. The roasting process softens the garlic to a butter-like consistency and creates a somewhat sweet and nut-like flavor. To roast garlic, remove the outer paper layers and place either the whole head or separated individual cloves on a piece of aluminum foil. Drizzle with olive oil, loosely wrap, and seal in the aluminum foil. Bake in a 400 degree oven until soft, 25 to 30 minutes.

3 large russet potatoes, peeled and cut into 1-inch cubes
1 teaspoon salt
½ cup milk
2 tablespoons chopped roasted garlic (about 4 cloves) (See accompanying instructions.)

2 tablespoons chopped roasted poblano chile or canned green chilies
4 tablespoons unsalted butter, melted
salt
freshly ground pepper

Cover potatoes with cold water and salt. Boil potatoes over medium-high heat until tender, about 15 minutes. Drain. Place potatoes in a large bowl, add milk, and mash with a potato masher. Add roasted garlic, roasted poblano, and butter. Blend with an electric mixer until smooth. Season with salt and pepper.

Potato Bake with Squash and Spinach

SERVES 8 TO 10

8 medium russet potatoes (about 2½ pounds)
1 cup sour cream
2 tablespoons milk
2 tablespoons plus 1 tablespoon plus 1 tablespoon unsalted butter, at room temperature
½ teaspoon plus ⅛ teaspoon plus ⅛ teaspoon salt

⅛ teaspoon freshly ground pepper
1 package (12 ounces) frozen squash, thawed and drained
1 large egg, lightly beaten
1 package (10 ounces) frozen chopped spinach, thawed and drained
2 teaspoons minced onion
1 ounce Cheddar cheese, shredded (¼ cup)

Place potatoes and enough water to cover in a large saucepan over high heat. Bring to a boil. Reduce heat to medium-low. Cover and cook 30 minutes, or until fork tender. Drain. Cool slightly and peel. Place potatoes, sour cream, milk, 2 tablespoons butter, ½ teaspoon salt, and pepper in a large bowl. Beat with an electric mixer at low speed until smooth and fluffy. Set aside.

Preheat oven to 350 degrees. Lightly grease a deep 2-quart baking dish or soufflé dish. Mix squash, 1 tablespoon butter, and ⅛ teaspoon salt in a small bowl. Set aside.

Thoroughly mix egg, spinach, onion, 1 tablespoon butter, and ⅛ tea-spoon salt in a second small bowl. Set aside.

Spread one-third of potato mixture in bottom of prepared dish. Add squash mixture, then spinach mixture. Repeat layers.

Bake 40 minutes, or until thoroughly heated. Remove from oven. Sprinkle Cheddar over top and let rest until cheese melts.

Baked Spicy Rice

1 tablespoon vegetable oil
½ cup raw long-grain rice
1 can (10 ounces) diced tomatoes
  with chilies
½ cup water

½ teaspoon salt
⅓ cup sliced pimento-stuffed olives
¼ cup chopped onion
2 ounces Monterey Jack cheese,
  shredded (½ cup)

Preheat oven to 350 degrees. Heat oil in a large skillet. Add rice and brown. Transfer to a 1-quart baking dish. Add tomatoes, water, salt, olives, onion, and cheese. Stir to combine. Cover. Bake 45 minutes. Uncover and stir. Bake an additional 15 minutes.

Carrot Mushroom Pilaf

4 tablespoons plus 4 tablespoons
  unsalted butter
1 bunch green onions, chopped
3 medium carrots, peeled
  and chopped
2 cups raw brown rice
4½ cups chicken broth
½ cup dry white wine
2 cloves garlic, minced
8 ounces fresh mushrooms, sliced

¾ cup chopped fresh parsley
¼ teaspoon freshly ground pepper
4 ounces Parmesan cheese,
  freshly grated (1 cup)
2 large eggs, beaten
1 cup half and half
½ teaspoon ground nutmeg

———

¼ cup chopped green onion

PARSLEY

The two most popular types of parsley are curly-leaf parsley and flat-leaf or Italian parsley. The stronger flavored Italian parsley is usually used in cooking, while the curly-leaf parsley is most often used as a garnish since it does not wilt as quickly.

Lightly grease an 8 by 12-inch baking dish. Melt 4 tablespoons butter in a large skillet. Add green onions and carrots. Sauté until tender, about 5 minutes. Add rice and cook 1 minute, stirring constantly. Stir in chicken broth and wine. Bring to a boil. Cover. Reduce heat and simmer 45 minutes, or until liquid is absorbed. Set aside.

   Preheat oven to 350 degrees. Melt remaining 4 tablespoons butter in a separate small skillet. Add garlic and cook 1 minute. Stir in mushrooms and cook 5 minutes. Drain. Stir in parsley and pepper.

   Spread half of rice mixture in bottom of prepared baking dish. Spread mushroom mixture over rice, then sprinkle with ½ cup Parmesan. Top with remaining rice mixture and sprinkle with remaining ½ cup Parmesan. Thoroughly mix eggs, half and half, and nutmeg. Pour over rice. Bake 30 minutes, or until thoroughly heated. Garnish with green onions.

May be prepared 24 hours in advance, covered, and refrigerated. Bring to room temperature before baking.

Almond and Red Grape Pilaf

SERVES 6

4 tablespoons unsalted butter
2 tablespoons minced onion
2 cups chopped celery
1 cup raw long-grain white rice
1 teaspoon salt
1 ½ cups chicken broth

1 ½ tablespoons chopped fresh chervil
1 ½ tablespoons minced fresh marjoram
freshly ground pepper
1 cup toasted slivered almonds
1 ½ cups halved seedless red grapes*

Melt butter in a large skillet. Add onion, celery, and rice. Cook and stir over medium heat, 3 to 5 minutes, or until rice becomes a pale wheat color. Add salt and chicken broth. Cover. Simmer over low heat 25 minutes, or until all liquid is absorbed. Remove pan from heat. Stir in chervil and marjoram. Season with pepper. Gently stir in almonds and grapes until combined. Serve immediately.

Green grapes or raisins may be substituted for red grapes.

Wild Rice Medley

SERVES 6

PERFECT RICE

To keep the wild rice from splitting during cooking, soak 8 hours or overnight, then rinse before cooking. Wild rice takes longer to cook than regular rice, about 50 minutes.

5 cups beef stock
1 cup raw wild rice
1 cup raw brown rice
2 tablespoons extra virgin olive oil
1 cup toasted walnuts
1 cup dried apricots, quartered

¼ cup golden raisins
¼ cup dried cranberries
1 cup minced celery
1 teaspoon salt
1 teaspoon freshly ground pepper

Combine stock and rice in a medium saucepan. Cover. Bring to a boil over high heat. Reduce heat. Simmer until rice is cooked, about 50 minutes. Heat olive oil in a skillet. Add walnuts, apricots, raisins, cranberries, and celery. Sauté gently 3 to 5 minutes. Stir walnut mixture into rice. Add salt and pepper. Stir to combine. Serve immediately.

Risotto Limone

SERVES 8 TO 10

6 cups chicken broth
4 tablespoons plus 4 tablespoons
    unsalted butter
1 small onion, chopped
2 cups raw Italian Arborio rice
8 ounces Parmesan cheese,
    freshly grated (2 cups)

¼ cup chopped fresh parsley
juice and grated zest of 1 lemon
salt
freshly ground pepper

Bring chicken broth to a slow boil in a medium saucepan. Set aside. Melt
4 tablespoons butter in a large saucepan over medium heat. Add onion.
Sauté until translucent. Add rice and stir to coat, 1 to 2 minutes. Add
½ cup broth. Stir while cooking until rice absorbs liquid. When the rice
dries out, add another ½ cup broth. Continue to stir. Continue adding
broth until all is used. Never drown rice. (Risotto is done when rice is
tender but al dente.) When rice is cooked, stir in Parmesan, remaining
4 tablespoons butter, parsley, lemon juice, and zest. Season with salt and
pepper. Cover and let stand a few minutes before serving. Risotto Limone
should have a creamy porridge-like consistency.

*Correct heat is very important. If the liquid evaporates too rapidly, the rice cannot cook evenly. Regulate
heat so risotto will cook in 30 minutes time. After 20 minutes, reduce the amount of broth to ¼ cup
at a time.*

RISOTTO

Risotto is a rice dish which originated in the Po Valley of northern Italy. The cooking technique involves constantly stirring the rice in a simmering broth so that the liquid is slowly absorbed. Risotto is not boiled rice. Italian Arborio rice is commonly used, but another short-grain, high-starch rice may be substituted.

Wild Mushroom and Onion Risotto

SERVES 4 TO 6

2 teaspoons olive oil
1 clove garlic, crushed
1 cup coarsely chopped onion
1 cup raw Italian Arborio rice
2¼ cups chicken broth
8 ounces fresh wild mushrooms,
    thinly sliced (shiitake, oyster,
    or cremini)

1 ounce Parmesan cheese,
    freshly grated (¼ cup)
2 tablespoons dry white wine
——
fresh parsley

Heat oil in a medium skillet over medium heat. Add garlic and onion.
Sauté until tender, about 5 minutes. Add rice. Stir until opaque, about
3 to 4 minutes. Add ½ cup broth and mushrooms. Bring to a boil. Reduce
heat and continue stirring. When liquid is absorbed, add another ½ cup
broth. Stir. Continue this process until all broth has been used. When
rice is done, remove from heat. Stir in Parmesan and wine. Garnish with
parsley and serve.

WILD MUSHROOMS

Although the inexperienced gatherer should be wary of poisonous mushrooms, mushroom gathering is a popular pastime in many countries as wild mushrooms are a delectable offering from the woods. The most common wild mushrooms include:

Boletus - Cèpes in French, porcini in Italian, these have a rich flavor.

Chanterelles - This orange-yellow mushroom can be sautéed and served alone.

Morels - With a conical cap that looks like a sponge, the dark brown morel is considered superior to the blond morel.

Oyster - Also cultivated, the mushrooms have a chewy texture and a neutral flavor.

Shiitake - An oriental variety that is cultivated, they have a strong, meaty flavor.

Baked Spinach

SERVES 8 TO 10

½ cup (1 stick) unsalted butter
½ medium onion, chopped
3 tablespoons all-purpose flour
3 packages (10 ounces each)
  frozen chopped spinach,
  cooked and drained

3 large eggs, lightly beaten
2 cups small curd cottage cheese
6 ounces Cheddar or Colby cheese,
  shredded (1½ cups)
salt
freshly ground pepper

Preheat oven to 350 degrees. Melt butter in a 7 by 11-inch Pyrex dish. Add onion. Stir in flour. Combine spinach, eggs, cottage cheese, and Cheddar or Colby cheese in a bowl. Season with salt and pepper. Spoon spinach mixture into onion mixture. Stir to combine. Bake uncovered 1 hour.

The casserole may be prepared a day ahead, refrigerated, and cooked the next day.

Spinach with Raisins and Pine Nuts

SERVES 4 TO 6

⅓ cup golden raisins
3 pounds fresh spinach, coarse
  stems discarded
2 tablespoons extra virgin olive oil

2 cloves garlic, minced
½ teaspoon salt
⅓ cup toasted pine nuts

Soak raisins in warm water 10 minutes. Drain. Steam spinach over medium-high heat until leaves are tender, about 2 to 3 minutes. Drain. Cool and pat dry.

   Heat olive oil in a large skillet over medium heat. Add garlic. Sauté until garlic begins to turn opaque. Add spinach. Cook, stirring frequently, 1 minute. Stir in salt, pine nuts, and raisins. Adjust seasonings. Continue to cook 3 minutes. Serve immediately.

Fried Green Tomatoes

SERVES 1 TO 2

**GREEN TOMATO
SANDWICH**

For a wonderful southern-style sandwich, layer slices of fried green tomatoes, basil, bacon, and mozzarella between two slices of toasted white bread.

¼ cup cornmeal
¼ teaspoon sugar
½ teaspoon salt
1 firm green tomato, cut into
  ½-inch slices

bacon fat from 4 slices of bacon
2 tablespoons peanut oil
———
coarse salt

Combine cornmeal, sugar, and salt. Dip each tomato slice into cornmeal mixture. Fry in hot bacon fat and oil until brown, turning once during cooking. Drain on paper towels. Sprinkle with coarse salt and serve hot.

Fried Green Tomatoes

One of the staples of the home garden, squash is cherished as much for its color and distinctive shapes as it is for its marvelous flavor. There's something enduring and essential about a basketful of fresh-picked squash in shades of green, gold, orange, and tan that calls to mind holiday feasts and family occasions. All squashes are members of the gourd family with seeds inside and protective skins outside. Delicately flavored summer squashes are picked early when the skins and seeds are edible and include yellow squash and zucchini. Others to try are the little green or yellow pattypan, shaped like a pie crust with scallops, or the delicious chayote from South and Central America, about the size of an avocado with one large seed, which is prepared the same way as summer squash. Winter squashes are golden with hard-shelled exteriors, picked when fully mature. Some varieties to look for include acorn, butternut, hubbard, and spaghetti squash, mini-pumpkins, and mottled orange-and-green turban squash.

Summer Vegetable Gratin

SERVES 10

2 tomatoes, thinly sliced
1 green bell pepper, seeded and
    thinly sliced
3 zucchini, thinly sliced
1 medium onion, thinly sliced
2 medium potatoes, thinly sliced
3 tablespoons minced fresh oregano
1 ½ teaspoons minced fresh thyme
1 tablespoon minced fresh basil
¼ teaspoon salt

½ cup plus ½ cup raw long-grain rice
¾ cup half and half
¼ teaspoon freshly ground pepper
2 tablespoons unsalted butter,
    cut into pieces
——
8 ounces Cheddar cheese,
    shredded (2 cups)
½ cup bread crumbs

Preheat oven to 350 degrees. Lightly grease a 2-quart baking dish. Combine tomatoes, bell pepper, zucchini, onion, and potatoes in a large bowl. Combine oregano, thyme, basil, and salt in a separate small bowl. Layer half of vegetables in the prepared baking dish. Sprinkle half of oregano mixture on top of vegetables. Add ½ cup rice. Repeat layers. Pour half and half over casserole. Season with pepper. Dot with butter. Cover with foil and bake 1½ hours.

Combine cheese and bread crumbs. Remove foil from casserole. Top with cheese mixture. Bake uncovered an additional 10 minutes.

Grilled Vegetables

SERVES 6 TO 8

1 cup olive oil
1 tablespoon dried thyme
1 tablespoon crushed garlic
1 teaspoon crushed red pepper
1 tablespoon dried tarragon
1 tablespoon dried basil
1 ½ tablespoons sun-dried tomatoes
    packed in oil, thinly sliced
——
1 large red bell pepper, seeded and
    sliced into 1 ½-inch strips
1 large yellow bell pepper, seeded
    and sliced into 1 ½-inch strips

1 zucchini, blanched and sliced
    lengthwise
1 yellow squash, blanched and
    sliced lengthwise
2 carrots, blanched and sliced
    lengthwise
8 ounces green beans, blanched
1 onion, sliced into ½-inch rounds
1 eggplant, sliced into ½-inch rounds
an assortment of whole fresh
    mushrooms
10 to 15 tiny new potatoes, unpeeled
    and steamed

Combine oil, thyme, garlic, red pepper, tarragon, basil, and tomatoes in a small bowl. Stir to blend. Combine bell peppers, zucchini, squash, carrots, green beans, onion, eggplant, mushrooms, and potatoes in a nonmetallic shallow baking dish. Pour marinade over vegetables. Toss to coat. Cover and refrigerate 1 to 2 hours. Bring to room temperature before grilling.

Prepare grill. Remove vegetables from marinade. Reserve marinade. Grill, basting with reserved marinade, until tender. Serve immediately.

Roasted Vegetables

SERVES 6 TO 8

10 tiny red new potatoes, unpeeled
   (if unavailable, cut large ones
   into quarters)
10 baby carrots
1 small white onion, cut into wedges
1 small red onion, cut into wedges
¼ cup olive oil
3 to 4 cloves garlic, minced
3 to 4 tablespoons fresh lemon juice
2 tablespoons chopped fresh oregano
   or rosemary, or a combination
1 teaspoon salt

1 teaspoon freshly ground pepper
½ teaspoon lemon pepper
½ small eggplant, peeled and diced
   (about 2 cups)
1 medium red bell pepper, seeded and
   cut into ½-inch strips
1 medium yellow bell pepper, seeded
   and cut into ½-inch strips
1 medium green bell pepper, seeded
   and cut into ½-inch strips
10 to 15 whole fresh mushrooms

Preheat oven to 450 degrees. Place potatoes, carrots, and onions in a 9 by 13-inch baking dish. Mix olive oil, garlic, lemon juice, oregano, rosemary, salt, pepper, and lemon pepper in a small bowl. Drizzle over vegetables and toss. Roast uncovered 20 to 30 minutes. Stir in eggplant, peppers, and mushrooms. Roast an additional 10 to 15 minutes, or until tender.

HIGH-HEAT ROASTING

High-heat roasting in a 425 to 450 degree oven is a cooking technique which produces a crisp outer layer and a moist inner layer. The result is delicious whether roasting meats, fish, or vegetables. When roasting vegetables, use a roasting pan large enough to keep them uncrowded and stir occasionally to prevent sticking. A nicely browned appearance will indicate doneness.

Yam and Butternut Squash Pudding

SERVES 10

1 whole butternut squash (about
   1½ pounds)
1½ pounds yams
1 cup milk
1 cup heavy whipping cream

6 large eggs, at room temperature
½ cup light brown sugar, firmly packed
1 teaspoon ground cinnamon
1 teaspoon ground nutmeg
½ teaspoon salt

Preheat oven to 400 degrees. Place squash and yams on a baking sheet. Bake until soft, about 1 hour. Cool to room temperature. Reduce oven temperature to 350 degrees. Grease an 8-cup soufflé dish.

Peel squash, discarding seeds. Purée pulp in a food processor until smooth. Transfer 1½ cups squash purée to a mixing bowl. Peel yams and purée in a food processor until smooth. Add 1½ cups yams purée to squash purée. Add milk, cream, eggs, brown sugar, cinnamon, nutmeg, and salt. Beat with an electric mixer until smooth. (The pudding can be prepared 1 day ahead to this point and refrigerated. Bring to room temperature before continuing.)

Pour pudding into prepared soufflé dish and place in a roasting pan. Add enough hot water to roasting pan to come 1½ inches up side of soufflé dish. Bake until pudding is firm to the touch, about 1½ hours. Serve hot.

Can also be baked in small ramekins. Decrease baking time to 30 to 40 minutes.

YAMS VS. SWEET POTATOES

Sweet potatoes are often mistaken for yams in the United States. Although the appearance and taste are similar, the sweet potato is a root vegetable and the yam is a tuber. Yams are native to Africa and are called nyami. *When slaves were brought to the United States from Africa, they mistook the American sweet potatoes for* nyami. *The name eventually evolved into yam, and so the confusion began.*

RISE AND SHINE

German Apple Pancakes

Mile High Biscuits

BETTER BISCUITS

◆ Stir the liquid into the flour until just moist. Excessive stirring makes the biscuits tough.

◆ Starting from the center, roll dough out in all directions. A back and forth rolling motion makes the biscuits tough.

◆ Plunge the cutter into dough and pull straight out. Twisting will cause the biscuits to not rise as high.

2 cups all-purpose flour
1 tablespoon sugar
1 tablespoon baking powder
1 teaspoon salt

1 cup heavy whipping cream, additional as needed
4 tablespoons unsalted butter, melted

Preheat oven to 425 degrees. Lightly grease a baking sheet. Combine flour, sugar, baking powder, and salt in a large bowl. Gradually mix in enough cream to bind. Turn dough out onto a floured surface. Knead about 30 seconds. Pat dough into a round ½ inch thick. Cut with biscuit cutter. Dip each biscuit into melted butter, coating top and sides. Place, buttered side up, on prepared baking sheet. Bake 12 minutes, or until light brown.

Mile High Biscuits may be prepared ahead, covered, and refrigerated for up to 2 hours before baking.

Whipping Cream Biscuits

1 cup heavy whipping cream   1 cup self-rising flour

Preheat oven to 425 degrees. Lightly grease a baking sheet. Mix whipping cream and flour in a medium bowl. Drop biscuits on prepared baking sheet. Bake 15 to 20 minutes, checking bottom for doneness. Serve immediately.

Biscuit dough can be rolled out onto a floured surface and cut with biscuit cutter.

Easy Corn Biscuits

1 can (8½ ounces) cream style corn
2¼ cups biscuit mix
½ cup (1 stick) unsalted butter

Optional Ingredients:
4 ounces Cheddar cheese, shredded (1 cup)
¼ cup minced fresh jalapeños

Preheat oven to 450 degrees. Combine corn and biscuit mix in a bowl plus any optional ingredients. Roll out to a ¼-inch thickness on a lightly floured surface. Cut biscuits with a 2-inch cookie cutter. (They may be frozen at this point.) Melt butter in a jelly-roll pan. Add biscuits, coating both sides with butter. Bake 10 minutes, or until golden brown.

Tender Scones

YIELDS 12 WEDGES

2 cups sifted all-purpose flour
½ teaspoon salt
1 tablespoon baking powder
2 tablespoons plus 2 tablespoons sugar
5⅓ tablespoons unsalted butter,
  at room temperature
1 large egg, beaten
½ cup plus 2 tablespoons heavy
  whipping cream

Optional Ingredients:
¾ cup chopped dried apricots, dried
  currants, dried cherries, dried cranberries, dried strawberries, seedless
  raisins, chopped chocolate, or chopped
  nuts, or ½ to 1 teaspoon ground
  cinnamon or ground nutmeg

Combine flour, salt, baking powder, and 2 tablespoons sugar in a large
bowl. Cut in butter with a pastry blender until it resembles small pebbles.
Mix in egg and ½ cup cream. Stir in any combination of the optional
ingredients, but the total amount should be ¾ cup.

Preheat oven to 400 degrees. Turn dough out onto a lightly floured
surface and knead lightly. Pat into a 9-inch circle and to a ½-inch thickness. Place on a baking sheet. Cut into 12 pie-shaped wedges. Brush tops
with remaining 2 tablespoons cream and sprinkle with remaining
2 tablespoons sugar. Bake 15 minutes, or until light brown.

English Scone Cake

YIELDS 16 TO 20 SQUARES

3 cups all-purpose flour
2 teaspoons baking powder
½ teaspoon salt
1 teaspoon ground nutmeg
1 cup sugar
3 tablespoons solid vegetable
  shortening

1 cup water, additional if needed
1 cup currants*
——
¼ cup sugar
½ teaspoon ground nutmeg
2 tablespoons unsalted butter, melted

Preheat oven to 350 degrees. Grease and flour a 9 by 13-inch baking pan.
Combine flour, baking powder, salt, nutmeg, and sugar in a large bowl.
Cut in shortening with a pastry blender. Add water to reach consistency
of drop biscuits. Stir in currants. Spread mixture in prepared pan. Bake
30 to 40 minutes.

Combine sugar and nutmeg in a small bowl. When cake tests done,
brush top with melted butter and sprinkle with sugar mixture.

Raisins may be substituted for the currants.

JAVA JIVE

Coffee is a sociable drink.
Even as far back as the
sixteenth century, travelers
to the Islamic world wrote
of coffeehouses where
customers would gather to
enjoy the brew and discuss
their affairs - and affairs
of state. In the fifties and
sixties, a pot of perked
coffee at the kitchen table
was an important part
of the day for suburban
housewives. Formal coffees
featuring an assortment
of coffees and homemade
baked goods are still good
get-togethers for bridge, for
investment or book clubs,
or for showers and house-
warmings. And as a perfect
ending to a wonderful
meal, there are few things
more deeply satisfying
than sipping a rich coffee
drink flavored with exotic
liqueurs as you sit back,
enjoy the conversation,
and savor the warm feelings
that coffee always seems
to inspire.

Coolrise Sweet Dough

6 to 7 cups all-purpose flour
2 packages dry yeast
½ cup sugar
1½ teaspoons salt

½ cup (1 stick) unsalted butter,
    at room temperature
1½ cups hot water
2 large eggs, at room temperature

Combine 2 cups flour, yeast, sugar, and salt in a large bowl. Stir to blend. Add butter and hot water all at once. Beat with a mixer at medium speed 2 minutes, scraping bowl occasionally. Add eggs and 1 cup flour. Beat at high speed 1 minute, scraping bowl occasionally. Gradually stir in enough remaining flour to make a soft dough that leaves sides of bowl. Turn dough out onto a floured board and knead 5 to 10 minutes. Cover loosely with plastic wrap, then a towel. Let dough rest 20 minutes on the board. Punch down.

This is the basic recipe for Coolrise Sweet Dinner Rolls, Coolrise Orange Rolls, and Coolrise Cinnamon Rolls. Coolrise Sweet Dough may also be shaped into 2 mini-loaves.

Coolrise Sweet Dinner Rolls

YIELDS 2 TO 2½ DOZEN ROLLS

1 recipe Coolrise Sweet Dough

Prepare Coolrise Sweet Dough as directed. Shape dough into any of the shapes described below. After shaping, cover loosely with plastic wrap and refrigerate 2 to 24 hours. Preheat oven to 375 degrees. Bake rolls 15 to 20 minutes.

Dinner Rolls: Pinch off a 2-inch piece. Roll into a ball. Roll until ball forms a log 4 inches long. Roll ends between hands to taper. Place on a greased baking sheet 2 inches apart.

Cloverleaf Rolls: Pinch off a 1-inch piece. Roll into a ball. Place 3 balls in each cup of a greased muffin pan. Balls should touch bottom of cups and fill them half full.

Pan Rolls: Pinch off 2-inch pieces and roll into balls. Place in greased round cake pan, letting balls touch each other. Do not place in center of pan.

Butter Horns: Roll dough to a ¼-inch thickness, brush lightly with melted butter, and cut into a 12-inch circle. Cut circle in 16 pie-shaped pieces. Starting at wide end, roll up. Place, point end down, on a greased baking sheet 2 inches apart.

Crescents: Same procedure as Butter Horns, but curve ends to form crescents.

YEAST

Yeast is a living, microscopic, single-cell organism that, as it grows, converts its food into alcohol and carbon dioxide, a process known as fermentation. The Egyptians are known to have used yeast as a leavening agent more than 5000 years ago. There are two types of yeast commercially available, baker's yeast and brewer's yeast. Baker's yeast, as the name implies, is used as a leavener. The most commonly used is active dry yeast, which is in the form of tiny, dehydrated granules in ¼-ounce envelopes. When mixed with warm water, the cells once again become active. Baker's yeast should be given a test called proofing before it is used. To proof, dissolve a small amount in warm water and add a pinch of sugar, then set aside 5 to 10 minutes. The yeast is alive and capable of leavening bread if it begins to swell and foam. Brewer's yeast is a non-leavening yeast used in beer making and also as a food supplement.

Coolrise Orange Rolls

1 recipe Coolrise Sweet Dough

Orange Filling:
3 cups sifted powdered sugar

1 tablespoon grated orange zest
6 tablespoons unsalted butter,
  at room temperature
¼ cup fresh orange juice

Prepare Coolrise Sweet Dough as directed. Combine powdered sugar, orange zest, butter, and orange juice in a large bowl. Divide Coolrise Sweet Dough in half and roll each piece into a 14 by 7-inch rectangle. Spread one-fourth of orange filling onto each rectangle, leaving a 1-inch margin on long sides. Roll dough jelly-roll fashion, starting at long side. Pinch seam to seal, but do not seal ends. Cut into 12 equal slices per roll. Place slices, cut side down, in greased muffin pans. Cover loosely with plastic wrap and place in refrigerator 2 to 24 hours. Preheat oven to 375 degrees. Bake rolls 15 to 20 minutes. Frost rolls with remaining orange filling while still warm, but not hot.

Coolrise Cinnamon Rolls

1 recipe Coolrise Sweet Dough

Cinnamon Mixture:
1 cup sugar
1 cup all-purpose flour
1 teaspoon ground cinnamon
⅔ cup ground pecans
½ cup (1 stick) unsalted butter,
  melted
2 egg whites, beaten until frothy

Icing:
4 tablespoons unsalted butter,
  at room temperature
4 cups sifted powdered sugar
2 large egg whites
1 teaspoon vanilla extract
¼ teaspoon cream of tartar
1 to 2 teaspoons milk

Prepare Coolrise Sweet Dough as directed. Combine sugar, flour, cinnamon, pecans, butter, and egg whites in a small bowl. Pinch off pieces of Coolrise Sweet Dough and shape into 1½-inch balls. Place on a greased baking sheet 3 inches apart. Press each ball down to flatten slightly. Make an indentation in center of each ball. Top with a spoonful of cinnamon mixture. Cover loosely with plastic wrap. Refrigerate 2 to 24 hours.

Preheat oven to 375 degrees. Cut butter into sugar, using a pastry blender, until mixture looks like cornmeal. Add egg whites, vanilla, and cream of tartar. Beat until thoroughly combined, adding milk to achieve desired consistency. Set aside. Bake rolls 15 to 20 minutes. Remove rolls from baking sheet immediately. Drizzle icing over rolls while still warm.

Dewberry Jewels

YIELDS 18 MUFFINS

DEWBERRIES

A cousin to boysenberries and youngberries, dewberries, also known as trailing blackberries, grow on plants which trail along the ground. Select plump berries with glossy, unbroken skins. Chill berries before washing in ice water.

½ cup (1 stick) unsalted butter,
  at room temperature
1 ¼ cups sugar
2 large eggs, at room temperature
2 cups all-purpose flour
2 teaspoons baking powder

½ teaspoon salt
½ cup milk
1 ½ cups fresh dewberries*
——
4 teaspoons Vanilla Sugar

Preheat oven to 375 degrees. Lightly grease muffin pan. Cream butter and sugar in a large bowl until light and fluffy. Add eggs, one at a time, beating well after each addition. Sift flour, baking powder, and salt into a small bowl. Add flour mixture to butter mixture, alternating with milk. Fold in dewberries. Divide batter evenly among muffin cups. Sprinkle tops with vanilla sugar. Bake 30 minutes, or until golden brown.

Blueberries, blackberries, raspberries, or pecan pieces may be substituted for the dewberries. (Frozen berries, thawed and drained, may be used.)

Vanilla Sugar:
1 or 2 vanilla beans
sugar

Place one or two vanilla beans in a container. Fill container with granulated sugar. Cover with plastic wrap and then lid. Sugar will be flavored within a few days.

USES FOR VANILLA SUGAR

Vanilla sugar has a wonderful aroma. It can be used for decorating cookies and cakes, sprinkled over fresh fruit, or stirred into coffee or tea.

Lemon Yogurt Muffins

YIELDS 2 DOZEN MUFFINS

3 cups all-purpose flour
¼ teaspoon salt
½ teaspoon baking powder
1 teaspoon baking soda
2 to 3 tablespoons grated lemon zest
1 cup chopped pecans
1 cup vegetable oil
1 ¾ cups sugar

3 large eggs
2 cups plain yogurt or sour cream
¼ cup fresh lemon juice

Glaze:
3 cups sifted powdered sugar
grated zest of 2 lemons, minced
juice of 1 ½ lemons

Preheat oven to 350 degrees. Lightly grease muffin pans. Combine flour, salt, baking powder, baking soda, lemon zest, and pecans in a large bowl. Combine oil, sugar, eggs, yogurt, and lemon juice in a separate bowl. Combine flour and egg mixtures, mixing until blended. Pour into muffin cups. Bake 25 to 30 minutes, or until muffins are slightly brown at the edges.

    Combine powdered sugar, lemon zest, and lemon juice in a small bowl. Spread glaze on warm muffins. Serve immediately.

Lemon Yogurt Muffins may also be made in mini-muffin pans. Decrease baking time to 10 minutes. Yields 6 dozen mini-muffins.

*Lemon Yogurt Muffins and
Tender Scones with Cherries*

Orange and Pecan Muffins

MASTERING MUFFINS

- Grease muffin pans with shortening or nonstick cooking spray,
  not butter.

- Vigorous stirring creates tough
  muffins with pointed tops. Stir
  only until dry ingredients are
  moistened. Lumps will disappear
  during baking.

- Never grease muffin cups that
  won't be used. Place an ice
  cube or several tablespoons of
  water in unused cups to prevent
  warping of the pan.

- Muffins are done when tops are
  domed and dry to the touch or
  when an inserted wooden pick
  comes out clean.

1 large egg, lightly beaten
½ cup vegetable oil
½ cup milk
1 ½ cups all-purpose flour
¼ cup sugar
¼ cup brown sugar, firmly packed
2 teaspoons baking powder
2 teaspoons grated orange zest
½ teaspoon ground cinnamon
½ teaspoon salt

Topping:
½ cup chopped pecans
½ cup brown sugar, firmly packed
¼ cup all-purpose flour
¼ teaspoon ground cinnamon
2 tablespoons unsalted butter, melted

Icing:
¾ cup powdered sugar
1 tablespoon fresh orange juice
½ teaspoon vanilla extract

Preheat oven to 400 degrees. Lightly grease a muffin pan. Combine egg, oil, and milk in a small bowl. Set aside. Combine flour, sugar, brown sugar, baking powder, orange zest, cinnamon, and salt in a large bowl. Add egg mixture to flour mixture. Mix until blended. Fill muffin cups two-thirds full.

Combine pecans, brown sugar, flour, cinnamon, and butter. Mix until crumbly. Spoon topping evenly over each muffin. Bake 20 minutes.

Combine powdered sugar, orange juice, and vanilla in a small bowl. Drizzle icing over muffins while still warm.

Bountiful Breakfast Muffins

1 ½ cups All Bran cereal
1 ¼ cups skim milk
2 large egg whites
⅓ cup applesauce
½ cup mashed banana
½ cup raisins
½ cup sugar
½ teaspoon salt

1 tablespoon baking powder
1 teaspoon vanilla extract
¼ teaspoon ground cinnamon
⅛ teaspoon ground nutmeg
⅛ teaspoon ground allspice
½ cup chopped pecans
1 ¼ cups sifted all-purpose flour

Preheat oven to 400 degrees. Lightly grease muffin pans. Combine All Bran and milk in a large bowl. Let rest 3 minutes. Add egg whites, apple-sauce, banana, raisins, sugar, salt, baking powder, vanilla, cinnamon, nutmeg, allspice, and pecans. Mix well. Gradually add flour and mix only until combined. Fill muffin cups two-thirds full. Bake 20 minutes.

Bountiful Breakfast Muffins are low-calorie and low-fat if pecans are omitted. Enjoy the guiltless delight.

Walnut Muffins

2 cups dark brown sugar,
  firmly packed
2 tablespoons unsalted butter,
  melted

4 large eggs
¼ teaspoon black walnut extract
1 ½ cups whole wheat flour
½ cup chopped walnuts

Preheat oven to 350 degrees. Grease mini-muffin pans. Mix brown sugar
with butter in a large bowl. Beat in eggs, one at a time, beating after each
addition. Add walnut extract. Stir in flour and nuts. Combine well. Fill
muffin cups half full. Bake 20 minutes, or until inserted wooden pick
comes out clean. Remove muffins from cups while still warm.

Fresh Rosemary Muffins

1 tablespoon chopped fresh
  rosemary
¼ cup golden raisins
¼ cup raisins
¼ cup currants
¾ cup milk
4 tablespoons unsalted butter
1 ½ cups all-purpose flour

½ cup sugar
2 teaspoons baking powder
¼ teaspoon salt
1 large egg, lightly beaten
4 ounces goat cheese (8 tablespoons),
  or 4 ounces cream cheese, cut into
  ¾-inch cubes

Preheat oven to 350 degrees. Lightly grease a muffin pan. Combine
rosemary, raisins, currants, and milk in a small saucepan. Simmer 2 to
4 minutes. Remove from heat. Add butter and stir until melted. Let cool.
(To cool quickly, place pan in refrigerator about 10 minutes.) Combine
flour, sugar, baking powder, and salt in a large bowl. Mix until combined.
Set aside. Slowly add beaten egg to cooled milk mixture. When combined, add to dry mixture. Mix until dry ingredients are moistened.
Spoon one-third batter into muffin cups. Place 2 teaspoons goat cheese
or one ¾-inch cube cream cheese in center of batter, dividing among
cups. Top with remaining batter. Bake 20 minutes, or until golden brown
and springy in centers. Muffins can be served hot or at room temperature.

Lemon Poppy Seed Tea Bread

YIELDS 1 LARGE LOAF OR 3 SMALL LOAVES

POPPY SEEDS

Poppy seeds are the ripe seeds of the opium poppy. They have a crunchy texture and a nutty flavor. Like other seeds and nuts, the poppy seed's flavor can be enhanced by toasting. There is no need to pre-toast poppy seeds that are to be used as a topping for baked goods. Seeds may be stored up to 6 months in an airtight container in the refrigerator.

6 tablespoons unsalted butter,
   at room temperature
1 cup sugar
1 tablespoon lemon extract
2 large eggs, at room temperature
1 ½ cups all-purpose flour
¼ teaspoon salt
1 ½ teaspoons baking powder

½ cup milk
grated zest of 1 lemon
1 tablespoon poppy seeds

Glaze:
½ cup super-fine sugar
3 tablespoons fresh lemon juice

Preheat oven to 325 degrees. Grease a 5 by 9-inch loaf pan. Cream butter and sugar in a large bowl until light and fluffy. Add lemon extract and eggs, one at a time, beating well after each addition. Sift flour, salt, and baking powder. Combine milk and lemon zest in a separate bowl. Stir flour mixture into butter mixture, ½ cup at a time, alternating with milk mixture. Stir in poppy seeds. Stir dough until blended. Pour into loaf pan. Bake 50 minutes.

Combine sugar and lemon juice. Remove loaf from oven. Loosen sides from pan. Spoon glaze over top, letting some run down the sides. Cool 10 minutes. Remove from pan and cool completely on wire rack.

English Muffin Bread

YIELDS 2 LOAVES

ZILLAH MAE'S JAM

7 cups sugar
4 cups fresh raspberries
2 cups fresh blueberries, stemmed
⅓ cup fresh lemon juice
6 ounces liquid fruit pectin

Crush raspberries and blueberries in a large saucepan. Add sugar and lemon juice, mixing well. Bring to a rapid boil. Stir while boiling 1 minute. Remove from heat. Stir in pectin, blending well. Skim foam, if necessary. Ladle into sterilized 1-cup jars leaving ½ inch on top. Seal with scalded hot lids. Store in refrigerator. Yields 5 pints.

3 cups plus 2½ to 3 cups
   all-purpose flour
2 packages dry yeast
1 tablespoon sugar
2 teaspoons salt

¼ teaspoon baking soda
2 cups milk
½ cup water
cornmeal

Lightly grease two 8 ½ by 4 ½-inch loaf pans and sprinkle them with cornmeal. Combine 3 cups flour, yeast, sugar, salt, and baking soda in a large bowl. Set aside. Heat milk and water in a small saucepan until very warm. Add milk mixture to flour mixture. Beat well. Stir in 2 ½ to 3 cups more flour to make a stiff batter. Spoon batter into pans. Loosely cover and let rise in a warm place for 45 minutes. Preheat oven to 400 degrees. Bake 25 minutes. Remove immediately and cool on wire rack.

This bread is delicious toasted and served with Zillah Mae's Jam.

Herbed Beer Bread

3 cups self-rising flour
3 tablespoons sugar
2 ounces Parmesan cheese,
 freshly grated (½ cup)
1 tablespoon minced fresh oregano

1 tablespoon minced fresh basil
1 tablespoon minced fresh thyme
12 ounces beer, at room temperature
2 tablespoons unsalted butter, melted
cornmeal

Preheat oven to 325 degrees. Grease a 5 by 9-inch loaf pan and sprinkle bottom and sides with cornmeal. Combine flour, sugar, cheese, oregano, basil, and thyme in a large mixing bowl. Stir in beer to produce a stiff batter. Pour batter into pan. Bake 1 hour and 5 minutes. Brush with butter and sprinkle with cornmeal. Remove from pan and cool on a wire rack.

Bread may be frozen, wrapped in an airtight package, for up to 3 months.

Fresh Herb Focaccia

1 teaspoon rapid rise yeast
⅔ cup warm water
2 cups all-purpose flour
¼ cup semolina flour

1 teaspoon coarse salt
2 tablespoons minced fresh
 rosemary or fresh sage
⅓ cup plus 1 tablespoon olive oil

Combine yeast and water in a small bowl. Set aside. Combine flour, semolina flour, salt, and rosemary or sage in a large bowl. Add ⅓ cup olive oil and yeast mixture to flour mixture. Knead dough about 10 minutes on a floured surface, adding more flour if necessary, until no longer sticky. Put dough in a large bowl. Let rise until doubled in size, about 1½ hours. (If you have a bread machine, add ingredients according to your machine's instructions on "dough" mode.) Roll out on a floured surface to a 12-inch diameter. Cover and let rise 30 minutes.

   Preheat oven to 375 degrees. Place dough on pizza stone or greased baking sheet. Brush with remaining 1 tablespoon olive oil. Bake 20 to 25 minutes, or until golden brown, misting oven with water 2 or 3 times during first 10 minutes of baking. Cool completely on a wire rack. Remove and cut into 8 wedges. Serve warm. May be made in advance and reheated.

FOCACCIA

This Italian flat bread originated on the Ligurian coast of Italy. Try dipping it in a mixture of olive oil and freshly ground pepper as a prelude to a meal.

Tomato Tart

1 unbaked 10-inch pie crust
pinch ground nutmeg

——

1½ pounds Roma tomatoes,
  thickly sliced
1 rib celery, coarsely chopped
1 carrot, peeled and
  coarsely chopped
1 medium red onion,
  coarsely chopped
1 clove garlic, minced
¼ cup coarsely chopped Italian
  parsley, firmly packed

2 tablespoons olive oil
2 tablespoons unsalted butter, melted
salt
freshly ground pepper
1 tablespoon minced fresh basil
4 large eggs, lightly beaten
2 ounces Parmesan cheese, freshly
  grated (½ cup)
1 large tomato, seeded and thinly sliced

——

fresh basil leaves
freshly grated Parmesan cheese

Place pie crust into tart pan. Dust with nutmeg and prick bottom with
a fork. Place aluminum foil with pie weights or dried beans over pastry.
Chill 30 minutes. Preheat oven to 425 degrees. Bake 10 to 15 minutes.
Remove foil and weights. Continue cooking until crust is golden and
dry in the center, about 5 minutes. Remove from oven and cool at least
15 minutes.

Place tomatoes, celery, carrot, onion, garlic, and parsley in a large
skillet. Drizzle olive oil over top. Cover and cook over medium-low heat
1 hour, stirring occasionally. Transfer mixture to a food processor. Process
until finely chopped. Add butter. Process to combine. Season with salt
and pepper. Transfer tomato mixture to a medium saucepan. Cook over
medium heat until thickened, about 15 minutes. Transfer to a bowl and
stir in basil. Set aside and allow to cool completely.

Preheat oven to 350 degrees. Add eggs and Parmesan to cooled
tomato mixture. Pour tomato mixture into pie crust. Arrange tomato
slices over filling. Bake 20 minutes, or until golden brown and filling is
firm in the center. Cool 12 to 15 minutes before slicing. Garnish with
basil and Parmesan.

Herb Tomato Onion Quiche

3 tablespoons unsalted butter
2 cups thinly sliced onion
1 tablespoon all-purpose flour
2 large eggs
1 cup milk
1 teaspoon salt
⅛ teaspoon freshly ground pepper
2 tablespoons chopped fresh parsley

1 tablespoon chopped fresh chives
1½ teaspoons chopped fresh tarragon
1½ teaspoons chopped fresh basil
4 ounces Cheddar cheese,
  shredded (1 cup)
1 unbaked 9-inch deep dish pie crust
1 tomato, thinly sliced

Preheat oven to 425 degrees. Melt butter in a large skillet. Add onions and sauté until tender. Stir in flour. Set aside. Beat eggs and milk in a small bowl. Add salt, pepper, parsley, chives, tarragon, and basil. Place sautéed onions and cheese into pie crust. Cover with egg mixture. Bake 15 minutes. Reduce heat to 350 degrees. Bake an additional 15 minutes. Arrange tomato slices on top of pie. Bake until tomatoes begin to brown, about 10 minutes.

Hash Brown Quiche

24 ounces frozen uncooked shredded
  hash browns, thawed
5⅓ tablespoons unsalted butter,
  melted
2 large eggs, beaten
½ cup half and half
½ teaspoon seasoned salt

4 ounces Jalapeño Jack cheese,
  shredded (1 cup)
4 ounces Swiss cheese, shredded
  (1 cup)
1 cup diced ham
———
fresh parsley

Preheat oven to 425 degrees. Press hash browns into quiche pan. Blot with paper towel to remove all moisture. Brush with melted butter. Bake 25 minutes. Remove from oven. Reduce oven to 350 degrees. Combine eggs, half and half, and salt. Place cheeses and ham in hash brown shell. Pour egg mixture over top. Bake 40 to 50 minutes. Garnish with parsley.

Yes, there really was a Johnny Appleseed. A God-fearing, apple-loving, Swedenborgian missionary, John Chapman was born in 1774 in Massachusetts. As early American pioneers moved westward along the Ohio River, he wandered with them, planting orchards, preaching the gospel, and giving away apple seeds and saplings. While the Swedenborgian gospel he spread may not be one of America's foremost religions, his love of apples is an important part of the American tradition. Apples are grown in every region of the country from late summer to winter, and the varieties are truly astonishing: from the plentiful Red and Golden Delicious, Jonathan, and Winesap to tasty antique kinds like Cox's Orange Pippin and Rhode Island Greening. Some are recommended for eating, some for cooking, and some for making cider or drying. Of course, the method beloved by most Americans is when they're seasoned with fragrant spices, baked in a golden crust, and topped with a scoop of slowly melting vanilla ice cream. Apple pie is a treat anytime.

Apple Raisin Quiche

SERVES 6 TO 8

1 unbaked 9-inch pie crust
½ cup raisins
2 teaspoons ground cinnamon
¼ cup light brown sugar, firmly packed
3 medium Granny Smith apples, peeled, cored, and thinly sliced

3 large eggs
1 cup heavy whipping cream
12 ounces Monterey Jack cheese, shredded (3 cups)

Preheat oven to 400 degrees. Place pie crust into pie pan. Scallop edges and prick bottom and sides with fork. Line snugly with foil. Bake 6 minutes. Remove foil and continue baking an additional 10 minutes. Remove from oven. Set aside. Combine raisins, cinnamon, and brown sugar in a small bowl. Place half of apple slices in pie crust. Cover apple slices with half of raisin mixture. Repeat layers. Beat eggs with cream in a small bowl. Pour egg mixture over layers. Top with cheese. Bake 1 hour, or until top is browned and apples are tender. Cool 10 minutes before slicing.

Confetti Eggs

SERVES 6

2 tablespoons unsalted butter
1 small onion, minced
1 red bell pepper, seeded and diced
1 green bell pepper, seeded and diced
5 large fresh mushrooms, diced
freshly ground pepper
4 ounces Colby cheese, shredded (1 cup)

6 large eggs
1 cup heavy whipping cream
¼ cup milk
salt
1¼ teaspoons ground cumin
¼ teaspoon crumbled dried thyme
⅛ teaspoon Tabasco Sauce

Melt butter in a heavy skillet over medium heat. Add onion, bell peppers, and mushrooms. Sauté until tender, stirring occasionally, about 7 minutes. Season with pepper. Set aside.

Preheat oven to 325 degrees. Generously grease a 9-inch square baking dish. Sprinkle cheese over bottom and sides of dish, pressing lightly. Combine eggs, cream, milk, salt, cumin, thyme, and Tabasco in a food processor. Process 5 seconds. Add two-thirds onion mixture and pulse to combine. Pour egg mixture into prepared dish. Bake until eggs are almost set, about 30 minutes. Sprinkle remaining one-third onion mixture over top. Bake until eggs are set, about 10 minutes more. Cut into squares and serve hot.

Savory Breakfast Strata

SERVES 6

5 cups cubed day-old bread
4 links Italian turkey sausage,
  casings removed, browned,
  and crumbled
¼ cup chopped sun-dried
  tomatoes packed in oil, oil reserved
½ cup chopped onion
1 to 2 tablespoons chopped
  fresh rosemary

4 to 6 ounces Monterey Jack cheese,
  shredded (1 to 1½ cups)
6 large eggs
1½ cups milk
1 teaspoon salt
¼ teaspoon freshly ground pepper
1 teaspoon dry mustard
¼ teaspoon ground nutmeg (optional)

Spray a 9-inch square baking dish with nonstick cooking spray. Sprinkle bread cubes in casserole. Sprinkle sausage evenly over bread cubes. Pour 1 tablespoon reserved sun-dried tomato oil into skillet. Add onions and sauté until tender. Add tomatoes and rosemary, stirring until blended. Place onion mixture over sausage. Cover with cheese. Whisk eggs, milk, salt, pepper, dry mustard, and nutmeg in a medium bowl until well blended. Pour egg mixture over casserole. Cover. Refrigerate 8 to 10 hours or overnight. Bring to room temperature before baking. Preheat oven to 350 degrees. Bake 30 to 45 minutes, or until set.

BRIE SOUFFLÉ

3 tablespoons unsalted butter, at
  room temperature
6 slices white bread, crusts removed
1½ cups whole milk
1 teaspoon Tabasco Sauce
3 large eggs
1 pound Brie, rind removed and
  thinly sliced

——

chopped red bell pepper
chopped fresh parsley

Preheat oven to 350 degrees. Grease a 1½-quart soufflé dish. Butter bread slices on one side and cut each slice into thirds. Combine milk, Tabasco, and eggs in a small bowl. Beat lightly. Place half of bread slices, butter side up, in prepared soufflé dish. Top with half of Brie. Repeat layers. Slowly pour egg mixture over layers. Let rest 30 minutes. Bake 45 minutes, or until golden brown. Garnish with bell pepper and parsley.

Vegetable Frittata

SERVES 6

2 tablespoons vegetable oil
¾ cup diced green bell pepper
¾ cup diced mushrooms
¾ cup diced zucchini
¾ cup diced onion
¾ cup diced pimento
6 large eggs
2 packages (8 ounces each) cream
  cheese, softened

¼ cup milk
2 cups cubed white bread
6 ounces Cheddar cheese, shredded
  (1½ cups)
1 teaspoon salt
½ teaspoon garlic powder
¼ teaspoon freshly ground pepper

Preheat oven to 350 degrees. Lightly grease a quiche or 9-inch springform pan. Heat oil in a large skillet. Add bell pepper, mushrooms, zucchini, onion, and pimento. Sauté until tender. Drain. Transfer to a large bowl. Beat eggs with cream cheese and milk until smooth. Add egg mixture to vegetable mixture. Stir to combine. Add bread, cheese, salt, garlic powder, and pepper. Combine well. Pour into prepared pan. Bake 30 minutes. Cool 10 to 20 minutes. Cut into wedges.

Sausage or bacon may be added.

THE ITALIAN OMELETTE

An Italian frittata has often been confused with the French omelette. A frittata is cooked slowly over low heat or in a moderate oven. Its texture is firm and set, not creamy and moist like an omelette.

Eggs Sardou

EGGS SARDOU

From New Orleans, where Creole is a prominent part of the cuisine, comes Eggs Sardou. A twist on the traditional Eggs Benedict, this recipe recalls the indulgence of the French Quarter.

Eggs can be poached up to 24 hours in advance. Poach eggs until set, but less done than desired. With a slotted spoon, remove eggs to a shallow pan. Cover eggs with cold water and plastic wrap. Refrigerate. When ready to serve, carefully place eggs into a pan of simmering water. Cook until warm, about 1 minute.

2 cups heavy whipping cream
4 large egg yolks, beaten
2 packages (10 ounces each) frozen chopped spinach, thawed and drained
1 teaspoon salt
¼ teaspoon white pepper
⅛ teaspoon ground nutmeg
dash Tabasco Sauce

——

2 cans (16 ounces each) artichoke bottoms, drained

Hollandaise Sauce:
2 large egg yolks
1 to 2 tablespoons fresh lemon juice
¼ teaspoon Dijon mustard
4 tablespoons plus 4 tablespoons unsalted butter

——

8 large eggs, poached

Preheat oven to 350 degrees. Bring cream to a boil in a medium saucepan. Reduce heat. Simmer uncovered 5 minutes. Spoon some cream into egg yolks, then stir egg yolks into cream. Return cream mixture to a boil, stirring constantly, until thickened, about 2 minutes. Add spinach, salt, pepper, nutmeg, and Tabasco, stirring until well blended. Set aside.

Bake artichoke bottoms in shallow baking pan until hot, 5 to 7 minutes.

Hollandaise Sauce: Whisk egg yolks, lemon juice, and mustard in a small saucepan until smooth. Add 4 tablespoons butter. Cook over low heat, stirring constantly, until butter melts. Add remaining 4 tablespoons butter. Continue stirring until butter melts and sauce thickens. Keep warm.

Arrange spinach mixture on a serving plate. Top with artichoke bottoms. Place a poached egg on each artichoke bottom. Spoon Hollandaise Sauce over eggs. Serve immediately.

German Apple Pancakes

2 tablespoons unsalted butter
6 large eggs
1 cup all-purpose flour
2 tablespoons sugar
½ teaspoon salt
1 cup milk

Cinnamon Apples:
4 tablespoons unsalted butter
2 large Granny Smith apples,*
  cored and sliced ¼ inch thick
  (peel if desired)
6 tablespoons sugar
1 ½ teaspoons ground cinnamon
2 teaspoons powdered sugar

Preheat oven to 400 degrees. Place butter in two 9-inch ovenproof skillets. Heat in oven until butter is melted. Spread butter evenly. Set aside. Process eggs, flour, sugar, salt, and milk in a food processor. Divide batter evenly between the prepared skillets. Bake 10 to 15 minutes, or until a deep golden brown. Remove from oven and immediately loosen pancake from pan and slide onto serving dish. Keep warm.

Cinnamon Apples: While pancakes are baking, melt butter in a large skillet. Add apples. Sprinkle sugar and cinnamon over apples. Stir to coat. Cook over medium-high heat until slices are tender, stirring occasionally, about 6 to 8 minutes. Pour apples onto pancakes. Sift powdered sugar over top and serve.

Pears may be substituted for the apples.

This recipe may be made using one German apple pancake pan. Bake at 400 degrees 15 minutes. Reduce oven to 325 degrees and continue to bake 40 to 45 minutes, or until deep golden brown.

Stone Ground Cornmeal Pancakes

1 cup all-purpose flour
1 teaspoon baking soda
2 heaping tablespoons baking powder
3 tablespoons sugar
¼ teaspoon kosher salt
3 heaping tablespoons wheat germ

3 heaping tablespoons stone
  ground yellow cornmeal
1 cup sour cream
1 large egg, lightly beaten
3 tablespoons unsalted butter, melted
½ to 1 cup milk

Combine flour, baking soda, baking powder, sugar, salt, wheat germ, and cornmeal in a large mixing bowl. Stir until well blended. Add sour cream and egg. Blend in melted butter. (Batter will be stiff.) Batter can be prepared in advance and refrigerated at this point, which will enhance the flavors. Thin batter with small amounts of milk until it runs slowly out of a cup. Cook on a lightly oiled hot skillet or griddle. Serve with butter and warm maple syrup.

PANCAKES

A stack of golden pancakes topped with maple syrup or honey (or any number of fresh fruits or dessert toppings) is a perfect way to start the day. For many, they're a favorite Sunday morning tradition as the cook, often the father, demonstrates his skill at the griddle while the rest of the family waits with mouths watering. Fortunately, the wait isn't long. And neither is the amount of time the pancakes spend on the plates; they're usually polished off in record time. Pancakes have been around in one form or another since ancient Egypt. They were a popular food in Western Europe by the ninth century as a substitute for meat in Lenten shriving practices. In America, pancakes have enjoyed widespread popularity since a commercial pancake mix was promoted at the 1893 Chicago World's Fair. Pancakes can be the highlight of the meal, cooked with ripe fruits like banana and berries or served simply with flavored syrup and plenty of butter.

Banana Pancakes

4 very ripe bananas
2 large eggs
2 tablespoons fresh lime juice
2 tablespoons sugar

1 teaspoon vanilla extract
1 cup all-purpose flour
½ cup vegetable oil, additional if needed

Mash bananas in a food processor. Add eggs, lime juice, sugar, and vanilla. Blend until smooth. Add flour, mixing well. Add water if necessary to make batter into a very thin consistency. Heat oil in a heavy skillet. Drop one tablespoon batter into oil. Turn once or twice until lightly browned all over. The pancakes should be crisp, similar to a fritter. Serve with butter and hot maple syrup.

This dish is nice accompanied by a fruit salad of mango, papaya, and kiwi.

PERFECT PANCAKES

- The griddle should be very hot. To test, sprinkle surface with water. If it "dances," the griddle is ready.

- Batter should be lumpy. Overbeating makes tough pancakes.

- Cook the first side until bubbles break all over surface. Flip and cook second side until golden brown.

- Never press down on a pancake with a spatula. This will compress it and make it heavy.

- If not serving immediately, keep warm by placing in a single layer on a dishtowel-covered baking sheet. Place in 200 degree oven.

Oatmeal and Berry Pancakes

2 cups rolled oats
2 cups buttermilk
2 large eggs, beaten
4 tablespoons unsalted
  butter, melted and cooled
½ cup all-purpose flour
1 tablespoon sugar
1 teaspoon baking powder

1 teaspoon baking soda
¼ teaspoon ground cinnamon
½ teaspoon ground nutmeg
½ teaspoon salt
1 ½ cups berries (blueberries,
  raspberries, blackberries, or
  a combination)

Place oats in a food processor and process 10 seconds. Combine oats and buttermilk in a large bowl. Cover and refrigerate overnight. Whisk eggs and butter into oat mixture. Combine flour, sugar, baking powder, baking soda, cinnamon, nutmeg, and salt. Add to oat mixture. Spray a griddle with nonstick cooking spray. Cook pancakes on a hot griddle until batter bubbles and the bottom is golden brown. Sprinkle a few berries on each pancake before turning. Turn and brown other side. Remove to individual plates. Garnish with fresh berries. Serve with hot maple syrup.

Orange Pecan Waffles with Orange Maple Syrup

SERVES 6

¾ cup pecans, lightly toasted
  and cooled
1¾ cups all-purpose flour
3 tablespoons sugar
2 tablespoons baking powder
¾ teaspoon salt
¼ cup freshly grated orange zest
3 large eggs

6 tablespoons unsalted butter,
  melted and cooled
1¼ cups club soda

Orange Maple Syrup:
1 cup maple syrup
¼ cup fresh orange juice

Process pecans, flour, sugar, baking powder, and salt in a food processor until pecans are finely ground. Transfer pecan mixture to a large bowl. Stir in orange zest. Whisk eggs and butter in a small bowl. Add egg mixture and club soda to flour mixture, stirring until just combined. Cook waffles on a hot waffle iron. Keep warm.

    Orange Maple Syrup: Heat syrup and orange juice in a saucepan. Stir until hot. Serve with waffles.

MAKING WAFFLES
- Never open the waffle iron during the first minute of cooking or the waffle will split apart.
- Waffles are done when the steaming stops, the lid rises, and the visible sides are golden brown.
- If there is resistance when the lid is lifted, the waffle is not done.

Sour Cream Pecan Waffles

SERVES 4

3 large eggs, separated
¾ cup milk
½ cup (1 stick) unsalted butter,
  melted and cooled
1 cup sour cream
1½ cups all-purpose flour

2 teaspoons baking powder
½ teaspoon baking soda
1 tablespoon sugar
½ cup chopped pecans, lightly
  toasted and cooled

Whisk egg yolks in a large bowl until light. Add milk, butter, and sour cream. Stir until smooth. Combine flour, baking powder, baking soda, and sugar in a separate large bowl. Sift flour mixture into egg mixture, blending well. Stir in pecan pieces. Beat egg whites until stiff. Carefully fold egg whites into the batter with a spatula. Spray a waffle iron with nonstick cooking spray. Cook waffles on a hot waffle iron until golden brown. Serve hot with maple syrup or fresh fruit.

SWEET TEMPTATIONS

Divine Espresso Ice Cream with Biscotti

Cameo Cake with White Chocolate Frosting

Cake:

1 ½ cups (3 sticks) unsalted butter

¾ cup water

4 ounces white chocolate, broken
  into pieces

1 ½ cups buttermilk

4 large eggs, lightly beaten

1 ½ teaspoons vanilla extract

½ cup plus 3 cups all-purpose flour

1 cup chopped toasted pecans

2 ¼ cups sugar

1 ½ teaspoons baking soda

White Chocolate Frosting:

4 ounces white chocolate

11 ounces cream cheese, softened

5 tablespoons unsalted butter,
  at room temperature

1 ½ cups sifted powdered sugar

1 ½ teaspoons vanilla extract

Preheat oven to 350 degrees. Grease and flour three 9-inch round cake pans. Melt butter in a medium saucepan. Add water. Bring to a boil over medium heat, stirring occasionally. Remove from heat. Add chocolate, stirring until it melts. Stir in buttermilk, eggs, and vanilla. Set aside. Combine ½ cup flour and pecans, stirring to coat. Set aside. Combine remaining 3 cups flour, sugar, and baking soda in a large bowl. Gradually stir in chocolate mixture. Fold in pecan mixture. (Batter will be thin.) Pour batter into prepared pans. Bake 20 to 25 minutes, or until cake tester inserted in center comes out clean. Cool in pans on wire racks for 10 minutes. Remove from pans. Let cool completely on wire racks.

White Chocolate Frosting: Melt chocolate in top of a double boiler over low heat, stirring constantly. Remove from heat. Set aside to cool, about 10 minutes. Beat cream cheese and butter. Gradually add chocolate, mixing constantly, until blended. Slowly mix in powdered sugar until smooth. Add vanilla. Mix until blended.

Spread frosting on tops of two layers then stack layers on a serving plate. Use wooden picks to stabilize the two layers. Add third layer. Frost top and sides of cake. Refrigerate until ready to serve.

Party Lemon Cake

SERVES 8 TO 10

Lemon Frosting:
3 cups sugar
1 cup all-purpose flour
4 large eggs, beaten
2 cups cold water
 juice and grated zest of 4 lemons
4 tablespoons unsalted butter
¼ cup bourbon

Cake:
1 cup (2 sticks) unsalted butter,
 at room temperature
2½ cups sugar
1 teaspoon vanilla extract
5 large eggs
1 teaspoon baking soda
1 cup buttermilk
2½ cups cake flour, sifted

——

sweetened whipped cream
lemon slices

Lemon Frosting: Combine sugar and flour in top of a double boiler. Blend in eggs, water, lemon juice, and zest. Cook until very thick. Remove from heat. Stir in butter and bourbon. Refrigerate until thoroughly chilled.

Preheat oven to 350 degrees. Grease and flour three 9-inch round cake pans. Cream butter and sugar until light and fluffy. Blend in vanilla. Add eggs, one at a time, blending after each addition. Dissolve baking soda in buttermilk. Alternately add flour and buttermilk to butter mixture, blending after each addition. Pour batter into prepared cake pans. Bake 20 minutes. Cool in pans on wire racks. Remove from pans. Let cool completely.

Place one cake layer on a serving plate. Tape a double foil collar, about 6 inches high, securely around single cake layer. Spread one-third chilled frosting over first layer. Repeat with second and third cake layers. End with a top layer of frosting. Refrigerate overnight with collar in place. Shortly before serving, remove collar and frost sides of cake with sweetened whipped cream. Garnish with lemon slices.

CAKE FLOUR

Cake flour contains less gluten than regular flour which is why it produces lighter cakes. If a recipe calls for cake flour and you don't have any, substitute 1 cup stirred all-purpose flour minus 2 tablespoons for 1 cup cake flour.

Mincemeat Cake

SERVES 8 TO 10

1 teaspoon baking soda
1 cup cold brewed coffee
½ cup (1 stick) unsalted butter,
 at room temperature
¾ cup sugar

1 large egg, beaten
⅔ cup maple syrup
8 ounces mincemeat, chopped
2 cups all-purpose flour
1 cup walnuts or pecan pieces

Preheat oven to 350 degrees. Grease and flour a Bundt pan. Dissolve baking soda in coffee. Set aside. Cream butter and sugar. Mix in egg. Add syrup, mincemeat, and coffee mixture. Combine well. Slowly add flour. Mix until blended. Fold in nuts. Pour batter into prepared pan. Bake 50 to 60 minutes, or until cake tester inserted in center comes out clean. Let cool completely.

MINCEMEAT

Mincemeat, a spicy preserve made of fruit, was first documented in the sixteenth century. Old-time mincemeats included minced, cooked lean meat, hence the name. Most modern versions do not contain meat. The ingredients are combined, then covered and allowed to marinate 1 month to allow the flavors to blend. Pies made of mincemeat had become a Christmas tradition in England by the 1700s.

*Birthday parties complete
with decorated cakes, light-
ed candles, and off-key
singing are a much-beloved
tradition. But like many
traditions, we owe it all
to the early Egyptians and
Greeks: to the Egyptians
who recorded and celebrated the births of male children and royalty, and to
the Greeks who adopted
the practice and added to
it the custom of a sweet
birthday cake to celebrate
the occasion. With the rise
of Christianity, birthdays
disappeared altogether.
Early church officials
considered them to be
pagan rituals. The older
practice was revived in the
fourth century when the
church began celebrating
Christmas as the birth of
Christ. Later, as parish
churches began recording
the birth dates of children,
the birthday cake reap-
peared, topped with candles
which were kept lit throughout the day until the cake
was eaten.*

Old-Fashioned Chocolate Layer Cake

SERVES 8 TO 10

Cake:
2 cups sugar
⅔ cup solid vegetable shortening
3 large eggs
2 cups all-purpose flour
¼ teaspoon salt
½ cup unsweetened cocoa*
2 teaspoons baking soda
2 cups buttermilk
1 teaspoon vanilla extract

Chocolate Frosting:
1 pound powdered sugar, sifted
6 tablespoons milk
1 teaspoon vanilla extract
4 tablespoons unsalted butter,
   at room temperature
1 tablespoon brewed coffee
⅓ cup unsweetened cocoa
1 teaspoon ground cinnamon

Preheat oven to 350 degrees. Grease and flour three 9-inch round cake pans. Cream sugar and shortening until light and fluffy. Add eggs, one at a time, beating after each addition. Set aside. Sift flour, salt, and cocoa in a separate bowl. Dissolve baking soda in buttermilk. Alternately add flour mixture and buttermilk to butter mixture, blending after each addition. Blend in vanilla. Pour into prepared pans. Bake 20 to 25 minutes, or until cake tester inserted in center comes out clean.

Chocolate Frosting: Mix powdered sugar, milk, vanilla, butter, coffee, cocoa, and cinnamon. Spread frosting on top of two layers, then stack layers on serving plate. (Hold together with wooden picks.) Add third layer. Frost top and sides.

*To make a darker, richer cake, use good quality imported cocoa.

Lemon Orange Pound Cake

SERVES 12

Cake:
½ cup solid vegetable shortening
½ cup (1 stick) unsalted butter,
   at room temperature
2 cups sugar
6 large eggs
3 cups all-purpose flour
½ teaspoon salt
½ teaspoon baking soda
1 teaspoon baking powder

1 cup buttermilk
1 teaspoon vanilla extract
1 teaspoon lemon extract

Glaze:
1 tablespoon grated lemon zest
1 tablespoon grated orange zest
3 tablespoons fresh orange juice
3 tablespoons fresh lemon juice
1½ cups powdered sugar

Preheat oven to 350 degrees. Grease a 10-inch tube pan. Cream short-ening, butter, and sugar until light and fluffy. Add eggs, one at a time, beating after each addition. Combine flour, salt, soda, and baking powder in a separate bowl. Alternately add flour mixture and buttermilk to butter mixture, blending after each addition. Mix in vanilla and lemon extracts. Pour batter into prepared pan. Bake 1 hour.

Combine lemon zest, orange zest, orange juice, lemon juice, and powdered sugar. When cake tests done, remove from pan and place on a wire rack positioned over a plate. While still hot, prick top of cake randomly with a fork. Drizzle glaze over cake. Let cool.

Apricot Delight

Cake:
½ cup plus ½ cup (2 sticks)
    unsalted butter,
    at room temperature
1 cup finely ground almonds
½ cup plus ⅓ cup sugar
2 tablespoons plus 2 tablespoons milk
2 teaspoons vanilla extract
1 large egg
2 cups all-purpose flour, sifted
2 teaspoons baking powder
½ teaspoon salt

Filling:
4 tablespoons unsalted butter,
    at room temperature
1 large egg yolk
1 cup powdered sugar
1 teaspoon vanilla extract
——
1 cup apricot preserves
——
powdered sugar

DIVIDING A
CAKE LAYER
When slicing the cake in half
horizontally, use a long serrated
knife. To remove the top layer
easily without breaking it, slide
the bottom of the springform pan
between the two layers as you
cut the cake.

Preheat oven to 400 degrees. Grease an 8-inch springform pan. Melt
½ cup butter in a saucepan. Blend in almonds, ½ cup sugar, 2 tablespoons
milk, and vanilla. Bring to a boil. Remove from heat. Set aside to cool.
Cream remaining ½ cup butter with ⅓ cup sugar until smooth. Slowly
beat in egg. Sift flour, baking powder, and salt in a separate bowl.
Alternately add flour mixture and remaining 2 tablespoons milk to butter
mixture, blending after each addition. Spoon batter into prepared pan.
Spread almond mixture over batter. Bake 25 minutes. Cool.

   Cream butter until soft. Beat in egg yolk. Add powdered sugar, 2 tablespoons at a time, and blend until fluffy. Add vanilla, blending well.

   Remove cooled cake from pan and slice in half horizontally. Spread all
filling on bottom layer of cake. Carefully spread all apricot preserves over
filling. Place top layer of cake over apricot preserves. Sprinkle top of cake
with sifted powdered sugar.

Amaretto Angel Food Cake

2 teaspoons vanilla extract
2 teaspoons fresh lemon juice
1 tablespoon Amaretto
14 large egg whites,
    at room temperature

1½ teaspoons cream of tartar
½ teaspoon salt
1⅔ cups sugar
1¼ cups sifted cake flour

Preheat oven to 300 degrees. Lightly grease a 10-inch tube pan. Place cooking rack in center of oven. Combine vanilla, lemon juice, and Amaretto
in a small bowl. Set aside. Beat egg whites in a large bowl until frothy. Add
cream of tartar and salt. Continue beating until soft peaks form. Add sugar,
⅓ cup at a time. Continue beating until stiff, but not dry. Fold in vanilla
mixture. Sift flour over egg whites and fold gently. Spoon batter into
prepared pan. Bake 1 hour, or until cake is golden brown and springy to
the touch. Cool completely while inverted. Remove from pan.

TYPES OF PEARS

Anjou - large, egg shaped, russet colored, with a sweet flavor

Bartlett - large, bell shaped, red or yellow green, with a musky sweet flavor

Bosc - long, thin necked, russeted golden skin, with a tart flavor

Comice - round, green, very juicy, with a sweet flavor

Forelle - like small Bartletts with red and yellow flesh

Nelis - large, round, dark green, very juicy, with spicy flavor

Seckel - tiny, with russet skin, spicy and sweet

Cake:
8 dried pear halves, finely chopped
3 to 4 Bartlett or Anjou pears,
   peeled, cored, and chopped
¼ cup pear brandy
⅔ cup (1 stick and 2⅔
   tablespoons) unsalted butter,
   at room temperature
¾ cup dark brown sugar,
   firmly packed
4 large eggs
⅔ cup honey
2½ cups all-purpose flour

1 teaspoon salt
1 teaspoon baking soda
1 teaspoon ground cinnamon
½ teaspoon ground allspice
½ teaspoon ground cloves
1 teaspoon grated orange zest

Glaze:
1½ cups powdered sugar, sifted
1 tablespoon pear brandy
2 teaspoons fresh orange juice

Combine dried pears, fresh pears, and brandy in a jar. Stir and cover tightly. Let rest at room temperature several hours or overnight.

Preheat oven to 350 degrees. Lightly grease a Bundt pan. Cream butter and brown sugar. Add eggs, one at a time, beating after each addition. Add honey. Mix well. Sift flour, salt, soda, cinnamon, allspice, and cloves in a separate bowl. Stir in orange zest. Add flour mixture to butter mixture. Blend well. Stir in pears. Pour batter into prepared pan. Bake 45 minutes to 1 hour, or until top springs back when lightly touched. Cool in pan about 45 minutes, then remove carefully to a wire rack.

Mix sugar, brandy, and orange juice. When cake has cooled completely, transfer to a serving plate. Drizzle glaze over top.

Woodford Pudding Cake with Vanilla Sauce

SERVES 8

Cake:
1 cup sugar
½ cup (1 stick) unsalted butter,
    at room temperature
3 large eggs, lightly beaten
1 cup buttermilk
1 cup all-purpose flour
1 teaspoon baking soda
½ teaspoon ground cinnamon
¼ teaspoon ground nutmeg
1 cup blackberry jam

Vanilla Sauce:
1 cup (2 sticks) unsalted butter,
    at room temperature
1½ cups sugar
1 large egg
1 cup heavy whipping cream
1 teaspoon vanilla extract

Preheat oven to 350 degrees. Grease and flour a Bundt pan. Cream sugar and butter until light. Add eggs, one at a time, beating after each addition. Add buttermilk to egg mixture. Mix well. Sift flour, soda, cinnamon, and nutmeg in a separate bowl. Mix dry ingredients into egg mixture. Blend in jam. Spoon into prepared pan. Bake 30 to 40 minutes, or until firm. Cool slightly. Remove from Bundt pan. Serve warm with Vanilla Sauce.

Vanilla Sauce: Cream butter and sugar. Add egg and cream. Mix well. Transfer to a double boiler and cook until thick, stirring constantly. Stir in vanilla.

Pudding can also be baked in miniature Bundt pans or an 8-cup shallow baking pan.

New Orleans Praline Ice Box Cake

SERVES 10 TO 12

1 cup (2 sticks) unsalted butter,
    at room temperature
1 pound powdered sugar
5 large eggs, separated
6 tablespoons praline liqueur
1 cup chopped pecans

6 dozen (3 packages) ladyfingers, split
——
1 cup heavy whipping cream
1 teaspoon vanilla extract
pecan halves

Cream butter and sugar until light and fluffy. Set aside. Beat egg yolks until frothy. Slowly add liqueur. Combine egg mixture with butter mixture. Beat egg whites in a large bowl until stiff, but not dry. Slowly fold egg whites and nuts into butter mixture.

Separate ladyfingers and arrange flat side down in a single layer in a 9-inch springform pan. A few will need to be cut in order to fit. Cover with layer of butter mixture, then layer of ladyfingers. Repeat layers, finishing with ladyfingers flat side up. Cover with plastic wrap. Refrigerate 12 hours.

Whip cream and vanilla until stiff. Remove cake from pan and place on a serving dish. Just before serving, frost cake with whipped cream. Garnish with pecan halves. Store in refrigerator.

SEPARATE EGGS -
THE EASY WAY

The easiest way to separate the egg white from the yolk is to break an egg into your "clean" hand and let the white part drip between your fingers.

Frozen Kahlúa Cake

SERVES 12

KAHLÚA

Kahlúa is a thick, coffee-flavored liqueur made in Mexico. Derived from a sugarcane base, Kahlúa can be used in baking, drizzled over ice cream, or added to hot chocolate or coffee.

Cake:
¾ cup (1½ sticks) unsalted
  butter, at room temperature
2 cups sugar
¾ cup unsweetened cocoa
4 large eggs, separated
1 teaspoon baking soda
2 tablespoons cold water
½ cup cold brewed coffee
½ cup Kahlúa
1⅓ cups all-purpose flour
2 tablespoons vanilla extract

Glaze:
1 cup powdered sugar
½ cup Kahlúa

Topping:
1 cup heavy whipping cream
1 teaspoon sugar
1 tablespoon Kahlúa

Preheat oven to 325 degrees. Grease and flour a Bundt pan. Cream butter and sugar. Mix in cocoa and egg yolks. Set aside. Dissolve baking soda in water. Stir in coffee and Kahlúa. Alternately add Kahlúa mixture and flour to butter mixture, blending after each addition. Mix in vanilla. Beat egg whites in a separate bowl until stiff. Fold egg whites gently into batter. Pour batter into prepared pan. Bake 1 hour.

Combine powdered sugar and Kahlúa, stirring to blend. When cake tests done, remove from pan to a serving plate. While still warm, randomly pierce cake with a fork. Pour glaze over top. Cool cake completely. Wrap cake in plastic wrap. Freeze several hours or overnight. Remove from freezer about 1 hour before serving.

Whip cream and sugar until stiff. Blend in Kahlúa. Slice cake and serve topped with whipped cream.

Kahlúa Gingerbread

SERVES 12

½ cup (1 stick) unsalted butter,
  at room temperature
¾ cup sugar
⅓ cup dark brown sugar,
  firmly packed
1 large egg
1 cup molasses
2 cups all-purpose flour

1½ teaspoons baking soda
1 teaspoon ground cinnamon
1½ teaspoons ground ginger
1 teaspoon ground cloves
½ teaspoon salt
⅔ cup hot water
⅓ cup Kahlúa
2 tablespoons cold brewed coffee

Preheat oven to 325 degrees. Grease a 9 by 13-inch baking pan. Cream butter and sugars. Thoroughly mix in egg, molasses, flour, baking soda, cinnamon, ginger, cloves, salt, water, Kahlúa, and coffee. Pour batter into prepared pan. Bake 30 to 35 minutes, or until cake tester inserted in middle comes out clean. Serve warm or cold with Key Lime Curd (page 262) or whipped cream.

Pumpkin Roll

SERVES 10

Cake:
¾ cup all-purpose flour
2 teaspoons ground cinnamon
1 ½ teaspoons ground ginger
1 teaspoon baking powder
1 teaspoon ground nutmeg
½ teaspoon salt
3 large eggs
1 cup sugar
⅔ cup pumpkin purée
1 teaspoon fresh lemon juice
powdered sugar

Filling:
8 ounces cream cheese, softened
4 tablespoons unsalted butter,
  at room temperature
1 cup powdered sugar
1 teaspoon vanilla extract
——
powdered sugar, sifted

Preheat oven to 375 degrees. Grease, flour, and line a 18 by 12-inch jelly-roll pan with wax paper. Sift flour, cinnamon, ginger, baking powder, nutmeg, and salt. Set aside. Beat eggs at high speed until creamy, 1 to 2 minutes. Add sugar slowly, beating an additional 3 minutes. Stir in pumpkin pureé and lemon juice. Fold in flour mixture until just incorporated. Spread batter carefully in prepared pan. Bake 15 minutes, or until cake tests done. Spread a tea towel on a flat surface and sprinkle liberally with powdered sugar. Turn cake out onto towel and remove wax paper. Roll cake in towel. Refrigerate 3 hours.

Mix cream cheese, butter, powdered sugar, and vanilla until blended. Unwrap chilled cake and remove towel. Spread filling carefully on cake. Roll back up. Cover top with sifted powdered sugar. Slice and serve.

MAKING VANILLA EXTRACT

A member of the orchid family, vanilla beans grow on climbing vines and were originally cultivated by the Aztec Indians. Always use pure vanilla extract or make your own by submerging a split vanilla bean, seeds intact, in a jar containing ¾ cup vodka. Seal and store in a cool, dark place for 4 months before using.

Banana Cake

SERVES 8 TO 10

Cake:
½ cup (1 stick) unsalted butter,
  at room temperature
1½ cups sugar
2 large eggs
3 large bananas, mashed
¾ cup chopped pecans
¼ cup milk
1 teaspoon vanilla extract

2 cups all-purpose flour
1 teaspoon baking soda

Frosting:
2 tablespoons unsalted butter, melted
2 cups powdered sugar, sifted
1 banana, mashed
——
½ to 1 cup chopped pecans

Preheat oven to 325 degrees. Grease and flour a 9 by 13-inch metal baking pan. Cream butter and sugar in a large bowl. Mix in eggs and banana. Add pecans, milk, and vanilla, blending well. Sift flour and baking soda. Add to banana mixture. Pour into prepared pan. Bake 30 to 35 minutes.

Cream butter, powdered sugar, and banana. Spread frosting on warm cake and sprinkle with pecans.

Boccone Dolce

SERVES 8

BEATING EGG WHITES

Egg whites should ideally be beaten in a copper bowl in order to achieve full volume. Since a copper bowl is not always available, a pinch of cream of tartar can be added. When beating egg whites, make sure that the bowl and beaters are clean and dry.

Meringue Layer:
4 large egg whites
⅛ teaspoon salt
¼ teaspoon cream of tartar
1 cup sugar

Filling:
6 ounces semi-sweet chocolate
3 cups heavy whipping cream
⅓ cup powdered sugar
1 teaspoon vanilla extract

———

1 pint fresh strawberries, hulled and sliced

Preheat oven to 250 degrees. Beat egg whites, salt, and cream of tartar until stiff. Gradually mix in sugar. Continue mixing until meringue is stiff and shiny. Line 3 baking sheets with wax paper. Trace 3 circles on paper, each 10 inches in diameter. Spread meringue evenly over circles to about a ¼-inch thickness. Bake 20 to 25 minutes. Remove from oven when meringue becomes pale gold, but still pliable. Cool. Carefully peel meringue off wax paper. Use cake racks to completely cool.

Melt chocolate in top of a double boiler. Set aside. Beat cream in a separate bowl until stiff. Gradually add sugar and vanilla, beating until very stiff.

Place one meringue layer on a serving plate. Spread with a thin coat of melted chocolate, then a layer of whipped cream about ¾ inch thick. Next, add a layer of strawberries. Add the second layer of meringue, spread with chocolate, another layer of whipped cream, and strawberries. Top with third meringue layer. Frost sides with remaining whipped cream. Decorate top by squeezing remaining chocolate through a pastry cone with a small opening or decorate with whole strawberries. Refrigerate 2 to 3 hours before serving.

Cookies and Cream Cheesecake

SERVES 8 TO 10

Crust:
3 cups Oreo cookie crumbs
9 tablespoons unsalted butter, melted
1 cup sugar

Filling:
4 packages (8 ounces each) cream cheese, softened
1½ cups sugar
6 large eggs
1 teaspoon vanilla extract or dark rum
1 ½ cups Oreo cookies, broken into large pieces

Combine cookie crumbs, butter, and sugar. Mix well. Press mixture into bottom and 2 inches up sides of a greased 9-inch springform pan. Chill. Preheat oven to 300 degrees. Beat cream cheese and sugar until smooth and fluffy. Add eggs, one at a time, beating well after each addition. Mix in vanilla. Carefully fold in broken cookie pieces. Pour batter into prepared crust. Bake 1 ½ hours. Turn oven off, open door slightly, and let cheesecake cool in oven an additional hour. Remove from pan. Chill before serving.

Chocolate-Glazed Three Layer Cheesecake

SERVES 12

Crust:
2 cups Oreo cookie crumbs
¼ cup sugar
5 tablespoons unsalted butter, melted

Chocolate Layer:
8 ounces cream cheese, softened
¼ cup sugar
1 large egg
¼ teaspoon vanilla extract
2 ounces semi-sweet chocolate, melted
⅓ cup sour cream

Pecan Layer:
8 ounces cream cheese, softened
⅓ cup dark brown sugar, firmly packed
1 tablespoon all-purpose flour
¼ cup chopped pecans
1 large egg
½ teaspoon vanilla extract

Sour Cream Layer:
5 ounces cream cheese, softened
¼ cup sugar
1 large egg
1 cup sour cream
¼ teaspoon vanilla extract
¼ teaspoon almond extract

Glaze:
6 ounces semi-sweet chocolate
4 tablespoons unsalted butter
¾ cup sifted powdered sugar
2 tablespoons water
1 teaspoon vanilla extract

Preheat oven to 325 degrees. Combine cookie crumbs, sugar, and butter. Mix well. Press crumb mixture into the bottom of a 9-inch springform pan and 2 inches up sides. Chill.

Beat cream cheese and sugar until light and fluffy. Add egg and vanilla, blending well. Mix in chocolate and sour cream. Spoon over crust.

Beat cream cheese, brown sugar, and flour until light and fluffy. Blend in egg and vanilla. Stir in pecans. Carefully spoon over chocolate layer.

Beat cream cheese and sugar until light and fluffy. Blend in egg, sour cream, vanilla, and almond extract. Spoon gently over pecan layer.

Bake 1 hour. Turn oven off and leave cheesecake in oven 30 minutes. Open oven door and leave cheesecake in oven another 30 minutes. Cool. Cover and chill 8 hours. Remove from pan and place on serving platter. Refrigerate.

Melt chocolate and butter in top of a double boiler. Add powdered sugar, water, and vanilla. Stir until smooth. Spread over chilled cheesecake while glaze is warm. Cheesecake should not be refrigerated after glazing, so glaze when ready to serve or shortly before.

Company Cheesecake

HOW TO PREVENT A CHEESECAKE FROM CRACKING

If a cheesecake cracks in the middle during baking, try baking it in a water bath the next time. The extra moisture will sometimes prevent this from happening. Wrap the springform pan tightly in foil to prevent water from seeping in. Place the pan in a large roasting pan and fill the larger pan with boiling water until it reaches halfway up the side of the springform pan. Bake as directed.

Crust:
1 cup graham cracker crumbs
¼ cup sugar
4 tablespoons unsalted butter, melted

Filling:
*5 packages (8 ounces each) cream
  cheese, softened*
¼ teaspoon vanilla extract
¼ teaspoon grated lemon zest
1 ¾ cups sugar

3 tablespoons all-purpose flour
¼ teaspoon salt
4 to 5 large eggs (1 cup)
2 large egg yolks
¼ cup heavy whipping cream

Topping:
½ cup currant jelly
2 teaspoons kirsch or brandy
2 pints fresh strawberries, hulled

Combine graham cracker crumbs, sugar, and butter. Press crumb mixture into bottom of a 9-inch springform pan. Set aside.

Preheat oven to 450 degrees. Beat cream cheese until light. Blend in vanilla and lemon zest. Continue beating while gradually adding sugar, flour, and salt. Add eggs and yolks, one at a time, beating after each addition, until just blended. Gently stir in cream. Pour filling into prepared crust. Bake 12 minutes. Reduce heat to 300 degrees and bake an additional 55 minutes. Cool 1 hour in pan on a wire rack. Loosen sides carefully with a spatula and remove from pan. Allow cheesecake to cool 2 more hours.

Melt jelly and kirsch over low heat. Cool slightly. Dip strawberries in topping and arrange, point sides up, on top of cheesecake. Chill before serving.

White Chocolate Snickers Cheesecake

Crust:

⅔ cup graham cracker crumbs

⅔ cup sugar

1 teaspoon ground cinnamon

3 tablespoons unsalted butter,
    at room temperature

6 large Snickers bars, chilled and
    finely chopped

Filling:

4 packages (8 ounces each) cream
    cheese, softened

⅔ cup sugar

3 large eggs

1 teaspoon vanilla extract

6 ounces white chocolate

¾ cup heavy whipping cream

———

Smooth Fudge Sauce

Carefully wrap the outside of a 10-inch springform pan with 2 or 3 layers of aluminum foil. (This will ensure that no water gets to crust while baking.)

Combine crumbs, sugar, cinnamon, and butter in a small bowl. Mix well. Line bottom of foil-wrapped pan with crust mixture. Place half of the chopped Snickers in a large mound in center of pan. Reserve other half.

Preheat oven to 350 degrees. Beat cream cheese 5 minutes. Scrape down sides of bowl and add sugar. Mix well. Add eggs, one at a time, mixing after each addition. Add vanilla and blend well. Melt chocolate in top of a double boiler. Add cream, stirring until well blended. Slowly add melted chocolate mixture to cream cheese mixture, mixing until completely combined. Pour filling into prepared crust. Place in a ½-inch water bath. Bake 1½ hours. Remove from oven. Let cool 2 hours before cutting. Top with Smooth Fudge Sauce and remaining chopped Snickers.

Smooth Fudge Sauce:

½ cup (1 stick) unsalted butter

4 ounces unsweetened chocolate

¼ teaspoon salt

3 cups sugar

1⅔ cups evaporated milk

1 tablespoon vanilla extract

Melt butter and chocolate in a large saucepan over low heat. Add salt, sugar, milk, and vanilla, one at a time, blending after each addition until smooth. Increase heat to medium and whisk, while bubbling, 1 minute. Remove from heat. Serve warm with White Chocolate Snickers Cheesecake or over ice cream. Yields 1 quart.

Pumpkin Walnut Cheesecake

Crust:
1½ cups vanilla wafer crumbs
¼ cup sugar
6 tablespoons unsalted butter,
    melted

Filling:
3 packages (8 ounces each) cream
    cheese, softened
¾ cup sugar
¾ cup brown sugar, firmly packed
5 large eggs
¼ cup heavy whipping cream
1 teaspoon ground cinnamon

1 teaspoon ground nutmeg
¼ teaspoon ground cloves
2 cups pumpkin purée, canned or
    freshly cooked

Walnut Topping:
6 tablespoons unsalted butter
1 cup dark brown sugar, firmly packed
1 cup coarsely chopped walnuts
    or
Sour Cream Topping:
1 cup sour cream
5 teaspoons sifted powdered sugar
freshly grated nutmeg

Combine crumbs, sugar, and butter. Mix well. Press firmly into bottom
and halfway up sides of lightly greased 9-inch springform pan. Chill.

Preheat oven to 350 degrees. Beat cream cheese. Add sugars and continue beating until light and fluffy. Add eggs, one at a time, beating after
each addition. Stir in cream, cinnamon, nutmeg, cloves, and pumpkin.
Blend well. Pour batter into prepared pan. Bake 1 hour. While cheesecake
bakes, prepare your choice of toppings.

Walnut Topping: Cream butter with brown sugar. Stir in walnuts.
Gently spoon topping over hot cheesecake. Return cheesecake to oven
15 minutes. Cool cheesecake completely in pan, then remove it carefully.
Cover and refrigerate overnight.

Sour Cream Topping: Remove cheesecake from oven and let cool slightly. Set oven on broil and move oven rack to its lowest position. Mix sour
cream and powdered sugar. Spread mixture lightly on top of cheesecake.
Place under broiler to set (harden). Watch cheesecake carefully as sour
cream burns easily. Remove to a cooling rack and cool to room temperature. Remove cheesecake from pan. Cover tightly and chill several hours
or overnight in refrigerator. Sprinkle lightly with nutmeg before serving.

Frozen White Chocolate Mousse Cake
with Raspberry Sauce

Crust:
1 cup vanilla wafer crumbs
3 tablespoons unsalted butter, melted

Mousse:
6 ounces plus 2 ounces white
  chocolate, chopped
¾ cup sugar
¼ cup water
4 large egg whites
⅛ teaspoon cream of tartar

1½ cups heavy whipping cream, chilled
1 tablespoon Grand Marnier
1 teaspoon vanilla extract
3 tablespoons chopped pistachios

Raspberry Sauce:
2 cups fresh or frozen unsweetened
  raspberries
¼ cup sugar
2 tablespoons Grand Marnier

WHITE CHOCOLATE

Not a true chocolate, white chocolate contains no cocoa bean paste. Never use white chocolate confection or imitation white chocolate in place of white chocolate as the taste and texture are not the same.

Combine crumbs and butter. (Do not use food processor.) Press evenly into bottom of a 9-inch springform pan. Refrigerate.

Melt 6 ounces white chocolate in top of a double boiler, stirring until smooth. Cool slightly. Bring sugar and water to a boil in a small saucepan, stirring until sugar dissolves. Continue boiling, without stirring, until a candy thermometer reads 238 degrees (soft-ball stage). Beat egg whites and cream of tartar until soft peaks form. Gradually beat hot sugar syrup into egg whites. Continue beating until mixture is stiff and glossy, about 3 minutes. Fold in warm chocolate. Refrigerate chocolate mixture until cool, but not set, about 5 minutes. Whip cream, Grand Marnier, and vanilla in a large bowl until soft peaks form. Gently fold cream into chocolate mixture. Fold in remaining 2 ounces white chocolate. Pour mousse into prepared crust and smooth top. Sprinkle with pistachios. Freeze until firm, about 6 hours. Cover with plastic wrap and return to freezer.

Raspberry Sauce: Purée raspberries in a blender. Strain purée to remove seeds. Stir in sugar and Grand Marnier. Refrigerate sauce at least 1 hour.

Remove mousse cake from freezer just before serving. To serve, spoon sauce onto individual plates and place a slice of cake on each. (Both mousse cake and raspberry sauce can be prepared up to 3 days before serving.)

Dutch Chocolate Mousse

SERVES 8

6 ounces semi-sweet chocolate chips
½ cup Vandermint liqueur, hot
   but not boiling
1 cup (2 sticks) unsalted butter,
   cut into pieces
4 large eggs, separated
2 tablespoons powdered sugar

———

1 cup heavy whipping cream
2 teaspoons vanilla extract
3 tablespoons powdered sugar

———

bittersweet chocolate curls

Combine chocolate and liqueur in a blender. Add butter and egg yolks. Continue blending until smooth. Beat egg whites in a separate bowl. Mix in sugar. Continue mixing until egg whites are stiff, but still moist. Gently fold chocolate mixture into egg whites. Pour into a 2-quart soufflé dish or individual soufflé dishes. Cover with plastic wrap and refrigerate until firm.

   Whip cream, vanilla, and sugar until firm peaks form. Top soufflé with whipped cream and shaved chocolate curls.

Low-Fat Flan

SERVES 6

**BAKING IN A
WATER BATH**

Baking a dish in a water bath helps to keep the food moist. It is a method often used when cooking such items as puddings. To create a water bath, place the baking dish in a larger pan. Pour water into the larger pan until it reaches halfway up the side of the baking dish. Place the pans in the oven and bake as directed.

½ cup sugar
¼ cup water
2 large eggs
3 large egg whites

1 can (14 ounces) low-fat sweetened
   condensed milk
1½ cups skim milk
1 tablespoon vanilla extract

Preheat oven to 325 degrees. Combine sugar and water in a small saucepan. Bring to a simmer over low heat, stirring occasionally. Increase heat to medium-high and cook, without stirring, until syrup turns a deep amber color, 5 to 8 minutes. Immediately pour syrup into a 1½ to 2-quart soufflé dish or 6 individual Pyrex custard cups. Tilt dish to coat with syrup. Whisk eggs and egg whites in a large bowl. Blend in sweetened condensed milk, skim milk, and vanilla. Pour egg mixture through a strainer into syrup-coated dish. Bake in a water bath 60 to 70 minutes. Cool to room temperature. Refrigerate at least 4 hours or overnight. Invert soufflé onto a platter. Serve immediately.

Low-Fat Flan

Chocolate Lovers Dream Cake

SERVES 8

Cake:
8 ounces semi-sweet chocolate
½ cup brewed strong coffee
1 cup (2 sticks) unsalted butter
1 cup sugar
4 large eggs, beaten

Frangelico Raspberry Sauce:
1 package (10 ounces) frozen
  raspberries, thawed

½ cup sugar
1 tablespoon Frangelico liqueur

Topping:
1 cup heavy whipping cream
2 teaspoons brandy (optional)
1 tablespoon powdered sugar
————
fresh raspberries
fresh mint sprigs

Preheat oven to 350 degrees. Invert a 5 by 9-inch glass loaf pan and cover it with foil. Place shaped foil inside loaf pan and grease well. Melt chocolate in coffee in top of a double boiler. Add butter and sugar, stirring until butter is melted and sugar is dissolved. Cool mixture 10 minutes. Beat in eggs, one at a time, mixing after each addition. Pour batter into prepared pan. Bake until a crust forms on top, approximately 45 minutes. Remove from oven. Set pan in enough cool water to come halfway up side of pan. Cool completely in water bath. (Cake will rise and fall as it cools.) Wrap pan with plastic wrap. Refrigerate at least 2 days or up to 2 weeks.

Frangelico Raspberry Sauce: Combine raspberries, sugar, and Frangelico in a small saucepan. Bring to a boil. Remove raspberry mixture from heat. Purée in a blender or food processor. Strain to remove seeds. Cover and refrigerate.

Whip cream, brandy, and powdered sugar until stiff. Cover each dessert plate with 2 tablespoons raspberry sauce. Place a slice of chocolate cake on raspberry sauce and top with whipped cream. Garnish with fresh raspberries and a sprig of mint. Serve immediately.

Iced Lemon Soufflé

SERVES 8

ZESTING

Citrus zest is only the colored portion of the skin of the fruit. Avoid the white inner portion or pith, which is very bitter. The best way to get citrus zest is to use a citrus zester. This tool has 5 tiny cutting holes that create threadlike strips of peel. Press firmly down on the zester as you scrape along the skin of the fruit.

2 tablespoons water
1 envelope unflavored gelatin
grated zest of 4 lemons
½ cup fresh lemon juice, strained

1 cup superfine sugar
7 large egg whites
1 cup heavy whipping cream

Combine water, gelatin, lemon zest, lemon juice, and sugar in a small saucepan. Stir over low heat until gelatin is thoroughly dissolved. Transfer to a large mixing bowl and chill until mixture reaches a syrup consistency. Beat egg whites in a separate bowl until stiff peaks form. Fold egg whites into chilled lemon mixture. Whip cream until stiff. Fold cream into lemon and egg mixture. Pour into a 1-quart soufflé dish. Cover and chill 5 hours or overnight.

Can be made 1 or 2 days in advance.

Bread and Butter Pudding

2 cups half and half

3 large eggs, at room temperature

5 tablespoons plus 1½ teaspoons
   sugar

½ teaspoon vanilla extract

3 to 4 slices white bread, crusts
   removed, buttered on both sides,
   and quartered

⅓ cup currants or raisins

Preheat oven to 275 degrees. Butter a 2-quart baking dish. Scald half and half in a saucepan. Set aside. Whisk eggs, 5 tablespoons sugar, and vanilla in a large bowl. Whisk in scalded half and half. Gently stir in bread and currants, submerging bread in liquid. Transfer mixture to prepared baking dish. Sprinkle remaining 1½ teaspoons sugar over mixture.

Set baking dish into a hot water bath ½ inch up sides of baking dish. Bake in water bath 1 hour and 15 minutes, or until center is set and top is lightly browned. Serve with Bourbon Sauce, Lemon Sauce, or Grand Marnier Sauce.

Bourbon Sauce:

6 tablespoons unsalted butter

½ cup brown sugar, firmly packed

1 teaspoon vanilla extract

2 tablespoons bourbon

Melt butter in a saucepan over medium-low heat. Add sugar and cook 2 minutes, stirring constantly. Remove from heat. Stir in vanilla and bourbon. Serve over Bread and Butter Pudding or ice cream.

Lemon Sauce:

2¼ teaspoons cornstarch

½ cup sugar

¾ cup boiling water

2 tablespoons fresh lemon juice

1 tablespoon unsalted butter

⅛ teaspoon ground nutmeg

⅛ teaspoon salt

½ teaspoon grated lemon zest

Mix cornstarch and sugar in a small saucepan. Add boiling water and cook until thick, stirring constantly. Stir in lemon juice, butter, nutmeg, salt, and lemon zest. Serve over Bread and Butter Pudding.

Grand Marnier Sauce:

1 tablespoon cornstarch

1 cup sugar

1½ cups milk

1 tablespoon vanilla extract

3 large egg yolks, lightly beaten

3 tablespoons Grand Marnier

Combine cornstarch and sugar in a small saucepan. Add milk and vanilla. Stir over medium heat. Whisk in egg yolks. Continue whisking until mixture begins to simmer. Do not allow to boil. When sauce thickens, remove from heat. Stir in Grand Marnier. Serve over Bread and Butter Pudding, ice cream, or fruit.

SCALDING MILK

Before heating milk for scalding, rinse out the pan with cold water. This makes cleaning the pan easier. The milk may be heated either over direct heat or in the top of a double boiler. Milk is scalded when tiny bubbles begin to form around the edge of the pan and the milk reaches 180 degrees. The reason for scalding milk is to keep it from souring.

Chocolate Bread Pudding with Brandy Cream

SERVES 12

VARIATION

Try topping this bread pudding with Cinnamon Ice Cream (page 277) for an extra special and very rich treat.

Brandy Cream:
3 large egg yolks
⅓ cup sugar
1 cup heavy whipping cream
⅓ cup milk
¼ cup brandy
⅛ teaspoon salt

Pudding:
1 loaf brioche (12 inches),
  cut into 12 slices, or
6 to 8 croissants, halved

1 cup (2 sticks) unsalted butter,
  melted
8 ounces semi-sweet chocolate, chopped
3 cups heavy whipping cream
1 cup milk
12 large egg yolks
1 cup sugar
2 teaspoons vanilla extract
⅛ teaspoon salt

Brandy Cream: Whisk egg yolks and sugar until well blended. Bring cream and milk to a boil in a heavy saucepan over moderately high heat. Whisk half of the hot cream into yolk mixture and then whisk yolks back into remaining hot cream in saucepan. Whisk mixture over low heat until thick, but not boiling. Remove from heat. Stir in brandy and salt. Strain Brandy Cream and chill overnight.

Preheat oven to 425 degrees. Brush bread slices with melted butter and toast on both sides until golden brown. Watch carefully so bottoms don't burn. Melt chocolate in top of a double boiler. Combine cream and milk in a separate saucepan, and heat until almost boiling. Whisk egg yolks and sugar in a mixing bowl. While whisking, slowly add hot cream mixture to egg yolk mixture. Strain mixture into a separate bowl and skim off foam. Slowly add strained mixture to melted chocolate, whisking constantly. Stir in vanilla and salt.

Arrange bread slices in a 9 by 13-inch baking dish, overlapping rows. Pour chocolate mixture over bread. Cover dish with plastic wrap, placing 2 small plates on top to weight it down. Press down every 10 minutes for 1 hour. This will allow the bread to totally absorb the liquid. (At this point, pudding can be refrigerated overnight, but bring it to room temperature before baking.)

Preheat oven to 350 degrees. Remove plastic wrap from baking dish and place in a hot water bath 1½ inches deep (½ inch, or slightly more, from top of baking dish). Bake 45 minutes, or until pudding looks glossy and liquid is absorbed. Serve with Brandy Cream.

White Chocolate Bread Pudding

Pudding:
4 ounces French bread, trimmed
    and cut into ¼-inch slices
1½ cups half and half
½ cup heavy whipping cream
1 large egg
4 large egg yolks
½ cup sugar

1½ teaspoons vanilla extract
4 ounces white chocolate, melted

White Chocolate Sauce:
¾ cup heavy whipping cream
4 ounces white chocolate, melted

———

shavings of dark and milk chocolate

Preheat oven to 350 degrees. Generously butter six ½-cup custard cups.
Cut bread slices into strips as wide as depth of custard cups. Put bread
strips on baking sheet and bake until golden, approximately 10 minutes.
Set aside.

Heat half and half and cream in a medium saucepan over low heat until
hot. Do not boil. Beat egg, egg yolks, and sugar in a small bowl. Whisk a
few tablespoons warm cream mixture into egg mixture. Whisk eggs back
into cream. Stir in vanilla. Place melted chocolate into a large bowl and
slowly whisk cream mixture into it.

Line sides of custard cups with bread strips, breaking strips as necessary
to get a neat fit. Strain custard into cups and let bread absorb liquid.
Add more custard as needed to fill cups to within ½ inch of rim. Place
cups in baking pan large enough to hold them with at least 1-inch spacing
between each. Fill pan with boiling water to within 1 inch of rims of the
custard cups. Bake until set and a tester inserted comes out clean, about
35 to 45 minutes. Check pan after 15 minutes. Add additional boiling
water if necessary to maintain water level.

White Chocolate Sauce: Heat cream until frothy, but not boiling. Whisk
warm cream into melted chocolate until smooth. Refrigerate until ready
to use.

Pudding may be served in cups or unmolded. To unmold, cover and
chill cups thoroughly, at least 1 hour. Loosen edges with a knife and invert
onto individual plates. Serve
with White Chocolate
Sauce. Garnish with
chocolate shavings.

CHOCOLATE GARNISHES

*The appeal of a dessert is always
enhanced by the presentation.
Chocolate garnishes are some of
the easiest to master. The following
are some suggestions:*

◆ *Melt chocolate in a glass bowl in
the microwave. The time depends
upon the quantity being melted.
Pour the melted chocolate into a
plastic bag and seal. Snip a small
corner of the bag to allow the
chocolate to escape in a small
stream. Drizzle the chocolate
over the entire dessert, over each
individual serving, or on the individual serving plates before placing the dessert. The chocolate
may even be drizzled onto wax
paper into desired shapes. When
hardened, remove from the wax
paper and place on the dessert.*

◆ *To make chocolate leaves, brush
melted chocolate onto the back
of a clean, non-poisonous leaf,
such as rose, lemon, or camelia
leaves. Peel the leaf away once
the chocolate has hardened.*

◆ *Grate chocolate and sprinkle over
the dessert.*

◆ *To make small chocolate curls,
run a vegetable peeler down the
side of a block of chocolate.*

◆ *To make the large, showy chocolate curls, spread melted chocolate on a baking sheet or marble
surface to a thickness of ¼ inch.
When hardened, scrape across
the chocolate in a long, slow
motion using a knife or metal
spatula held at a 45 degree angle.*

Spiced Bread Pudding

SERVES 6

SOUR MILK

To make sour milk, bring milk to room temperature and add 1 table-spoon lemon juice or distilled white vinegar. Stir to combine. Let stand 5 minutes.

10 slices white bread with crust
1 ½ cups brown sugar,
    firmly packed
1 teaspoon baking soda
1 teaspoon ground cloves
1 teaspoon ground nutmeg
1 teaspoon ground cinnamon

1 ½ cups sour milk
½ cup sour cream
1 large egg
1 cup raisins
——
Vanilla Sauce

Preheat oven to 325 degrees. Grease a 2-quart casserole or pudding dish. Combine bread, sugar, baking soda, cloves, nutmeg, and cinnamon. Mix well. Add milk, sour cream, and egg. Continue mixing until well blended. Stir in raisins. Pour pudding into prepared dish. Bake 1 hour. Serve with Vanilla Sauce (page 233).

French Country Cherry Pudding

SERVES 6

1 package (16 ounces) frozen
    cherries, thawed and drained
2 tablespoons plus 1 tablespoon sugar
1 tablespoon kirsch
3 large eggs, separated
1 teaspoon vanilla extract
juice and grated zest of 1 large lemon

½ cup sugar
7 ½ teaspoons all-purpose flour
7 ½ teaspoons cornstarch
1 teaspoon baking powder
——
sweetened whipped cream

Preheat oven to 350 degrees. Grease a 10-inch round baking dish. Combine cherries, 2 tablespoons sugar, and kirsch in a small bowl. Set aside. Beat egg yolks, 1 tablespoon sugar, vanilla, lemon juice, and lemon zest 3 minutes with an electric mixer at medium speed. Beat egg whites in a separate bowl until stiff. Add ½ cup sugar, a little at a time, beating after each addition. Combine flour, cornstarch, and baking powder in a small bowl. Fold egg yolk mixture into egg whites. Add flour mixture and fold in just until ingredients are incorporated.

    Pour batter into prepared baking dish. Spread cherry mixture on top. Do not stir. Bake 35 minutes, or until the top is lightly browned. Serve warm with whipped cream.

Banana Pudding

2 cups vanilla wafers
¼ cup rum
¼ cup bourbon

————

1 ¼ cups plus 1 tablespoon sugar
¾ cup all-purpose flour
½ teaspoon salt
4 cups milk

8 large egg yolks, beaten
2 teaspoons plus ½ teaspoon
  vanilla extract
8 ripe bananas, sliced
1 cup plus ½ cup crumbled chocolate-
  covered toffee bars
2 cups heavy whipping cream

**PERFECT WHIPPED
CREAM**

*Always chill cream, bowl, and
beaters before whipping cream.*

Place vanilla wafers in a shallow bowl and sprinkle with rum and bourbon. Set aside.

Combine 1¼ cups sugar, flour, salt, milk, egg yolks, and 2 teaspoons vanilla in top of a double boiler. Place over simmering water. (Do not let water boil or touch bottom of top pan.) Stir continuously until thick enough to heavily coat back of a metal spoon. Place top of double boiler in a bowl of ice water. Stir about 5 minutes to stop the cooking.

Layer half of vanilla wafers, half of bananas, half of custard, and ½ cup crumbled toffee bars in an 8 by 12-inch glass baking dish. Repeat layers.

Whip cream, 1 tablespoon sugar, and ½ teaspoon vanilla. Spread whipped cream over pudding. Sprinkle remaining ½ cup crumbled toffee bars over top. Refrigerate before serving.

Bananas Foster Shortcake

SERVES 6 TO 8

BANANAS FOSTER VARIATION

Roll 1 tablespoon vanilla ice cream in crêpe. Place banana slices on either side of crêpe on an individual serving plate. Top with sauce and drizzle with melted chocolate. Serve immediately.

Shortcake:
2½ cups all-purpose flour
2 teaspoons baking powder
¾ teaspoon salt
¾ cup (1½ sticks) unsalted
   butter, chilled and cut into pieces
1 cup puréed banana

Sauce:
2½ cups heavy whipping cream
2½ cups dark brown sugar,
   firmly packed
7½ teaspoons dark rum
7½ teaspoons banana liqueur
5 bananas, peeled and cut into
   ¾-inch rounds
2 quarts butter pecan ice cream,
   slightly softened

Preheat oven to 400 degrees. Sift flour, baking powder, and salt in a mixing bowl. Cut in butter until mixture resembles coarse pebbles. Lightly stir in banana purée to make a damp dough. Turn mixture out onto a floured surface. Roll or pat to a 1-inch thickness. Cut dough into 2½ to 3-inch rounds with a floured biscuit cutter. Place rounds on an ungreased baking sheet. Bake until golden brown, about 30 minutes. Set aside.

Combine cream and brown sugar in a large saucepan. Cook over moderate heat, stirring constantly, until slightly thickened, about 10 to 12 minutes. Allow to cool 10 minutes. Stir rum, banana liqueur, and sliced bananas into warm sauce.

Split shortcake and place on individual plates. Scoop ice cream onto bottom half of shortcake, top with banana sauce, and add top half of shortcake. Serve immediately.

Ice Cream Tortoni

SERVES 6 TO 8

⅓ cup chopped toasted almonds
3 tablespoons unsalted butter,
   melted
¾ cup plus ¼ cup vanilla
   wafer crumbs

1 teaspoon almond extract
3 pints vanilla ice cream, softened
1 jar (16 ounces) apricot preserves

Combine almonds, butter, ¾ cup crumbs, and almond extract. Press firmly into bottom of a 9-inch square dish which has been lined with aluminum foil. Layer 1 pint ice cream topped with one-third apricot preserves. Repeat layering and top with remaining ¼ cup crumbs. Freeze. When ready to serve, remove from freezer to soften before cutting into squares.

Plum Dandy

SERVES 6 TO 8

½ cup (1 stick) unsalted butter,
  at room temperature
1 cup sugar
1 cup all-purpose flour, sifted
1 teaspoon baking powder
⅛ teaspoon salt
2 large eggs
24 pitted purple plum halves*

Topping:
1 tablespoon sugar
1 tablespoon ground cinnamon
1 tablespoon fresh lemon juice

Preheat oven to 350 degrees. Cream butter and sugar. Thoroughly blend in flour, baking powder, salt, and eggs. Spoon batter into a 9-inch spring-form pan. Place plum halves skin side up on top of batter. Set aside.

Combine sugar and cinnamon. Sprinkle evenly over plums, then drizzle with lemon juice. Bake 1 hour. Cool slightly, then remove from pan. Serve warm with vanilla ice cream or sweetened whipped cream.

*Peach halves or quarters may be substituted for the plums.

BAKING POWDER

When making a recipe that calls for baking powder, get it into the oven as quickly as possible after mixing, because baking powder starts acting as soon as it is mixed with liquid ingredients.

Pecan Torte

SERVES 8

4 large eggs, separated
¼ teaspoon cream of tartar
6 tablespoons unsalted butter,
  at room temperature
1½ cups dark brown sugar,
  firmly packed

1 teaspoon vanilla extract
3½ cups finely ground pecans
1 cup heavy whipping cream
2 tablespoons powdered sugar

——

½ cup chopped pecans

Preheat oven to 350 degrees. Grease two 8-inch round cake pans. Line bottoms of greased pans with wax paper. Lightly grease wax paper. Beat egg whites and cream of tartar in a large bowl until stiff. Beat egg yolks in a separate small bowl until frothy. Cream butter and sugar in a separate bowl. Add egg yolks, vanilla, and pecans. Gently fold pecan mixture into egg whites. Pour batter into prepared pans. Bake 40 minutes, or until surface springs back when gently pressed. Remove cake layers to wire racks. Remove wax paper. Cool completely.

Whip cream with powdered sugar until stiff. Place one cake layer on a serving plate, bottom side up. Spread half of whipped cream over cake. Arrange second layer on top, right side up. Spread remaining whipped cream on top and sprinkle with chopped pecans. Refrigerate until ready to serve.

Sides of torte may also be iced with additional whipped cream if desired.

TORTES

A torte is similar to a cake, except that in place of flour, dry bread crumbs, ground nuts, or a combination of the two are used. Tortes are almost always baked in a springform pan with a removable bottom, as tortes are very delicate in texture and cannot withstand much handling.

Apple Walnut Pie

FREEZER PIE DOUGH

4 cups all-purpose flour
2 teaspoons salt
1 tablespoon sugar
1¾ cups solid vegetable shortening
1 large egg
1 tablespoon distilled white vinegar
½ cup water

Sift together dry ingredients. Blend in shortening. Beat egg, and add water and vinegar. Pour over flour mixture, and mix with a fork. Dough will keep up to 1 month in the freezer. Dough must be chilled overnight before rolling and cutting. Makes 5 single pie crusts.

1 unbaked 9-inch pie crust

Filling:
2 ½ pounds Golden Delicious
   apples, peeled, cored, and thinly
   sliced (about 5 to 6 medium)
2 tablespoons fresh lemon juice
½ teaspoon grated lemon zest
½ teaspoon ground nutmeg
1 ¼ teaspoons ground cinnamon
1 cup sugar
3 tablespoons cornstarch, blended
   with ¼ cup cold water

Topping:
¾ cup all-purpose flour
¾ cup dark brown sugar, firmly packed
¾ cup walnuts, chopped
½ cup (1 stick) unsalted butter,
   at room temperature
——
1 cup heavy whipping cream, whipped
   to soft peaks

Preheat oven to 350 degrees. Prepare a 9-inch pie crust and bake until almost done, about 12 to 15 minutes.

Place apples in a large skillet and sprinkle with lemon juice. Set aside. Combine lemon zest, nutmeg, cinnamon, and sugar. Sprinkle over apples. Bring apples to a boil over moderate heat. Adjust heat so mixture bubbles gently. Cook uncovered, stirring occasionally, 10 to 12 minutes, or until apples release their juice. Increase heat to high. Boil uncovered, stirring occasionally, an additional 5 minutes, or until liquid is reduced by half. Reduce heat to low. When apples stop bubbling, stir in cornstarch mixture. Continue cooking, stirring just until mixture clears and turns very thick, about 2 minutes.

Combine flour, sugar, and walnuts. Add butter and toss with a fork until crumbly.

Spoon apple filling into partially baked pie crust, mounding in center. Crumble topping over apples, but do not pack down. Bake 30 to 40 minutes, or just until the filling bubbles over and topping is crisp. Cool several hours before cutting. Top each slice of pie with a spoonful of whipped cream.

Blueberry Glaze Pie

Filling:
¼ cup plus 4 cups fresh blueberries
¼ cup plus ½ cup sugar
7½ teaspoons cornstarch
¼ teaspoon salt
⅓ cup cold water
7½ teaspoons fresh lemon juice

2 tablespoons lemon-flavored
 gelatin powder
1 tablespoon unsalted butter
——
1 9-inch pie crust, baked and cooled
——
sweetened whipped cream

Purée ¼ cup blueberries, ¼ cup sugar, cornstarch, salt, water, and lemon juice in a blender or food processor. Transfer to a heavy saucepan. Cook over moderate heat until thick, stirring constantly. Remove from heat. Sprinkle gelatin powder over hot mixture and stir to combine. Stir in remaining ½ cup sugar. Add butter and stir until butter melts. Gently fold in remaining 4 cups fresh blueberries. Pour mixture into prepared pie crust. Refrigerate 3 to 4 hours before serving. Top with sweetened whipped cream.

Purple Plum Pie

2 unbaked 9-inch pie crusts
——
1 cup sugar
¾ cup all-purpose flour
¼ teaspoon salt
4½ cups pitted purple plums,
 quartered

1 tablespoon fresh lemon juice
4 tablespoons unsalted butter, at room
 temperature and cut into pieces
——
1 brown paper supermarket sack
2 paper clips

PURPLE PLUMS

There are several varieties of purple plums including Damson, Emily, Italian, and President. Select firm plums that give slightly to pressure. Ignore any pale gray coating on the skin which is natural. Ripe plums should be stored in a plastic bag in the refrigerator for up to 5 days. One pound of plums yields 3 cups sliced.

Preheat oven to 425 degrees. Line a 9-inch pie pan with one pie crust.

Combine sugar, flour, salt, and plums in a large bowl. Pour plum mixture into crust and sprinkle with lemon juice. Dot with butter. Cover with second crust. Flute edges together and cut 3 long steam vents. A light sprinkling of sugar may be added on top crust.

Place pie in paper sack. Be sure it is large enough to loosely cover pie. The sack catches any juices that bubble over and prevents edges and top of pie from browning too much. Fold open end of sack over twice to close and fasten with paper clips. Place sack on a baking sheet. Bake 1 hour. Remove sack from oven. Place on a cooling rack and let rest unopened 5 minutes before removing pie. Serve pie warm or cold.

VANILLA

A close cousin of chocolate, vanilla has its own sweet seductions. It's the favorite flavoring of ice cream and just about any dessert you can think of. Vanilla is a product of a tropical orchid that blooms for a single day and must be pollinated by hand. In large doses, the scent of vanilla is so intoxicating it sometimes has an effect like a drug. First harvested from wild plants in the jungles of Central and South America, vanilla was prized by Aztec dignitaries to add even more flavor to their favorite drink of cocoa sweetened with honey. Mexico is still a major producer of vanilla beans along with Madagascar and Tahiti. Cooking with vanilla beans instead of the commercial extract is well worth the slight effort it takes. You can find vanilla beans packaged in clear tubes in the spice section of supermarkets and specialty cooking shops.

Lemon Sponge Pie

SERVES 8

1 cup sugar
3 tablespoons all-purpose flour
juice and grated zest of 2 lemons
2 large eggs, separated
1 tablespoon unsalted butter, melted

⅛ teaspoon salt
1 cup milk
——
1 unbaked 9-inch pie crust

Preheat oven to 350 degrees. Combine sugar and flour. Mix in lemon juice, lemon zest, slightly beaten egg yolks, butter, and salt. Stir in milk and mix well. Beat egg whites in a separate bowl until stiff, then fold carefully into lemon mixture. Pour batter into pie crust. Bake 40 minutes until set, or until a tester inserted in center comes out clean. Serve immediately.

Raspberry Cream Pie

SERVES 8

1 cup sugar
⅓ cup plus ⅓ cup all-purpose flour
2 large eggs, lightly beaten
1⅓ cups sour cream
1 teaspoon vanilla extract
3 cups fresh raspberries
⅓ cup brown sugar, firmly packed
⅓ cup chopped pecans

3 tablespoons unsalted butter,
    at room temperature
——
1 unbaked 9-inch pie crust
——
Sweetened Sour Cream
raspberries

Preheat oven to 400 degrees. Blend sugar, ⅓ cup flour, eggs, sour cream, and vanilla until smooth. Fold in raspberries. Spoon filling carefully into pie crust. Bake 30 to 35 minutes or until center is firm. Combine additional ⅓ cup flour, brown sugar, pecans, and butter while pie is baking. Sprinkle mixture evenly over hot pie when pie tests done. Continue baking an additional 10 minutes, or until topping is golden. Remove pie from oven and allow to cool completely on a wire rack. Garnish with Sweetened Sour Cream and additional fresh raspberries.

Sweetened Sour Cream:
1 cup sour cream
¼ cup brown sugar, firmly packed
¼ teaspoon vanilla extract

Mix sour cream, sugar, and vanilla in a small bowl. Cover and chill. Yields 1 cup.

Use Sweetened Sour Cream in place of whipped cream as a topping. Can be flavored with rum, Kahlúa, or Grand Marnier.

Coconut Buttermilk Pie

1 unbaked 9-inch pie crust

―――――

3 tablespoons all-purpose flour
1 cup sugar
½ cup (1 stick) unsalted butter,
  melted
3 large eggs

1 cup buttermilk
1 cup flaked coconut
1½ teaspoons vanilla extract
½ teaspoon almond extract

Prepare 9-inch pie crust and chill. Preheat oven to 425 degrees. Combine flour and sugar in a large bowl. Beat in melted butter, eggs, and buttermilk. Add coconut and vanilla and almond extracts. Blend well. Pour into chilled pie crust. Bake 10 minutes. Reduce oven to 350 degrees and continue to bake 35 minutes. Do not open oven when lowering temperature. (Pie will puff up as it bakes and collapse as it cools.) Serve at room temperature.

COCONUT

Packaged coconut is available shredded or flaked; dried, moistened, or frozen; and sweetened or unsweetened. Using fresh coconut, however, is worth the effort. Select a heavy coconut with a distinct sloshing of liquid inside. To crack the shell, pierce the three eyes with an ice pick and drain the liquid. Place on a dishtowel and with a hammer, hit around the middle until it splits. Hammer into smaller pieces. Separate the flesh from the shell with a small knife and peel off the brown skin with a vegetable peeler.

Praline Pumpkin Pie

2 cups plus 1 cup brown sugar,
  firmly packed
⅔ cup finely chopped pecans
4 tablespoons plus 1 tablespoon
  unsalted butter,
  at room temperature
2 large eggs, slightly beaten
1 can (16 ounces) solid
  pack pumpkin
½ teaspoon salt

2 teaspoons ground cinnamon
½ teaspoon ground nutmeg
½ teaspoon ground ginger
¼ teaspoon ground cloves
1 tablespoon all-purpose flour
1 can (12 ounces) evaporated milk

―――――

2 unbaked 9-inch pie crusts

Preheat oven to 425 degrees. Combine 2 cups brown sugar, pecans, and 4 tablespoons butter. Sprinkle evenly over 2 pie crusts. Bake 10 minutes. Remove from oven and reduce oven to 350 degrees. Combine 1 cup brown sugar, 1 tablespoon butter, eggs, pumpkin, salt, cinnamon, nutmeg, ginger, cloves, flour, and milk in a large bowl. Mix well. Divide evenly between 2 pie crusts. Bake 30 minutes, or until a tester inserted into center of pie comes out clean.

Sweet Potato Pecan Pie

CHANTILLY CREAM

⅔ cup heavy whipping cream
1 teaspoon vanilla extract
1 teaspoon brandy
1 teaspoon Grand Marnier
¼ cup sugar
2 tablespoons sour cream

Combine cream, vanilla, brandy, and Grand Marnier in a small bowl. Beat on medium speed 1 minute. Add sugar and sour cream. Continue beating until soft peaks form, about 3 minutes. Do not overbeat. Yields 2 cups.

Note: Overbeating will make cream grainy, which is the first step leading to butter. Once grainy, it cannot return to its former consistency. If this happens, enjoy on toast.

Crust:
3 tablespoons unsalted butter,
  at room temperature
2 tablespoons sugar
¼ teaspoon salt
½ large egg, beaten until frothy
2 tablespoons cold milk
1 cup all-purpose flour

Filling:
2 to 3 sweet potatoes, baked and
  peeled (1 cup pulp)
¼ cup light brown sugar,
  firmly packed
2 tablespoons sugar
½ large egg, beaten until frothy
1 tablespoon heavy whipping cream
1 tablespoon unsalted butter,
  at room temperature

1 tablespoon vanilla extract
¼ teaspoon salt
¼ teaspoon ground cinnamon
⅛ teaspoon ground allspice
⅛ teaspoon ground nutmeg

Pecan Syrup:
¾ cup sugar
¾ cup dark corn syrup
2 large eggs
1½ tablespoons unsalted butter,
  melted
2 teaspoons vanilla extract
⅛ teaspoon salt
⅛ teaspoon ground cinnamon
¾ cup pecan pieces or halves

———

Chantilly Cream

Beat butter, sugar, and salt on high speed until creamy. Add ½ egg and beat until blended. Add milk and beat slowly for 2 minutes. Add flour and beat until blended (overmixing will produce a tough dough). Remove dough from bowl and shape into a 5-inch round about ½ inch thick. Lightly dust round with flour and wrap in plastic wrap. Refrigerate at least 1 hour, preferably overnight. (Dough will last up to 1 week refrigerated.)

Grease and flour a 9-inch deep dish pie pan. Roll dough out on a lightly floured surface to a ¼-inch thickness. Very lightly flour top of dough and fold into quarters. Carefully place dough in pie pan so that corner of folded dough is centered in pan. Unfold dough and arrange to fit sides and bottom of pan. Press firmly into place. Trim edges. Refrigerate 15 minutes. Preheat oven to 325 degrees.

Combine sweet potatoes, sugars, remaining ½ beaten egg, cream, butter, vanilla, salt, cinnamon, allspice, and nutmeg. Beat at medium speed until mixture is smooth, 2 to 3 minutes. Do not overbeat. Set aside.

Pecan Syrup: Mix sugar, corn syrup, eggs, butter, vanilla, salt, and cinnamon at low speed until syrup is opaque, about 1 minute. Stir in pecans and set aside.

Spoon filling evenly into dough-lined cake pan. Pour pecan syrup on top. Bake 1 hour and 45 minutes, or until a tester inserted in center of pie comes out clean. Cool and serve with Chantilly Cream (see accompanying recipe).

Pecans will rise to top of pie during baking. Store pie at room temperature for first 24 hours, then refrigerate.

Toffee Chocolate Pecan Pie

SERVES 8

1 unbaked 9-inch pie crust

——

4 ounces chocolate-covered
  toffee bars, chopped (3 bars)
4 large eggs, lightly beaten
1 cup light corn syrup

4 tablespoons unsalted butter,
  melted
½ cup sugar
1 tablespoon vanilla extract
¾ cup semi-sweet chocolate chips
1 cup pecans, coarsely chopped

Preheat oven to 350 degrees. Cover bottom of a 9-inch pie crust with chopped chocolate-covered toffee bars. Combine eggs, corn syrup, butter, sugar, and vanilla. Mix well. Stir in chocolate chips and pecans. Pour mixture over broken chocolate-covered toffee bars in pie crust. Bake 50 to 55 minutes or until done.

BREAKING CHOCOLATE

To break chocolate-covered toffee bars, hit wrapped bars against the side of a counter top.

Creamy Fudge Pie

SERVES 6 TO 8

6 tablespoons unsweetened cocoa
6 tablespoons all-purpose flour
1½ cups sugar
3 large eggs, well beaten
1½ teaspoons vanilla extract
¾ cup (1½ sticks) unsalted
  butter, melted

——

1 unbaked 9-inch pie crust

——

Raspberry Cabernet Sauce

Preheat oven to 350 degrees. Sift together cocoa, flour, and sugar, removing any cocoa lumps. Mix in eggs and vanilla. Blend in butter. Pour into pie crust and bake 30 to 35 minutes. Inside of pie will be creamy with a crusty top. Serve with Raspberry Cabernet Sauce.

Also good with peppermint ice cream.

Raspberry Cabernet Sauce:
1 bottle Cabernet Sauvignon or
  other red wine
1 package (12 ounces) frozen
  raspberries, thawed
1 cup sugar

Combine wine, raspberries, and sugar in a large saucepan. Bring to a vigorous boil over high heat and cook until only 2 cups remain, about 30 minutes. As sauce begins to thicken, stir to prevent scorching. Strain liquid through a sieve to remove seeds. Refrigerate at least 3 hours. Sauce will last 1 month in refrigerator. Yields 1⅔ cups.

Chocolate Mousse Pie with Caramel Pecan Topping

SERVES 6 TO 8

FOLDING

To fold one mixture into another (usually beaten egg whites or whipped cream), use a whisk, large spoon, or rubber spatula and gently work the ingredients together in a figure-eight motion. Turn the bowl slowly as you are folding, working quickly and stopping when no streaks remain. The idea is to release as few air bubbles as possible, creating a lighter product.

Crust:
6 ounces chocolate wafer crumbs
  or graham cracker crumbs
4½ teaspoons sugar
3 tablespoons unsalted butter, melted

Caramel Pecan Topping:
1 cup light brown sugar,
  firmly packed
⅛ teaspoon salt
½ cup (1 stick) unsalted butter
¼ cup plus 2 tablespoons heavy
  whipping cream
2 tablespoons dark rum
1 cup chopped pecans

Mousse:
8 ounces semi-sweet chocolate,
  cut into ½-inch chunks
2 large egg yolks
3 tablespoons strong brewed coffee
¼ cup sugar
1 cup (2 sticks) unsalted butter,
  cut into pieces
3 large egg whites
2 teaspoons lukewarm water
½ cup pecan halves

Preheat oven to 350 degrees. Combine crumbs, sugar, and butter. Press crumb mixture into bottom and up sides of an 11-inch fluted tart pan with removable bottom. Chill crust 5 minutes, then bake 5 minutes. Cool.

Caramel Pecan Topping: Stir sugar, salt, and butter in a saucepan over medium heat until sugar dissolves. Stir in cream and rum. Bring to a boil. Lower heat and simmer until caramel thickens to a consistency that coats back of a spoon. Transfer half of caramel to another saucepan and set aside. Stir chopped pecans into remaining caramel. Immediately spread pecan caramel over bottom of crust. Refrigerate until caramel sets.

Grind chocolate in a food processor to small bead consistency. Add egg yolks and blend. Combine coffee, sugar, and butter in a medium saucepan over low heat until sugar dissolves. Heat to simmering. Slowly add hot coffee mixture in a thin stream to food processor while machine is running. Stop and scrape sides with a spatula, then process 5 seconds longer. Transfer mixture to a mixing bowl. Set aside. Beat egg whites with water in a separate bowl until stiff peaks form. Fold egg whites into chocolate mixture and refrigerate until partially set.

Spread chilled mousse over caramel-covered crust. Refrigerate until firm. Reheat remaining caramel over low heat. Add 2 tablespoons cream to thin if necessary. Cool slightly. Arrange pecan halves decoratively on mousse. Gently spread caramel evenly over mousse and pecans. Refrigerate at least 2 hours. Cut pie with a clean, hot knife.

Chocolate Toffee Pie

Crust:
¼ cup sugar
4 tablespoons unsalted butter,
    at room temperature
2 tablespoons water
2 cups finely chopped pecans

Filling:
14 ounces semi-sweet chocolate
2 tablespoons vegetable oil
2 cups heavy whipping cream

Cream Topping:
¾ teaspoon unflavored gelatin
4½ teaspoons cold water
1½ cups heavy whipping cream

⅓ cup powdered sugar
½ teaspoon vanilla extract

Sugared Pecans:
1 large egg white
1 teaspoon cold water
1 pound pecan halves
1 cup sugar
⅛ teaspoon salt

Toffee Sauce:
½ cup (1 stick) unsalted butter
1 cup sugar
1 cup heavy whipping cream
——
sweetened whipped cream

CHOCOLATE

The botanical name for the cocoa tree translates to "food of the gods" and who would disagree! The largest crops of cocoa beans come from Brazil and Africa. Beans are fermented, dried, roasted, and ground into a paste which is the heart of chocolate's flavor. Chocolate should be stored in a cool, dry place and never refrigerated. If stored in damp or cold conditions, sugar crystals will form on the surface of the chocolate.

Preheat oven to 325 degrees. Grease a 12-inch pie pan. Heat sugar and butter in a small saucepan, whisking until a thick paste forms. Remove from heat. Add water and pecans. Press mixture into prepared pan. Bake until golden brown, about 15 minutes. Cool.

Melt chocolate and oil over low heat, stirring constantly. Remove from heat. Whip cream until stiff. Fold into chocolate. Chill 2 hours. Whip again and spread over cooled crust.

Melt gelatin and water in small saucepan, heating gently until dissolved. Cool. Add 1 to 2 tablespoons cream. Whip remaining cream with sugar and vanilla until soft peaks hold. Beat in gelatin mixture until stiff. Spread over filling.

Sugared Pecans: Preheat oven to 225 degrees. Beat egg white with water. Add pecans, sugar, and salt. Spread on baking sheet and bake 1 hour, turning occasionally.

Toffee Sauce: Heat butter and sugar over medium heat, stirring constantly, until rich brown color is achieved. Mixture will bubble. Be careful not to burn. Remove from heat and whisk in cream.

Place a spoonful of Toffee Sauce on plate. Place a piece of pie on top of sauce. Garnish with additional piped whipped cream and Sugared Pecans.

Coffee Ice Cream Pie

SERVES 10 TO 12

Crust:
20 Oreo cookies
5⅓ tablespoons unsalted butter,
   melted

1 tablespoon unsalted butter
⅔ cup evaporated milk

———

2 pints coffee ice cream, softened

———

Sauce:
2 ounces unsweetened chocolate
½ cup sugar

1 cup heavy whipping cream
2 tablespoons coffee liqueur

Crush cookies in a food processor to a fine crumb consistency. Add butter and mix well. Press mixture into bottom of a 10-inch pie pan. Freeze.

Melt chocolate, sugar, butter, and milk in top of a double boiler. Cook over boiling water until sauce thickens slightly, stirring continuously. Cool.

Spread ice cream carefully onto crust. Return to freezer. Whip cream with liqueur until stiff, but not dry.

Pour cooled chocolate sauce evenly over ice cream, then spread whipped cream topping over chocolate sauce. Cover with plastic wrap and freeze 4 hours or overnight. Remove pie from freezer 20 minutes before serving.

Lime Tart

Crust :
1 ¼ cups all-purpose flour
2 tablespoons sugar
½ teaspoon salt
½ cup (1 stick) unsalted butter,
   chilled and cut into pieces
1 large egg yolk
1 tablespoon cold water

Filling:
½ cup heavy whipping cream
2 tablespoons cornstarch
2 large eggs
6 large egg yolks
¾ cup sugar
¾ cup fresh lime juice
¾ cup fresh orange juice
4 tablespoons unsalted butter

———

lime peel strips, rolled in sugar
sweetened whipped cream

Combine flour, sugar, and salt in a food processor. Add butter and pulse until mixture resembles coarse meal. Add egg yolk and water and process until dough begins to hold together. Form dough into a ball and flatten into a disk. Cover dough in plastic wrap and refrigerate 30 minutes.

Roll dough out on a lightly floured surface to a 13-inch round. Roll dough onto a rolling pin and transfer to a 9-inch tart pan with a removable bottom. Press dough onto bottom and up sides of tart pan, then trim edges. Freeze until firm, about 1 hour.

Preheat oven to 400 degrees. Line crust with foil. Fill with pie weights or dried beans. Bake until crust is set on edges, about 12 minutes. Remove weights and foil from crust. Return crust to oven. Bake until center of crust is golden, about 14 minutes. Cool on a wire rack.

Whisk cream and cornstarch in a bowl. Let rest 1 minute. Whisk again, blending in eggs and yolks. Combine sugar, lime juice, orange juice, and butter in medium saucepan over medium heat. Stir until sugar dissolves and butter melts. Bring to a boil. Remove from heat. Whisk juice mixture into egg mixture. Return combined mixture to saucepan and boil 1 minute, whisking constantly. Strain into a bowl and cool slightly. Pour filling into tart shell. Chill 8 hours or overnight. Garnish tart with lime peel and whipped cream.

If tart crust is too crumbly to work with, simply press it into tart pan by hand. A graham cracker crust or ready-made pie crust can be substituted. Individual tart shells may even be used if desired.

Key Lime Tartlets

LIMES

The two main varieties of limes are the Persian lime, which is the most common, and the Key lime from Florida. The Key lime is smaller, rounder, and more yellow than the Persian lime. The peak season for Persian limes is from May through August. Look for brightly colored, smooth-skinned limes that are heavy for their size. Small brown areas on the skin won't affect flavor, but a hard, shriveled skin will.

Key Lime Curd:
1 tablespoon grated Key lime zest
⅔ cup fresh Key lime juice
2 cups sugar
1 cup (2 sticks) unsalted butter
4 large eggs, lightly beaten

Crust:
⅔ cup (1 stick and 2⅔ tablespoons)
  unsalted butter, chilled
1½ cups all-purpose flour
½ cup powdered sugar
½ teaspoon salt
2 tablespoons water
1 teaspoon vanilla extract

———

½ cup whipped cream

Key Lime Curd: Combine lime zest, juice, sugar, and butter in top of a double boiler and cook over simmering water, stirring constantly, until butter melts. Gradually stir about one-fourth of lime mixture into eggs. Add this mixture back into top of double boiler, stirring constantly. Cook over simmering water, stirring constantly, until mixture thickens and coats a spoon, about 15 to 25 minutes. Remove from heat and strain if necessary. Cool, cover, and refrigerate. (Key Lime Curd will keep in refrigerator up to 2 weeks.)

Cut butter into flour, sugar, and salt. Sprinkle water and vanilla over flour mixture. Stir well to mix. Divide dough into 2 balls and put in plastic wrap in refrigerator to firm, about 15 minutes. Preheat oven to 325 degrees. Roll dough out onto floured surface about ⅛ inch thick and cut with round cookie cutter. Place in miniature muffin tins or 3 to 4-inch tart pans and prick with a fork. Bake 13 to 15 minutes, or until light brown. (Can be frozen.) Fold 1 cup Key Lime Curd into ½ cup whipped cream and spoon into tartlets.

Pear and Almond Crisp

4 pears, peeled, cored, and sliced
2 tablespoons fresh lemon juice
¾ cup sliced blanched almonds
¾ cup milk
6 tablespoons plus 2 tablespoons
  unsalted butter, melted and cooled

3 large eggs, lightly beaten
½ teaspoon vanilla extract
½ teaspoon almond extract
¾ cup self-rising flour
½ cup plus 2 tablespoons sugar
dash salt

Preheat oven to 400 degrees. Grease a 1-quart baking dish. Add pears and lemon juice. Toss to coat. Set aside. Grind almonds in a food processor (not to point of almond butter). Reserve ¼ cup. Add milk, 6 tablespoons butter, eggs, vanilla, and almond extract to blender. Blend until smooth. Set aside. Combine flour, ½ cup sugar, and salt in a large bowl. Stir in almond mixture. Combine. Pour batter over pears, drizzle with remaining 2 tablespoons butter, sprinkle with remaining 2 tablespoons sugar, and top with remaining ¼ cup almonds. Bake 40 minutes, or until golden brown. Cool on a wire rack 15 minutes. Serve warm.

Apple Cranberry Crisp with Almond Streusel Topping

SERVES 6 TO 8

1 cup cranberries, fresh or frozen
¼ cup plus ¾ cup sugar
¼ cup currants
¼ cup dark rum
6 to 7 medium Granny Smith apples,
  cored, peeled, and sliced ¼ inch
  thick (6 cups)
1 tablespoon fresh lemon juice
1 teaspoon grated orange zest
½ teaspoon ground cinnamon
3 tablespoons all-purpose flour

Topping:
4 tablespoons unsalted butter,
  at room temperature
¼ cup all-purpose flour
¼ cup brown sugar, firmly packed
½ cup blanched slivered almonds
¼ cup rolled oats

Preheat oven to 350 degrees. Toss cranberries with ¼ cup sugar in a small bowl. Set aside. Combine currants and rum in a separate small bowl. Set aside. Toss apples with lemon juice in a large bowl. Stir in remaining ¾ cup sugar, orange zest, and cinnamon. Fold in cranberries and currants. Stir in flour until mixture is combined. Set aside.

Mix butter, flour, and brown sugar in a large bowl until mixture resembles coarse meal. Stir in almonds and oats. Spoon apple mixture into a 2-quart soufflé dish and top with topping. Bake 45 minutes. Cool at least 20 minutes before serving.

Rhubarb Crumble with Bourbon Cream

SERVES 4 TO 6

Crumble:
1 cup plus ⅓ cup sugar
1 tablespoon ground cinnamon
½ teaspoon ground nutmeg
4 cups rhubarb, cut into 1-inch
  pieces
⅔ cup all-purpose flour
⅓ cup rolled oats

1 teaspoon baking powder
⅛ teaspoon salt
3 tablespoons unsalted butter,
  at room temperature

Bourbon Cream:
2 cups vanilla yogurt, chilled
2 tablespoons bourbon

Preheat oven to 400 degrees. Generously grease a 9-inch square glass baking dish. Combine 1 cup sugar, cinnamon, and nutmeg in a large bowl. Gently toss rhubarb into sugar mixture. Spread rhubarb mixture evenly in prepared baking dish. Combine flour, oats, baking powder, salt, and remaining ⅓ cup sugar. Cut in butter until mixture resembles coarse meal. Sprinkle evenly over top of rhubarb. Bake 20 to 25 minutes, or until rhubarb is tender and crumbs are browned.

Bourbon Cream: Beat yogurt until very thick. Stir in bourbon. Serve Rhubarb Crumble warm, topped with Bourbon Cream.

RHUBARB

There are two types of rhubarb available. Hothouse rhubarb has pink or pale red stalks and yellow-green leaves, and field-grown rhubarb has cherry red stalks, bright green leaves, and a stronger flavor. Select rhubarb with crisp, bright stalks. Refrigerate, tightly wrapped in a plastic bag, for up to 3 days. Remove all leaves and wash stalks just before using. All fibrous strings should be removed from the field-grown rhubarb. One pound rhubarb yields 3 cups chopped.

Fresh Peach and Blueberry Crêpes

SERVES 6 TO 8

CRÊPE USES

Crêpes are best described as very thin pancakes. They can be combined with a variety of main course or dessert fillings to create an elegant course. Try some of the following fillings or experiment with your own favorites.

◆ *Chicken à la King*

◆ *Lobster or crab in a sherried cream sauce*

◆ *Ground beef browned with onion, garlic, and chili powder and topped with taco sauce, grated cheese, and sliced olives*

◆ *Scrambled eggs, cheese, and Picante sauce*

◆ *Creamed spinach*

◆ *Broccoli with cheese sauce*

◆ *Fresh fruit and crème fraîche (page 102)*

◆ *Ice cream and a favorite topping*

◆ *Sautéed apples with raisins, brown sugar, and cinnamon, topped with whipped cream*

Filling:
6 large peaches, pitted and diced
   into ½-inch pieces
3 tablespoons Grand Marnier
5 tablespoons sugar
½ cup fresh blueberries
3 tablespoons fresh orange juice
grated zest of 1 orange

Crêpes:
1 cup all-purpose flour
2 tablespoons sugar
⅛ teaspoon salt
2 large eggs
1 tablespoon vanilla extract
2 tablespoons Grand Marnier
¼ cup water
milk
1 tablespoon vegetable oil

Combine peaches, Grand Marnier, sugar, blueberries, orange juice, and orange zest in a large bowl. Cover and let flavors marinate at least 30 minutes.

Crêpes: Combine flour, sugar, and salt in a blender or a food processor. Add eggs. Pulse twice. Combine vanilla, Grand Marnier, water, and enough milk to make 1⅓ cups total liquid. Add half liquid mixture to flour mixture and process 2 seconds. Add remaining liquid and oil to flour in food processor. Process until thoroughly mixed. Strain if necessary to remove any lumps. Cover batter and refrigerate 2 hours or overnight. Crêpe batter should be like heavy cream. Thin with extra liquid if necessary. Preheat a lightly greased crêpe pan or heavy griddle over medium-high heat. Using about 2 tablespoons batter per crêpe, cook crêpes on one side only until firm and slightly golden. (If crêpes are cooked in advance, place wax paper between each and stack. Wrap crêpes in an airtight bag and refrigerate up to 4 days, or freeze for longer storage.)

Preheat oven to 400 degrees. Butter a shallow casserole dish. If crêpes have been chilled, allow them to return to room temperature. Place 2 tablespoons marinated fruit, drained, off center in each crêpe and fold into quarters or roll into cylinders. Arrange crêpes seam side down in prepared casserole. Spoon remaining marinade over crêpes. Bake 10 minutes. Remove from oven and sift powdered sugar over crêpes. Place under broiler 2 to 3 minutes to brown sugar, watching carefully to avoid burning.

Serve with Vanilla Sauce (page 233) or crème fraîche (page 102).

Chocolate Toffee Brownies

YIELDS 2 DOZEN BROWNIES

9 ounces chocolate toffee bars, chopped, reserving ½ cup
½ cup (1 stick) unsalted butter
2 ounces unsweetened chocolate
2 large eggs

¾ cup sugar
½ teaspoon vanilla extract
¼ teaspoon salt
1 cup all-purpose flour, sifted
¾ cup toasted pecan halves or pieces

Preheat oven to 350 degrees. Place oven rack in bottom third of oven. Spray an 8-inch square baking pan with cooking spray. Place a piece of wax paper, cut to fit, in bottom of pan, and spray again with cooking spray. Set aside.

Melt butter and chocolate in a double boiler until smooth. Set aside. Beat eggs, sugar, vanilla, and salt with an electric mixer set at medium speed until mixed. Add melted chocolate and flour, beating on low speed. Stir in pecans and all but reserved ½ cup toffee bars. Pour into prepared pan and spread evenly. Sprinkle remaining toffee bars on top. Bake 25 to 30 minutes, or until tester inserted in center comes out barely clean. Transfer to rack to cool. Turn upside down on baking sheet. Remove wax paper, then turn brownies upright. Refrigerate 1 hour. Cut into 24 small brownies.

Pecan Chocolate Chunk Brownies

YIELDS 4 DOZEN BROWNIES

1 cup (2 sticks) unsalted butter, melted
2 cups sugar
4 large eggs, lightly beaten
½ cup unsweetened cocoa
1 tablespoon vanilla extract

⅓ cup all-purpose flour
½ teaspoon salt
7 ounces semi-sweet chocolate, coarsely chopped
½ cup chopped pecans

Preheat oven to 350 degrees. Spray a 9 by 13-inch pan with nonstick cooking spray. Whisk butter, sugar, eggs, cocoa, and vanilla in a large bowl. Slowly add flour and salt, mixing until batter is smooth. Stir in chocolate and pecans until combined. Pour batter into prepared pan and spread evenly. Bake 35 to 40 minutes, or until tester inserted in center comes out clean. Cool on rack before cutting.

Kahlúa Brownies with Buttercream Frosting and Chocolate Glaze

YIELDS 3 DOZEN BROWNIES

UNSWEETENED CHOCOLATE

Unsweetened chocolate is also known as baker's chocolate and is cocoa solids with no additional flavorings or sugar. In a pinch, 3 tablespoons unsweetened cocoa powder plus 1 tablespoon unsalted butter can be substituted for 1 ounce unsweetened chocolate.

Crust:
⅓ cup light brown sugar,
  firmly packed
5 ⅓ tablespoons unsalted butter,
  at room temperature
⅔ cup all-purpose flour, sifted
½ cup finely chopped pecans

Filling:
2 ounces unsweetened chocolate
¼ cup solid vegetable shortening
4 tablespoons unsalted butter
2 large eggs
½ cup sugar
½ cup light brown sugar,
  firmly packed
1 teaspoon vanilla extract

¼ cup Kahlúa
½ cup all-purpose flour, sifted
¼ teaspoon salt
½ cup chopped pecans

Buttercream Frosting:
6 tablespoons unsalted butter,
  at room temperature
2 cups sifted powdered sugar
1 tablespoon Kahlúa
1 tablespoon heavy whipping cream

Glaze:
2 ounces semi-sweet chocolate
1 ounce unsweetened chocolate
2 teaspoons solid vegetable shortening

Preheat oven to 350 degrees. Grease and flour a 9-inch square baking pan. Cream sugar and butter until light and fluffy. Slowly add flour and continue to mix until blended. Add pecans. When completely combined, press crust into bottom of prepared pan. Set aside.

Combine chocolate, shortening, and butter in a small saucepan over low heat. Stir until chocolate is melted and mixture is smooth. Cool. Combine eggs, sugars, and vanilla in a large bowl. Mix until blended. Stir into cooled chocolate mixture. Add Kahlúa. Slowly add flour and salt, mixing until batter is smooth. Stir in pecans. Pour filling into prepared crust. Bake 25 minutes, or until tester inserted in center comes out clean. Be careful not to overbake. Let cool.

Buttercream Frosting: Cream butter, sugar, Kahlúa, and cream in a small bowl until smooth and creamy. Spread over cooled filling mixture and refrigerate 30 minutes. More Kahlúa may be added to make spreading easier. For a less sweet brownie, use half of Buttercream Frosting.

Melt chocolates and shortening over low heat, stirring constantly. Cool and spread over Buttercream Frosting.

Kahlúa Brownies with Buttercream
Frosting and Chocolate Glaze

White Chocolate Brownies with
Vanilla Ice Cream and Chocolate Sauce

YIELDS 1 TO 1½ DOZEN BROWNIES

MINT

*The most common varieties of mint
include spearmint, peppermint,
apple mint, lemon mint, and
chocolate mint.*

Brownies:
7 tablespoons unsalted butter
4 ounces plus 4 ounces white
  chocolate, finely chopped
2 large eggs
⅛ teaspoon salt
½ cup sugar
1½ teaspoons vanilla extract
1 cup all-purpose flour
4 ounces bittersweet chocolate,
  finely chopped

Chocolate Sauce:
½ cup heavy whipping cream
3 tablespoons unsalted butter,
  cut into pieces
⅓ cup sugar
⅓ cup dark brown sugar, firmly packed
⅛ teaspoon salt
½ cup sifted unsweetened cocoa
¼ cup strong brewed coffee

———

1 quart vanilla ice cream
fresh mint
fresh berries

Preheat oven to 350 degrees. Line an 8-inch square pan with foil. Lightly grease foil.

Melt butter over low heat in a small saucepan. Remove butter from heat and add 4 ounces white chocolate. Do not stir. Beat eggs and salt at high speed until frothy, about 30 seconds. Continue to beat eggs, about 2 to 3 minutes, while gradually adding sugar. Add butter mixture and vanilla. Blend well. Slowly add flour. Beat quickly until smooth. Fold in remaining 4 ounces white chocolate and bittersweet chocolate. Pour batter into prepared pan and bake 35 minutes. Allow to cool in pan on a wire rack.

Chocolate Sauce: Combine cream and butter in a small saucepan. Cook over moderate heat, stirring constantly, until butter melts and cream begins to boil. Add sugars and stir until dissolved. Reduce heat. Add salt and cocoa. Whisk until smooth. Remove from heat. Thin with coffee if desired. Serve warm or at room temperature.

Coat bottom of a dessert plate with chocolate sauce. Place a brownie in center of plate and top with a scoop of vanilla ice cream. Garnish with fresh mint and fresh berries.

Mint Chocolate Cupcakes

2 cups cake flour

1 teaspoon baking soda

¼ teaspoon salt

½ cup unsweetened cocoa

⅔ cup (1 stick and 2⅔ tablespoons)
  unsalted butter,
  at room temperature

1½ cups superfine sugar

3 large eggs

2 teaspoons peppermint extract

1 cup milk

Frosting:

3 ounces semi-sweet chocolate

4 tablespoons unsalted butter

1 teaspoon peppermint extract

SUPERFINE SUGAR

Also called caster sugar, superfine sugar is granulated sugar that has been milled further. It is ideal for use in meringues, angel food cakes, or any recipe where coarser sugar might affect the consistency of the finished product.

Preheat oven to 350 degrees. Line muffin cups with paper liners. Sift flour, baking soda, salt, and cocoa. Set aside. Cream butter and sugar until light, about 5 minutes. Add eggs, one at a time, beating well after each addition. Beat in peppermint extract. Slowly blend in flour mixture, alternating with milk, until blended. Spoon batter into paper liners, filling each cup three-fourths full.

Bake 12 to 15 minutes, or until cake tester inserted in center comes out clean. Do not overbake. Cool cupcakes in pan on a wire rack 5 minutes. Remove cupcakes to wire rack to cool completely.

Melt chocolate and butter in a medium saucepan over low heat. Stir until smooth. Remove saucepan from heat and stir in peppermint extract. Cool frosting until spreadable. Frost cupcakes.

Chocolate-Covered Almond Macaroons

Almond Macaroons:
1½ cups blanched almonds
1½ cups powdered sugar
3 large egg whites,
    at room temperature

Chocolate Buttercream:
7 tablespoons sugar
7 tablespoons water
4 large egg yolks

⅔ cup (1 stick and 2⅔ tablespoons)
    unsalted butter
4 teaspoons unsweetened cocoa

Frosting:
5 ounces semi-sweet chocolate
1 tablespoon plus 2 teaspoons
    solid vegetable shortening

Preheat oven to 350 degrees. Line baking sheets with wax paper. Grind almonds in a food processor. Add powdered sugar and pulse until completely combined. Set aside. Beat egg whites until stiff, but moist. Sprinkle almond mixture over beaten egg whites, one-third at a time, folding in each addition until blended. Drop dough by rounded tablespoons onto prepared baking sheets. Space cookies 1 inch apart. Bake 15 to 18 minutes, or until lightly browned. Cool cookies on baking sheets 5 minutes, then transfer to racks. Cool completely.

Chocolate Buttercream: Combine sugar and water in a small saucepan. Bring to a boil over high heat, stirring constantly. Continue to boil without stirring until syrup reaches 230 to 234 degrees on a candy thermometer (soft-thread stage). Before syrup has reached its target temperature, beat egg yolks in small bowl until blended. Beating constantly at medium speed, slowly add hot syrup to eggs in a thin, steady stream. Beat until mixture is thick and lemon colored and has cooled to room temperature. Beat in butter, 1 tablespoon at a time, until just blended. Stir in cocoa. If mixture gets dark and runny from overbeating, refrigerate it, then beat again.

Spread 2 tablespoons buttercream on bottom of each cooled cookie. Then place cookies, buttercream side up, in a single layer on a plate and refrigerate until buttercream is firm, at least 15 minutes.

Combine chocolate and shortening in top of a double boiler. When chocolate melts, stir mixture until smooth. Remove from heat and let cool, stirring occasionally, until lukewarm (80 to 85 degrees). Dip each cookie, buttercream side down, in chocolate to coat completely. Place macaroons on a plate, chocolate side up, and refrigerate until chocolate coating is set, at least 10 minutes. Store in refrigerator.

Biscotti

2½ cups all-purpose flour
2 cups finely chopped almonds
½ teaspoon baking powder
1½ cups sugar
¼ teaspoon salt
½ teaspoon grated lemon zest
3 large eggs
½ cup (1 stick) unsalted butter,
  at room temperature

½ teaspoon anise extract or
  1½ teaspoons almond extract
1 large egg white, lightly beaten

Chocolate Biscotti Variation:
omit lemon zest
add ¼ cup Dutch processed cocoa
use 1½ teaspoons almond extract

BISCOTTI

Biscotti are twice-baked Italian cookies. These crunchy cookies are delicious eaten alone or dipped in coffee or sweet wine.

Preheat oven to 375 degrees and grease a baking sheet. Combine flour, almonds, baking powder, sugar, salt, and lemon zest until blended. Cream eggs, butter, and anise extract on low speed until smooth. Slowly add flour mixture to egg mixture and blend well. (Dough will be sticky.) Divide dough equally and form each half into a "log" about 12 to 14 inches long and 3 inches wide. Place logs on prepared baking sheet and brush with egg white. Bake 30 minutes, or until golden brown. Remove from oven. Test for doneness. Reduce oven temperature to 325 degrees. Cut biscotti on the diagonal into ½-inch slices. Lay slices on their sides and return to oven. Bake an additional 12 to 15 minutes, or longer for a drier cookie. Cool on wire racks and store in an airtight container.

Biscochitos

1 cup (2 sticks) unsalted butter,
  at room temperature
½ cup plus 2 tablespoons sugar
1 teaspoon anise seed
1 large egg yolk, lightly beaten
3 cups all-purpose flour

4½ teaspoons baking powder
½ teaspoon salt
¼ cup water
½ teaspoon ground cinnamon

ANISE SEED

One of the oldest spices, anise is a botanical relative of caraway, cumin, dill, and fennel. Ribbed, fuzzy, and pale brown, the seeds are the most flavorful part of the anise plant.

Preheat oven to 400 degrees. Cream butter, ½ cup sugar, and anise seed. Blend in egg yolk. Sift flour, baking powder, and salt in a separate bowl. Mix water into flour mixture. Combine butter mixture with flour mixture and knead well. Roll dough out on a floured surface until ⅛ inch thick. Cut out cookies with a biscuit or cookie cutter. Cookies can be cut into any size.

    Combine 2 tablespoons sugar and cinnamon. Sprinkle on top of cookies. Place 1 inch apart on greased baking sheets and bake 10 to 15 minutes, or until golden brown. Remove cookies carefully from baking sheets and allow to cool completely on wire racks.

These will keep for weeks in an airtight container. Delicious with hot chocolate.

Traditional Mexican Christmas Cookies

YIELDS 2 DOZEN COOKIES

*1 cup (2 sticks) unsalted butter,
   at room temperature*
½ cup powdered sugar
2 tablespoons milk
1½ teaspoons vanilla extract
½ teaspoon ground cinnamon
*1½ cups plus ¼ cup all-purpose
   flour*

1 teaspoon baking powder
sugar

Topping:
1 cup sugar
1 ounce semi-sweet chocolate, grated
½ teaspoon ground cinnamon

Preheat oven to 325 degrees. Beat butter, sugar, milk, vanilla, and cinnamon until light and fluffy. Gradually add 1½ cups flour and baking
powder, beating at low speed until well blended. Stir in additional ¼ cup
flour if dough is too soft to shape. Roll dough into 1¼-inch balls. Place
3 inches apart on ungreased baking sheets. Flatten each ball into 2-inch
rounds with bottom of a glass which has been buttered and dipped
in sugar. Bake 20 to 25 minutes, or until edges are golden brown.

Combine sugar, chocolate, and cinnamon in a small bowl. Three or
four minutes after removing cookies from oven, coat both sides of cookies
with this mixture, one at a time. Cool on wire racks.

Lemon Pecan Wafers

YIELDS 6 DOZEN COOKIES

*½ cup (1 stick) unsalted butter,
   at room temperature*
1 cup sugar
1 large egg
1 tablespoon grated lemon zest

1 tablespoon fresh lemon juice
2 cups all-purpose flour
⅛ teaspoon salt
1 teaspoon baking powder
1 cup pecans, toasted and chopped

Cream butter and sugar until light and fluffy. Beat in egg, lemon zest,
and lemon juice. Combine flour, salt, and baking powder in a separate
bowl. Gradually blend flour mixture into butter mixture. Stir in nuts
(mixing with your hands if necessary to distribute nuts evenly). Shape
dough into 2 rolls, 1½ inches in diameter each. Wrap in wax paper and
refrigerate until firm, about 2 hours. (Dough may be stored in refrigerator
up to 3 days.)

Preheat oven to 375 degrees. Grease a baking sheet. Unwrap dough
and, using a sharp knife, cut into ⅛-inch slices. Place slices 1 inch apart
on prepared baking sheet. Bake 12 minutes, or until edges are lightly
browned. Transfer to racks to cool.

Santa Fe Chocolate Chip Cookies

¾ cup (1½ sticks) unsalted
   butter, at room temperature
¾ cup dark brown sugar,
   firmly packed
⅔ cup powdered sugar
1 large egg
1 teaspoon vanilla extract
2½ cups all-purpose flour

½ teaspoon ground cinnamon
1 teaspoon baking soda
1 teaspoon salt
2 cups milk chocolate or semi-sweet
   chocolate chips
1 cup chopped pecans
⅓ cup toasted pine nuts, chopped

BROWN SUGAR

Brown sugar is granulated sugar that has been flavored with molasses. The difference between dark brown and light brown sugar is determined by the amount of molasses they each contain. Brown sugar should always be measured firmly packed unless specified otherwise.

Cream butter and sugars until light and fluffy. Beat in egg and vanilla. Sift flour, baking soda, cinnamon, and salt in a separate bowl. Slowly add flour mixture to butter mixture and beat until blended. Stir in chocolate chips, pecans, and pine nuts. Place 2 sheets plastic wrap on a work surface. Spoon half of dough into a 12-inch strip down center of each plastic sheet. Form each dough strip into a 12-inch log. Wrap with plastic and refrigerate 1 hour. (Dough can be prepared up to 3 days ahead and kept refrigerated.)

   Preheat oven to 325 degrees. Using a sharp knife, cut chilled cookie dough into ¼-inch slices. Place dough slices on large baking sheets. Bake until cookies are light golden brown, about 14 minutes. Remove baking sheets from oven and place on cooling racks 5 minutes. Remove cookies from baking sheets. Transfer to wire racks to cool completely. Store in air-tight container.

A⁺ Cookies

3 large eggs
1 cup light brown sugar,
   firmly packed
1 cup sugar
2 teaspoons vanilla extract
2 teaspoons baking soda
½ cup (1 stick) unsalted butter,
   at room temperature

1½ cups chunky or smooth peanut
   butter
4½ cups rolled oats
½ pound semi-sweet chocolate chips
½ pound M & M chocolate candies,
   peanut or plain

Preheat oven to 350 degrees. Whisk eggs in a large bowl. Add sugars, vanilla, baking soda, butter, and peanut butter, one at a time, blending well after each addition. Stir in oats, chocolate chips, and M & M's until well blended. Form large tablespoons of dough into balls. Place on an ungreased baking sheet 4 inches apart. Bake 12 to 15 minutes. Do not overbake. Cool on wire racks.

Coconut Crisps

1 cup (2 sticks) unsalted butter,
  at room temperature
1 cup plus ¼ cup sugar
1 cup dark brown sugar,
  firmly packed
1 large egg
1 cup vegetable oil
1 teaspoon vanilla extract
1 teaspoon salt

1 teaspoon baking soda
1 teaspoon cream of tartar
3½ cups all-purpose flour
1 cup rolled oats
1 cup flaked coconut
1 cup crispy rice cereal

Cream butter, 1 cup sugar, and brown sugar until light and fluffy. Mix in egg, oil, and vanilla, blending well. Add salt, baking soda, and cream of tartar. Slowly mix in flour, 1 cup at a time, until batter is smooth. Stir in oats, coconut, and cereal. Dough will be soft. Cover and chill several hours.

   Preheat oven to 350 degrees. Form teaspoons of dough into 1-inch balls and place on ungreased baking sheets. Flatten dough with bottom of glass which has been buttered and dipped in sugar. Bake 12 minutes.

Pecan Crisps

COOKIE BAKING

The most common mistake made by cooks when baking cookies is to overbake them. Cookies cook in a short time, usually at 350 degrees to 375 degrees. A few degrees and a few extra minutes can make a difference. Often cookies look undercooked when they are actually perfectly done. Watch for browning on the edges which indicates that cookies are baked.

1 large egg white
¼ teaspoon baking soda
¼ teaspoon salt

1 cup dark brown sugar, firmly packed
2 cups chopped pecans
2 teaspoons vanilla extract

Preheat oven to 325 degrees. Place a piece of aluminum foil, dull side up, on baking sheets and grease well.

   Beat egg white, baking soda, and salt with an electric mixer at high speed until stiff peaks form. Stir in sugar, pecans, and vanilla. Drop by teaspoons onto prepared baking sheet. Bake 15 to 20 minutes. Remove foil from baking sheet and place on cooling rack. Peel cookies off aluminum foil by hand when cookies have cooled.

Peanut Butter Swirls

½ cup (1 stick) unsalted butter,
  at room temperature
1 cup sugar
½ cup peanut butter
1 large egg

2 tablespoons milk
1¼ cups all-purpose flour
½ teaspoon salt
½ teaspoon baking soda
6 ounces semi-sweet chocolate chips

Cream butter and sugar. Beat in peanut butter, egg, and milk. Set aside.
Sift flour, salt, and baking soda into a separate bowl. Stir flour mixture
into butter mixture. Combine well. Chill several hours. Place dough on
floured wax paper and roll into a 15 by 8 by 4-inch rectangle. Melt chocolate in top of a double boiler. Cool slightly. (Chocolate should not be so
hot that it melts dough, nor should it be so cold that it will not spread.)
Spread chocolate on dough mixture. Using wax paper to help, roll dough
up jelly-roll style. Place a baking sheet under roll to help transfer it to
refrigerator. Chill 8 hours or overnight.

Preheat oven to 375 degrees. Slice roll into ¼-inch slices with a very
sharp knife. Bake 8 minutes on an ungreased baking sheet. Cool cookies
slightly before removing from baking sheet. Cool on wire racks.

CARAMEL POPCORN

2 cups brown sugar, not packed
½ cup light corn syrup
¾ cup (1½ sticks) unsalted
  butter
1 gallon popcorn or 2 bags
  microwaved popcorn

Preheat oven to 225 degrees.
Combine sugar, corn syrup, and
butter in small saucepan. Heat
until sugar dissolves and liquid is
bubbly. Place popcorn in a large
bowl and remove any unpopped
kernels. Pour sugar mixture over
popcorn and stir gently to coat.
Place popcorn in a shallow baking
pan and bake 2 hours, stirring occasionally. Cool on wax paper and
store in an airtight container. Yields
1 gallon of popcorn.
Makes a great gift!

Chocolate-Covered Peanut Butter Triangles

½ cup creamy peanut butter
½ cup sifted powdered sugar
2 tablespoons unsalted butter, melted
1 teaspoon vanilla extract
7 sheets frozen phyllo dough,
  thawed (page 55)

Topping:
5 tablespoons unsalted butter, melted
½ cup semi-sweet chocolate chips,
  melted
¼ cup chopped pecans

Preheat oven to 400 degrees. Combine peanut butter, sugar, butter, and
vanilla. Mix until well blended. Set aside. Brush 1 sheet phyllo dough
with melted butter. (Keep remaining sheets covered with a damp towel to
prevent them from drying out.) Cut phyllo sheet lengthwise into 4 long
strips. Place 1 slightly rounded teaspoon of peanut butter mixture about
1 inch from the end of one of the strips. Starting at end with the filling,
fold a corner of dough over filling so it lines up with other side of strip,
forming a triangle. Continue folding like a flag, in a triangular shape,
using the entire strip. Repeat with remaining 3 strips. Repeat with
remaining sheets of phyllo, butter, and filling.

Place triangles on an ungreased baking sheet, seam side down. Brush
each triangle with melted butter. Bake 6 to 8 minutes, or until golden
brown. Cool on wire racks. Frost cookies with melted chocolate and
sprinkle with chopped pecans. Cool until chocolate is set. Serve immediately or cover and refrigerate up to 2 days.

Pecan Pralines

YIELDS 4 DOZEN PRALINES

SOFT-BALL STAGE

The soft-ball stage is reached when the mixture being cooked measures a temperature of 234 to 240 degrees. This is best determined using a candy thermometer. If no thermometer is available, the cold water test may be used. Use a fresh cup of cold water for each test. Drop a small amount of the mixture into the cup. It will form a soft ball that flattens of its own accord when removed from the water.

2 cups sugar
¼ cup light corn syrup
⅛ teaspoon salt
1 tablespoon unsalted butter

6 tablespoons milk
¼ cup bourbon
2 cups pecan pieces

Cook sugar, corn syrup, salt, butter, and milk over medium-high heat until mixture reaches soft-ball stage (begins at 234 degrees on candy thermometer). Watch carefully. Do not stir. Remove praline mixture from heat. Stir in bourbon and pecans. Stir until thick. Drop by rounded teaspoons onto waxed paper. Let cool. Store in an airtight container.

Golden Caramels

YIELDS 60 TO 64 PIECES

1 can (14 ounces) sweetened condensed milk
½ cup (1 stick) unsalted butter

1 cup dark brown sugar, firmly packed
½ cup Lyle's golden syrup*

Spray an 8-inch square pan with nonstick cooking spray. Line with foil and spray again. Combine milk, butter, sugar, and syrup in a saucepan over low heat, stirring constantly. Once sugar is dissolved, increase temperature to medium-high. Bring to a boil, stirring constantly, about 15 minutes, or until mixture is a rich brown color and leaves sides of pan when you stir. It should form a firm but chewy ball when a little bit is dropped in a cup of ice water. A candy thermometer would read 234 to 240 degrees, or soft-ball stage. Mixture will bubble. Pour caramel mixture into prepared pan. Cool completely. Cut caramel into 1-inch squares with a lightly oiled knife, cleaning knife between cuts if necessary. Wrap each square individually in colored cellophane or wax paper.

*Lyle's golden syrup can be found at specialty stores, or corn syrup can be substituted.

Can be dipped in melted milk chocolate.

Making candy involves some trial and error. If your mixture never gets firm enough, cook a little longer next time and use this batch over ice cream. Don't try to heat it too quickly (on high heat) because it is easy to burn.

Divine Espresso Ice Cream

YIELDS 1 QUART

1 can (14 ounces) sweetened
  condensed milk
2 cups heavy whipping cream
½ cup very strong espresso, cooled

2 teaspoons vanilla extract
½ cup chocolate-covered espresso
  beans, coarsely crushed (3 ounces)

Combine condensed milk, cream, espresso, and vanilla in a medium bowl. Blend well. Cover and refrigerate 4 hours, or until very cold.

Beat chilled milk mixture at medium speed 6 to 8 minutes, or until thick and custard-like. Transfer mixture into an ice cream freezer and process according to manufacturer's instructions until partially frozen. Stop machine and quickly stir in crushed chocolate-covered espresso beans. Finish processing. Do not overprocess.

Cinnamon Ice Cream

YIELDS 2½ QUARTS

6 large eggs
2 cups sugar
8 cups half and half

3 tablespoons ground cinnamon
2 tablespoons vanilla extract

Beat eggs lightly in a large bowl. Add sugar, half and half, cinnamon, and vanilla. Blend well. Transfer mixture to an ice cream freezer and process according to manufacturer's directions. When completed, place ice cream in freezer to harden further.

Cinnamon Ice Cream is a great dessert to serve after a Mexican meal.

Fresh Strawberry Ice Cream

YIELDS 3 QUARTS

4 pints fresh strawberries, hulled
juice of 2 lemons
3¼ cups sugar

4 cups heavy whipping cream
2 cups half and half

Chop strawberries in a blender or food processor. Add lemon juice and sugar. Process to combine. Cover and chill. Add whipping cream and half and half. Mix thoroughly. Transfer to an ice cream freezer. Freeze according to manufacturer's directions.

Grape Sherbet

YIELDS 1 GALLON

Sherbets, sorbets, and ices are all frozen, made of water, sugar, and a liquid flavoring such as fruit juice.

Sherbets differ from sorbets and ices in that sherbets contain either milk or egg whites. Sherbet is lighter than ice cream but richer than a sorbet or an ice. Since sorbets do not contain dairy products, they tend to be fat free. Both sherbets and sorbets are made in ice cream makers which give them their fine, smooth consistency. Ices are made by pouring the mixture into a shallow pan and stirring only occasionally during freezing. The less ice is stirred, the more coarse and crunchy its texture.

32 ounces grape juice
1 to 2 teaspoons fresh lemon juice

2 ¼ cups sugar
6 cups milk

Combine grape juice, lemon juice, and sugar in a large saucepan over low heat. Stir until sugar melts. Remove from heat. Cool completely, then stir in milk. (Mixture will curdle if sugar mixture is too warm.) Transfer to an ice cream freezer and prepare according to manufacturer's directions.

Lemon juice cuts the tartness of grape juice.

Coconut Sorbet

YIELDS 1 ½ QUARTS

Sugar Syrup:
3 cups water
¾ cup sugar
————

2 ½ cups cream of coconut
3 cups sugar syrup
3 tablespoons fresh lemon juice

Combine water and sugar in a medium saucepan over medium-high heat. Stir slowly with a wooden spoon until sugar dissolves. Bring syrup to a boil. Boil, without stirring, 5 minutes. Remove from heat. Cool completely. Cover and refrigerate until ready to use.

Combine cream of coconut, sugar syrup, and lemon juice. Stir well. Transfer mixture to an ice cream freezer. Freeze according to manufacturer's directions. Process until sherbet is white in color and solid. Place sherbet in freezer 2 to 3 hours to harden.

Cabernet Ice

SERVES 4 TO 6

1 pint fresh strawberries, hulled
½ cup sugar
2 tablespoons fresh lemon juice
1 cup Cabernet

————
peppermint sprigs

Purée strawberries, sugar, and lemon juice in a blender or food processor. Stir in wine. Pour into a large container. Cover and freeze 8 hours or overnight until completely frozen.

Spoon into serving bowls and garnish with a sprig of peppermint.

Lemon Frozen Yogurt

1 cup fresh lemon juice
  (about 8 lemons)
3 cups sugar
4 cups plain nonfat yogurt

2 cups plain whole milk yogurt
5 cups skim milk
2 teaspoons almond extract
1 tablespoon grated lemon zest

Thoroughly combine lemon juice, sugar, yogurts, milk, almond extract, and lemon zest. Transfer to an ice cream freezer and prepare according to manufacturer's directions. Keep yogurt frozen until serving time.

Strawberries and Creamy Vanilla Sauce

1 pint fresh strawberries, hulled
1 cup Cointreau

½ pound powdered sugar
1 teaspoon vanilla extract
1 cup heavy whipping cream

Creamy Vanilla Sauce:
8 ounces cream cheese, softened

Place strawberries in a shallow bowl and cover with Cointreau. Stir to combine well. Cover and refrigerate.

Combine cream cheese, sugar, and vanilla in a blender. Pour in cream and continue mixing until well blended. Serve sauce over strawberries.

Butterscotch Sauce

1½ cups sugar
1½ cups light corn syrup
4 tablespoons unsalted butter, melted

⅔ cup heavy whipping cream
¼ cup bourbon

Heat sugar in a nonstick skillet over medium-high heat, stirring constantly, until sugar is melted and turns a dark caramel color. Stir in corn syrup. Remove from heat. Blend in butter, cream, and bourbon. Spoon warm sauce over vanilla ice cream. Serve immediately.

THE JUNIOR LEAGUE OF HOUSTON, INC.

The Junior League of Houston was founded in 1925 by a dozen civic-minded women with the desire to serve their community and its citizens through the action and leadership of trained volunteers. The emphasis then was on children's health and the main source of revenue was a small Tea Room set up in the basement of an obliging local bank.

Today, the Junior League of Houston continues its tradition as an organization of women committed to promoting voluntarism, developing the potential of women, and to improving the community through the effective action and leadership of trained volunteers. Since committing its first volunteers to a well-baby clinic, the Junior League has expanded its focus to address a broad spectrum of community needs. You'll find League members counseling teenage mothers, juvenile delinquents, and troubled families; helping protect children from abuse and neglect; working in health clinics; tutoring disadvantaged children; delivering food and friendship to the housebound; or volunteering in one of the many diverse activities the League supports. The essence of the Junior League is its ability first to identify a community problem, then to develop a project to address that problem, and finally, to make the project successful through the ongoing work of trained volunteers.

In its own quiet way, the Junior League is having a positive impact on the lives of the people it serves directly and the thousands of people its members may never know. As the city grows and changes, the Junior League will continue to identify critical needs and to participate in finding solutions.

OUR TEA ROOM

The Junior League of Houston Tea Room started modestly enough in 1925 as the newly chartered group's first fund-raising project. Funds collected from dues to the Luncheon Club, as it was then called, were used to support the League's community projects. With donations from the members' own homes and a staff of volunteers, the Luncheon Club opened in downtown Houston. Somehow, 170 people were served lunch that first day in a room that was equipped to seat only 45. But from that time on, the Junior League of Houston Tea Room has enjoyed continuing success.

Bouquets of Rosemary

To the following individuals, without whose generous contributions of time, energy, expertise, and guidance, *Stop and Smell the Rosemary* could never have been realized:

KAY ADAMS AND JODI LOE
Our friends from *Southern Living* magazine, who gave us so much support and guidance in the development of this book.

ROBERT MCGRATH
From The Phoenician Hotel, for giving his time, recipes, and cooking expertise.

THE HILL GROUP
For their never ending enthusiasm, patience, and creativity from the very inception of this project.

LINDA HOFHEINZ
For her constant smile, her creative genius and drive to push us to go the extra mile to strive for perfection, and for her food styling in the photographs of "A Harvest Feast for the Senses."

MIRIAM WESTMORELAND
Our friend from Open Season on Flowers, who never minded getting the perfect "uncommon" flower for our photography shoot. Her arrangements truly make our book special.

PHYLLIS TUCKER
Of Phyllis Tucker Antiques, for sharing her prize sterling silver pieces with us for our photography shoot and also for sharing her wealth of wisdom and proper tea etiquette tips.

ELIZABETH SWIFT AND PAIGE DEBOBEN
Of Elizabeth Swift Catering, for preparing and styling the appetizers for the photographs of "A Spirited Gathering".

MALCOLM ROWLAND
Our true and constant friend at the Junior League, for helping us every step of the way.

OUR FAMILIES
Our heartfelt thanks and love must go to our wonderful families for all of their endless sacrifices and constant support and encouragement for this seemingly never ending project.

Underwriters

The Junior League of Houston, Inc. wishes to thank our generous members and friends who helped underwrite the production costs of *Stop and Smell the Rosemary*.

Nancy O'Connor Abendshein
Dorothy Mathias Ables
Barbara Beardmore Adams
Doris Fondren Allday
Bonnie Blades Allen
Helen H. Allen
Mary Kay Anderson Allen
Mrs. Nancy C. Allen
Holly Teas Anderson
Marilyn Flaitz Andrews
Sondra Haynes Appel
Mrs. Daniel C. Arnold
Veronica "Roni" Obermayer Atnipp
Deedo Bering Bailey

Peggy Cope Bailey
Gail Spies Baker
Ruth Houston Baker
Mary Delmore Balagia
Janice H. Barrow
Nancy Scott Beck
Lizinka Mosley Benton
Louise W. Berry
Barbara Underwood Blackbird
Eloise Hand Blades
JoEllen Lenoir Blunk
Caroline E. Boone
Jane White Braden
Lisa Hansen Braly
Allison Miller Brandt
Pamela Jordan Brasseux
The Brown Foundation
Laura Shepherd Bruce
Boone B. Bullington
Belinda Benning Burbach
Elizabeth Malone Burdine
Sue Williams Butler
Ginger Roberts Buttery
Sandy Hannegan Calderwood
Lisa Boettcher Caledonia
Marilyn Dull Callender
Maurie Ankenman Cannon
Ethel G. Carruth
Margaret D. Cashman
Kristi Shipnes Cassin
Ray Taggart Chilton
Catherine Christopherson
Marian Russo Cisarik
Lisa Gholston Clarke
Betty Walker Cochran
Meredith Cocke
Anne and Claude Cody
Barbara Miller Collie
Allyson Priest Cook
Kelly Elizabeth Andrews Coselli
Mary Frances Bowles Couper
Ann Synnott Cox
Alice Picton Craig
Mrs. O. H. Crosswell
Susan Dearien Crouch
Sally Malott Curtis
Julia Vinson Dabney
Holly Willis Darby
Kathryn Buckley Davis
Diane Purcell Dean
Terry Hastings Dean
Laurie De Lio
Catherine "Kit" Newman Detering
Deborah Detering
Kimberly Gabriel Dominy
Eleanore Banks Donnelly
Verlinde Hill Doubleday
Kelly Morrell Duenner
Dianne Duperier
Sally Barnes Earl
Elaine McHard Eisemann
Frances Simmons Ellis
Katherine Black Ellwood
Lesha P. Elsenbrook
Nancy White Flagg
Marian Fleming
Julia Anderson Frankel
Anne Pearce French
Carol Hanley Garcia
Melissa Garlington
Marilyn V. Georges
Sara Moore Greene
Mrs. Pat M. Greenwood
Jan Havens Greer
Beverle Gardner Grieco
Lennie Sargent Grimes
Elizabeth Gilmer Hagens
Joanie Amacker Haley
Margie Whilden Halverson
Diana and Russell Hawkins
Eleanor Stanley Haynes
Anne McCauley Hedgcoxe
Kari M. Herrera
Courtney Leggett Hoffman
Peggy Cullinan Hoffman
Carol Jones Hoppe
Tany Pollard Hopper
Mary Knight Hughes
Clare Wiggins Jackson
Louise Davis Jamail
Stephanie Stewart Jamison
Margaret Lea Jeter
Barbara Ivy Jogerst
Mrs. Raleigh W. Johnson, Jr. (Marjorie Bintliff)

Mrs. Robert M. Johnson (Mary Louise)
Dr. Frances M. Jones
Margaret Newell Jones
Melissa Baker Jones
Carolyn Craig Keeble
Mickey Wier Kelsey
Andrea Jones King
Rosalie Meek King
Sarah Pennington King
Anne A. Kirkland
Francita Stuart Koelsch
Mr. Victor and Dr. Lucy Kormeier
Lucy Neblett Kuhn
Mary K. Pederson Kyger
Susan L. Lawhon
Judy and Frank Lee
Lesley Kay Heck Lilly
Sara Houstoun Lindsey
Pamela House Lovett
Evelyn Sanford Luckett
Pat Dayvault Luther
Shelley Branch Mackay
Denis Davis Mayfield
Susan Ray Mayfield
Jacqueline "Jackie" Gilbert McCauley
Susan "Susie" Bailey McGee
Beth Connelly McGreevy
Kate Normile McNair
Linda Duyck McReynolds
Lynne Fryer Michels
Cara Okoren Moczulski
Rhue McCullough Monroe
"Mare" Dorrance Monteith
Julie Held Moorhead
Nancy Bowne Morgan
Jan Foster Morrell
Ann Kelsey Nance
Bobbie Brinkman Nau
Susan Nunchuck-Schumski
Lisa Launius O'Leary
Anne Bradley O'Neill
Zillah Turman Oden
Jane Maffett Osborne
Ann Hill Painter
Martha Perkins Waldron Perrin
Mary Leslie Gayle Plumhoff
Joann Melcher Porter
Carol Gloyna Prince
Anne W. Pullen
Hilary Strong Purcell
Nancy Morriss Reed
Cara Wallin Reid
Jo Ann Gaido Riddle
Meg Bryce Robertson
Deborah Brown Robinson
Susan Scott Ross
Nancy Morgan Runnells
Vale Asche Russell
Florence Jones Rutherford
Caroline Jogerst Sabin
Zillah Mae Ford Schirmeyer
Lisa Manchester Schroeder
Sue Simpson Schwartz
Susan C. Sciullo
Mr. and Mrs. Daniel S. Searight
Mrs. Gretchen Gilliam Simmen
The L. E. Simmons Family Foundation
Allene Davison Skalla
Marie Louise Lester Smith
Mary Bone Smith
Mary Glenn Yeager Smith
Terry Pressler Smith
Betsy Milam Sobral
Anne Halliburton Stewart
Donna Lucas Stovall
Kim Mason Strange
Diane H. Strong
Anne Arnold Suman
Judy Ohlrogge Tandy
Carla Oden Tenison
Sarah Elizabeth Terry
Martha Reed Thayer
Meredith Key Thompson
Sandy Settegast Thompson
Martha Thomson Thorsell
Patricia Francis Thrash
Sally Gresham Tinkham
Deborah Kay Putzka Touchy
Ann Gordon Trammell
Nancy Nisbet Trice
Lynda Knapp Underwood
Sydney Ann Whitehead Uthoff

Blake Campbell Vaughan
Susan Westbrook Vaughan
Leslie Neumann Wahl
Mary Jane Moody Wakefield
Janet Schooley Walker
Pamela Osenbaugh Walker
Julia Picton Wallace
Elizabeth Cowden Walter
Stephanie Alison Washington
Joan Wier Weatherly
Sharyn A. Weaver
Camille Skalla Weisberger
Phoebe C. Welsh
Edith "Shug" Allen Wheless
Mrs. James L. Whitcomb
Terry Pepin Wichelhaus
Elizabeth H. Wilkens
Gwendolyn "Wendy" Wilkins-Burks
Peggy Lynn Williams
Carol Shannon Willis
Diane Schmidt Winter
Debra Lee Wolcott
Celine F. Womack
Peggy Gottlich Wright
Sally Holland Young
Michelle S. Zschappel

Special Thanks

We wish to thank the following businesses which so generously donated food or services for the production and marketing of *Stop and Smell the Rosemary*. We are deeply indebted to you for all of your support and enthusiasm for this project. Our deepest gratitude goes to all listed here:

American Photo Copy
American Student Travel
Brennan's - Houston
Chroma Copy International
Colors of the Sun Festive Foods
Cooke's Gourmet, Inc.
Coosemans Houston, Inc.
Crowded House Moving
Elizabeth Swift Catering
Glazier Food Company
Lake Austin Spa Resort
Martin Food Service Company
McGowen Cleaners
Open Season on Flowers
Randalls Food Markets, Inc.
Susan Mayfield Catering
Technigrafiks

Special thanks also goes to St. Joseph's Hospital for providing the nutritional analysis on selected recipes and to Kyle Britt and Raymond D. Watts for sharing their expertise and knowledge of pairing wine with food.

We are also indebted to the 1994-95 and 1995-96 Junior League Board of Directors for their abiding support and constant enthusiasm for this project.

Special Friends

The Junior League of Houston, Inc., wishes to thank the many friends and businesses who, by their participation, have made possible this cookbook. We are grateful for your expertise, counsel, support, and your generous donations of the props for our photography.

Nancy O'Connor Abendshein
Dorothy Mathias Ables
Acura Southwest
Veronica "Roni" Obermayer Atnipp
Barney's New York-Galleria

Elizabeth "Betsy" Baxter
Beacon Hill Showroom
Bering's Distinctive Gifts and Hardware
Pamela Jordan Brasseux
Brian Stringer Antiques
Boone Boies Bullington
Classic Gifts and Antiques
Craftsman Glass and Mirror, Inc.
Crate and Barrel
Crowded House Moving
Crowe and Company
Terry Hastings Dean
Paige Deboben
Distinctive Details
Events
Expressions Custom Furniture
Trebie Perry Francisco
Anne Pearce French
Gallery Americana
The Garden Gate
Marilu Barnes Garza
Goode and Company
Beverle Gardner Grieco
David Hale
Susan Ganchan Hancock
Hart Galleries
Cristi Sowell Harvey
Diana Mayor Hawkins
Ken Hoffman
Linda Hofheinz
Home Treasures
Carol Jones Hoppe
Howard M. Graetz Antiques
Marcia Huggins
Clare Wiggins Jackson
Junior League Kitchen Staff
Junior League Tea Room Staff
Sharron Kinnaird
Krispen (Antiques, Accessories, Floral, Fine Linens)
David Lackey Antiques and China Matching Service
Linda H. Lamb
Linens By Littwitz
Longoria Collection
Margaret K. Reese Antiques
The Market
Susan Ray Mayfield
Carolyn McCairns
Ellyn Mead
Laura Lamb Menegaz
Meredith Long & Company
Mes Amis
Kristin Mills
Cara Okoren Moczulski
Moore & Shaffer
Neiman Marcus
Maconda Brown O'Connor
Ralph S. O'Connor
Barrett S. Oden
Zillah Turman Oden
Pappas Family Restaurants
Evelyn Cave Pearce
Suzanne Penn
Phyllis Tucker Antiques
Lillian "Lili" McDonald Pickard
Pier 1 Imports
Pillsbury Michel Silver
Pottery Barn
R.N. Wakefield and Company
Robert E. Alker Fine Art
Deborah Brown Robinson
Malcolm Rowland
Janet Schindler
Smith and Hawken
Spruzzare, Inc.
Surroundings
Taft Symonds
Teas Nursery Company, Inc.
Carla Oden Tenison
Tiffany & Company
Carolyn Spann Utt
Williams-Sonoma
Bertha Stambulie
Margaret Blackshear Watson
Raymond D. Watts
Isabel Brown Wilson
Lisa Macon Wilson
Ivory Woods

Recipe Donors

The Junior League of Houston, Inc., gratefully thanks its members, families, friends, and Junior League Tea Room Patrons who contributed recipes to our book. It is our sincere hope that no one has been overlooked.

Nancy O'Connor Abendshein
Dorothy Mathias Ables
Carroll Ann Adams
Marion Adkins
Lisa Jolley Agnew
Dede Ryan Ale
Barbara R. Allen
Mary Kay Anderson Allen
Jeanne Richey Amacker
Marilyn Flaitz Andrews
Sondra Haynes Appel
Jennifer Stewart Arnold
Lucy Gray Arnold
Lillian Arnoldy
Deirdre Dickinson Arthur
Sylvia Ashbaugh
Robin Rushton Ashe
Gayle Lynn Athy
Martha Anthony Athy
Vicki Richards Atkinson
Veronica "Roni" Obermayer Atnipp
Theresa Hall Attwell
Julie Deane Ayres
Bettye Z. Baccus
Candy Irvan Bagby
Allison Arnspiger Bailey
Melissa Piper Bailey
Elizabeth Sloan Bainum
Martha C. Bair
Gail Spies Baker
Robbin White Baker
Marguerite Emmert Baldwin
Sally Polsfoot Baldwin
Virginia Bargfrede
Bobbie Barksdale
Georganna Allen Barnes
Nadine A. Barr
June I. Barrett
Ann Baudette
Susan Heuer Bazelides
Laura Thorsell Beavers
Lauren Beck
Sue Ledbetter Bell
Mary Lee Cottingham Benedict
Kathryn Giddens Bennett
Shawn Bennett
Leslie Berardo
Mariene Bercovitch
Melinda Wynn Berkman
Linda Bertetti
Nancy Sellingsloh Bertin
Mrs. Legare H. Bethea
Margaret E. Biehl
Alice Bing
Beth Ringham Bittson
Martha W. Black
Brenda Casimir Blackwood
Collier Wheelus Blades
Elizabeth R. Blaine
Marie Sharpe Blaine
Rosanna Deane Blalock
Betty Elizardi Bland
Martha Upchurch Blecher
JoEllen Lenoir Blunk
Judy Bobbett
Janet Reid Bodin
Nanci Silver Boice
Nancy McFarlane Bonner
Caroline Boone
Christopher Boone
Sue Zanne Myers Boone
Vicky Boone
Kathy Fountain Boss
Rene Gillean Boudloche
Kim Boudreau
Jennifer Justice Bowen
Martha Elledge Bowen
Mrs. Ted Bowen
Lavinia Price Boyd
Janie Park Boyles
Jane White Braden
Lisa Hansen Braly
Jayne Winslow Brandon
Pamela Jordan Brasseux
Carol Haugh Brejot
Karen Murphy Brennan
Shirley Brewer
Marianna Hawley Brewster
Patricia Richardson Brice
Barbara Ledbetter Britt
Robin Burke Britt
Judy Pond Britton
Anne Broady
Virginia "Vicky" Gaylord Brod
Sally Kerbow Brollier
Jane Moody Brooks
Rae Broussard
Carol Anne Browder
Laurie Sowell Brown
Sarah Mendell Brown
Elizabeth Barrow Brueggeman
Catherine Cage Bruns
Melanie Buchanan
Sharrie Farrar Buck
Amy Bulger
Adrienne Estes Bullard
June E. Buongiorno
George Anna Lucas Burke
Kathy Sellers Burney
Dawn Motsinger Burns
Shirley Patton Bushong
Judy James Bute
Mayde W. Butler
Mary Hancock Cain
Sandy Hannegan Calderwood
Carol Clayton Callaway
Allison Ashbaugh Callender
Bettye Callier
Billye Callier
Pam Jolley Calvin
Cathy Kyle Camalier
Marty Cameron
Mrs. K. Ray Campbell
Paula "Dede" Capps
Nancy Hoyt Cardiff
Elizabeth Carl
Patricia Summers Carlin
Florine F. Carr
Catey Van der Naillen Carter
Amy Carver
Karen Letsos Case
Ann Casimir
Cristina Celeste Cassin
Jo Anne Sharman Cassin
Barbara Scott Catechis
Barbara Bowen Cauble
Trish Perry Chambers
Sara Robinson Chambless
Rosabel Chandler
Anne Trumbull Chapin
Mary Thuss Cheney
Dorothy Chernosky
Mary Jence Montgomery Childers
Ray Taggart Chilton
Marian Russo Cisarik
Dolores Clark
Elizabeth "Betty" Sellingsloh Clarke
Lisa Gholston Clarke
Lynn Mottek Clayton
Lollie Lauderdale Cluett
M. Carol Coale
Christina Codner
Anne Turpin Cody
Jana Manicom Cody
Muriel Helen Furstenau Cody
Shelba Coe
Sandy Conner
Cynthia Seba Cook
Paula L. Coons
Elizabeth Swift Copeland
Colleen Cordts
Katherine Anderson Cornell
Carroll A. Corson
Sylvia Schmidt Couch
Carol Cogdell Courtney
Jane Warner Covault
Marjorie Cowell
Diana Cox
Marge Cross
Carolyn Carolla Crosswell
Mrs. William E. Crouch
Aggie Crump
Dorothy Mewbourne Cuenod
Sandra Garbade Cumley
Jann Curry
Lisa Curry
Sally Malott Curtis
Faye Cutter
Judith Anderson Dabney
Betty Dale
Pamela Hindman Daley
Sue Dalton
Jennifer Bridges Darwin
Autumn Love Davidson
Myrna Lynn Davidson
Dorothy Dunn Davis
Ellen Smith Davis
Kathryn Buckley Davis
Peggy Kerr Davis
Susan Johnson Davis
Kathleen Coghlan Dawson
Barbara Day
Terry Hastings Dean
Carmalee DeGeorge
Carol Lovelady Dehan
Clare Delicioso
Marilyn Gracey DeMontrond
Christi Fields DeSpain
Catherine "Kit" Newman Detering
Leslie Gowan Devillier
Elizabeth Lipscomb Dice
Mrs. Leo Dicianne
DeVaun Dickson
Julie Weiss DiFonzo
Christina M. DiMaria
Rue Ann Wood DiVita
Ione Masterson Doggett
Betty Finnegan Doherty
Cheryl Grimm Doland
Kimberly Gabriel Dominy
Donna Donelson
Lisa Castle Donnell
Nancy Feldon Doss
Ouie Dossett
Barbara Wiessing Doyle
Dana Dry
Mercedes Romero Duggan
Ann Christine Kingdon Dull
Barbara Bering Dundas
Jana Guzzi Dundas
Ione Vega Dunn
Dianne Duperier
Toni Walsh Duperier
Sallie Dupree
Anice Shelton Duytschaever
Sandra McLemore Earle
Kathy Allen Eason
Ann Bowie Eiser
Courtnay Tartt Elias
Louise Pincoffs Ellingson
Jennifer Crouch Ellis
Lisa Lindgren Eriksen
Louise Ewing Erwin
Mrs. Harvey Evans
Marsha Ewart
Barbara Fallon
Margaret Smith Farese
Janet Beard Farr
June Farren
Catharine Clark Faulconer
Tricia Avis Feagan
Mary Feehan
Marlene Feurbach
Joni Hruska Fichter
Agnes Finch
Lois Cochran Finch
Michelle Fisher
Mrs. James C. Fitzgerald
Marjorie M. Flanagan
Mrs. Don D. Ford
Mrs. William R. Foreman
Holly Harris Forney
Karin Fortur
Allison Smith Fowler
Yolanda R. Franzen
Melanie Frazier
Jane Ann Smeck Freeman
Patricia Barrett Freeman
Nelda B. Frels
Judy Claman French
Jewel Ullrich Frnka
Frances Bell Froelich
Dr. Gerri Lee Frye
Connie Johnson Funk
Mary Moritz Fusillo
Grace G. Gage
Waverly White Gage
Nancy Crisler Galante
Lisa Melancon Ganucheau
Carol Hanley Garcia
Nancy Penix Gardere
Melissa Ann Garlington
Susan Hollis Garrett
Marilu Barnes Garza
Catherine McCleskey Gassman
Beverly Gaucher
Jane Heyck Gaucher
Susan Gaucher
Isabell Akin Gerhart
Stephanie Denise Gibson
Elizabeth Schwartz Giles
Rita Smith Giles
Linda Gillbreath
Eileen Cummings Gillespie
Karen Gillett
Karen Brookshire Gilliam
Gail Braden Goodwin
Betty Ridley Gosse
Lillian B. Gough
Leslie A. Gowen
Doris Rother Grainger
Suzanne Grant
Francel Coleman Gray
Susan Brooks Green
Elaine Greenberg
Cody Caldwell Greenwood
Ann Painter Greer
Beverle Gardner Grieco
Rogene Larson Griffey
Marilyn Otteman Griffin
Margaret Hixon Griffith
Lennie Sargent Grimes
Elizabeth Prince Groff
Allison Hall Grove
Neat Eddleman Grubbs
Barbara Birdsey Gustafson
Catherine Fairleigh Haley
Joanie Amacker Haley
Betsy Hall
Jean Ham
Ann Lowdon Hamilton
Carolyn Burton Hamilton
Jacqueline Hamilton
Sandy Doss Hamilton
Hazel Hammond
Deanna Escamilla Hamrick
Julia Hartman Hancock
Laura Linden Hand
Peggy Dun Haney
Kelley Morgan Hann
Jinny E. Hardesky
Lizzy Greene Hargrove
Dianna McDermott Harper
Christine R. Harris
Ellen Baumgardner Harris
June Harris
Sue Williford Harris
Marian Powell Harrison
Margaret Davidson Harvie
Susi Huffman Haveman
Nancy Cousins Haverland
Diana Mayor Hawkins
Elizabeth Bixby Hawkins
Barbara Hay
Helen Rau Hayne
Charlotte Head
Laurie Howard Hembree
Ann Whitley Henneman
Janis Frank Henry
Virginia Byrd Henry
Sabrina Sanders Hergert
Laura Jane Hermes
Kari Musgrove Herrera
Carrie Lou Hester
Merry Fawley Heyne
Kyra Timkovsky Hidalgo
Lesley Bolton Higginbotham
Dorothy Hildebrand
Glendora M. Hill
Chris Hill
Anna Cowley Hodges
Mathilde Conway Farrell Hoefer
Courtney Leggett Hoffman
Linda Hickerson Hofheinz
Carolyn Knapp Hohl
Carol Crump Holcomb
Billie Musgrove Hollingsworth
Penny Hollyfield
Mary Jane Holm
Barbara Brennan Holmes
Lillian Hoover
Carol Jones Hoppe
Karen Horsley
Charlotte Wood Horton
Louise Moraghan Howell
Robin Odenweller Howell
Sara Hinchman Howell
Juli Hruska
Juliet Greer Hubbell
Cynthia "Cynthe" McWhirter Hughes
Tamara Stern Hundley
Martha Brannon Hunt
Elizabeth Painter Hutchins
Margaret Lee Isaacks
Clare Wiggins Jackson
Jennifer Morrow Jackson
Karen Loos Jaggers
Louise Davis Jamail
Kathleen Page Janik
Karen Murphy Jensen
Debbie Adams Johnson
Inez P. Johnson
Kathy Knowles Johnson
Mary Louise Tatum Johnson
Nancy B. Johnston
Frances M. Jones
Judy Felton Jones
Karen Kimball Jones
Margaret Newell Jones
Martha McKay Jones
Elizabeth Hughes Jordan
Mary McGill Jornayvaz
Nancy Reeves Jungman
Sandra Dunnam Justice
Amy Stovall Karges
Margie Scott Keeland
Gwen Clark Keeling
Virginia Meek Keenan
Nancy Wilson Kelley
Elizabeth Kladar Kelly
Karen Kelly
Ruth Hollins Kelly
Ruth Parkey Kelly
Janet Kepner
Cindy Van Keppel
Ellen Paull Ketchum
Mary Jo Kidd
Janet Tarbox Kiersted
Linda Raymond Kimball
Janet King
Jennifer King
Rosalie Meek King
Sarah Pennington King
Mrs. John Henry Kirby
Russel Knott
Carol Settegast Kobb
Cindy Krist
Holly Moore Kropschot
Lucy Neblett Kuhn
Kay Lynn Thompson Kuper
Mary K. Pederson Kyger
Merrily Doran Labarthe
Lauri Floyd Lafitte
Fredrica Lanford Lake
Carolyn Piro Landen
E.J. Landry
Victoria Venn Lange
Claudia Nelson Laswell
Fanelle Logue Laughlin
Jeanette Launey
Susan Harvin Lawhon
Eslie Landram Layton
Mary Farish Leatherwood
Nancy Leaton
Harriet Harrison Leavell
Carolyn Brown Lee
Frank Lee
Judy Oliver Lee
Barbara "Bootsie" Richardson LeFeuvre
Amy Pickett Leibman
Colette Flowers Leonard
Janine Thomas Levitch
Lucy Hamilton Lewis
Bessie Smith Liedtke
Lesley Kay Heck Lilly
Julianna Springman Lind
Martha Ann Knapp Linden
Elisabeth "Bet" Pannell Lindgren
Sara Houstoun Lindsey
Lisa Pooser Linker
Kathryn V. Lippincott
Cynthia Neill Liska
Katherine Keith Little
Robin M. Little
Kittie Jinkins Livesay
Dana Gipson Livingston
Florence Livingston
Melinda Heath Livingston
Sonya Baker Lloveras
Mrs. John W. Lloyd
Robin Hill Lloyd
Mary Schilling Long
Sara Sudenga Lowman
Cindy Seaboch Lucia
Evelyn Sanford Luckett
Ruby Luedemann
Shelley Branch Mackay
Mary Clarke Jarvis Mackenzie
Laura Gibbs Maczka
Donna Magill Maddox
Becky Scott Mahoney
Cheryl Zeringue Mahoney
Juneid Majors
Ellie Joyce Malavis
Jane S. Currie Marcinko
Donna Dwelle Marcum
Leigh Sumner Marcus
Mary Carol Markham
Elizabeth Bonnet Markland
Molly Wehner Marks
Faerie Marston
Susan Arnold Martin
Anne Elise Mumford Matthews
Constance "Connie" Wilson Mayfield
Sheila Earthman Mayfield
Susan Ray Mayfield
Richard Blair Mayor
Heather Donald Mayor
Randi Carol Mays-Knapp
Sheri Upchurch Mazy
Cynthia Norton McAndrew
Pinet Braun McBride
Carolyn McCairns
Alice McCake
Eleanor Montague McCarthy
Maura Aiken McCarthy
Missie Powers McCarty
Karen Short McCarver
Jacqueline "Jackie" Gilbert McCauley
Judy Ditto McCloud
Kirby Cohn McConnell
Jane Ingle McCord
Kimberly Von Eiff McCoy
Karen Price McCurley
Elizabeth Buongiorno McDaniel
Robert McGrath
Evelyn Schuster McGraw
Kathryn McGraw
Beth Connelly McGreevy
Jean McHenry
Mary Ann Smith McKeithan
Connie Howell McKenzie
Sidney McKenzie
Marcia McClain McKinzie
Leta "Lee" McManus
Sarah Watts McMurrey
Coleta McNabb
Willa Faye McNair
Judy Ross McNeely
Martha W. Means
Missy Medary
Carol Walker Meek
Tina Lundy Melo
Betty Mendell
Marsha Adams Mengle
Marilyn Merchant
Mary Merrem
Pauline Pape Mertensotto
Lynne Fryer Michels
Susan Reeder Miclette
Dale Porter Miller
Stephanie McLaughlin Milligan
Cara Okoren Moczulski
Ann Moebius
Luisa Albarran Molina
Sarah Lawson Molke
Corinne Mamo Montandon
Dian H. Montegret
Cheryl Phillips Monteith
Morgan Kennedy Moody
Anne Moore
Joan Lewis Moore
Roxanne Sittig Moore
Therese McNellis Moore
Julie Held Moorhead
Ellen Whittington Moreton
Melanie Patton Morgan
Nancy Bowne Morgan
Ellen Sampson Morris
Stella Morris
Sara White Morrison
Ann Alexander Morton
Mallie Mountain
Claudia Moursund
Joanne Mueller
Lura Jane Handley Munford
Kathleen Dies Munger
Alice Mae Murphey
Sharon Murphy
Virginia M. Murphy
Dorothy "Dee" Daniels Murtaugh
Sue Musslewhite
Bobbie Brinkman Nau
Leslie Surles Nelson
Laura Wyatt-Brown Neuhaus
Rebecca C. Nevill
Mary Wood Newell
Mary Ann Jameson Newman
Betty Sue Newton
Clare McFadden Neyland
Glenda Gayle Nicholson
Allyson Collette Nixon
Athena Walters Noal
Karen Hankins Noel
Lynn Norvell
Ann Allison Norwood
Dianna Kemp Nussbaum
Anne Bradley O'Neill
Anita Grubbs O'Shaughnessy
Mary Oblinger
Zillah Turman Oden
Sarah Okon
Lynne Okoren
Ann Clary Fancher Old
Jane Hix Oliver
Ann Williams Olson
Kali Orexsi
Gail Wolf Orr
Dianne Becker Orth
Phyllis W. Osborne
Kipper Dunn Oyanguren
Debbie Millican Padon
Liz Hatch Padon
Lynne Murphy Paine
Reese Broussard Palmer
Dana Painter Parkey
Ellen Wayne Ormond Parkey
Dianna Burnett Patterson
Jane Suzanne Patterson
Anne Berry Patton
Anna H. Payne
Joy Payne
Suzanne Penn
Erma Penns
Carrie Bratton Pepi
Janice Campise Perez
Kim Maresh Petersen
Susan Morgan Peterson
Jana Laird Phillips
Kathryn Reed Phillips
Larry B. Phillips
Virginia Phillips
Margaret Miller Pierce
Elizabeth Wiemer Pipkin
Laura Templeton Pipkin
Linda Pollard
Antoinette Post
Nedaye Gray Potts
Kathy King Powell
Peggy Powell
Christina Zinn Powers
Nancy Poynor
Kathleen Trotman Pressler
Nancy Avery Pressler
Sue Harrington Price
Charlotte Duggan Priest
Ann Herron Purcell
Hilary Strong Purcell
Mary Quoyeser

Lynn Rutland Rafferty
Jane Inglish Raine
Kelly Williams Raley
Celeste Ried Reavis
Allison Hood Redepenning
Leone Guthrie Reeder
Margaret Kenyon Reese
Ebby Davis Reeves
Cara Wallin Reid
Suzann Cooley Richardson
Jacquelyn Brown Richey
Elizabeth Winfield Rigney
Diane Slattery Riley
Mary Marshall Burlew Rives
Noel Roberts
Deborah Brown Robinson
Marty Roessler
Lucy Smith Rogers
Sally Grumman Root
Karen Campbell Ross
Susan Scott Ross
Elizabeth Hoover Rotan
Linda Ewan Roudebush
Sandy Rouse
Malcolm Rowland
Wick Nalle Rowland
Bette Rudolph
Ginnie Russell
Lynn Fawcett Russell
Ruth Arbuckle Russell
Florence Jones Rutherford
Patricia Quin Sachtleben
Elsie M. Sams
Kathy Steel Sangalis
Nancy Santamarie
Susan Saurage-Altenloh
Sandy Smith Scarborough
Cindy Clowers Schell
Mary Schiflett
Zillah Mae Ford Schirmeyer
Laurie Schmid
Marta Gray Schrader
Marjorie Barnum Schubert
Laura Griffin Schuhmacher
Karen Ann Colao Schulte
Sarah Scott
Eloise "Pinkie" Pollard Searls
Cherry Harmon Sears
Kari McGuirt Seger
Molly Mehring Shaffer
Richard Shaffer
Stephanie Box Shanks
Bess Baker Sharman
Kathleen Riley Sharman
Catherine Sharp
Rebecca Crowder Shatto
Cynthia Skiff Shealor
Suzanne Skipton Shelton
Ann Faber Shepherd
Celeste Kreidel Shepherd
Marilyn Edwards Shepherd
Mildred Wood Sherwood
Lisa Naugle Short
Carey Chenoweth Shuart
Bobbie Shurden
Chelle Deane Shutts
Gretchen Gilliam Simmen
Judy Fernbach Simon
Elizabeth Scott Sims
Anna Sinclair
Gayle Ramey Singer
Eugenia Fuchs Skarke
Cathy McLeod Skelton
Sue Long Skilling
Cindy Wait Sloan
Ellen Deming Small
Ann Shannon Smith
Babs Hartung Smith
Carol Galt Smith
Harriet Hill Smith
Marsha Gostecnik Smith
Mary Bone Smith
Mary Glenn Yeager Smith
Nancy Ann Smith
Lisa Kraus Smolen
Frances Agee Snelling
Hazel Snodgrass
Virginia Milam Sobral
Susan Shillings Solcher
Sherra Cassin Sowell
Amy Alise Spence
Mary Jeanette Sponsel
Lisa Springer
Amie Jones Springmeyer
Jean Squires
Dr. Bette Stead
Betty Steffan
Anne Halliburton Stewart
Jane Peden Stewart
Jeannette Andrews Stewart
Patti Phillips Stiernberg
Carolyn Hogan Stiles
Katherine McKenna Stotler
Marceil N. Straley
Ione Monroe Strange
Kim Mason Strange
Mrs. George E. Stroud, Jr.
Barbara Duke Stryker
Robin Peake Stuart
Leigh Heckmann Stubbs
Sandra Nell Sturgis
Laura Elliott Suffield
Anne Arnold Suman
Diane Keil Summerville
Kay Gibson Surles
Marilyn M. Svruters
Susan Archer Swann
Mary Talamini
Judy Ohlrogge Tandy
Kathleen Tangrey
Meg Estes Tapp
Fannie Louise Scott Tapper
Betty Keenan Taylor
Johnnie Skalla Taylor
Patricia Reckling Taylor
Ruth C. Taylor
Sara Cave Taylor
Jean Dooley Tellkamp
Lou Temple
Julie Ann Templin
Carla Oden Tenison
Alison Watts Tennant
Joan Woodruff Tenney
Martha Reed Thayer
Gene Hunt Thomas
Kakki Park Thompson
Laurel Rae Thompson
Meredith Key Thompson
Seliece Caldwell Thompson
Susan Savage Thompson
Carin Coleman Thorn
Grace Beth Feagin Thorn
Ramona Meyers Thornton
Ann S. Thurmond (Mrs. Gerald P.)
Lisa Timmons
Betti Belardi Tiner
Ellen Chernosky Tippetts
Jane Tolson
Jo Lynn Beeler Towns
Ann Gordon Trammell
Marybeth Bartolomeo Trevino
Nancy Nisbet Trice
Ellie Truvillion
Dorothy Ann Tucker
Georgia Tucker
D. Tupper
Diana C. K. Untermeyer
Sydney Ann Whitehead Uthoff
Carolyn Spann Utt
Mary Catharine Van der Naillen
Evelyn Mertes Van Os
Cecilia Gleeson Van Riet
Carolyn Eddleman Vandervoort
Courtney Samuel Vandiver
Kitty Gallagher Vann
Joan O. Varner
Joan Vaseliades
Laura Ehrhardt Vaughan
Louise Villerit
Becky Virtue
Leslie Garst Vogl
Portia Waddell
Karen Wilson Wagner
Carl Walker
Tammy Walker-Smith
Kathie McKeen Wall
Marna Wall
David L. Walton
Mary Knobelsdorf Walton
Susan Walton
Margaret Blackshear Watson
Heather Heath Weatherly
Joan Wier Weatherly
Susan Coale Weaver
Lucia Detrick Weihe
Camille Skalla Weisberger
Sheila McGinnis Weitzel
Mary Church Weyel
Rosemary Whalen
Melanie Wheat Whatley
Nancy Park Wheless
Carolyn McElroy Whitaker
Gina Gutekunst White
Linda Gale White
Martha Walton White
Sue Trammell Whitfield
Emmy Lou Whitridge
Teresa Hentschel Wichelhaus
Valerie White Wier
Susan Wiewall
Jane Ashby Wiggins
Routh Trowbridge Wilby
Ann Johnston Wilde
Gwendolyn "Wendy" Wilkins-Burks
Karen Connell Wilkinson
Ann Catlett Williams
Merle Hendershot Williams
Mrs. Robert Guy Williams
Susan Forbes Williams
Keri Nordbrock Williamson
Cora Lynn Basse Wilson
Debora Koerner Wilson
Nancy Norville Wilson
Suzie Gorman Wilson
Shirley Winn-Bannerot
Virginia Winston
Diane Winter
Gaile Bering Withers
Michele Zaboroski Womack
Robin McCuistion Wombwell
Kimberly Clark Wood
Mrs. Johnie Woodfin
Diana Woodman
Angela Woodruff
Ann Johnson Wooldridge
S. Jill Davis Wooten
Mary Barden Attwell Worrell
Beth Wray
Linda Tucker Wukasch
Mary Peyton Grubbs Yehle
Jan Gipson Young
Karen Koonce Ytterberg
Catherine Callery Zdunkewicz
Yvonne Valdez Ziegler
Eleanor Lee Zook

Recipe Testers

To the many members and friends who hosted Testing Parties and tested recipes. Our sincere gratitude for your time, money, advice, and discerning tastes ensuring our recipes are fabulous.

Nancy O'Connor Abendshein*
Anne Fawley Adams
Liz Marshall Albritton
Mary Kay Anderson Allen
Twyla O'Sullivan Alletag
D'Anne Brownell Anderson
Genie Anderson
Catherine Oldham Andrews
Deirdre Dickinson Arthur
Robin Rushton Ashe
Vicki Richards Atkinson
Carrie Campbell Atmar
Veronica "Roni" Obermayer Atnipp*
Theresa Hall Attwell
Virginia King Avant
Jana Fay Paxton Bacarisse
Gail Spies Baker
Marguerite Emmert Baldwin
Kimberly Pratt Bashaw
Betsy Goodrich Baxter
Carol L. Beauchamp
Cissy Morgan Beeler
Elisabeth Lange Belton
Molly Bates Bentsen
Cindy Hanson Bernard
Jo Ann Jester Berry
Moppy Black
Collier Wheelus Blades
Susan Traylor Boelsche
K.C. Bogaucius Boles
Jane Shanks Bonham
Caroline Boone
Gregorie Trant Bouline
Heather Margaret Bowen
Lavinia Price Boyd
Karen Murphy Brennan
Marianna Hawley Brewster
Lori Brookshire Britton*
Sally Kerbow Brollier
Diane Mathews Broocks
Donna Temple Brown
Margaret Warren Brown
Sarah Mendell Brown
Laura Shepard Bruce
Jo O'Neal Brueggeman
Adrienne Estes Bullard
Boone Boies Bullington
Belinda Benning Burbach
Elizabeth Malone Burdine
Linda Bush Burdine
Martha Burgher
Dawn Motsinger Burns
Courtenay Browning Butler
Kathy Simmons Butler
Carol Clayton Callaway
Jean Huffman Carter
Hally Randall Carver
Trish Perry Chambers
Stacy Scott Cheesman
Carol Rubarts Christ
Marian Russo Cisarik*
Meredith Finck Cocke
Anne Turpin Cody
Jana Manicom Cody
Cynthia Seba Cook
Kimberly Clark Cooper
Kelly Elizabeth Andrews Coselli
Anne Zelsman Coskey
Jane Warner Covault
Malinda Russek Crain
Susan Chriss Cravens
Annalee Degregory Crespy
Ann Criswell
Cutler Bellows Crockard
Emily Attwell Crosswell
Jennifer O'Donnell Curry
Lisa Curry
Sally Malott Curtis
Mary Helen Yearout Darden
Ellen Smith Davis
Kathryn Buckley Davis
Kathleen Coghlan Dawson
Terry Hastings Dean
Carol Lovelady Dehan
Christi Fields DeSpain
Julia Gregg DeWalch
Elizabeth Lipscomb Dice
Sara Paschell Dodd
Ione Masterson Doggett
Betty Finnegan Doherty
Heidi Ziegler Doll
Ellen Cluett Donnelly
Verlinde Hill Doubleday
Allison Drake Doyle
Kimberly Olsen Drew
Elizabeth Montgomery Dukes
Karla Steinhauser Dulaney
Jana Guzzi Dundas
Deborah DeFord Dunkum
Toni Walsh Duperier
Robin Owen Dyer
Sandra McLemore Earle
Kathy Allen Eason
Susan Paulus Ehrhardt
Katherine Black Ellwood
Lesha Pulido Elsenbrook
Gay Gooch Estes
Joni Hruska Fichter
Barbara Bennett Finkel*
Dianne Dreyling Forgason
Holly Harris Forney
Allison Smith Fowler
Betty Carpenter Frankhouser
Anne Pearce French*
Judith Claman French
Pam Post Fullenweider
Kelly Leslie Funderburk
Ruby Jo Dabney Gano
Carol Hanley Garcia
Melissa Ann Garlington
Kathy White Gibson
Karen Brookshire Gilliam
Alicia Gist
Kathryn Ellen Goodrich
Gail Braden Goodwin
Barbara Bienvenu Grady
Lynn Williams Graves
Franny Coleman Gray
Beverle Gardner Grieco
Margaret Hixon Griffith
Elizabeth Prince Groff
Allison Hall Grove
Dorris Collie Hall
Margie Whilden Halverson
Kathy Russo Hamilton
Deanna Escamilla Hamrick
Gigi Hancock
Laura Linden Hand
Peggy Dun Haney
Kelley Morgan Hann
Laura Hutchinson Hannon
Lynn Porch Hardaway
Dianna McDermott Harper
Eve Lieber Harrell
Cristi Sowell Harvey
Lyl Coxe Harvin
Susi Huffman Haveman
Diana Mayor Hawkins*
Ria Butler Henderson
Sabrina Sanders Hergert
Kari Musgrove Herrera
Lesley Bolton Higginbotham
Melinda Budinger Hildebrand
Tamara Hindley
Courtney Leggett Hoffman
Carol Crump Holcomb*
Barbara Brennan Holmes
Carol Jones Hoppe*
Sally Holm Hopper
Louise Moraghan Howell
Robin Odenweller Howell
Sara Hinchman Howell
Terri Fisher Huguenard
Cynthia "Cynthe" McWhirter Hughes
Carolyn Hay Humphries
Amy Billingsly Imber
Clare Wiggins Jackson
Louise Davis Jamail*
Stephanie Stewart Jamison
Tamara Cocke Jenkins
Jill Flake Jewett
Kathy Knowles Johnson
Mary Louise Tatum Johnson
Judy Felton Jones
Susan Carter Jones
Mary McGill Jornayvaz
Nancy Reeves Jungman
Lisa Wallace Kanaly
Alafair Benbow Kane
Gwen Clark Keeling
Chaille Cage Kelly
Karen Kelly
Janet Tarbox Kiersted
Rachel Snell Kimball
Sarah Pennington King
Carmen Moure Knapp
Frances McIntyre Knight
Holly Moore Kropschot
Merrily Doran Labarthe
Carolyn Piro Landen
Angela Bellfore Landowski
Diane Stone Langdon
Claudia Nelson Laswell
Mary Farish Leatherwood*
Carrie Brown Lee
Janey Shappell Lee
Judy Oliver Lee*
Mary Beth Larrabee Leonard
Lorie Leyendecker
Lesley Kay Heck Lilly
Patricia Pinson Lind
Sara Houstoun Lindsey
Cynthia Neill Liska
Sonya Baker Lloveras
Kathy Clark Lord
Allison Griffin Lorenzo
Julie Hall Lynch
Laura Gibbs Maczka
Cheryl Zeringue Mahoney
Ellie Joyce Malavis
Molly Wehner Marks
Susan Cregor Mathews
Susan Ray Mayfield*
Heather Donald Mayor
Richard Blair Mayor
Patti Cunningham McBride
Ann Mouton McCarroll
Eleanor Montague McCarthy
Maura Aiken McCarthy
Karen Short McCarver
Jacqueline "Jackie" Gilbert McCauley
Barbara Barrow McCelvey
Dana Livingston McClaren
Sally Wall McCollum
Kirby Cohn McConnell
Elizabeth Buongiorno McDaniel
Virginia Holt McFarland
Beth Connelly McGreevy*
Constance Daily McMaken
Martha Means
Julie Koppenberger Mitchell
Cara Okoren Moczulski*
Cheryl Phillips Monteith
Julie Held Moorhead
Madeline Stevens Morgan
Melanie Patton Morgan
Ellen Sampson Morris
Stephanie Kendrick Morris
Lura Jane Handley Munford
Timmie Perry Murphy
Bobbie Brinkman Nau
Leslie Surles Nelson
Allyson Collette Nixon
Athena Walters Noal
Karen Hankins Noel
Kelly Norton
Dianna Kemp Nussbaum
Anita Grubbs O'Shaughnessy*
Zillah Turman Oden
Ann Clary Fancher Old
Gail Wolf Orr
Kipper Dunn Oyanguren
Debra Millican Padon
Ann Hill Painter
Jane Suzanne Patterson
Anne Berry Patton
Camille Cocke Patton
Eydie Pengelly
Carrie Bratton Pepi
Janice Campise Perez
Susan Morgan Peterson
Chrissy Reddick Petrov
Lili McDonald Pickard
Elizabeth Wiemer Pipkin
Jill Baldwin Plumb
Mary Leslie Gayle Plumhoff
Kathy King Powell
Christina Zinn Powers
Kathleen Trotman Pressler
Nancy Avery Pressler
Charlotte Duggan Priest
Mimi Payne Prioleau
Hilary Strong Purcell
Katherine Kemper Putnam
Kellye McDade Pyle
Linda Kay Rader
Kelly Williams Raley
Nancy Raymond Raper
Peggy Bellah Rathmell
Galen Beveridge Reckling
Allison Hood Redepenning
Ebby Davis Reeves
Eugenia Head Reynolds
Suzann Cooley Richardson
Jacquelyn Brown Richey
Stacy Wharton Riddick
Diane Slattery Riley
Noel Duvic Roberts
Deborah Brown Robinson
Peggy Ratcliffe Roe
Karen Campbell Ross
Elizabeth Hoover Rotan
Linda Ewan Roudebush
Wick Nalle Rowland*
Gretchen Kraeger Ruddy
Patricia Quin Sachtleben*
Frances Bedford Sampson
Jeanie Eddleman Sanders
Kathy Steel Sangalis
Zillah Mae Ford Schirmeyer
Virginia Pipkin Schneider
Tamra Hogg Schoen
Lisa Manchester Schroeder
Cordelia Simpson Schroer
Marjorie Barnum Schubert
Laura Griffin Schuhmacher
Cherry Harmon Sears
Pamela Wilmore Sengelmann
Cynthia Skiff Shealor
Madeleine Topper Sheehy
Patty Davis Shepherd
Lisa Naugle Short
Gretchen Gilliam Simmen
Allene Davison Skalla
Sue Long Skilling
Cindy Wait Sloan
Ellen Whiting Deming Small
Betsy Deal Smith
Claire Furman Smith
Laura Leigh Gardere Smith
Mary Bone Smith
Sherron E. Smith
Terry Pressler Smith
Leslie MacKay Sprague
Anne Halliburton Stewart
Anne Lund Stewart
Donna Lucas Stovall
Annette DeWalch Strake
Kim Mason Strange
Vanessa Stock Stuckey
Susan Archer Swann
Mary Ann Swick
Clair Talley
Kendall DiRaddo Tamlyn
Johnnie Skalla Taylor
Patricia Reckling Taylor
Carla Oden Tenison
Alison Watts Tennant
Martha Reed Thayer
Kim Snively Thomas
Sandy Settegast Thompson
Susan Savage Thompson
Judy Fleming Thomson
Martha Thomson Thorsell
Lisa Timmons
Ellen Chernosky Tippetts
Helen Lawrence-Toombs
Nancy Nisbet Trice
Carolyn Spann Utt
Laurie McCrimmon Vander Ploeg
Kitty Gallagher Vann
Sue Nesbit Verhyden
Laura Smelly Visage
Karen Wilson Wagner
Caro Ivy Walker
Margaret Blackshear Watson
Diane Brockenbush Wattenbarger
Sharyn Aydam Weaver
Lucia Detrick Weihe
Camille Skalla Weisberger
Alta Jean Weyland
Nancy Park Wheless
Carolyn McElroy Whitaker
Teresa Hentschel Wichelhaus
Emily Tuttle Wilde
Tricia Tribble Wilkens
Keri Nordbrock Williamson
Kim Rogers Wilson
Lisa Macan Wilson
Mary Kerr Winters
Shelly Wood
Diana Woodman
Mary Peyton Grubbs Yehle
Catherine Callery Zdunkewicz

* *We gratefully acknowledge those who opened their homes for a Testing Party.*

285

Low-Fat Analysis

A selection of low-fat recipes from each section of our book based on a single serving.

	Recipe Name	Calories	Fat Count	Calories from Fat
Page 56	Roasted Bell Pepper and Artichoke Pizza	150	5 Grams	28%
Page 56	Garlic Chicken Bites with Tomato Raisin Sauce	113	2 Grams	17%
Page 63	Summertime Cooler	142	.2 Gram	1%
Page 74	Carrot Orange Salad with Fresh Dill	93	.4 Gram	4%
Page 87	Seafood Salad with Papaya Salsa	311	8 Grams	23%
Page 94	Roasted Vegetable Sandwich	271	7 Grams	22%
Page 103	Smooth Black Bean Soup	376	2 Grams	5%
Page 118	Light Pasta with Tomato Basil Sauce	143	3 Grams	19%
Page 142	Lamb Stew with Rosemary	553	9 Grams	16%
Page 155	Champagne Chicken	295	5 Grams	15%
Page 156	Lime Grilled Chicken with Mango Salsa	321	6 Grams	16%
Page 177	Thai Shrimp	269	2 Grams	6%
Page 181	South Texas Crawfish Boil	1068	8 Grams	6%
Page 186	Sweet and Sour Braised Red Cabbage	61.4	.3 Gram	4%
Page 196	New Potatoes with Herbs	248	6 Grams	21%
Page 214	Bountiful Breakfast Muffins	121	3 Gram	17%
Page 231	Amaretto Angel Food Cake	245	.1 Gram	0%
Page 242	Low-Fat Flan	331	8 Grams	20%
Page 253	Blueberry Glaze Pie	242	8 Grams	30%
Page 263	Rhubarb Crumble with Bourbon Cream	277	7 Grams	22%
Page 279	Lemon Frozen Yogurt	224	1 Gram	5%

Healthy Substitutions

1 cup butter - 498 mg. cholesterol	=	2 sticks (1 cup) margarine - 0 mg. cholesterol
1 cup heavy cream - 823 calories, 268 mg. cholesterol	=	1 cup evaporated skim milk - 176 calories, 8 mg. cholesterol
1 medium whole egg - 274 mg. cholesterol	=	¼ cup egg substitute, 0 mg. cholesterol *(Some egg substitutes do contain cholesterol. Check label to be sure.)*
1 cup whole milk yogurt, plain - 250 calories	=	1 cup part skim milk yogurt, plain - 125 to 145 calories
1 cup sour cream - 416 calories	=	1 cup blenderized low-fat cottage cheese - 208 calories
1 ounce baking chocolate - 8.4 grams saturated fat	=	3 tablespoons cocoa powder plus 1 tablespoon polyunsaturated oil - 2.8 grams saturated fat

Bibliography

Chalmers, Irena. *The Great Food Almanac, A Feast of Facts from A to Z.* San Francisco: Collins Publishers, 1994.

Frencey. Prosper Montagne, trans. *Larousse Gastronomique - The Encyclopedia of Food, Wine and Cookery.* New York: Crown Publishers, 1961.

Herbst, Sharon Tyler. *The Food Lover's Tiptionary.* New York: William Morrow and Company, Inc., 1994.

Herbst, Sharon Tyler. *The New Food Lover's Companion.* New York: Barron's Educational Second Edition Series, Inc., 1995.

Ortiz, Elizabeth Lambert. *The Encyclopedia of Herbs, Spices and Flavorings - A Cook's Compendium.* New York: Dorling Kindersley, Inc., 1992.

Panati, Charles. *Panati's Extraordinary Origins of Everyday Things.* New York: Harper & Row Publishers, Inc., 1987.

Pennington, Jean. *Bowes and Church's Food Values of Portions Commonly Used.* New York: 16th ed. JB Lippincott Co., 1994.

Toussaint-Famat, Maguelonne. Anthea Bell, trans. *History of Food.* Cambridge, Mass.: Blackwell Publishers, 1992.

WINE

A bottle of wine to one person may be just a small part of a festive meal, yet to another it may be THE most important part of the meal.

Selecting an appropriate wine need not be an intimidating event. The most important consideration is the wine YOU enjoy. Forget the old rule of white wines with white meat or fish and red wines with red meats. One should consider lighter wines (both white and red) for lighter foods, or alone, and heavier or full-bodied wines for heavier or richer foods.

Since few have total confidence in their knowledge of wines, the following will provide some suggestions to help when one wonders what type of wine will go with what type of food. The suggestions are types of wines, not brand names. Keep in mind that the classification of wines is subjective. A reputable wine store with a knowledgeable staff will be able to further guide you to specific wines within your taste preferences and budget.

ALONE OR WITH APPETIZERS
Red - Beaujolais-Villages, Piedmont Dolcetto, Pinot Noir, Côtes du Rhône, Sangiovese

White - Sauvignon Blanc, Chablis, Pouilly Fuissé, Riesling, Pinot Blanc, Champagne or Champagne types

SEAFOOD
Red - Pinot Noir, Burgundies, Merlot

White - Vouvray, Pouilly Fuissé, Meursault, White Graves, Fumé Blanc, Sancerre, Sauvignon Blanc, Soave, Montrachet, Pinot Grigio, Chablis, Chardonnay

GAME BIRD/POULTRY
Red - Pinot Noir, Burgundy, Merlot

White - Sauvignon Blanc, Fumé Blanc, Pouilly Fuissé, Chardonnay, Riesling, Pinot Blanc, Gewürztraminer

BEEF
Red - Cabernet Sauvignon, Bordeaux, Pinot Noir, Burgundy, Petite Syrah, Hermitage, Merlot, Shiraz, Rioja

LAMB
Red - Bordeaux, Burgundy, Cabernet Sauvignon, Merlot, Brunello

PORK
Red - Pinot Noir, Burgundy, Beaujolais, Sangiovese

White - Johannisberg Riesling Kabinett, Australia Semillion/Traminer, Gewürztraminer, White Burgundy

VEAL
Red - Burgundy, Pinot Noir

White - Sauvignon Blanc, Graves, Meursault, Riesling, Puy d'Oc, White Burgundies: Montrachet, Chablis, Fouligny, Pouilly Fumé, Chassagne-Montrachet, Batard-Montrachet, Corton-Charlemagne

GAME
Red - Petite Shiraz, Hermitage, Barbaresco, Cabernet Sauvignon, Pinot Noir, Petite Syrah, Zinfandel, Burgundy, Merlot, Bordeaux, Brunello, Piedmont

SALADS
Red - Côtes du Rhône, Beaujolais, Sangiovese

White - White Burgundy Sancerre and Fumé Blanc, Sauvignon Blanc, Riesling, White Bordeaux Graves, Soave

CHEESE
Red - Cabernet Sauvignon, Bordeaux, Burgundy, Shiraz, Port

White - Riesling, Kabinett, White Burgundy, Chardonnay, Sauternes, Champagne

FRUITS
Red - Port wines

White - Riesling: Auslese and Fein-Auslese and Trocken, Vouvray, Chenin Blanc, Gewürztraminer, demi-sec Champagne

DESSERTS
Red - Port wines

White - Barsac, Riesling, Sauternes, demi-sec Champagne

BEER

Beers, in general, are versatile. Combining beers with food seems by far more flexible than with wines. While there are no rules to select a particular beer with a certain food or menu, the following may provide helpful information on beer categories and styles. A reputable wine, beer, and spirits store should be able to recommend specific beers available in your area.

The four basic beer categories are Ales, Lagers, Combination Styles, and Specialty Beers.

ALES
Ales, the oldest of the brewing styles, tend to be smooth with a sweet, fruity flavor. Generally higher in alcohol content than lagers, they may be served between 50 degrees F and 60 degrees F. Ales are top-fermented, taking only a few days to mature.

LAGERS
Lagers are clear, crisp, and noticeably carbonated. Lower in alcohol content than most other beers, this malty flavored beer should be served between 40 degrees F and 50 degrees F. Lagers are bottom-fermented and take up to 6 weeks to mature.

COMBINATION STYLES
Combination styles incorporate the features of both the lager and ale beers. Brewing techniques and/or ingredients from the lager and ale beers are combined.

SPECIALTY BEERS
Specialty beers may be any of the above three categories but with additional flavorings, such as fruit, wood smoke, or herbs and spices. Uncommon brewing techniques may be applied as well.

HERB AND SPICE SUBSTITUTIONS

Herbs and spices each have their own flavor and aroma. The following substitutions are only recommended for emergencies and may change the intended flavor of the recipe.

1 tablespoon fresh herbs	=	1 teaspoon dried herbs
1 teaspoon allspice	=	1 teaspoon equal parts cinnamon, nutmeg, and cloves
1 teaspoon basil	=	1 teaspoon oregano
1 teaspoon caraway	=	1 teaspoon anise
1 teaspoon cayenne	=	1 teaspoon chili peppers
1 teaspoon chervil	=	1 teaspoon parsley or tarragon
1 teaspoon fennel	=	1 teaspoon anise or tarragon
1 small garlic clove	=	⅛ teaspoon garlic powder or 1 teaspoon garlic salt (reduce salt by ½ teaspoon)
1 tablespoon fresh ginger	=	1 teaspoon powdered or candied ginger with the sugar washed off
1 tablespoon mustard	=	1 teaspoon dried mustard
1 teaspoon nutmeg	=	1 teaspoon mace
1 small fresh onion	=	1 tablespoon dehydrated minced onion
1 medium fresh onion	=	1 tablespoon onion powder
1 teaspoon oregano	=	1 teaspoon marjoram
1 teaspoon sage	=	1 teaspoon thyme
dash cayenne or red pepper	=	few drops hot pepper sauce
fines herbs	=	equal parts of parsley, chives, tarragon, and chervil
bouquet garni (herbs wrapped in cheese cloth)		
classic	=	2 sprigs parsley, ½ bay leaf, 1 sprig thyme or ⅛ teaspoon dried thyme
for lamb	=	rosemary, parsley, and celery
for veal	=	parsley, thyme, and lemon rind
for beef	=	basil, parsley, bay leaf, and clove

MEASUREMENT EQUIVALENTS

LIQUID MEASURES

1 gallon	=	4 quarts	=	8 pints	=	16 cups	=	128 fluid ounces
½ gallon	=	2 quarts	=	4 pints	=	8 cups	=	64 fluid ounces
¼ gallon	=	1 quart	=	2 pints	=	4 cups	=	32 fluid ounces
		½ quart	=	1 pint	=	2 cups	=	16 fluid ounces
		¼ quart	=	½ pint	=	1 cup	=	8 fluid ounces

DRY MEASURES

1 cup	=	8 fluid ounces	=	16 tablespoons	=	48 teaspoons
¾ cup	=	6 fluid ounces	=	12 tablespoons	=	36 teaspoons
⅔ cup	=	5⅓ fluid ounces	=	10⅔ tablespoons	=	32 teaspoons
½ cup	=	4 fluid ounces	=	8 tablespoons	=	24 teaspoons
⅓ cup	=	2⅔ fluid ounces	=	5⅓ tablespoons	=	16 teaspoons
¼ cup	=	2 fluid ounces	=	4 tablespoons	=	12 teaspoons
⅛ cup	=	1 fluid ounce	=	2 tablespoons	=	6 teaspoons
				1 tablespoon	=	3 teaspoons